THE BRUTAL TAKEOVER

THE BRUTAL TAKEOVER

The Austrian ex-Chancellor's
account of the Anschluss of Austria
by Hitler

KURT VON SCHUSCHNIGG
Translated by Richard Barry

Atheneum
New York
1971

Printed in Great Britain

CONTENTS

PREFACE

Why has this book been written? Any author of a serious work tries to prove some theory, to demonstrate some cause-and-effect relationship or to describe in their correct historical perspective the events of some limited period of time, in this case the years 1918 to 1938 in Austria, as he saw and experienced them. Much has been written, including much that is valid, about the tragic events in Austria of March 1938, their antecedents and their sequel; much also that still requires corroboration and finally much that is little better than sheer special pleading. Something undoubtedly still remains to be said.

It must not be forgotten that in March 1938 Austria was not faced with a simple alternative – independence or Anschluss; there was a third actual and dangerous possibility – partition.

The fate of Austria at that time is therefore only comprehensible against the background of Austrian and European development in its entirety ever since 1918. Nothing is achieved by mutual reproaches and *post hoc* recrimination. Everyone must answer before history for the part he played and, taken overall, the long-term outlook is an optimistic one. The purpose of this book is to show that this is so and, in so far as it lies within the author's power, to prove it. In fifty or a hundred years' time all these developments and events will probably be visible in clearer historical outline.

My special thanks are due to Professor Ludwig Jedlicka, Director of the Institute of Contemporary History at the University of Vienna, for much assistance in tracing sources and for permission to make large-scale use of many of his own publications; with him I include Dr Gerhard Jagschitz, his assistant at the Institute. My thanks are also due to Dr Mommsen, the President, and Dr Volker Wagner of the Federal Archives, Koblenz, for permission to examine the voluminous material in their files, also to the Austrian State Archives and in particular Professor Hanns Leo Mikoletzky, the Director-General, and Professor Walter Goldinger of the General Administration Archives. I received valuable assistance from Dr Helmut Krausnick of the Institut für Zeitgeschichte, Munich, and from the former Director of Innsbruck University Library, Dr Josef Hofinger, and his staff. Finally all my thanks go to Fräulein Erna Lippert for her tireless efforts in preparing the manuscript.

In the English edition, for which I am indebted to Weidenfeld & Nicolson, London, certain cuts have been made both in the text and in the documentation; they concern details of minor interest for the non-Austrian reader. There have also been a few small additions.

I am also indebted to Cassell & Co. Ltd for permission to quote from Winston Churchill, *The Second World War – The Gathering Storm* (published in America by the Houghton-Mifflin Company, Boston).

THREE FLASHBACKS

*With Guido Zernatto[1] in my office in the Ballhausplatz about 7.0 p.m.
11 March 1938.*

No further doubt about the future now. The battle was over.

The history of events has long since been written. Their
significance for the future lies, not in what happened, but in how
it did so. With the passage of time and the opening of the archives
the major repercussions fall into perspective; as they do so, the
clearer it becomes that 11 March 1938 was a turning point – and
not for Austria alone; it was another of those moments when,
in Hebbel's words, 'the small world submits the great world to
a test'. This does not imply, however, that the manœuvres required to achieve the German objective, the elimination of
Austria, were any the less remarkable. Based on memory, shorthand notes and subsequent accounts, a precise picture of their
broad outline can now be reconstructed.

Early that afternoon (shortly after 2.0 p.m.) Berlin issued its
ultimatum demanding resignation of the Austrian government
and the appointment of Seyss-Inquart as Federal Chancellor;
otherwise the German *Wehrmacht* would march in that very
evening.

This ultimatum was telephoned through to Seyss-Inquart despite the fact that at about 2.0 p.m. Austria had accepted an earlier
ultimatum, similarly transmitted, demanding cancellation and
postponement of our proposed plebiscite.

Reports from the frontier and from our Consulate-General in
Munich combined with the attitude of Seyss-Inquart and Glaise-

Horstenau showed that the threat was no bluff. Moreover Glaise-Horstenau had only just arrived from Berlin and had been present in the Reich Chancellery on the previous evening when Hitler had taken his decision.[2]

The decision to invade Austria had been made, but for the benefit of the outside world a pretext was still being sought. The only counter we could make was to refuse to provide this pretext and so expose the German blackmail. By this time it was clear that we could expect no effective help from outside.

So shortly after 4.0 p.m. the government resigned; there was now no doubt that Seyss-Inquart would ultimately be appointed Federal Chancellor, though as the result of extreme pressure and in violation of all international law. The ultimatum's time limit (6.30) had now expired. From the legal point of view this made not the smallest difference. The German attitude to the law was conclusively demonstrated by the announcements issuing from the German radio:

First: 'The reports current abroad about troop movements on the Austrian frontier and the closing of the border are tendentious and fictitious; they originate from the state of hysteria of the Vienna government which, as a result of labour unrest, no longer has the situation under control.'

Later: 'The Reich government wishes to emphasise that the rumours of delivery of an ultimatum to Vienna by the German government are entirely without foundation.'

The Austrian President (Miklas) asked for clarification of this obvious discrepancy. Lieutenant-General Muff, the German Military Attaché in Vienna, thereupon handed over the formal ultimatum: Seyss-Inquart must forthwith be nominated Federal Chancellor, otherwise 200,000 men of the German *Wehrmacht* would move into Austria.

About the same time the German radio announced that a bloody communist rising had broken out in Austria; there were hundreds of dead; the Austrian government was no longer in control of the situation. This was pure invention. Nothing had happened which could conceivably justify armed intervention in the eyes of international law. Berlin was merely searching for anything which would serve as an even semi-plausible excuse for military action.

In this unequal struggle the Austrian object was to make it abundantly clear, for the sake of the future, that here was a glaring breach of the law. About 8.0 p.m., therefore, I broadcast a short message:

> 'The German government today handed to President Miklas an ultimatum with a time limit attached, ordering him to nominate as Chancellor a person to be designated by the German government and to appoint members of a cabinet on the orders of the German government; otherwise German troops would invade Austria. I declare before the world that the reports issued about Austria concerning disorders created by the workers and the shedding of streams of blood, and the allegation that the situation has got out of control of the government were lies from A to Z. President Miklas asks me to tell the people of Austria that *we have yielded to force* . . .'[3]

Next day the German News Agency denied the facts given in this message. There had been no ultimatum, it said, and no threat; instead there had been a spontaneous Austrian popular uprising.

Other details are well known – Göring, for instance, demanded a telegram from the new Austrian Chancellor asking for military assistance.[4] At 8.45 p.m. Hitler issued written orders to the *Wehrmacht* to move – in other words, after my broadcast and before the telegram demanded by Göring could have been sent.[5]

Two days later (9.15 a.m. 13 March) Göring from Berlin telephoned Ribbentrop in London to give him the following talking points:

> *Göring:* I really wanted to talk to you about the political things: well, the story about our having given an ultimatum to Austria is of course nonsense. The ultimatum was given to the Schuschnigg government by the National-Socialist ministers in the Cabinet and by the people's representatives. Later on more and more prominent people took up our point of view. The only thing which these Austrian ministers asked us, of course, was that we should back them up if necessary so that they would not be completely trampled down

once more . . . therefore Seyss-Inquart – who at this time was already in charge of the government – asked us to invade immediately . . . we could not know in advance whether there would be civil war or not. . . . The Führer thought that you, now that you are over there anyway, might tell the people a bit how things really are, and tell them especially that if they think that Germany gave an ultimatum to Austria, they were completely misinformed.

Ribbentrop: Yes, I did that already when I talked at great length with Chamberlain and Halifax. It was quite clear. . . .

Göring: I just wanted you to tell them again – no, not again – I mean, to tell Halifax and Chamberlain these things: It is not true that Germany gave any sort of ultimatum to Austria. That is a lie of Schuschnigg's, because the ultimatum was issued by Seyss-Inquart, Glaise-Horstenau and Jury. Secondly, it is not true that we issued an ultimatum to the President of Austria. That was done by the others and I believe a German Military Attaché accompanied them on Seyss' request because of some technical detail or other. . . . Furthermore I want to make it quite clear that it was Seyss-Inquart who had asked us, both orally and by telegram, to send troops. . . . So you see, the entry of our troops into Austria took place on the express demand of Seyss.[6]

Under cross-examination in Nuremberg on 6 July 1946 Seyss-Inquart admitted that on the evening of 10 March he had reached a large measure of agreement with the Chancellor (myself) on the subject of the plebiscite. On the morning of 11 March, however, he had received by courier a letter from Hitler demanding the postponement of the plebiscite, the holding of elections supported by demonstrations from the (Austrian) Nazis, and hinting at the possibility of a German invasion.[7]

Glaise-Horstenau arrived on the morning of 11 March by the same aircraft as the Berlin courier. When I met him in Nuremberg in November 1946 he told me that Hitler had been convinced that the Austrian plebiscite would be a success and was therefore determined to stop it, come what might. Hitler had therefore commissioned him (Glaise) to hand over the ultimatum in Vienna. Glaise had, however, pointed out that, as an Austrian Minister, he was not a suitable emissary; a courier had therefore been sent with him.

4

On 6 July 1946 Göring himself stated in the witness box:

> 'I regarded the invasion of Austria as absolutely essential and I was
> the one who gave the order to move. . . . I had always held the view
> that Austria belonged to and should be incorporated into the German
> Reich. This was my view even in Imperial times. . . . I was therefore
> opposed to all compromise agreements, except in so far as they could
> be of use for purposes of foreign policy cover.'[8]

The very foundation of the Berchtesgaden agreement of 12
February 1938 had been German recognition of the continued
validity of the Agreement of 11 July 1936; Germany had also
explicitly renewed her assurance of non-interference in internal
Austrian affairs. This had been confirmed in an identical communiqué issued by both parties on 15 February 1938 and a short
reference to it had been made in Hitler's Reichstag speech of 20
February.

In the 11 July 1936 agreement the German government had
'recognised the full sovereignty of the Federal State of Austria in
accordance with the statements made by the Führer and Chancellor on 21 May 1935'. It had further been agreed that each of the
two governments would regard 'the internal political structure of
the other country, including the question of Austrian National-
Socialism, as an internal affair of the other country, which it will
influence neither directly nor indirectly'.

Hitler's statement to the Reichstag on 21 May 1935, upon
which the agreement of 11 July 1936 was based, was as
follows:

> 'Germany has neither the intention nor the desire to interfere in
> internal Austrian affairs, to annex or incorporate Austria. . . .'

German military intervention and the resulting take-over of
Austria by force had been occasioned by the decision to hold a
plebiscite. For the Third Reich, however, the Anschluss in some
form or another was only a question of timing; indeed, as German
political tactics from February 1938 onwards conclusively prove,
merely a question of weeks.

To provide some pretence of legality for this unilateral renunci-

ation of a treaty, once the Austrian State had disappeared the story
ran that Austria had 'broken the Berchtesgaden agreement'.
There might have been some sense in this, had there been either
written or verbal agreement on mutual consultation. Such an
obligation, however, whether direct or indirect, had never been
discussed – and could not be, since non-interference in internal
political matters had been explicitly laid down and agreed.

The proposed wording of the plebiscite, originally accepted
even by Seyss-Inquart, had been: 'For a free, German, independent, social, christian and united Austria – for our daily bread and
peace at home.'[9]

In Hitler's eyes the Austrian question was not a foreign policy
problem; it was an entirely internal, or in the Berlin jargon of the
time 'racio-political' [*volkspolitische*], matter. The Wilhelmstrasse
was not therefore concerned; Ribbentrop, the Foreign Minister,
had gone to London early in March. Subsequently his Permanent
Secretary recorded:

> 'On Friday 11 March we were still in London with no direct news
> from Berlin; we could only follow developments on the radio. . . .
> I was deeply ashamed when I heard Schuschnigg's farewell message.
> The union of these two German states, with a thousand years of
> common history behind them, might have been an act of liberation.
> Now the Anschluss was the result of blackmail and force. The in-
> credible blunder of the military invasion demonstrated to the entire
> world that this was no spontaneous development.'[10]

The invasion of Austria started a chain reaction, beginning in
Vienna on 12 March 1938. It led through 29 September 1938 (the
Munich Agreement) to 15 March 1939 (entry into Prague) and
thence to 1 September 1939 (invasion of Poland), 9 April 1940
(invasion of Denmark and Norway), 10 May 1940 (attack on
Belgium and Holland), 14 June 1940 (occupation of Paris), 6 April
1941 (attack on Jugoslavia and Greece), 22 June 1941 (attack on
Russia) and finally to 9 May 1945 (capitulation).

At the end of all this we find the German question unsolved,
Berlin divided, an ideological frontier running through the heart
of Europe – and a resurrected free republic of Austria.

Gabriel Puaux, French Minister in Vienna in 1938 and a great friend of and authority on Austria, says in his memoirs: 'I remember 11 March 1938, when I could only watch the Austrian agony as a helpless bystander, as a day of shameful defeat.'[11]

The actual course of events has long been established beyond doubt or disputation. To describe the fog of perplexity, however, which, on that late evening of 11 March 1938 in the Ballhausplatz, prevented any glimpse into the future is another matter. Paralysis does not deprive a man of capacity for logical thought; he merely knows that he cannot move. The majority of those who witnessed events on the spot were in this state; in so far as they were Austrians this applied both to the vanquished and to the momentary victors. Seyss-Inquart was only the loud-speaker for telephoned orders from Berlin; Glaise-Horstenau had long since become nothing but a silent witness. Perhaps, therefore, the account of an actual participant in these events may be welcome as a complement to the black-and-white picture which the future historian will create based on documents. Personal experience may produce lights and shades which may not only sharpen the outlines but increase the human interest and so assist realistic judgement.

Outwardly nothing had yet changed. The files still lay on the desk; the engagement diary was still full; the Empress Maria Theresa still looked down from the damask-hung wall above the death-mask of Engelbert Dollfuss.

Since midday comings and goings had been continuous. In the intervals one had looked out through the tall windows on to the Hofburg opposite, on the Hochhaus and across to the Heldenplatz. It all seemed different; the familiar outlines were blurred; one gazed into space.

About 7.0 p.m. on that 11 March innumerable others were feeling similarly, including many who stifled their fear in jubilation next day. It was a moment of shock when scarcely any knowledgeable Austrian could see his way clearly. People felt that an epoch of history was at an end. That life must go on was clear, but how and at what price no one could be sure. For some a

7

world was sinking to which they had clung with all their heart and mind in spite of its much-lamented inadequacies. They included many who held no brief for the State in its present form. How should Austria organise her existence and what should be the Austrians' future? For others the hour of fulfilment had struck – but not in the way they had expected. Basically, apart from the extremist activists, no one had wanted a *diktat* from without; even the Anschluss disciples had not objected when the extremists had been summoned back to Germany.[12]

Disillusionment soon followed when exactly that occurred which we had feared earlier but which had been dismissed at the time as political propaganda: Austria was not to unite with the Reich; she was to disappear as a national and international entity.

The President wished for 'business as usual' until the new government had been appointed, but it was useless to shut one's eyes to the fact that a revolution directed from 'over there' was in progress and that its pitiless motto was *Ceterum censeo Austriam esse delendam* (I think that Austria should be wiped out anyway).

In the late afternoon of 11 March 1938 the only outstanding question was whether National-Socialism would come to power in Austria as the result of pressure from the streets or illegal pressure from without. For Hitler and his people it was important to present the upheaval as the result of an internal Austrian revolution. From the Austrian viewpoint, therefore, it was imperative that this should not occur and that the Third Reich should be seen to all the world as the disturber of the peace; at the same time, however, any risk of senseless casualties was indefensible. In the event Hitler disregarded his own ultimatum and, in spite of its acceptance, at 8.45 p.m. ordered the troops to move on the morning of 12 March. At the time, however, we did not know this in Vienna. The self-sacrificing President, doing his duty by straining every nerve to find a solution, did not know. The rest of us, who knew how threatening the situation was, were trying to stop the invasion and make the legal position unequivocally clear. Not even Seyss-Inquart knew; invasion seemed to him both undesirable and unnecessary. Many, both at home and abroad, having no alternative but to look for an alibi, simply accepted the story hammered home by every conceivable means that 'the fault was not that of the murderer but of his victim'.

So we sorted the drawers of the desk, extracting and subsequently destroying anything personal in the files. This included a recent exchange of correspondence with Archduke Otto, extracts from which were later published, and of which I subsequently obtained copies. In a sense these letters are epoch-making documents since they reflect the tension as it rose to fever heat; they show, perhaps more clearly than many an official international document, the desperation with which Austrians were battling for Austria in face of an impenetrable future. I therefore quote the letters *in extenso*:

'Abroad   17 February 1938

Dear Herr von Schuschnigg,
The events of the last few days force me to write to you.

I do not wish to discuss the past. You know only too well that I have always expressed to you the view that the earliest re-establishment of the legitimate monarchy would be the best ultimate guarantee of our independence. In spite of your loyal legitimist convictions (which I have never doubted and do not doubt today) you have thought it your duty to postpone this long-term settlement of the Austrian problem. You know also that I have never agreed with either the form or content of the 11 July 1936 Agreement. Finally you know that I have always been in favour of a far-reaching policy of conciliation *vis-à-vis* the mass of the workers but have always opposed a policy of appeasement towards the murderers of Dollfuss and the National-Socialist traitors to their people and country.

With the events of the last few days a new phase in the life of our people has begun.

By an unexampled act of force Austria's enemy has succeeded in forcing your government into an untenable position which dangerously inhibits further resistance on our part. He has succeeded in dictating to us a new agreement which throws the door open to interference by him. A precedent has been created which any Austrian must regard with the greatest anxiety.

In this situation I must speak – and speak to you, for today you carry the major responsibility for my country before God and before the people.

9

It is a terrifying responsibility. You are responsible first to the people, for they believe in you as the champion of independence and they want to support you in this policy. Secondly you are responsible for the concept of Austria, the supra-national unifying power which for centuries has held together a strong united Danube basin and even today is potent enough for reconstruction to be possible. Thirdly you are responsible for the true concept of the German race; in face of the degenerate neo-pagan tendencies in the Reich, only in Austria is this to be found today in all its old strength, as when it formed the basis of the Holy Roman Empire of the German Nation. Only in Austria can Germanism continue to exist and so be the saviour of Germany; otherwise the German race will go down in fearful chaos. Finally and most important of all, you are responsible for our greatest heritage, the Catholic faith. In the German Reich a systematic struggle against Catholicism is raging and in the long run this must lead to its disappearance among wide sections of the population. For the German area as a whole Austria is today the last stronghold of Catholicism and by it our people will stand or fall. If this last bastion falls, the church in central Europe, the sole source of happiness, will lie waste and millions of souls, which may still be saved for eternity, will be lost for ever.

But this responsibility is not yours alone. I carry part of it. As the legitimate heir of a dynasty which guarded Austria for 650 years, as son of my father, now asleep in God, who gave his life for his people on a distant island, I cannot and must not be untrue to my inherited duty.

I consider it my duty, dear Herr von Schuschnigg, to put to you the following plan for the salvation of my gravely threatened country; I, as the legitimate Emperor of Austria, assume responsibility for it. I do this in full knowledge of the implications of what I am about to say to you and after mature consideration of the great responsibility which I thereby assume.

The first point in my plan concerns foreign policy. Today we in Austria are exposed to the pressure of a mighty neighbour who wishes to deprive us of our existence. We must therefore look around for Powers who will counterbalance this pressure. Our choice must inevitably fall upon the Western Powers since they have always regarded our country with sympathy. Admittedly we do not consider their internal organisation ideal but in a matter of life and death this cannot enter into consideration. We must of course keep this vital approach to the Western Powers secret as long as we can. It must therefore be made by you personally, not only because the Western Powers trust you but also because I cannot feel any confidence in Guido Schmidt. He is obviously disliked by these Powers and I know that he has not always been loyal to you; moreover I am well aware of his pro-German tendencies. It is therefore imperative that you yourself should carry out this policy, by-passing the official channels. Be assured that in this I shall at all times be ready to help you, since I know that this is the only way to secure our position externally.

Militarily Austria must do her utmost to rearm and, however pressing other financial demands may be, they must be subordinated to this overriding duty. Once we have a strong army, the risks we run will not be as great as in the past. In this connection I congratulate you on your determination in maintaining General Zehner in his post despite all pressure. He constitutes a guarantee that the army will remain an Austrian army.

Turning now to internal policy, to save the country we must work in three directions and this you are in a position to do with your plenary powers as leader of the "Fatherland Front". First, we must work vigorously to pacify the Left. In the last few days the workers have shown that they are patriots. This section of the population cannot be infected with National-Socialism and therefore is the most likely to stand up for Austria; as a *quid pro quo* the government must give them the opportunity to participate in the organisation of the country, which they are ready to defend. Another force, not yet expended, is the legitimist. This movement – and this I guarantee – will go through hellfire for you, if they are assured that they are thereby working for the independence of Austria. I ask you to support this movement as best you may, for every additional legitimist is a further guarantee of the independence of our country. Finally, and this I hardly need emphasise to you, from the outset it will be of the greatest importance to take discreet measures against the pernicious activities of the ultra-nationalists.

In my view these are the measures which must be taken at once to save Austria from the danger of *Gleichschaltung* [absorption]. I am convinced that you will agree with me.

Now for the future:

The decisive moment will come when Germany demands further concessions from us, using threats and blackmail. I am sure that I am right in assuming that you, like me, think that Austria has reached the utmost limit of concessions to Germany. Any further step backwards would imply the annihilation of Austria and the annihilation of your and Dollfuss' painstaking work of reconstruction. My father, the Emperor, would have died in vain, hundreds of thousands would have fallen in vain, the post-1933 sacrifices would have been made in vain. We Austrians cannot allow this. Anything is preferable to losing our Fatherland.

I have heard that you, my dear Herr von Schuschnigg, have said that you would be unable to withstand further German pressure and in that event would resign your responsible office. I therefore address myself to you now as a man who has been steadfastly loyal to his Emperor and his people and I beg you before God to accede to my request.

First: So long as you are still Federal Chancellor I ask you to make no further concessions of any sort to Germany or to the Austrian ultra-nationalists.

Second: Should you have the impression that further German demands or threats against Austria are imminent, I ask you to inform me forthwith.

Third: What follows may surprise you but in these dark days of extreme danger it has been the subject of mature reflection – should you feel unable to withstand further pressure from the Germans or the ultra-nationalists, I ask you, whatever the situation, to hand over the office of Chancellor to me. I am determined to go to the limit to protect the people and the State; I am convinced that the people would respond. Since restoration of the monarchy would entail a prolonged process of recognition by the Powers, which the situation would not permit, I am not asking you for that. I urge you merely to hand over to me the Chancellorship, so that we may reap the same advantages as would ensue from formal re-establishment of the monarchy, but *without* altering the constitution and *without* fresh recognition, at least at the decisive moment. I would stress once more that I assume full responsibility for this momentous decision before God, the people, the world and history.

I have felt it my duty in this fateful hour to write you all this. I am convinced that thus I most nearly fulfil my duty as son of the martyred Emperor Karl, as a burning Austrian patriot and as the legitimate Emperor of my country. By your oath sworn as an officer, by your great services to the legitimist cause and by your selfless patriotism I implore you, my dear Herr von Schuschnigg, to grant my request. Do not imagine that this letter stems from the lust for power of a young ambitious man. Such ambition as I ever had would be stilled by the fearfulness of the situation and the weight of responsibility. I am acting thus only because I regard it as my duty, for if Austria is in danger, the heir to the House of Austria must stand or fall with his country.

No one besides myself knows of the contents of this letter. I have not even given a hint of any sort to my confidant, von Wiesner. For your part I ask you equally to mention this letter to no one, to answer it in writing as soon as possible and despatch your reply by the same method as I have used.

I assure you of my confidence in you and of my resolve to assist you in everything during this difficult time. May God bless you and show you the right path for the benefit and salvation of our homeland.'

'Vienna   2 March 1938

Your Majesty,

I confirm receipt of the letter of 17 February which Your Majesty was good enough to send me.

The supreme duty of any responsible leader of the State is to preserve the country. Anything which serves that end is good, anything which imperils the country is bad and should be left out of consideration. Account must be taken of the overall international situation which alters from time to time. The basic principle of Austrian ideology is: service to peace. Should Austria find it necessary, in order to preserve her existence, to be the instigator of an international war, she would no longer be true to this mission. Moreover a war could only be waged if, contrary to the conditions of 1914, there was a chance of success. Finally one should only count on help from abroad if one is sure of it.

Both the geographical and geo-political situation of the country make peace with Germany imperative. This is dictated not only by serious psychological considerations but also by sober economic calculation; since 12 February, for instance, even the staunchly conservative farming community, including that in the Tyrol, has expressed its opinion unequivocally on this subject. A country can only remain in existence if a minimum economic subsistence level is guaranteed.

I find myself compelled to agree with this view by the mood of the country and by actual conditions -- and upon these, in my humble view, Your Majesty has never been correctly, or at least fully, informed.

In particular I would regard it as entirely fatal for the dynasty if a temporary or provisional restoration, only to be bought at the price of severe casualties and with foreign assistance, were to take place. I am profoundly convinced that this would at the same time seal the fate of Austria.

Austria has offered prolonged, honourable and stubborn resistance to any further step backwards. Even if, however (which God forbid), this were to occur and Austria be forced to yield to force, it is still better that this should happen without the dynasty being implicated. At some time the resurrection of Austria might become possible as part of a complete reorganisation of Europe; tragic though it may be, it is probable that this could only ensue after another major war. Under no circumstances can it be reasonable in my view to lead the country into a struggle which is hopeless from the outset. I know what war means; I have also seen civil wars. I know therefore that it is my duty to do my utmost to save our country from such a situation. Anyone who has the future of Austria at heart cannot and must not think about defeat with honour; he must mobilise all his forces to keep the country in honourable existence so as to be equipped for better times to come, as come they must one day.

I am no pessimist but I cannot ignore the gravity and significance of the situation. I also cannot ignore the fact that much of the legitimist talk has largely contributed to the aggravation of the situation between the two states and has not been helpful to the continuance of a free Austria; I have repeatedly warned against it but unfortunately in vain. Our policy must be geared to the present; the concept of Austria, and of the House of Austria, cannot, in my view, be judged through the spectacles of a single generation. These concepts must remain, though we passing creatures may perish.

Such, Your Majesty, is my opinion.

My views and convictions are based on precise knowledge of the international and internal situation. I am profoundly distressed that I have not contrived to convey them to Your Majesty in a form which carries conviction. I earnestly request you to believe me now when I say that the stake is enormous, perhaps total, and that any attempt at restoration, whether in the recent past or the immediately foreseeable future, would, with one hundred per cent certainty, imply the ruin of Austria.

I need hardly add that I should be only too happy if things were different, but I can only implore Your Majesty to believe me that this is so.

I am of course only too ready to keep Your Majesty informed, so far as I may, of possible changes in the situation. Meanwhile I can only say: What happened had to happen and it was right. Had it not happened, no responsible Austrian would today be in a position to communicate with Your Majesty. This applies also and in particular to the 11 July 1936 Agreement.

I would most urgently ask Your Majesty to consider that in the case of such fundamental decisions, what is advisable or inadvisable can only be judged on the spot; it is difficult to do so from a distance. In this highly involved and difficult period no one can say with certainty that he will succeed in reaching his goal. On the other hand there is no doubt that for us there is no other realistic or practical way. Our duty can only be to hold the door open for some future development; anything lost now will be impossible to recapture for as long as anyone can see.

Finally may I respectfully point out to Your Majesty that adherence to the constitution is the only legal and practical procedure for all of us and that according to this constitution dismissal and appointment of the Federal Chancellor is the prerogative of the President.

With the heartfelt desire that God may protect Your Majesty and the House of Austria,

In the firm conviction that, whether with or without setbacks, the development of Austria's cause will be of historical significance,

Finally with the assurance that the sole motive for all my decisions will, as my duty demands, be the struggle for the country and my responsibility to every Austrian,

I remain . . .'[13]

Meanwhile in the ante-room – the room in which Dollfuss died – the members of the government, leading politicians and senior officials had assembled.

Once again the German radio announced that a bloody communist rising had broken out in Vienna and throughout Austria; the government was no longer in a position to control the situation; hundreds of dead . . .

Hans von Hammerstein-Equord, a trusted senior official and descendant of an ancient German family, clenched his fists; the blood mounted to his cheeks; normally so calm, dignified, balanced and thoughtful, he was barely recognisable. With a sob, half choked with rage, there burst from him: 'I am ashamed to be a German!' No one contradicted him.[14]

29 April 1945 – Niederdorf in the Pustertal, South Tyrol

'Final halt', the SD escort commander[15] had said; the five or so trucks and buses with SS markings were parked on the open road some half a mile short of the village. We were 136 prisoners in all of seventeen different nationalities. They included: three ex-Prime Ministers (one of them was Léon Blum), seven RAF officers (including Wing Commander H. M. A. Day who had been shot down in October 1939 and had to his credit five attempts at escape, including the spectacular one of 23 March 1944 from Stalag Luft III), five Greek, one Italian and two Russian Generals, a Dutch Minister, a French Catholic Bishop, a Czech university professor, Richard Schmitz, ex-Vice Chancellor of Austria and Burgomaster of Vienna, and his friend from the Dachau days, Prince Xavier of Bourbon-Parma. The Germans included Pastor Niemöller, Johannes Neuhäusler, ex-Suffragan Bishop of Munich, Dr Josef Müller, a leading Catholic resister and later Bavarian Minister of Justice, Fabian von Schlabrendorff, the lawyer, Dr Hjalmar Schacht, ex-President of the Reichsbank and Reich Minister, Colonel-General Franz Halder, ex-Chief of the General Staff, General Alexander von Falkenhausen, ex-Governor-General of Occupied Belgium, General Georg Thomas, ex-Head of the *Wehrmacht* Economic Office, Colonel (still on the General Staff list) Bogislav von Bonin, Operations Officer of Guderian's Army Group, Fritz Thyssen, the great industrialist, together with a considerable number of people under so-called 'kith and kin' arrest including nine members of the Stauffenberg family, seven of the Goerdeler family and two Hammerstein-Equords.

On 27 April we had been moved from Dachau when it was apparently only a question of twenty-four hours before the US Third Army reached the Munich area.

And now it was the 'Final Halt'.

Ambiguous words – 'final' could mean the end of us all. Most of us knew that ominous intentions were abroad but we had little idea whether or how we could deal with them. On paper our convoy was under command of *Untersturmführer* [2nd Lieutenant] Stiller, an Austrian by birth from the staff of Dachau concentration camp. He seemed somewhat unsure of himself and outwardly anxious to please but only shortly before had said that he believed the great turning point would come with the advent of the promised 'miracle weapons'. So far as we could see there was little to fear from him and his men, some thirty of them, elderly and in many cases press-ganged into the SS. The SD escort, however, was another matter; it consisted of some twenty men armed to the teeth under command of *Untersturmführer* Bader, formerly on the staff of Buchenwald; he was notorious as the commander of special liquidation squads for undesirable prisoners; he and his men made no secret of the fact. 'The total number of SS men available to guard the prisoners in Niederdorf was eighty-six.'[16]

On the evening of our arrival one of our number, Captain S. Payne Best, of the British SIS, who had been in German captivity since November 1939, had obtained from one of the SD men a hint that the RSHA (*Reichssicherheitshauptamt* – Reich Central Security Department), Berlin, had issued a liquidation order.[17]

Ex-Captain Wichard von Alvensleben, of Headquarters C-in-C South-West, who eventually disarmed the SS escort, confirms that a liquidation order applicable to all concentration camp prisoners in this convoy had been issued by SS Headquarters; it was found in the briefcase of the responsible SS officer and included a list of names with priorities for execution. Von Alvensleben's report continues:

'Though the SS unit in Niederdorf was 86 men strong, we succeeded in dealing with it with only eight NCOs, pending the arrival by road of a company from Toblach which I had ordered up on my own initiative; the SS men were ultimately removed without a struggle. All this was possible solely thanks to Karl Wolff (then an SS General and SS C-in-C in Italy). Contrary to the views of Army

Group South-West, when the Commandant telephoned, Wolff authorised him to act against the SS on his own initiative.'[18]

By good fortune immediately after arrival at Niederdorf two of our fellow-prisoners, Colonel Bonin and General Thomas, had managed to telephone General Hans Röttiger, Chief of Staff to General Heinrich von Vietinghoff commanding in Bolzano; they had asked for *Wehrmacht* assistance to stop this eleventh-hour threat of a massacre of prisoners or in the current jargon 'dirty business'. The telephone call, which had gone unnoticed by the SS, had been possible owing to the presence of a *Wehrmacht* staff in the place and had been helped by the friendly attitude both of the local population and the *Wehrmacht* personnel.

Nevertheless we passed an anxious night. We were given temporary lodgings in the village. Few of us were either ready or able to think much about the situation; I certainly could not.

Our company came from the most varied backgrounds; it mirrored the disorder of international society. For many of us personal contact with our fellow-prisoners had been forbidden for years, so our first conversations in Dachau during the last few weeks had been of special interest. The human links forged by our common experiences in concentration camps overshadowed all earlier enmities and produced real personal friendship. The professional soldiers perhaps took their fate the hardest. Admittedly their thinking had been wooden – they had thought that the valley of the Austrian Inn would form a good defensive frontier, for instance, and so had been all for its acquisition. In many respects they were poles apart from us in their opinions, their tradition and their historical ideas. In every case, however, these anti-Nazi German officers with whom we had been imprisoned during these final weeks, were upright, decent-thinking men, devoted to their duty; all had a strong sense of their human responsibilities; all regarded Hitler as a national disaster; militarily, they said, the Führer was a dilettante; he was to blame for embarking on this war which the overall situation showed could not be won.

Though basically opposed to the policy of the military, in the final analysis Schacht thought the same.

I asked him whether, when he visited Vienna as President of the Reichsbank in 1936, he had been convinced that Adolf Hitler's policy was right.

He had been convinced, he said, that Germany must be made strong externally and crisis-proof internally; to this end the most important step was the elimination of unemployment which constituted the primary social and political danger to the nation. He had never overrated Hitler but for a long time had the impression that he believed what he said. Meanwhile of course he had realised that Hitler never spoke the truth, always thought something different from what he said or wrote, never adhered to a point of view and was impervious to all factual argument.

I then asked whether he had thought war unavoidable. Of course not, he replied. On the contrary. War could and should have been avoided by any responsible leader because in the long run Germany could never hold out.

Had he put this view to Hitler, I asked. Of course, and not only to Hitler but also to the military; most of them too were deaf to argument.

Why had he not drawn the logical conclusions earlier? Because he had good reason to hope, he said, that he could win Hitler over to his views. He had done all he could to interest Hitler in the question of colonies. Once Germany had colonies, it would have been easy to divert to Africa all National-Socialism's urge for adventure and its day-dreamings, an innocuous outlet would have been provided for the entire rearmament effort and Europe would have been left in peace.

Early in 1938 Austrian hopes were similar. We were then playing for time and banking on a detente in Europe. . . .

But in fact even then the die had already been cast, though the world did not know it. Schacht had gone to Paris and London, he said, where he had conducted laborious but promising negotiations for the restitution of the German colonies. When he reported to Berlin, however, he was told: 'We have no interest in colonies, only in revision in Europe.'

As it so happened, in Paris Schacht had been negotiating with Léon Blum who was then head of the government, and on the colonial question he confirmed Schacht's statements word for word.

Blum was a sterling character, in appearance more like an English conservative peer than a radical labour leader. With his imperturbable calm, deliberately relaxed attitude and kindly approach he was a sort of sheet-anchor amid the tribulations and upheavals around him. He spoke little of what had happened to him in the last few years – though it was a lot. Smilingly he re-called that when we had met ten years before during the Austrian State visit to Paris of 1935, a great gulf had been fixed between us. A gulf should never be so deep, however, he said, that one should lose faith in the possibility of bridging it. As before, Blum was still a convinced socialist, a believer in evolution. On many subjects of course our views differed. But, for instance, even when discussing State subsidies to Church schools and expressing an opinion diametrically opposed to my own, he did so without offensiveness or asperity and with respect for his opponent's views. He taught one the superiority of discussion and that attempts to dictate, however well-meaning, seldom achieve their object.

These various encounters between men free of national preju-dices seemed to provide a glimpse into a better, in other words more human, future. This same hope was keeping millions alive and saving them from despair.[19]

That 30 April was a Sunday. During it the fortunes of our prisoner convoy finally took a turn for the better thanks to the pertinacious efforts of Colonel von Bonin and the highly adroit manoeuvres of Toni Ducia, the contact with the Tyrol resistance movement who with his assistant, Dr Thalhammer, communicated in every direction. Captain Wichard von Alvensleben and his cousin Captain Gebhard von Alvensleben arrived from Sexten with a *Wehrmacht* company, disarmed the SS and took over protection of the prisoners, who were now to all intents and purposes free. At Ducia's suggestion we were accommodated in the Prags Wildsee Hotel, some five miles from Niederdorf and recently derequisitioned. There, on 4 May, we were taken over by a com-pany of 339 US Infantry Regiment under command of Captain John Atwell from New York. We remember with gratitude the unselfish assistance given us both by the Germans of Alvensleben's company who now became prisoners of war, and the American GIs and officers, the latter including a youngster from Vienna.

Various partially contradictory stories about our liberation were later in circulation. There were three more or less distinct chains of events: first the action of Colonel von Bonin, then Ducia's circumspect leadership of the Tyrolese Resistance and finally an entirely separate initiative by a group of Italian partisans in liaison with General Garibaldi and Lieutenant-Colonel Ferrero who had been with us in Dachau. On arrival in Niederdorf these two succeeded in striking off on their own and gaining contact with the Italian partisan organisation operating in the surrounding mountains.

About midday on 30 April I was visited in my billet in Niederdorf by Lieutenant-Colonel Ferrero in full uniform. He urged me to place myself and my family forthwith under the protection of the partisans who had a completely secure head-quarters in Cortina. Transport would be arranged at once. He pointed out the uncertainty of the situation and pressed for an immediate decision. There seemed to be no question of liberating the entire convoy and the impression given was that this was an isolated enterprise. There were several weighty considerations against this, primarily that only the day before we had all agreed to take no individual initiative – in the common interest. The British Captain Best was at the time acting as spokesman for the entire group and we knew from him that he and Colonel Bonin were taking care of the protection and accommodation of the convoy.[20]

I therefore declined the offer, referring to the solidarity agreed upon by the entire group and the consequences for the others which any deviation from this rule might have.

Later it emerged that General Garibaldi had planned to occupy Niederdorf the following night (30 April–1 May) with his parti-sans, liberate the prisoners and cart them all off to the partisans' headquarters in the Dolomites. The British and German spokes-men for the convoy, however, argued him out of his plan, saying that a smooth hand-over of the whole convoy to the Americans must not be jeopardised and that the latter were expected in the immediate future. Ferrero at first insisted but eventually an amicable agreement was reached and they left our group and went their own way. On 3 May, however, Italian partisans reappeared in the Prags Wildsee Hotel itself where they contacted Léon Blum and Vassili Kokorin, a Russian Air Force Lieutenant and a nephew of Molotov. Blum refused their invitation and remained in the hotel; Kokorin went with them and so regained his freedom – but not for long; he had been badly frostbitten and without medical attention proved unable to withstand the hardships of winter in the partisan camp.

Independently of this proposed action by the partisans a somewhat similar enterprise by the South Tyrolese resistance in Niederdorf was under way for the night of 29–30 April. It was not surprising that the Italian partisans and the (German-speaking) 'South Tyrolese Sharpshooters' concentrated around Niederdorf knew little of each other or at least had no touch with each other. Ever since 1919 the Pustertal, as part of South Tyrol, had belonged to Italy; for the partisans therefore it was part of their country; for the South Tyrolese it had always been their home, particularly now in the confused atmosphere of the recent collapse. The South Tyrolese resisters had obviously been alerted by Ducia and were now ready for anything; moreover many had arrived of their own accord when the villagers, who were clearly on the side of the prisoners and against their guards, realised the nature and destination of the convoy.

Eventually on his own initiative Colonel Bonin telephoned the German Army Group in Bolzano and this finally led to the intervention of Alvenleben's company. That we were finally liberated on 4 May 1945 by the advanced guard of a division of US Fifth Army was due to the combined efforts of Alvensleben, Bonin and Ducia (in alphabetical order).[21]

USAF Rehabilitation Camp, Capri – 15 May 1945

Our treatment was most friendly and generous and the atmosphere one of humanity such as we had not known for seven years. Nevertheless it was a golden cage since our freedom of

movement on the island was limited. This could hardly be otherwise pending the completion of 'screening' and the necessary
bureaucratic procedures in each case. This lasted for three months
– by international standards not excessive; the situation was
exceptional; there were no records, precedents or analogies.

Some ninety of us from the Dachau convoy still remained;
twenty-nine of these were women including my own wife and
daughter, now four years old.[22] Despite the near-miraculous turn
in our fortunes we were all mere flotsam, living on our hope of an
early return home.

As early as 4 May, immediately after our liberation in the Prags
Wildsee, our first question had naturally been: when could we go
home. The US Brigadier-General Gerow, whose responsibility it
was to organise the evacuation of our convoy, gave the understandable reply that, in view of the uncertainty of the situation,
this was at the moment neither possible nor advisable.

After repeated enquiries on our arrival in Capri a British Major
from the staff of Allied Headquarters Caserta eventually told us
that it would be at least six weeks before there could be any
question of a return home. In fact this situation lasted two years.
Both for realistic and personal reasons I had never had any
thought of re-entering politics. I did not know at the time that, on
the recommendation of its political advisers, the US Military
Government had placed a veto on political activity by any member of the last Austrian government, including initially Julius
Raab. I had recently been reinstated on the Tyrolese Chamber's
roll of attorneys, of which I had been a member until struck off
by the Nazi authorities; but even if I returned home as a private
citizen, I would inevitably be burdened with troubles which at
this time I felt physically incapable of facing. First of all I had
neither house nor furniture and I had my family to consider.[23]

In 1947 therefore I accepted a private invitation to the United
States, there to start a new life. Good fortune led us, in June 1948,
to St Louis, Missouri, where we were welcomed by a university
professor friend who had been forced to emigrate from Innsbruck
in 1938 and held a teaching professorship in the School of
Dentistry at St Louis (Catholic) University.[24]

2

A PEOPLE IN AFFLICTION

The words 'people', 'state' and 'nation' mean different things to different people. It is no accident that these differences have been particularly marked in the central European area and are far older than the Republic of Austria.

Before 1918 an 'Austrian' would talk of the 'multi-racial' empire when referring to his country, which was supra-national; its mere title was a reminder of the imperial tradition. The phrase 'Austrian nation' was hardly ever used except internationally, when it also covered Hungary.[1] In English and French the word 'nation' means a people politically organised as a state, in other words the nation-state. These days we refer to the 'United Nations', meaning an international community of states, adherence to which is voluntary. Historically the English, French, Spaniards and Russians have been ahead of the Italians and Germans in modern nation-building, but this does not prevent the German word 'nation' meaning primarily a people politically organised as a state and therefore the sovereign state. This is also its normal meaning under international law. Austria, therefore, has her legitimate place among the nations; from 1918 to 1938 she was a legal entity, just as she became again in 1945 after her liberation.

It is a fact, however, that these words as normally used before 1938 did not represent the legal position. There were political reasons for this and, as we shall see, they were closely connected with the Anschluss movement. The acid test once more proved what experienced Austrians had always known and had emphasised often enough – in view of the facts of life (and not solely European facts) the concept of the ethnically national unitary state was utopian. In those days the Austrian who talked of 'the nation' meant a cultural community transcending political frontiers, a community to which the 'Austrian type' felt that he belonged. Today the word 'nation' is currently used to denote the nation-state of which every citizen is a national.

All this must be clearly understood if misunderstandings are to be avoided. The German language now has no equivalent to the French *Ethnie française* which denotes a cultural and linguistic association with kindred groups outside the frontiers of France;[2] the English-speaking world, both Old and New, uses the words 'Anglo-Saxon civilisation' to indicate common customs and a common cultural background. The constitutions of various Latin American states include provisions which testify to their links with Spain – preferential terms for naturalisation, for instance. One of the duties of consuls abroad is to ensure that their former nationals do not lose their cultural links with their country of origin, even though they may long since have become citizens of their country of residence.

The situation with regard to German culture and the German nation as a cultural entity is precisely similar. The German language possesses no other term than 'nation' but in this sense the word has no political connotation and the German-speaking Austrian feels that he belongs to the German 'nation' as a cultural entity just as do the German Swiss and the German minorities which have survived unassimilated within the political boundaries of other nations.

In the post-1918 period many proclamations were made and many votes cast in favour of the union of Austria with Germany; in 1938 Austrians greeted the invading Germans with apparently genuine jubilation. These two facts have been adduced to support the theory that the Anschluss,* though it may perhaps have had superficial blemishes, was basically right since it was an expression of the will of the people.

---

* The German word *Anschluss*, meaning literally union or accession, is commonly used to denote the union of Austria with Germany, which was one of the problems of the inter-war period. It will be used throughout this book. (Translator)

What was the truth about the Anschluss idea?

Two things are indisputable: first, the answer to this question will differ according to the period to which it applies; secondly, everyone committed to the Anschluss programme – and this included all shades of Austrian National-Socialist opinion – had visualised something quite different from the eventual reality. The final outcome, probably inevitable, was seen only when the ultimate test came.

Up to 1918 there was no serious or numerically significant Anschluss movement either in Austria or Germany, in spite of Georg von Schönerer's[3] nineteenth-century cries that only through union with the Hohenzollern empire could Austrian Germanism be saved from perdition. The main points in Schönerer's Pan-German programme were violent opposition to the dynasty and the Catholic Church ('Away from Rome') together with racial anti-semitism as a national imperative. He and his Pan-Germans made some impact on the student bodies (the *Burschenschaften*), but in general response was confined to a small section of the population, primarily in the minor towns. In 1897 Schönerer's following in the Vienna Chamber of Deputies was only five out of a total of 524 and in the first parliament elected by universal suffrage (1907) he was supported by only three of the twelve German Radicals out of a total of 516 members.

Unconnected with Schönerer's Pan-Germans a German Workers Party had existed in Bohemia and Moravia since 1903. At a Party congress in Vienna in May 1918 it re-christened itself National-Socialist German Workers Party (NSDAP – the official title of the later Nazi Party). In the last Chamber of Deputies elected under the monarchy (1911) it had three representatives. Its programme demanded abolition of the Austro-Hungarian monarchy, 'concentration of the entire German settlement area in Europe into a democratic, socialist German Reich' and the democratisation of Germany. After the war one of its founder members, Rudolf Jung, moved from Czechoslovakia to Munich and in 1919 participated in the formation of the NSDAP, member No. 7 of which was Adolf Hitler.[4]

Before World War I, apart from the infiltration of a few antimonarchical and anti-Catholic pamphlets, the loud but generally inconsequential and discordant Pan-German propaganda noises issuing from Austria evoked little response from Germany. On 31 August 1919, however, the Pan-German League, formed in 1894, included the incorporation of Austria into the German Reich as one of its aims when redrafting its statutes.[5]

In 1918–19 and subsequent years Germany, for obvious reasons, took no official initiative on the Anschluss question and left the running to Vienna. Nevertheless even during the war some sections of German opinion regarded the possible incorporation of Austria as offering some hope. In Le Temps of 30 April 1938, for instance, Vladimir d'Ormesson quoted a remark said to have been made in 1916 by Prince Bernhard von Bülow, the ex-Reich Chancellor and German Ambassador in Rome: 'Even if we lose this war, we shall have won the rubber provided we can annex Austria.'[6]

By October 1918 it was obvious that the war was lost and the Austro-Hungarian monarchy beyond salvage, at least in its previous form. Ever since the Lansing Declaration of May 1918 it had been clear that the destruction and dismemberment of the Danube monarchy and the creation of new national states were among the Entente's war aims. An additional – and most important – objective was the curtailment of German influence and the consequent prevention of German political and economic hegemony in Central Europe. It was therefore clear that union of the rump of Austria with Germany formed no part of the victor powers' concept of Europe. It was also clear that, so far as the German question was concerned, the decisive voice on future political organisation in the Danube basin was that of France.[7]

The Emperor's manifesto of 16 October 1918 called for a nationally-based federated Austria; its publication coincided, however, with Woodrow Wilson's rejection of the Austro-Hungarian Peace Note and this he based on the desire of the Czechs and southern Slavs for independence. On 21 October the German-speaking members of the 1911 Austrian Chamber of Deputies met and constituted themselves the Provisional National Assembly for German Austria. Of a total of 232 deputies 102 belonged to the German National Union, 72 to the Christian

Socials and 42 to the Social Democrats. In a proclamation the Provisional National Assembly opted for the formation of an independent German-Austrian State and a general election for a Constituent National Assembly. All the major parties declared themselves ready to join with the national states now in process of formation in a federation based on self-determination. Dr Viktor Adler, the Social Democrat leader who died shortly afterwards, emphasised his Party's readiness for federation if neighbouring countries wanted it; if they did not, German Austria should be incorporated into the German Reich as one of its component states. Only two small splinter groups, one of which was the National-Socialist, demanded immediate union with Germany. The alternative therefore seemed to be: a Danube Federation or Anschluss.

In the next ten days, however, events moved fast. On 28 October the Czechoslovak Republic was proclaimed in Prague; on the 29th the southern Slav areas, represented by a Croat assembly in Zagreb, announced their union with Serbia. On the same day the newly-formed Hungarian National Council under the chairmanship of Count Michael Karolyi recalled Hungarian troops from the front. The army collapsed.

Against this desperately gloomy background the first German-Austrian government assembled under the presidency of Dr Karl Renner. In view of the general trend, forces in the ascendancy were obviously those which could point to their programme as including opposition to the *ancien régime* and dissociation with the war. These were the Social Democrats and they now hoped to show that their ideological alternative was both right and practicable and do so without producing a carbon copy of the Russian revolution.

Viktor Adler was in charge of foreign affairs until 11 November 1918; his place was then taken by Dr Otto Bauer[8] who, however, resigned on 26 July 1919 before the formation of Renner's third Social Democrat–Christian Social government. Even before the end of the war, foreseeing imminent collapse, Bauer had rejected any idea of federation and called for an immediate Austro-German union. His main motive was ideological.

On 1 November 1918 the Social Democrat Party Rally in Vienna demanded a republican form of government. On 3 November the armistice agreement was signed in the Villa Giusti near Padua. On 11 November the Emperor announced his withdrawal from all official business and, although he did not explicitly abdicate, stated that he would accept in advance any decision on the future form of the Austrian State. On 12 November the Provisional National Assembly passed unanimously the law on the State and governmental structure of German-Austria; Article 2 laid down that German-Austria was an integral part of the German Republic.

In spite of an abortive attempt by left-wing radicals to storm the parliament building and establish a soviet dictatorship (an evil omen for the future) the session proceeded calmly. The official record shows the following extract from Renner's governmental statement on the law:

'A particularly vital feature of this statute is Article 2 which says that the German-Austrian Republic is an integral part of the German Republic; this is essential because of the race to which we belong. (Cries of 'Hear, hear'.) The great German people is in misery and distress. This people which has always prided itself as the home of poets and thinkers, our German people which is wedded to humanism and international amity, this our German people now has its back bowed. But at this moment when it would be so easy, so comfortable and perhaps so tempting to think only of our own affairs ('Hear, hear'), perhaps to snatch some advantage from the wiles of our enemies, at this moment our German people everywhere should know: We are a single race, a community in face of destiny. (Standing ovation. Loud and prolonged applause and clapping from the floor and galleries.)'[9]

The 12 November 1918 law therefore proclaimed Austria's desire for union, or at least that of her Provisional National Assembly. But it was a unilateral declaration of declamatory significance only and without practical effect. As Head of Foreign Relations, however, Otto Bauer sought agreement with the German government, initiating personal negotiations with Ulrich Count von Brockdorff-Rantzau, the German Foreign Minister. It was agreed to conclude a treaty admitting Austria as a member state of the German Reich with specific reserved rights roughly on the lines of those of Bavaria. A secret protocol to this effect was signed on 2 March 1919.

At a session of the newly-elected Constituent National Assembly[10] held in Vienna Bauer stated:

'Today we reconfirm as our programme the union of German-Austria with the Great German Republic. . . . With good reason the German Reich is being careful to avoid anything which might give the impression that our decisions are being influenced by the Reich in any way, particularly the decision for the Anschluss. We can and should enter the Reich only of our own free will, entirely uninfluenced by them. (Loud applause.)'

So on 12 March 1919, with only a few negative votes, the Constituent National Assembly once more decided that German-Austria should be an integral part of the German Republic. In his opening speech to the Weimar Constituent National Assembly Philipp Scheidemann, the German Chancellor, had already said: 'May the time be near when our Austrian brothers can once more take their place in the great community of the German people.' Article 61 of the Weimar Constitution stated: 'After its union with the German Reich German-Austria will have the right to the number of votes in the *Reichsrat* [Upper House] to which its population entitles it. Until then the representatives of German-Austria will act in an advisory capacity.'

The Austro-German Anschluss Treaty, however, was never concluded. Both Vienna and Weimar were aware of France's hostility to it; in December 1918 Stephan Pichon, the French Foreign Minister, had categorically reaffirmed France's position. Nevertheless, initially the Allies were not entirely at one on the Anschluss issue. Washington and London were not altogether opposed to it and definitely did not regard the problem as important as did the French; after some vacillation Italy decided to follow the French line. The successor states (Jugoslavia, Rumania, Czechoslovakia – the so-called Little Entente) were firm supporters of Paris in matters of foreign policy; an enlarged Germany was as unwelcome to them as a Danube Federation which, they considered, carried with it the danger of a Habsburg restoration.

In any case, before the Austrian peace delegation had even arrived in Paris, the Allied and Associated Powers had agreed on an absolute ban on the Anschluss. This was not unknown in Vienna.

Friedrich Funder says in his memoirs that on 16 April 1919 Colonel Cunningham, the Head of the British Military Mission in Vienna, had let it be known unofficially that Austria could expect appreciably better peace terms both territorially and economically if she were prepared to renounce all ideas of union with Germany. On this question views both in Britain and the US had changed, he said; there was no desire for a Danube Federation either; people would prefer Austria to remain neutral. Vienna should take note that this was not a question of emotion or of party politics. The Anschluss would be banned in the peace terms. . . .

A similar, even more urgent, warning came from Henri Allizé, the French Minister in Vienna. He had been active in arranging French deliveries to relieve the catastrophic Austrian food situation and was regarded as a sincere friend of Austria.[11]

But in Austria these warnings fell on deaf ears. Anschluss propaganda continued unabated in the press, at meetings in the provinces and even in parliament. Official quarters were still in touch with Berlin preparing for union with the Reich. Regional plebiscites were arranged to impress the Entente with the people's determination.

Tyrol and Salzburg actually voted on 24 April and 18 May 1921 respectively with a 90 per cent poll in favour of the Anschluss. Votes were also proposed in other areas, including Styria where the Governor Dr Anton Rintelen was heavily involved in the Anschluss movement; but these had to be abandoned in view of the threatened repercussions. On 1 October 1920 the Constituent National Assembly unanimously accepted a Greater-German proposal that, to demonstrate the will of the people, a nation-wide vote should be taken, but this was similarly shelved.

Meanwhile Lefèvre-Pontalis, the French Minister, had handed

to Dr Michael Mayr, the Federal Chancellor, the following declaration on behalf of his government: 'Should the Austrian government be unable to stop the present machinations in favour of Anschluss with the German Reich, the French government would suspend aid to Austria and the full authority of the Reparations Commission would be re-established.' The British and Italian representatives had associated themselves with this statement.[12]

In the German Peace Treaty signed on 28 June 1919 Anschluss with Austria was forbidden and Germany undertook to recognise Austrian independence as inviolable unless any change were agreed by the League Council. Under the rules of the League unanimity was required for any decision by the Council.

The ban on the Anschluss was not included in the original drafts of the Austrian Peace Treaty (Treaty of Saint Germain) of June and July 1919; in the final draft, however, it appeared as Article 88 – on French *and* British insistence. Austria undertook 'to refrain from any action which directly, indirectly or in any way . . . might endanger her independence, unless agreed by the League Council'. The articles on the Anschluss were deleted from both the Austrian and German constitutions.

In addition, in December 1919 the Supreme Council of the Allied and Associated Powers formally declared that they would 'oppose any attempt, direct or indirect, aimed against the inviolability of the territory of the Austrian State, against the provisions of Article 88 of the Treaty of Saint Germain or against the political or economic independence of Austria'. This decision was never revoked in later years.[13]

At the elections for the National Diet held on 17 October 1920 the Christian Socials emerged as the strongest party with 41·82 per cent of the vote as against 35·91 per cent for the Social Democrats. The two parties' seats in the House were 85 and 69 respectively. This laid the foundation for undisputed leadership both of the Christian Socials and of the Republic by the Christian Social leader, Mgr Ignaz Seipel, an ex-Minister under the Empire. He did not, however, form his first government until 31 May 1922.

The aims of Seipel's policy were preservation of the State, a new sense of purpose for Austria and maintenance of the population's standard of living. He succeeded in obtaining a loan from the League of Nations to deal with the bleak economic situation and avert the threat of famine, but with this went an aggravation of the internal political disagreements in Austria which were ultimately to lead to a permanent breach with the Social Democrat opposition.[14]

Under the Geneva Protocols Austria had pledged herself 'in accordance with the terms of the Peace Treaty not to divest herself of her independence' during the twenty-year period of the loan and to refrain from all negotiations and from any economic or financial undertaking which might adversely affect this independence either directly or indirectly.

On the Anschluss question Seipel was in fact in a difficult situation. He had never been an Anschluss man. As Chancellor of a coalition government, however, representing initially some 66 per cent of the electorate and only 58 per cent after the October 1923 elections, he had to take account of his Greater-German partners – and the demand for the Anschluss was still in the forefront of their party programme. Hence the witticism attributed to Seipel: 'Always talk about it, never think about it.'*

Seipel, of course, never said this. The story originated during the political argument over the Geneva Protocols when Karl Renner, speaking for the opposition, had said:

'Our signature in Saint Germain was obviously given under the irresistible pressure of force of arms and of exhaustion; we signed under protest and such signatures have their part to play in history. The glorious French nation has taught us how signatures such as that on the Peace Treaty of Frankfurt should be regarded. In the case of Saint Germain irresistible pressure and unavoidable necessity could be our excuse. But this is something quite different. . . . What justification could we have for denouncing this part of the agreement [the Geneva Protocols], gentlemen of the German Nationalist Party?

* An inversion of Léon Gambetta's remark: 'Always think about it, never talk about it' – he was referring to *revanche* for the annexation of Alsace Lorraine after the French defeat of 1870–1.

How could we denounce it when we have voluntarily accepted it [the ban on the Anschluss]? . . . I have already mentioned the Treaty of Frankfurt and in that connection I would observe that on the subject of Alsace the French said at the time: "Always think about it, never talk about it"; and now we ourselves have written all this into a protocol which we have voluntarily accepted. It seems to me that, as far as the Anschluss question is concerned, the Ballhausplatz has adopted a different version: "Always talk about it, never think about it."

If we voluntarily and happily sign this, if this House underwrites it, then for at least twenty years we must say goodbye to the idea which has been dominant in every citizen of this country from the birth of this Republic to the present day. We can foresee the tragic consequences of that. Twenty years! That is longer than any of us here present expect to live. . . .'[15]

Any objective appreciation of the situation is bound to reach the conclusion that, in the case of the Geneva rescue operation of 1922, the alternatives were not independence or Anschluss; Austria's very existence was at stake, the alternative being foreign occupation in case of imminent internal collapse. It must also be remembered that internal conditions in the major neighbouring states (Germany, Italy, Hungary) were still fluid and the future therefore obscure; moreover, in view of the catastrophic economic situation, it was by no means certain that, when the crunch came, the Social Democrat leaders, however well-meaning, would be able to withstand the repeated demand of their more radical supporters for a trial of the soviet dictatorship system. The conviction therefore grew that, despite all its drawbacks, the best service to peace and to the interests both of the Austrians and the Germans and of other peoples as well, lay in the existence of an independent Austria, in other words maintenance of the *status quo* guaranteed by the League.

The background to the tense atmosphere in Austria with all its political phobias was primarily sociological, but sociological not in the class warfare sense, since after 1918 real class distinctions hardly existed any more. The capitalistic bourgeois layer was thin, the major landowners practically without significance.

Politically neither played anything like the role which propaganda attributed to them. The really dangerous, the decisive, wave of feeling was caused by the economic extinction of the middle class as a result of defeat in war and the post-war inflation. The resulting general proletarianisation, fear of its ultimate consequences and, more important than all, lack of career prospects for most of the younger generation, led to an emotional extremism in all shades of political opinion; people were dissatisfied with the existing system and turned to 'self-help'. Basically and from the very start the Austrian trauma was an ideological one and in it, whatever the indications to the contrary, the Anschluss problem and its motivation played a decisive role.

Julius Braunthal, one of the most eminent and competent journalists among the left-wing Austrian *émigrés* wrote in retrospect:

'It must be realised that the German-Austrian working-class attitude to the Anschluss was not primarily determined by their sense of nationality. German nationalism had been the ideology of their class enemies in society, Habsburg patriotism that of their class enemies in the State. The German-Austrian worker hated one as much as the other. The idea of socialist internationalism was perhaps more deeply rooted in the German-Austrian working class than in any other in Europe. . . .

When, long before 1918, Otto Bauer put forward the idea that the Anschluss was a necessity, he accordingly evoked no great response from the Austrian workers. He reported that the mass of the workers were still unenthusiastic about the Anschluss idea, despite the fact that its first protagonists had been Social Democrats.

With the disappearance of the Kaiser, however, and the seizure of power in Germany by a socialist regime supported by workers' and soldiers' councils, the German revolution seemed to have overhauled our own at one stroke; the mass of the workers then began to think that the great highly-industrialised Reich offered far better conditions for pursuit of the fight for socialism than little German Austria, helplessly dependent on its agricultural neighbours and itself at least 50 per cent agricultural. Economic, patriotic and socialistic motives therefore combined to drive all classes of the German-Austrian people towards Anschluss with Germany.'[16]

This was tantamount to looking at the Anschluss primarily from the viewpoint of class interest. There were others, however, who rejected the theory of class warfare and class domination; they by no means subscribed to the notion that the old Austria had never been a home to the German-Austrians and that they had never looked upon it as their Fatherland.

About 1922 the elections had produced a 60–40 ratio between the ideological adversaries. With the consolidation of the state and financial stabilisation, the believers in Austrian independence increased in numbers and confidence, although economic recovery was long in coming; Anschluss propaganda decreased in virulence. At the same time, unfortunately, the internal political climate became increasingly tense.

The reason initially given for the necessity for the Anschluss was the economic non-viability of Austria; apart from a few lone voices this was regarded as unarguable dogma.[17] It was propounded in parliament, at public meetings, in the press, in technical magazines (Gustav Stolper in *Volkswirt*, for instance) and in university lecture halls. The size of the economic base, lack of raw materials, absence of a flourishing export industry, inadequate food and feeding stuffs production and divorce from Austria's natural markets were all cited as proof.

Up to 1922 hardly a voice was raised to question this theory. Although history has proved it untrue, from the point of view of those at the time it was understandable. The dismemberment of the old economic area, the exaggerated protectionism of the successor states, the modest scale of international aid and the policy of the victors did not, in fact, augur well for the future.

Had there been a European Recovery Programme or Marshall Plan after the First World War, the problem of Austria's non-viability would have been solved far more rapidly and satisfactorily; Austria in particular and the world in general would have been spared much. Comparison is convincing: the Geneva aid agreement was concluded some three years after our first defeat; it produced in 1923 a League of Nations loan of 650,000,000 gold kroner at an average rate of interest of $7\frac{3}{4}$ per cent against the security of customs and tobacco monopoly receipts. In 1948, three years after our second collapse, the US economic aid programme started with special reference to Austria; by 30 June 1954 Austrian industry had received in ERP credits alone a total of 6·4 milliard schillings.[18]

Nevertheless, difficult though conditions were, Austria did prove that she was economically viable after 1922. By 1923 electrification of the railways had begun, water power was being developed and a comprehensive road-building programme had been planned; agricultural production had risen rapidly and was capable of meeting a large proportion of the population's food requirements; by 1927 cereals, cattle and milk production had passed the pre-war figures.[19] By 1937 Austria was self-sufficient as to 70 per cent in cereals, 90 per cent in meat and fats and 100 per cent in potatoes, sugar and milk products. The budget was balanced and the currency sound. In March 1938 the gold and currency reserves seized by the Reichsbank from the Austrian National Bank amounted to 410,700,000 schillings (2,772 gold oz.).

All was not, of course, entirely rosy; unemployment, for instance, reached its peak in 1933. But even the United States was in a similar predicament; there the world economic crisis had begun on 24 October 1929 with the New York Stock Exchange's 'Black Friday' and unemployment reached phenomenal heights both in the United States and the United Kingdom. Obviously this development, together with its accompaniment of bank crashes, was bound to have severe repercussions on Austria, as it did throughout the world.

In October 1929 the Austrian *Bodencreditanstalt* ran into serious difficulties and, to avoid complete collapse, was taken over by the *Creditanstalt*. In May 1931 the *Creditanstalt* crashed and, to protect its customers, the Federal authorities assumed a large share of the liability. A few months later the German Damat-Bank (*Darmstädter- und Nationalbank*) suffered the same fate; a year later its affiliated Dresdner Bank could only be kept afloat by a rescue operation assisted by the Reich authorities. Inflation reached its peak in Germany in November 1923 when the gold mark was worth one billion (one thousand million) paper marks.[20] The situation was saved in August 1924 by currency reforms, including the creation of a new Reichsmark, introduced by Hjalmar Schacht, the President of the Reichsbank.

The collapse of the *Creditanstalt* threatened Austria with a renewed currency crisis. It was countered only by the grant of a further League of Nations loan of 300,000,000 schillings for a term of twenty years. Among the conditions was a renewed ban on the Anschluss or a customs union with Germany until the loan was repaid. In contrast to the Geneva Protocols this 'Treaty of Lausanne' encountered bitter opposition not only from the Social Democrats but also from the Greater-Germans in parliament. On 23 August 1932 the agreement was accepted by the National Diet but only by 82 votes to 80. Austria's viability was assured for a time but the Austrian economy still had a long and unrewarding row to hoe and this inevitably led to further deterioration of the political climate.

League financial control ended in 1936. Unemployment was still far too high – a monthly average of 406,000 in 1933, 350,000 in 1936 and 321,000 in 1937; to these figures must be added some 40–50 per cent of insured persons not on national assistance. Nevertheless unemployment was falling, and not merely because insurance conditions were being more strictly applied, as one view has it;[21] this is disproved by the rising figures of sickness insurance for workers and employees.

Subsequent tendentious statements notwithstanding, the truth is that from 1932 until the Anschluss Austria was following a slow but sure path to economic recovery and was holding her own with other states of similar size and in a similar position. Industrial production was rising and by 1937 was approaching that of 1929, the last boom year.

Up to 1922 there had hardly been any real dialogue on the Anschluss question. Supporters and opponents were both swayed by emotion. The entire argument took place in an atmosphere in which, for various reasons, the overriding consideration was a complete break with the past. Between 1918 and 1930 the public debate, when there was such a thing, attracted little attention – the provincial plebiscites held in 1919 and 1920 were more in the nature of protests against the Peace Treaty and the desperate economic situation.

The situation changed visibly when sentimental reasons and long-term political aims gave way to a stern, ruthless nationalist ideology which would brook no compromise. Hitler had categorically demanded the Anschluss in *Mein Kampf*. In 1928 the Nazi Party had declared that it would not forgo 'a single German . . . in the League of Nations colony of Austria'. As early as 1923 Hitler had decided that, if necessary, the National-Socialists must take over the government in Austria by force.[22]

National-Socialism, hitherto a politically non-negotiable raw material 'made in Austria', was now re-exported to Austria from Germany as a gospel to cure all ills. By 1932–3 the situation was serious. In view of the National-Socialist menace the leaders of both the major Austrian parties executed an about-turn; whatever their previous attitude to the Anschluss, the subject was now taboo, for no one wanted what was now in prospect.

The average Austrian, who had been indoctrinated for fourteen years and as a rule had been taught little at school calculated to inspire him with faith in Austria, was now expected to forget all the slogans of the past. For this time was required. In general he succeeded, although naturally some were discontented with one thing and some with another after 1933. The point was that, like their parents in 1918, they were now expected to repudiate what yesterday had ranked as gospel.

Seen from Hitler's headquarters things looked quite different, and that long before his seizure of power on 30 January 1933. After all, had not the Austrians been demonstrating in favour of the Anschluss ever since 1918? At that time their national desires could not be met for external political reasons. Things would soon be quite different. Therefore National-Socialist politicians in Austria or speaking about Austria had only one object – to force through the Anschluss. Everything else was a side issue.

Accordingly in 1932 a bitter struggle began in Austria; as with certain more recent political problems in other areas, it was initiated with a policy of terror. That this would inevitably lead to 'counter-terror' was not only foreseen but desired; the subsequent question, which came first, the hen or the egg, would receive a far more potent answer from the German side than the Austrian. In any case this was merely a tactical problem to be answered according to the international situation at the time and which no one took seriously.

Leaving aside the political manœuvring, how did the Anschluss question really stand at this time?

The arguments used by Anschluss supporters on both sides of the frontier were based partly on emotion and partly on reason, the former more on the Austrian side and the latter on the German. The Austrian Anschluss man longed for Germans to be united. Old Austria was gone; many who had loyally served their country and its monarchy now decided to survive its interment as Germans of the Reich. Before 1932, however, many had understandably come to the conclusion that, because of the world situation, the Anschluss was apparently impossible for a long time to come and at best must remain a long-term objective. The results were declarations and statements of programme which people soon ceased to take seriously.

Up to 1933 Berlin's policy was equally governed by the realisation that the Anschluss was impossible for the foreseeable future. Over there emotional impulses such as the dream of German unity played a secondary role from the outset, although use was made of them to popularise the idea. From the German point of view the Anschluss was obviously welcome as some compensation for the loss of power imposed by the Peace Treaty; in principle, therefore, all political groups in the Reich together with their leaders were in favour of it. Every German ambassador in Vienna up to 1938, whatever his background, regarded the Anschluss as rational, made no secret of his opinion and quoted in support of his views the will of the Austrian people. Every German chancellor and every foreign minister thought the same way but, until Hitler came, none of them saw any possibility of implementing it in the foreseeable future. None of them was prepared to accept responsibility for the risk of international conflict or to disregard the rules and precepts of international law.

For reasons of political common sense and respect for the law all Hitler's predecessors as chancellor accepted the existence of an independent sovereign Austria. This statement is not invalidated by the fact that Julius Curtius, the German Foreign Minister, and Johannes Schober, the Austrian Foreign Minister, signed an Austro-German Customs Union Treaty on 19 March 1931.[23] Moreover, some time before, Dr Lindner, head of the Austrian Desk in the German Foreign Ministry, had submitted a detailed memorandum setting out the legal and political implications of a Customs Union.[24] His paper, which was 'confidential' and dated 20 August 1927, was entitled 'Notes on the Question of an Austro-German Customs Union'; it includes the following:

'The negotiations between Germany and Austria-Hungary which ended in mid-1918 were an attempt (basically successful) to fuse two states in some degree into a single economic area, while preserving their economic and political independence both internally and externally. There can be no doubt, however, that the signatory powers of the Treaty of Saint Germain and of the Geneva Protocols would regard the conclusion of an Austro-German customs union as a measure likely to endanger the independence of Austria in the sense of that word used in the special conditions, however capable of a wider interpretation these conditions may be; in view of the generally antagonistic attitude to the Anschluss on the part of the Powers, the necessary agreement of the League Council would be obtainable either not at all or only at the price of impossible concessions. Any favourable politico-economic terms granted to Austria by Germany would probably be regarded with suspicion; it would not be necessary to refer to the Peace Treaties to invalidate them; they could be dealt with as violations of the Most Favoured Nation clause.

A satisfactory solution to the problem can only be achieved by means of a carefully prepared agreement taking account of the over-all external political situation; the initiative must come from the Austrian side. So far no Austrian government has taken the view of Riedl, the Austrian ex-Ambassador, who remarked that, if necessary, the agreement of Geneva must be obtained by the "water-dropping-on-a-stone" method.'

In Austria the attitude of people on both sides of the fence was primarily governed by emotion, in which the refusal of the right to self-determination and a romanticised picture of the unitary national state played an important part. We shall never know exactly how many Austrians really wanted the Anschluss and how many were opposed to it in principle. In any case this is largely a question of what period we are considering.

It may well be, and rightly so, that in a hundred years' time the two World Wars – and, please God, this is all there will be – will be referred to historically as *the* Twentieth-Century World War covering the Russian revolution, the entry of the United States into the war, the dissolution of Austria-Hungary, and then, after a short pause, the fall of Germany as a world power, the liquidation of the Western colonial empires, the rise of Russia as a super-power, the shift of imperialism from West to East, the balkanisation of Central Europe and finally the crippling of Europe as a power.

Of course we now have UNO, thanks be. But, despite its open diplomacy, for really thorny problems UNO has proved hardly more effective than the old Concert of Powers.

What is all this to do with our subject? Merely that there is a direct connection between the Russian October Revolution, the fall of Austria-Hungary and the cultural and political situation of the Austrian Republic within Central Europe during the inter-war period – and the latter led to the Anschluss with Germany and so direct to the Second World War. To disregard this connection is like looking into a concave mirror which must inevitably distort the historical picture.

The contribution made by the old Austria together with the countries under the Crown of St Stephen was:

1. For centuries it had held together an organised Central Europe, holding both Eastern and Western expansionism at bay by offering to the multifarious languages and nationalities of Central and East-Central Europe a common home and a common economic and cultural area.

2. It was not invariably trailing behind, as the popular belief is; in many ways it was ahead of its time as a real factor for

regional integration. Despite its ups and downs, until 1918 it functioned; until it was defeated in war, the majority of its inhabitants never questioned its existence.

3. It may be assumed that, had it survived, it would have acted like other states and would not have closed its doors to economic and social progress or to political reform.

4. The Austrians were not an ethnic community united by language; they formed a multi-national political association like the Swiss, Belgians, Canadians and even more the Russians today.

Because there was no true national majority and for historical reasons, the strongest links holding the State together were the dynasty, the army, the administration and the Church.

It is idle to speculate whether, had there been no war and no defeat, this state had a chance of long-term survival. It may well be that Austria-Hungary was in any case nearing the end of her career, but this was no reason for anyone to refuse to respect her importance and her achievements in the past. This, however, was what the Anschluss movement on both sides of the frontier studiously did.

Among the various arguments in favour of the Anschluss the historical was one of the weakest. Neither 1848 nor 1866 provides any sound basis for the 'back to the Reich' cry simply because there was no such thing as a unified German national state. The dream of many people in 1848 never became a political reality; 1866 and Bismarck's ideas did nothing to change this.

On the other hand there did exist a long-standing economic and cultural community bound by common interests which could not fail to find some expression politically. From the Austrian point of view Hitler represented, not the continuation and completion of some arrested historical development, but precisely the opposite – a break with history.

In National-Socialist jargon anyone who opposed the idea of the Anschluss was a traitor to his country and a separatist. Austria's very existence was described as a menace to Germanism. The phrase 'two German states', so frequently used in Austria at the time, must be construed with this background in mind. In addition Austria had long been regarded as the cultural centre for the German minorities in the successor states; up to 1933 the Germans of the old Austro-Hungarian Empire, now 'Germans abroad', still looked to Vienna, whether from the Sudetenland, South Tyrol, the Banat, Siebenburgen or Poland. One of the Third Reich's first acts of aggression against Austria was to search the house and confiscate the papers of the honorary Austrian consul in Danzig.

Shortly after 1933 Austria had already lost this position as a sort of protecting power for the Germans of the old Empire; the Third Reich with its League for Germanism Abroad [*Bund für das Deutschtum in Ausland*] had stepped in. Austria could not compete with the money and propaganda resources available to Germany. As time went on, however, Austria in general and Vienna in particular became a centre for all those German cultural forces and tendencies which, for political or racial reasons, had lost their old home in the Reich. Major German publishing houses continued to do business in Vienna; well-known artists and scientists escaped to the freedom of Austria. Austria had become the second German state in fact, because there German culture, now homeless in its old home, found a new country. The more violent the opposition to German National-Socialism, the more justified became the Austrian claim to be the representative of the now homeless German culture and of the higher values of Germanism. To all intents and purposes Weimar had been exiled from the Third Reich and had found its home in Vienna.

The political revolution of November 1918 was established fact to which practically everyone had resigned themselves. The only possible outcome was a democratic republic. Only the 'romantic revolutionaries' thought that it would lead straight to the 'dictatorship of the proletariat' on the lines of the Russian revolution of October 1917, in other words to a soviet rather than a parliamentary democratic republic. Among the romantics, of course, were the communists, who had formed an Austrian communist party in November 1918; numerically it was weak. Its first leader was an ex-bank official named Franz Koritschoner; in the spring of 1919 he was succeeded by Ernst Bettelheim, an emissary of Béla Kun charged with the preparation and execution of the Vienna communist *putsch* of 15 June 1919; a soviet dictatorship was to be proclaimed on the Hungarian model.

There were, of course, workers' and soldiers' soviets in which communists and Social Democrats discussed passionately the pros and cons of setting up a soviet republic in Austria and the prospects of seizing power by force. The chairman of the executive committee of the workers' and soldiers' soviets was Friedrich Adler,[25] one of the leaders of the Social Democrat Party.

The undisputed theorist and political leader of Austrian Marxism was Otto Bauer. Contrary to the views of the hotheads he by no means held the view that Austria should take her cue from the Russian revolution; he was too well aware of the sociological and economic differences between the two countries.

The majority of Austrians felt no urge for further revolution and social upheaval. They were convinced that revolution would lose them more than it could gain.

Otto Bauer was by no means the uncompromising advocate of force which many, both of his supporters and opponents, thought him. Probably it was his misfortune to be heard too much and read too little. He was, of course, a radical; he was convinced of the validity of dialectical materialism and believed in the victory of scientific socialism in the struggle for a complete new order of society. This could never come, he concluded, without ruthless class warfare. Success in this struggle, however, postulated solidarity within the proletarian fighting front. As the communist manifesto of 1848 had said, the communists were no party of their own, different from and opposed to the other workers' parties; they were rather the activist advanced guard. Accordingly in Austria successful efforts were made to preserve the single-class character of the Party and prevent the fragmentation which occurred in Germany and other countries both before and after 1918. Austro-Marxism's particular contribution, therefore, lay in the unity of the socialist-proletarian movement and its projection to other countries. This was the basis of Bauer's political theory

45

and practice as the movement's leading representative. His arguments were clear but they were frequently obscured by the emotional over-simplification of political oratory.

Political revolution, people thought, was no more than a single day's work; at one stroke the republic had been proclaimed and privilege swept away. Now they thought that social revolution was equally simple; all the workers had to do was to take over factories, mines, offices, banks and property one day; the directors and capitalists would simply be turned out and what had belonged to capitalists and landowners in the morning would be public property by the evening.

But things were not quite as easy as that. The problems of gross national product and distribution of goods remained. Socialism was primarily concerned with fair distribution, in other words a redistribution of income; but this did not mean equal shares for all. The hard worker was still entitled to a larger slice of the national cake than the indolent; the idler should get nothing at all. An end should be put to unearned income, in other words interest and dividends from inherited or acquired property.

The problem remained, however, that socialist society must produce more, not less, goods than the capitalist; otherwise, despite the redistribution of income, the individual would earn less than before. Socialist society's most urgent task, therefore, was to organise a fair redistribution of the national product without reducing its total volume.[26]

This shows how far Otto Bauer's ideas of the time (1919–21) were divorced from the Soviet Russian doctrine of dictatorship of the proletariat. Later, when an émigré in Brno, he revised his views on the Soviet form of socialism, describing it as the supreme historical example of the triumph of socialist society.[27] But this was in 1936.

However this may be, Otto Bauer, Max Adler and Friedrich Adler, the main Marxist theorists in Austria during the early postwar years, clung to the theory that the ultimate aim of a socialist order of society could be achieved only if the political revolution was followed by the social. But this could not be done by means of a political coup taking place overnight. It was analogous to a socio-biological process, implying a gradual, though radical, transformation of existing society and this required time. In addition the permanency of any revolution depended on the historical and economic situation of the time.

The prerequisite for the social revolution which must come one day, they said, was the capture of political power by the proletariat and this was possible only by the use of revolutionary methods.[28]

So far so good. Next on the programme would come expropriation and socialisation of heavy industry, first the iron and coal mines, then the iron and steel industry. The next stage of the victorious social revolution would be the democratisation of the lower-level administrative areas, including local administration, then the constitution of elected economic and works councils. All forestry and all estates over 300 acres were to be socialised together with the mortgage banks; then would follow all financial institutions. Building land and the housing industry was to be communalised.[29]

In 1918 and 1919 it was generally assumed that seizure of power by a 'proletarian dictatorship' was technically possible but equally generally realised that it would not be allowed to last long. Austria was still under threat of blockade by the victors and she had to have imports both to feed the population and keep her industry going.

The way to Germany was barred. 'When Czechoslovakia stopped one or two Vienna coal trains on the frontier, the city was without electricity for days and the trams could not run; when Jugoslavia stopped food trains from Trieste, the meagre flour and fat ration upon which the hungry urban population depended could not be maintained during the following weeks. . . . In this situation and in view of the victor powers' explicit veto, the working class did not dare push the revolution beyond the democratisation already achieved.'[30]

This was a desperate situation if ever there was one. In the last analysis, moreover, even without outside intervention any extension of the revolution in Austria would have suffered the same fate as the attempts in Hungary and Bavaria in March and April 1919.

Safety valves were required and tactical manœuvres, not recognisable as such, were necessary. But threat was implicit in everything people read, heard and understood. Threats were so continuous and so violent – mobs, strikes, boycotts, marches and counter-demonstrations – that people eventually became so habituated to the use of strong words that no one took them seriously any more. Nevertheless the atmosphere was close and oppressive; tension was in the air for years until it was almost a normality. The worst aspect, however, was that human contacts were lost as a result, as always happens when invective takes the place of argument. No one was prepared to admit that he was not invariably right and his opponent not invariably wrong; people preferred to be 'wrong together with their friends than right in the company of their opponents'. So long as this situation persisted the prospects of collaboration and the possibility of peaceful compromise between differing points of view were problematical. Often enough matters threatened to reach an impasse.

Proportional representation had produced a balance of political forces such that any real effective majority seemed out of the question; the result was that both Right and Left pursued the struggle for power using non-parliamentary methods. All across the board the Centre, though probably supported by the majority of the electorate most of the time, was not strong enough to curb the extremism of the various parties' wings.

In addition to the permanent threat of the mass use of force, individual acts of violence stood out as warning signs: on 1 June 1924 Seipel, the Federal Chancellor, was severely wounded by revolver shots on the Vienna Southern Railway Station; the assailant, Karl Jaworek, a young Social Democrat, thought that he was thereby serving his party's cause: on 3 October 1933 Rudolf Drtil, a young National-Socialist, attacked Chancellor Dollfuss with a revolver in front of the parliament building. Between these two dates came 15 July 1927; 1934 was not far off. Both attacks were the work of individuals, as also was the case in other countries and under other political systems in the tense political atmosphere of those years.[31]

When an act of violence is the work of a lone wolf, he and no one else is, of course, directly responsible; the background against which the act takes place, however, must also be considered. In any case assassinations and attempted assassinations have never yet served the cause for which they were intended. On 3 October 1933 Chancellor Dollfuss was only slightly wounded but, as I can vouch from personal experience, the attack caused him to think – and his thoughts were directed not to his attacker and his possible Austrian backers; as with any fanatic his only complaint against them was lack of understanding and he had no fear of them. He was far more worried by the following report dated 5 October 1933 from Stefan Tauschitz, the Austrian Minister in Berlin:

'Zl 85/pol.
Comments by a senior Propaganda Ministry official
on the attack on Chancellor Dollfuss.

Top Secret

Chancellor,
A senior Propaganda Ministry official expressed himself as follows in conversation about the attack made on you on the 3rd of this month: "So you've gone and chosen the wrong man all over again in Vienna; at the decisive moment the f—ing fool gets it wrong and misses. To my mind you want three well-aimed shots in Vienna – for Dollfuss, Starhemberg and Fey."

When my informant commented that Dr Dollfuss was a national-ist who favoured an understanding between Germany and an inde-pendent Austria, the official replied: "What! Nonsense! Anyone who is not a National-Socialist is a swine and should be done away with. Austria has now reached the stage when she can be worn down by terrorism. Over the years we managed to wear down a much larger state than that and we must do the same with Austria. Once half the people have been won over politically, then is the time to start terrorism."

He then drew a comparison with the action of von Papen in the Beuthen case,[32] saying: "If Papen had had the National-Socialists hanged after the Beuthen case, we should have been able to make play with such an act of violence in order to rouse people on the side of the National-Socialist movement. Since, however, he sang small and could not summon up the courage to carry out the sentence, we made him look ridiculous and so gained our point that way. One must always be able to turn every case, whatever it may be, to the advantage of the Movement. The decisive moment in Vienna must come in late autumn."

My informant is definitely of the opinion that there is some connection between Dertil [sic.], the assassin, and certain circles in the National Socialist Party; he thinks that the fact that Dertil may not have been a National-Socialist himself supports this view, since it is more prudent to choose tools which are not obvious beforehand. This information is completely authentic and reliable.

I have the honour to be, Chancellor, your obedient servant
Tauschitz.'[33]

This report requires no comment. It merely shows that from beginning to end of the First Republic the spectre of the Anschluss was there, whether as a beckoning vision or a menacing warning. The picture of Austria in the period between the Habsburgs and Hitler may be drawn in red with black shadows or vice versa, but, whether consciously or inadvertently, it lacks perspective and so becomes a picture puzzle. It comes to life only if the Nazi in the background is neither disregarded nor belittled. He influenced everything, as a potential threat from the early 1920s and a menacing reality from about 1931. Initially Anschluss propaganda seemed to act as a unifying factor internally, though the ideological and political motives from which it sprang were very varied;[34] it became a factor for disunity once it was clear that the continued existence of Austria depended not upon internal Austrian politics, but on European policy. That this was so was proved, first in 1922 with the Peace Treaty and the Geneva Protocols, then in 1931 with the abortive Customs Union, and finally in 1933 when Germany launched her cold war against Austria with the Thousand-mark Blockade,[35] and Austria, in view of her geographic and economic position, became wholly dependent on Italian support.

The magnitude of Austria's problems and their apparent insolubility produced a creeping crisis of confidence. First came the external problem created by the Peace Treaty: little mutilated

Austria had to learn how to make her way in the new European order; resignation or yearning for the past were frowned upon, but ahead was nothing but a void. Then there was the internal problem: put baldly – was parliament or the mob to rule, in the theoretical language of political society – community of the people or class warfare, in terms of the political battle – democracy or dictatorship. But if it was to be democracy – how long for? If it was to be dictatorship – whose and for whom?

It is an indisputable fact that initially (and this does not apply to Austria alone) the word 'dictatorship' meant 'dictatorship of the proletariat', not dictatorship pure and simple. It is also true that in Austria the political theorists stood out against it when for a short moment it seemed a possibility; moreover they never thought of it in terms of the immediate future. Nevertheless stress was laid on the extremist connotation of the word and according to the laws of political acoustics extremist voices invariably awake echoes; the louder the argument, the smaller the prospect of compromise.

Christian Socials and Social Democrats struggled for an absolute majority without ever achieving it. Neither side questioned the legitimacy of this as an aim. On what was to happen once this aim had been achieved, however, their views were very different. One side would have given democracy a (possibly short-lived) chance; the other would have seen the green light for social upheaval leading to their ultimate goal – a classless socialist society.

Insecurity both external and internal, together with the violence of the propaganda slogans, produced a fruitful breeding ground for the development of self-defence formations. Additional factors were the military restrictions of the Peace Treaty, the existence of uncontrolled stocks of weapons from the demobilisation period and the examples set by neighbouring countries. Initially the formations on both sides of the barricades were genuinely for self-defence, 'defence' being the operative word. The *Arbeiterwehren* [Workers' defence forces] were intended to defend the achievements of the revolution, the *Bürger- und Bauernwehren* [Citizens' and Peasants' defence force] to stop the revolutionary excesses which threatened in the turbulent years 1918–19. In 1923 the

Arbeiterwehren and *Ordnertruppen* [law and order squads] formed themselves into the republican *Schutzbund*[36] [Defence League]; the Austrian *Heimwehr* [Home Defence] movement grew gradually from the *Bürger- und Bauernwehren*.

The existence of paramilitary formations was certainly no indication of a normal healthy domestic political situation, particularly seeing that on both sides they consisted of armed men[37] not directly under control of the State. Unless called out as government auxiliaries, these self-defence formations remained private associations of equal status in law and therefore subject to the same legal regulations. The political parties used them for their own purposes and did their best to maintain their influence over them – in which the Left was more successful than the Right. The *Heimwehr* in particular was seldom a uniform body; it was plagued by territorial problems of organisation, differing ideological and political trends in the various provinces and the resulting leadership squabbles. Throughout its existence it never rid itself entirely of these troubles.

It must be admitted that both the formation and the subsequent actions of these self-defence organisations were products of the abnormal conditions of the time, for which they were not responsible. The climate of those turbulent years, extra-parliamentary pressure (extra-parliamentary opposition in present-day terms) and the notorious weakness of the forces of law and order produced a situation of which people were forced to take notice and no one could see how or whether it could be dealt with by the forces available. In similar circumstances and for similar purposes similar organisations were formed in almost all neighbouring states and even in the far-off Baltic Republics.[38]

In its early years the *Heimwehr* was certainly not fascist. Instead it was seriously concerned to defend hearth and home and the social order in which it believed. Conversely the republican *Schutzbund* stood ready to defend the revolution's achievements; the working class intended to gain power by legal means and the *Schutzbund* would protect it against the inevitable counter-revolutionary assault.[39] The real background to the self-defence movement on both sides was mistrust, mistrust of the existing political set-up and its institutions, but above all mistrust of each other; each was positive that the other was set on establishing his dictatorship, by legal means if possible but, if not, by force. Opinion was further inflamed by violent speeches and articles, both perfectly legal under the rule of freedom of expression. If his opponent refused to be convinced, everyone was ready to force him to conform for his own good. People were not all fascists on one side and bolshevists on the other. A contemporary writer says: 'If there is talk of fascism in Austria, in the interests of historical accuracy and the honour of our people it should be stated that the first Austrian fascists were extreme left-wingers and that they were directly responsible for the emergence and formation of the other brand of fascism.'[40] In particular, so far as the later development of the *Heimwehr* movement is concerned, once the nationalist groups had divorced themselves from the Austrian ultras, it became a strong, important and reliable factor in the struggle for Austrian independence and against National-Socialism.

The kaleidoscopic history of the self-defence forces played a significant role in pre-1938 Austrian politics. From 1921 to 1929 they were on the upgrade; after a recession in 1929–31 they reached their peak in 1933–4, gradually levelling off thereafter until their original *raison d'être* vanished in April 1936 with the introduction of universal military service. The outside world became aware of the Austrian *Heimwehr* movement only in the spring of 1928 as a result of the unhappy and discouraging picture presented by Austrian internal politics about the time of the burning of the Vienna Law Courts on 15 July 1927. First Hungary and then Italy became interested for reasons of foreign policy. So far as Count Bethlen, the Hungarian Minister-President, was concerned any leftward swing in Vienna would endanger Hungarian treaty revision policy which was directed in the first instance against Czechoslovakia and then against the Little Entente as a whole. Both for economic and political reasons he was opposed to any extension of German influence in Central Europe; Weimar Germany did not encourage Hungarian agricultural exports and Budapest feared that with a left-wing government in Austria, that market too might be lost to Hungary. The plan for a

Hungarian-Austrian-Italian economic bloc, first seriously discussed in 1928, accorded with Mussolini's ideas on Italian leadership in the Danube basin. Italy too, therefore, wished to prevent any increase of German influence. Budapest's fears about possible anti-Hungarian tendencies on the part of a left-wing Austrian regime were reinforced by Béla Kun's stay in Vienna in the spring of 1928. Mussolini also had no wish to find neighbouring Austria pursuing an anti-fascist and anti-Italian policy. Bethlen's proposals therefore met with a favourable reception in Rome. Italy and Hungary agreed to combine in preventing a socialist government coming to power in Vienna and to support the *Heimwehr* both politically and materially.

In September 1929 Dr Johannes Schober, the Vienna Police President, was appointed Federal Chancellor, an office which he had already held twice before. His relations with the *Heimwehr* were excellent and he was looked upon as their man. In December 1929 the National Diet, after wearisome negotiations, took a decision on the government's proposal for constitutional reform aimed at an increase in the authority of the State and the powers of the Head of State, together with introduction of a corporate representational body alongside parliament. The proposal failed to gain the necessary two-thirds majority and so, to enable some decision to be taken, the more drastic proposals such as the introduction of corporate representation and limitation of the powers of parliament were dropped.[41] Much subsequent misery might have been avoided, had the original ideas been accepted.

The *Heimwehr* were determined, if necessary, to insist on suspension of the constitution and thought that they were assured of the Chancellor's support. They were bitterly disappointed when the subject was never mentioned. A breach was opened between government and *Heimwehr*. In addition opinion among the Christian Social leaders, primarily those of the Peasants' League and the Christian Workers' Movement, was turning increasingly against the *Heimwehr* until the low point was finally reached on 18 May 1930 with the announcement of the so-called Korneuburg programme.[42]

The most striking phrases in this programme as announced by

Dr Steidle were: 'We are aiming at power in the State. We reject both democracy and the parliamentary system. We acknowledge the principles of fascism.' Steidle himself was still a Christian Social member of the Federal Diet; later he tried to qualify these statements and many of his supporters had no great liking for the programme. The split in the non-socialist camp was now plain for all to see. The Korneuburg gaffe also had pregnant consequences for the *Heimwehr* movement. Starhemberg called the proclamation 'obscure verbiage'. Steidle resigned and, after violent arguments particularly with the Styrian leader Pfrimer, Starhemberg was appointed Federal Leader.

The *Heimwehr* had initially been recruited primarily from the urban middle class, ex-servicemen, students and farmers. It was designed as a defensive formation and its common bond was anti-Marxism, a negative creed. In contrast to its opponents it had no real ideology and only very vague ideas about its social and political programme. Finally it adopted in its entirety Othmar Spann's[43] doctrine of the 'real state' based on corporations. This was hardly calculated to make any greater impact on the mass of its supporters than the Korneuburg tub-thumping.

In the early days of the *Heimwehr* movement (up to about 1931) people of every shade of political opinion and ideology had foregathered in its ranks, always provided that they were anti-socialist. Anschluss supporters and German radicals rubbed shoulders with Austrian legitimists, liberals with conservatives, non-believers with devout Catholics – as in the old army. But all this was to change under the pressure of events and developments both inside and outside the frontiers of Austria.

In May 1931 internal crises led to Starhemberg's resignation from the leadership. This brought Pfrimer, the Styrian nationalist, to the top once more. After the so-called Pfrimer *putsch* of September 1931, a comic-opera affair stifled at birth, it was clear that the movement had passed its prime. The mere threat of the use of Federal forces had sufficed to stop the proposed march on Vienna before it had ever begun.

The *putsch* plan had been confined to Pfrimer's Styrian *Heimwehr*, but the result was a split in the Austrian movement as a whole. In May 1932 the Styrians under Pfrimer and Rauter placed themselves under the NSDAP in Munich and became an integral part of the Hitler movement. The Austrian loyalist members of the Styrian *Heimwehr* assembled under a new provincial leader appointed by Starhemberg, Graf Stürgkh.

Starhemberg's *Heimwehr* and Starhemberg himself were now definitely committed to Austria. In 1934 and subsequent years, however, conflicts and rivalries among the leaders, primarily between Starhemberg and Major Emil Fey, the Vienna *Heimwehr* leader, led inevitably to a weakening of the movement's political position. Finally, on the introduction of universal military service all the defence formations were disbanded and their responsibilities taken over by the Front Militia which was in close touch with the Federal army.

It would be both unjust and inaccurate to deny the considerable contribution and the great sacrifices made by the Austrian *Heimwehr* under Starhemberg in defence of the concept of Austrian independence and in the cause of freedom. This does not alter the fact that in the early years (1928–9), for which Starhemberg bears no responsibility, the actions and aims of the various *Heimwehr* leaders were sometimes calculated to bring them into conflict with the responsible State authorities, with public opinion and, most important of all, with the policy of maintenance of Austria's independence.

Though Seipel, Schober and later Dollfuss gave the *Heimwehr* temporary support for reasons of internal political tactics, none of them approved of its foolhardy plans to set up a *Heimwehr* dictatorship. It would have been something very different from the later 'corporate state' and would have been opposed by the majority of the *Heimwehr* members themselves, particularly the peasant element.

A fact generally disregarded for various reasons is that the pluralist nature of Austrian society was largely reflected in the right of association and in the formations themselves; recognition of the Austrian State was obligatory, as was renunciation of all direct or indirect support from those forces, whether inside or outside the frontiers, the declared aim of which was the incorporation of Austria into the Third Reich. During the years of cold war Austria was struggling for her very existence. Choice of weapons is largely imposed upon the defender by the attacker, particularly when he is indisputably the stronger and, as it proved, recognises no legal or other restrictions.

The struggle was not directed against individuals but against the 'system' whose servants they were, a system which the Nazis maintained was the obstacle to the 'return to the Reich' and the 'German victory'. In the circumstances, however, the only alternative 'system' was a full-blooded socialist one and of this there could be no question for international reasons. In fact therefore there was nothing to be done but cling together, support each other and sit it out or alternatively abandon the whole idea of Austria.

On 26 March 1933 Lothar Egger, the Austrian Minister in Rome, reported as follows to the Chancellor:

'On the 18th of this month, two days after the arrival of the British Ministers in Rome, an article appeared in the *Popolo d'Italia* entitled "The Austrian crisis and the absurdity of class warfare". The article would have been of no more than normal interest, had it not ended with these words: "As far as we are concerned the problem might arise whether a socialist Austria was not preferable to Austria as a province of Hitler's Reich." '[44]

In December 1935 the British government enquired of Selby, its representative in Vienna, whether, in view of the international political situation, the moment had not arrived to take some initiative in Austria with a view to democratisation of the system. Selby's reply was that he 'was by no means of this view. Instead he would urge that, so long as the Austrian government was involved in so serious a struggle with Germany for the preservation of its independence, it should be left in peace'.[45] And Selby was no particular friend of the Right in Austria.

On 28 May 1936 General Jansa, who had been Chief of the Austrian General Staff since May 1935, wrote as follows to Ambassador Hornbostel:

'My friend,

I hear on good authority that the Führer himself will decide on the timing for the occupation of Austria.

The reoccupation of the demilitarised zone [the Rhineland] was planned for 1937 but the situation was favourable and it has now taken place. The same may happen with Austria. It may not come for years, but it could come overnight.

For the moment Hitler has ordered that acts of violence in Austria should cease and martyrs should not be created; only grapevine propaganda is to continue.

The Austrian Legion, which will be used for the occupation of Austria, is about 25,000 strong. These people receive a two-year training and are then placed in civilian jobs. Nevertheless the Austrian Legion can be mobilised in 24 hours.

Besides the Legion a sort of Cheka is being prepared which will constitute the political security force on the occupation of Austria.'[46]

On 1 September 1937 von Papen reported on the situation in Austria to the German Foreign Minister, von Neurath:

'At present he [the Federal Chancellor] was convinced by hundreds of reports that, if not the leaders of the Reich, at least very strong and influential groups in the Party considered the absorption of Austria into the German Reich to be the immediate political task. Knowledge of this fact prevented him from proceeding in many fields as he might perhaps do under other circumstances.

Then followed some very long statements regarding the well-known complaint that the Reich had never ceased to exert its influence on the Austrian National-Socialists in all ways. . . . For the rest Austria had not undertaken and never would undertake to carry out any foreign policy which would injure the Reich, and it was also incorrect, if I had made the statement, that the Austrian Army was being armed against Germany. The principal theme of his objections was the increasing acuteness, as he said, of the cultural situation in the Reich. All in all his replies were *completely negative*, so that no change in his political course is to be expected.

The question now arises . . . whether, if and when we have reached the conclusion that the policy of July 11 cannot be developed with Federal Chancellor Schuschnigg, we ought not, with the co-operation of the external and internal factors, to consider bringing about a change of chancellors. It is certain that the President of the Republic has for a long time been sharply critical of the policy of Schuschnigg. He might be used as an opening wedge. It is also certain that people in the Clerical *Heimwehr* camp, such as Gleissner and . . . Schmitz, are striving to bring about the fall of the Federal Chancellor. Possibly the Chancellorship would first be entrusted to one of these men. That would mean an intensification of the course of the Fatherland Front in all matters and therefore would start anew the course of developments (with the prospect of a change). But it might also be that we could get the President of the Republic to place at the head of the Government a more objective man with fewer political liabilities, one more inclined to cooperate with the workers, a man who would, above all, undertake to further energetically the gradual *rapprochement* of the two states through the conclusion of binding treaties. In this connection former Federal Chancellor Ender is being proposed by many groups (including the Austrian NSDAP) as a useful personality. He was the Chancellor of the Customs Union, and I believe that he does not hold to the "Austrian ideology" so fanatically as the present Chancellor.

I bring up the question of this cabinet change because I am convinced that with a continuation of the Schuschnigg methods we shall *very soon* be in an untenable position. One could perhaps take the viewpoint that the increasing gravity of the tension would give us the opportunity to attempt to solve the Austrian question by other means [!]. But quite apart from the fact that, viewed historically, it would always appear to me to be a mistake to seek a violent solution instead of one presented by Austrian *domestic* developments, I should like to think that it would certainly be preferable for the general European situation to adopt the course I have in mind. But then one would have to have clearly in mind *now* the course to be followed in the near future, if one is not to be subjected to surprises; all the more so since, as I assume, the Duce will also treat of the German-Austrian question. As far as those conversations are concerned, in my opinion the advantage to be derived for us from the policy of the "Axis" must after all, be realised in some way. The Duce could probably be pledged to certain fundamental principles in the further treatment of the Austrian question. . . .

To supplement the facts of the situation, I add the further information that the State Secretary, with whom I had already discussed in detail the complex of problems and from whom I really expected support *vis-à-vis* the Chancellor, in no way differed from the latter's negative statements.

For the present, most cordial greetings and Heil Hitler!

Your

Von Papen.'[47]

On 20 and 21 May 1937 von Kanya, the Hungarian Foreign Minister, met Count Ciano, the Italian Foreign Minister; Kanya's notes record Ciano as saying: 'Rome continues to insist on Austrian independence and will only abandon this principle: 1. If Austria restores the monarchy; 2. If a Popular Front government came to power in Vienna; 3. If in foreign policy Austria adhered to the Paris-Prague-Moscow axis.'

Neither the Italian nor the Hungarian views were new nor were they unknown to the Ballhausplatz.[48]

All these documents speak for themselves. They show that at the time it was not as simple as it later appeared to distinguish between 'anti-State' and 'anti-government' tendencies.

Later critics[49] have accused the Austrian government of resisting Hitler only to save their own skins, not for the sake of Austria; some have even referred to a token resistance. This overlooks the fact, however, that any sudden move towards a parliamentary coalition (and there could have been no question of anything else) would have provoked counter-pressure from within; externally it would have been the sort of experiment, like an attempted restoration, for which Hitler was waiting. It also overlooks the fact that, had the new corporate constitution, as planned for 1938 and publicly announced in Innsbruck on 17 September 1937 been fully implemented, this would have been the start of a development which would largely have cut the ground from under the feet of the revolutionary socialists. After all, the struggle against National-Socialism was one for the continued existence of the Austrian State and not for or against some future social revolution – and the chances of the latter were by no means brighter in 1938 than in 1918.

Josef Buttinger (alias Gustav Richter, leader of the illegal revolutionary socialists) says that in spring 1938, when an *émigré* in Paris, he openly rejected all idea of reconstituting an independent Austria in the event of the fall of Hitler; Bauer and Adler were at one with him in this and Bauer drafted Austrian socialism's first political manifesto after the Anschluss. This, the so-called Brussels Resolution, called for a socialist revolution of all Germans. Should Hitler's regime be brought down by war, the right of self-determination should be demanded for Austria; the brighter the prospects for a German socialist revolution, the more important was it to resist any re-establishment of Austrian independence.[50]

In retrospect the period of the defence formations (*Wehrverbände*), including the Republican *Schutzbund*, seems like a bad dream, whichever way one looks at it. Nevertheless at the time they had their use, for they acted as a corrective to the disorder of the new-born republic's early years.

The post-November 1918 ideological differences were crystallised and accentuated by the fact that both sides possessed considerable stocks of weapons; on demobilisation infantry weapons had been distributed by the Inter-Allied Military Commission to 'People's and Citizens' Defence Forces, factories, railway stations, military authorities, etc.'. Available returns show that at 30 November 1918 the following had been handed out:

    1,156 machine guns
    80,345 automatic rifles
    13,627 rifles with considerable quantities of rifle ammunition.[51]

The Federal army being limited to 30,000 men, it may be assumed that most of these weapons passed into the hands of the 'volunteer formations', initially the *Arbeiterwehren* and on the other side the *Bürgerwehren*.

In July 1932 a Jewish ex-Servicemen's League was formed and a year later it could boast 8,000 members. According to the Jewish religious authorities' figures on 10 March 1938 there were 180,000 Jews in Austria of whom 165,000 were in Vienna; this compares with a figure of 220,000 in 1923.[52] These are numbers of practising Jews only, however; the total Jewish population in Austria in the inter-war period is estimated at about 300,000, of whom 250,000 were in Vienna.

As in other European countries there were anti-semitic tendencies in pre-Hitler Austria too. Formerly political forces, together with the official authorities, had been sufficiently strong to prevent any excesses and nip any outburst in the bud apart from some verbal invective. Karl Renner says:

'It is true that . . . Dr Karl Lueger (Mayor of Vienna 1897–1910), who had to keep his eye on the German Nationalists when dealing with the Jewish element, to placate his opponents announced the principle that "Jews and Social Democrats will not be employed". In his usual humorous manner, however, he added: "I will decide who is a Jew." Throughout the Christian Social period in power no harm came to a single Jew in Vienna; in fact the Jewish element made far greater progress in the press, literature, theatre and business worlds than in the previous so-called liberal period. . . . It must not be forgotten, however, that Vienna was the entry point for Jews from the East who did not assimilate easily; some popular opposition to the entry of these people was understandable since the general standard of living was lowered thereby.'[53]

In the old Austria there had been two currents of anti-semitism: radical 'racial anti-semitism', the protagonists of which were the Pan-Germans; it had also strong anti-Catholic overtones and its primary political objective was the absorption of Austria into a 'racially homogeneous' Germany. Then there was 'religious anti-semitism' which believed in Austria and aimed at social reform; for economic reasons, however, it was opposed to 'Jewish-liberal' preponderance and to the increased competition resulting from Jewish immigration. Richard Charmatz, perhaps over-generalising, regarded political anti-semitism in Austria as 'largely a product of the capitalist economy', an expression of middle-class helplessness in face of advancing industrialisation.[54]

Dr Oskar Karbach,[55] the Jewish-nationalist writer opposed to the policy of assimilation, regards the historic urge of many German Austrians for Anschluss with Germany as the mainspring of Austrian anti-semitism. The Pan-Germans, he considers, were only secondarily anti-semites. They merely thought to further their nationalist ideas by adroit use of the anti-semitic card. The other side (the Christian Socials) regarded anti-semitism more as an academic matter; they had never made any attempt to define who should really be regarded as a Jew. Nevertheless in his judgement these so-called moderate anti-semites unquestionably carry some share of the blame for the poisoning of the atmosphere in Austria, although naturally they have their alibis ready.[56]

In the Vienna of the First Republic a tendency to anti-semitism was particularly marked in years of economic upheaval, between 1921 and 1923 for instance, during the period of inflation and of the Geneva rescue operation with its political and economic repercussions. At the time organised anti-semitism was definitely led by the newly-formed National-Socialist movement, which stressed the racial and *völkisch* aspects and linked the problem with the Anschluss movement; politically its targets were the governments, first of Schober (June 1921–May 1922) and then of Seipel (from May 1922). Vienna police headquarters files show that speakers included Dr Walter Riehl (Austrian National-Socialist leader), Rudolf Jung, a Sudeten German politician, and from Bavaria Anton Drexler, Adolf Hitler and Julius Streicher. As early as 1923 there were student disturbances in the Vienna Institute of Commerce and World Trade and the police confiscated some inflammatory anti-semitic posters of National-Socialist origin.

In the turbulent years after 1933 anti-semitic slogans were current among the small shopkeepers of Vienna, as they had been sixty years before; they were directed primarily against the big department stores. In glaring contrast to the racial anti-semitism of the National-Socialists, however, the background to this movement was purely economic. No legal restrictions were placed on Jews nor were any economic handicaps imposed, though Jews were sometimes accepted into the public service but only in proportion to their ratio of the population. There was never any discrimination in the schools, and in the academic professions, the business world and cultural life Jews continued to play their respected, even leading, role. Terms such as 'half-Jew' and 'half-caste' were never used.

During the inter-war period, moreover, the background to anti-semitism was largely political; the target was not the Jews as a race or religious community but the party which was to a great extent inspired by Jews and which had sold its soul to Marxism. So to a considerable extent anti-semitism was synonymous with anti-Marxism. Josef Buttinger says that 80 per cent of the intellectuals who joined the Social Democrat Party were Jews; of the 200 Social Democrat lawyers, the 400 members of the Social Democrat Legal Association and the 1,000 Social Democrat doctors in Vienna almost all were Jews, as were the vast majority of the 450 members of the socialist high-school-teachers union, 90 per cent of the editorial staff of the *Arbeiterzeitung* and other Party newspapers and eight out of the ten lecturers employed by the Social Democrat educational organisation. Among post-war Central Europe's homeless intellectuals who had taken root in Vienna, almost all the revolutionary reformers were Jews.[57]

In 1934 Dr Emmerich Czermak, an ex-Minister of Education, together with Dr Oskar Karbach attempted to initiate discussions with the true, in other words practising, Jews, naturally making it clear that they were opposed to racial anti-semitism. Czermak says:

'In discussion with these Jews we found that both sides set far more store by racial solidarity and the predestined community of a people than by an artificially propagated and totally unworkable internationalism; also that life and experiences shared in common were a goal far superior to divisive and destructive class warfare. . . . We respect the Jewish people and its national religion and wish to see both preserved, but we also wish to protect ourselves – not from those who recognise the Jewish race and religion, but from the parasites who have neither national nor religious roots and neither understand nor respect the qualities of their own or their host nation.'[58]

Between 1933 and 1938 no serious difficulties with Jewish organisations arose, in particular none with the religious community. Representatives of Austrian Jewry on various official bodies were outstanding – Dr Desider Friedmann as President (elected) of the religious community, Dr S. Frankfurter and Dr Jakob Ehrlich on the Council of State [*Staatsrat*], Federal Council of Culture and Vienna Municipal Council. On his own initiative Dr Friedmann attempted via Geneva to obtain international Jewry's help and support for Austria's struggle against the Nazis for her independence; he also refuted the story spread about in the West for obvious political and personal reasons about the Austrian government's anti-Jewish attitude. Of this he assured me personally.

During the same period numbers of scientists, artists, writers and publishers who had suffered or were threatened with racial persecution, took up residence in Austria. Between 1934, when the emergency legislation came into force, and March 1938 deliberate acts of terrorism against Jews ceased.

Following the tragic events of 12 February 1934[59] the propaganda story was spread abroad that, as far as anti-semitism was concerned, the 'Austro-fascist dictatorship' was indistinguishable from National-Socialist Germany. On 15 February, for instance, the *Daily Herald* reported a mass flight of Jews to Prague and Warsaw. Georg Franckenstein, the Austrian Minister in London, reported to Vienna that the Jewish central organisation had been in touch with him and considered that this press report must be regarded 'as a manœuvre by the Labour Party here to rouse public opinion against the Austrian government'. He asked for instructions. The Austrian Foreign Ministry replied by coded telephone message that there was 'naturally no question of any anti-semitic agitation or of the resulting mass flight'.[60] Even in 1947 there was still talk in the United States of 'the violent anti-semitic policies of the Dollfuss regime'.[61]

In his five-volume book *Österreich von Habsburg bis Hitler* [Austria from Habsburg to Hitler] Charles Gulick, referring to a speech by Emmerich Czermak on 29 November 1933, comments that 'The Christian Socials were worthy competitors of the Nazis in anti-semitism'; he also cites economic 'victimisation of Jews' and anti-Jewish discrimination in Vienna schools.[62] On 26 March Göring declared at the Vienna North-West Station that Vienna was no German city because it was totally judaised. This applied to trade, banking, culture and the previous government. 'The Jew must go. . . . By the time the Four-Year Plan is complete, there must be no more Jews in Vienna.'[63] The difference between Gulick and Göring is ghoulish but obvious.

Dr Oskar Karbach, who was no particular friend of the Austrian government system, comments on this subject:

'In retrospect it must be admitted that under the corporate state the position of the Jews in political and legal matters was unaffected – the position was undoubtedly different in so far as economic affairs are concerned. . . . On the other hand there was good reason for Austria to resist any temptation to imitate the anti-Jewish trend in the Third Reich or to produce some specifically Austrian and catholic form of anti-semitism; for overriding internal and external political reasons the harassed Alpine Republic simply could not afford to undertake risky experiments in this field. The government was only too well aware that adventures of this sort would not prolong the life of the corporate state by a single day and might well shorten it.'[64]

The corporate state was by no means designed as the dictatorship which history – with some apparent justification – has labelled it; history, after all, can describe only the actual developments and happenings of the years 1934–8. Political controversy has also attached the same label to it.

However, even during this period, when the transitional constitution was in force, a number of features differentiated it from a real dictatorship: a considerable degree of separation of powers, maintenance of the federal principle, a fully independent Chamber of Public Accounts, a non-political supreme court combining the previous administrative and constitutional courts, in which highly qualified lawyers practised without interference. The 1934–8 constitution was never designed as a definitive stage; it was a transitional phase provided for by the 1 May 1934 constitution on severely practical grounds and established as transitional in constitutional law. It is a fair question whether this period of four years was not unduly long despite the cold war with the Third Reich and its consequent external political repercussions. It must be admitted in this connection that development did not always proceed with sufficient rapidity and some acceleration would have been beneficial.

The most difficult task proved to be the organisation of the new professional corporations in which employers and workers from the various trades were to sit in separate sections. By 1938 we had succeeded in reorganising only agriculture and the public services. The first free elections took place in Vorarlberg in April 1936, when the farmers and agricultural workers voted. In the same year factory council elections were held in industry. Today it is said[65] that the illegal socialist trade unions exploited these elections to infiltrate their people into influential posts; whether this is true or not the councils functioned excellently and served their purpose. The same is true of the Trade Unions Association; after some initial hesitation on the part of former Social Democrat trade unionists this made rapid progress under its provisional leadership, finally reaching and even exceeding the earlier figure for membership. The tempo of social reform, social policy and social legislation, particularly important during the period of economic depression, admittedly left much to be desired. But this is a complaint common to all periods and all countries.

Dr Otto Ender, an ex-Chancellor and for many years Governor of Vorarlberg, was responsible for drafting the constitution. On 16 December 1937 he spoke to the Foreign Press Association and on 4 February 1938 in the Urania, Vienna; he stated on both occasions that corporation elections would take place in 1938 and that these would bring the provisional constitution to an end. It was firmly intended that the remaining conditions for implementation of the corporate constitution should be fulfilled in that year. The first official announcement to this effect was made in September 1937; it was seriously meant and practically feasible. No one can today say with certainty how the corporate state experiment would have worked out in the 1930s, had its development been normal, had it been allowed to overcome its teething troubles and had it reached completion. It was an experiment; there were no precedents and it was in no sense a copy of some foreign model. There was no intention to dictate to corporations and syndicates from above, any more than there was to establish a fascist parliament and totalitarian state authority.[66]

It may be that the legal basis for the new corporate constitution was 'very questionable and probably inadequate'; it may also be that 'the last sitting of the National Diet [30 April 1934] and everything to do with it was highly questionable'.[67] Opinions on these questions differed and still do. Complete agreement is unlikely to be reached on what to do to counter a State emergency in any given historical situation. There is a built-in resistance to recognition of the fact that a government crisis can become a real State emergency. When this happens, however, it is in practice impossible to meet all possible contingencies by legal preventive and protective measures.

'The Austrian experiment in liquidating the democratic constitution and replacing it by an authoritarian and markedly catholic regime had only one overriding purpose – to prevent the Anschluss. It is questionable whether this short-lived innovation was ever intended as anything more than an attempt to avert catastrophe at a tragic moment. Under the circumstances of the time it is understandable that it was not the perfect catholic state about which there had been such tempestuous theoretical argument for years before. A mighty opponent stood at the door; he had a numerically strong and fanatically devoted fifth column in the country; for a brief period it was thought that his victory, which all feared, could be averted; later it became daily more imminent. What began as an attempt to salvage Austria's independence was deliberately turned into a delaying manœuvre for the benefit of the entire world.' – Oskar Karbach.[68]

CIVIL WAR – ACTUAL AND POTENTIAL

The early 1930s were a period of turmoil in many European countries. In France Daladier's government, though possessing an adequate parliamentary majority, yielded to pressure from extra-parliamentary forces – the first in the history of the French Republic to do so. On 6 February 1934 the first street battles between Right and Left took place in Paris. The *Croix de Feu*, the *Jeunesses Patriotes* and the various French paramilitary formations grouped under the title *Action française* went into action. In England there was much talk, primarily among Oxford students, about organised propaganda against military service and all forms of discipline. The United States were busy with their own affairs and determined to adhere to their traditional isolationist policy. In Italy the ex-socialist and anti-clerical fanatic Benito Mussolini (editor of the Milan *Avanti* from 1912 to 1914) and his fascists had been in power since 1922 as a result of the impossibility of forming a parliamentary coalition. In the Far East the Sino-Japanese conflict was smouldering. In the USSR Stalin was busy with his Five Year Plans and internal purges.

Disarmament conferences met endlessly in Geneva; a Babel of voices, the most convincing and most honest being British, spoke of the necessity and advantages of peace. Stress was laid on the observance of treaties, with the finger pointed at the smaller states – who could, after all, be coerced if necessary. And in the midst of all this Hitler had begun a massive rearmament.

Such were the 1930s. As seldom before, appearances were belied by the reality. Little Austria was no exception.

It is no exaggeration to say that for most of its span of life the

First Austrian Republic lived under the shadow of potential civil war, though on neither side of the ideological barricades did the responsible leaders want it. The basic cause of this civil-war potential with its paralysing repercussions was the existence of two camps of approximately equal strength and separated by insoluble ideological differences, the one based primarily on the industrial workers and the other on the peasantry; each suspected the other of planning to seize power by force, in other words of preparing for open civil war. Their attitudes to the old Austria and its First World War defeat differed. Class warfare led to a friend/foe relationship in politics; consciously or unconsciously politics became coloured by the hatred born of fear. 'Hatred undoubtedly provides a powerful impulse for a political mass movement, but for political leaders it is a bad counsellor. It always carries people too far.'[1] Its worst feature is that it is never without response; imperceptibly the distance separating one point of view from another and one set of men from another widens.

In 1919 the communists had been defeated despite their expenditure of lung-power. Nevertheless, as a compromise to avert the communist menace, Friedrich Adler had recommended something very akin to the soviet system. In the words of the liberal *Volkszeitung* the impression given was that Austria had settled for rule by both sides as 'a half-way house between a parliamentary and a soviet republic'.

On 11 June 1920 Renner's third coalition government resigned because of differences over the constitution of the army. Four months later the coalition of the two major parties split irretrievably – and so it remained until the German *Wehrmacht* moved in in March 1938.

The reason for the break was a fundamental difference of view on which direction to take and so the political machine ground to a standstill. The brakes were still functioning but the steering was dangerous. The violent conflict about the future of the armed forces, the outcome of which was still in doubt, had led both sides to form armed Party guards, the blueprints for which had been in existence ever since 1918–19. This meant that a potential civil-war situation was a permanency, carrying with it the threat of actual civil war. 'The supporters of militant socialism wished to ensure that the proletariat could defend itself.'[2] The militant opponents of the class struggle were determined to break the monopoly of the agitator and insist on freedom of association in the factories.

General disarmament at home would obviously have been the most sensible solution. Julius Deutsch suggested it in 1923, Karl Renner in 1928 and Schober in 1930. But there were never any serious negotiations. As with the higher-level international disarmament conferences progress was blocked by one overriding factor – mistrust.

According to Otto Bauer by 1924 the Social Democrats had every chance of capturing the additional 320,000 votes necessary to obtain an absolute majority and so take over power. The Left was therefore to come to power peacefully and through the electoral system. But the bourgeoisie were unlikely to sit with folded hands and watch the workers proceed on their peaceful crusade to capture power. As soon as the ruling classes realised, he maintained, that their hegemony was coming to an end, they would seek to preserve it by force and to bring down the Republic which would then no longer be theirs. This was why the capitalists and monarchists had built themselves so strong a position within the Christian Social Party and this was why they maintained their armed formations.[3]

If the working class was to be voted into power, however, it must be in a position to defend the republican constitution against the armed formations of the Right. The vital requirement, therefore, was an army upon which it could rely, its own instrument, not an unthinking tool in the hands of reactionary officers. Soldiers and workers must therefore think alike and the army's officers and men be drawn from the ranks of convinced republicans. The working class, be it noted, had no intention of using the army for its seizure of power; it needed the army, however, to protect it from the counter-revolution which would attempt to snatch the voting papers from it when victory was within its grasp.[4]

In addition the workers themselves must be ready to ward off the fascist and monarchist threat. This was the job of the Republican *Schutzbund*. If the soldiers and at least some of the police and gendarmerie were on their side and a strong *Schutzbund* was on guard, the reactionaries would not dare to attack. The working class would then be able to take over power without the use of force and without civil war, simply by use of the legal power of the vote. The 1918 revolution had not freed the working class from the tyranny of the bourgeoisie but it had given it the opportunity of obtaining a majority in parliament. The members of the executive were at liberty to exercise their political rights; they were therefore fair game for working-class propaganda, might be won over and organised; with them a force could be created strong enough to prevent the reactionaries depriving the workers of their victory or snatching the fruits from them once they had won it.[5]

The communists, Otto Bauer continued, thought differently. Their obsession with the Russian Revolution was such that they thought nothing any good which was not a copy of it. They thought that the workers could seize power only by means of civil war and could keep it only by dictatorship and terror. In support of this view Otto Bauer claimed that in many countries where the proletariat was still living under the bourgeois yoke, force was the only method of breaking the power of the bourgeois regime; also that even in Austria exceptional circumstances such as a war might compel the proletariat to resort to force. As an example he quoted the case of a restoration in Hungary followed by combined efforts on the part of Hungarian and Austrian monarchists to re-establish an Austro-Hungarian dynasty. In such a case, it would be the duty of the Austrian proletariat to use dictatorial methods in organising the defence of the country, to exterminate the monarchist traitors and to ally themselves with neighbouring states opposed to a Habsburg restoration.

All these ideas were echoed in the Social Democrat Party programme announced in Linz on 3 November 1926.[6] It said nothing about 'dictatorship of the proletariat', although the words had been frequently used by Max Adler during negotiations at the Party rally. Otto Bauer came out unequivocally against it; according to his academic theory of the law of historical development, dictatorship of the proletariat was not essential in order to bring about a socialist order of society. A better solution would result from the imminent socialist victory at the elections – better because it did not involve the use of force. Nevertheless he thought it certain and a proven historical fact that the enemy would offer active or passive resistance to a socialist victory; then, and only then, was the use of force necessary and justified. The Linz programme's political strategy, therefore, was based on the inevitable use of force but for defensive purposes only.

The Linz programme said nothing about violent overthrow of the existing order; it did, however, refer to the necessity for class warfare and the aim 'of the working class to capture the dominant position in the democratic republic', using democratic methods 'to demolish the class tyranny of the bourgeoisie'.[7]

Allowance must be made for the fact that this was a Party declaration in the language of an election manifesto; nevertheless it was a precise reflection of Bauer's thinking. Both personally and intellectually he was an honest man, convinced that his views were 'scientifically' correct. But this does not alter the fact that from the point of view of the other side, however these words were interpreted, they were bound to impair even further the already strained relations between the two political extremes.

No one was thinking about a *putsch* to forestall a working class victory; this was proved seven years later, in September 1931, when the authorities dealt with Pfrimer's adventure.[8] There was no particular reason to fear any overwhelming socialist victory at the elections. It soon became clear that, in spite of substantial gains, both the Social Democrats and their opponents had a long way to go before obtaining an absolute majority. At elections for the National Diet the Social Democrat share of the poll was:

October 1923	39·6	per cent
April 1927	42·0	per cent
November 1930	41·15	per cent

Moreover from 1931 onwards the Social Democrat vote was on the downgrade – and not in Austria only. Not until the first national elections after the war, in November 1945, did it once more reach 44·6 per cent.

In 1926 and the subsequent turbulent years the Linz programme seemed to the other side to be a battle cry born of knowledge that Social Democrat strength was intact, confidence in victory and the conviction that socialist theory was correct. It could be argued, of course, that it visualised only a militant defence against possible counter-revolutionary manœuvres. But was not this the language of any potential aggressor and could not the 'pre-emptive attack' always be classified as 'defence'? Neither side could have guessed that a bare seven years later Fierlinger, the Czechoslovak Minister in Vienna renowned for his close contacts with the opposition, would have handed to his French colleague Clauzel a memorandum by Otto Bauer declaring himself ready 'in the name of the Social Democrat Party, to refrain from collective agreements etc.'. The official Austrian comment was: 'Clauzel remarked that the Social Democrats were singing quite small.'[9]

But in 1926 this situation had not been reached by a long chalk. At that time many of the bourgeoisie, and not only the hotheads and *condottieri* who are always to be found anywhere, were becoming increasingly mistrustful of contemporary democracy and increasingly anxious about the future. Their reasons:

1. If the socialists' optimistic forecasts proved correct and the Social Democrats did actually obtain their additional 320,000 votes, and therefore an absolute majority, in the near future, their leaders would clearly regard this as a mandate to proceed to the ultimate phase, the inauguration of a socialist society; they had left no doubt about the upheaval implicit in this – 'resistance would not be tolerated'. There were plenty of foreign examples to show what was meant by 'deliberate sabotage of the economy and suppression of violent opposition'.

2. If, however, this optimistic forecast proved false and there was still a bourgeois majority, the Linz Programme with its deification of the principle of class conflict had removed the possibility of any constructive collaboration with the opposition in future; the final victory of the proletariat could be assured only

by consistent resistance to a bourgeois regime. The Linz Programme, therefore, put out of court the pragmatic solution of a major coalition because it would be contrary to class interests and so postpone the final victory. Bourgeois democracy was regarded only as a transitional phase; class harmony was therefore neither possible nor desirable.

At a critical moment (June 1931) Seipel made a last attempt to form a coalition government including the Social Democrats, offering them four seats in a cabinet of nine which included three Christian Socials, one Greater-German and one *Landbund* representative.[10] But it was doomed to failure. Even had the attempt succeeded, it is more than doubtful whether it could have averted subsequent developments. Its failure, however, undoubtedly contributed to a further reduction of the waning confidence in the vitality of Austrian parliamentary democracy.

At the turn of the year 1926–7 public affairs were ostensibly conducted strictly in accordance with the rules of the legally established parliamentary state. Nevertheless, both on the surface and in practice, democracy had already become fragile. There were too many people on all sides who no longer believed in it and regarded it merely as a stepping-stone to fulfilment of their own political dreams. Once they had the essential 51 per cent of the votes and thus the free hand which a majority would give them, they thought, it would not be difficult to brainwash the other 49 per cent or whatever the figure turned out to be.

These 'others', the bourgeoisie, did indeed possess a majority which was subject to minor variations upwards or downwards every three years but was never less than 58 per cent. It was a coalition, however, united for negative rather than positive aims, for defence rather than attack. Its most vulnerable point, perhaps, was its lack of a clear common concept of Austria, valid both for the present and the future.

The original Christian Social programme of 15 December 1918 had given cautious and limited acknowledgement to the Anschluss but it was expunged from the Party programme of November 1926; the cry then was for 'equality of status for the German people within the European family of nations' and 'regularisation of the relationship to the German Reich on the basis of the right of self-determination'.[11] In 1933, influenced by events in Germany, the Social Democrats too deleted the Anschluss paragraph. In the critical years following 1926, however, the Anschluss was by no means an out-of-date notion.

In fact all thoughts turned on what seemed the pressing requirement of the moment. One side was convinced that the other was arming for civil war, the other that its outbreak could be prevented only by arming itself. Both were agreed that rule by the other would be calamitous and must be prevented or, if electoral results made this impossible, paralysed.

The prospect held out by the Linz Programme in the event of a left-wing victory was certainly not encouraging for the opponents of a socialist state and society. It was far more radical than the normal simple opposition between workers and non-workers, proletarians and capitalists, revolutionaries and reactionaries. Moreover the greater the emphasis placed by the Left on the well-known phrase about 'all wheels grinding to a halt', the greater the temptation for the Right to prove that they were equally adept at using extra-parliamentary methods of pressure.

One side threatened a general strike indicating that the primary aims would be paralysation of traffic and stoppage of electricity and gas supplies; the other countered with a threat to nip it in the bud by force; so tempers rose on either side. And all this was happening before Austria found herself battling for her economic existence in the wake of the world crisis, before the 'Third Reich' had cast its shadow over the country, and under the eye of neighbours (Italy, Hungary, Jugoslavia and Czechoslovakia) ready to invade and, in the case of Jugoslavia and Hungary, by no means adverse to picking up territorial gains at Austria's expense.

It is a fact often overlooked that the alternative did not lie simply between independence and Anschluss; there was a third possibility – partition following a military invasion. This would have become actual if, for instance, the government had resigned and a new government proved incapable of coping with the internal situation. The social revolution desired by one side and feared by the other could not take place without civil war, and any prolonged civil war would have spelt the end of Austria. In the highly charged atmosphere at the end of the Austrian Republic's first decade of existence this aspect received too little consideration by either side.

In retrospect the 'Arsenal affair', which seemed so deadly serious at the time, looks like a comedy. It does, however, illustrate the mortally dangerous crisis through which Austria was then living.

The case concerned the first major round-up of weapons by the official authorities. Under the old regime the sprawling Vienna Arsenal had been a military establishment producing infantry rifles. It was known that, ever since demobilisation, secret stocks of weapons had been located there, guarded under an agreement made with the coalition government by the Social Democrat occupants of the Arsenal area – administered in trust as it were. In the highly charged political atmosphere of 1926 the War Ministry received a report that these stocks were to be moved and issued to the Republican *Schutzbund*. On 2 March 1927 the army took over 12,000 rifles but it was officially admitted that considerable further stocks probably existed in secret caches somewhere in the Arsenal. After detailed negotiations the opposition declared themselves ready to hand the remaining stocks over to the Federal government and not to move any of the known dumps. It soon became clear, however, that clandestine movement of weapons was still going on and that the quantities were nothing like so paltry as the Arsenal staff had originally maintained. Eventually on 17, 18 and 20 May the army took over without serious friction a further 20,000 rifles, 665 machine guns, 400,000 rounds of ammunition and 20,000 rebored carbines of Italian origin.

On 6 March 1927, when excitement was at its height, the independent *Volkszeitung* published a leading article headed 'The *Schutzbund* on the alert':

'If there are no weapons concealed in the Arsenal, no one need get excited and our leaders are playing an irresponsible game with the people's peace and quiet. If weapons are secretly hoarded in the Arsenal, however, then they must go. Vienna does not need dumps of weapons within its walls; the population should not be threatened on pretext of protecting it; the Arsenal should be neither red nor black; the streets should not belong either to the Social Democrats or the Christian Socials. What we want is peace and quiet and those politicians and demagogues who refuse to leave this exhausted city in peace carry a heavy responsibility. We need no para-military formations either on the Right or the Left and if the Republic is unable to protect itself with the forces of law and order, it will not be able to do so by violence and tampering with the law. *People avoid playing with fire because they cannot tell how far the fire will spread nor what victims it will claim in the process.'*[12]

In fact no one was thinking of playing with fire, though there were widely differing opinions on how to avert the danger. One side was thinking primarily of preventing catastrophe by isolating the supposed source of conflagration; the other was mainly concerned with gaining control of certain fundamental social developments which it considered inevitable, with the object of preventing unnecessary destruction and exploiting them in the cause of progress. The only parties who initially believed full-scale destruction to be essential were the ostensible enemies but actual allies – the National-Socialists and the communists. Germany before the seizure of power was soon to give vivid illustration of that fact.

The fatal error on both sides was the failure to cry a firm halt to the advocates of force and total destruction; to this extent they were playing with fire. They did not ally themselves with the fire-raiser but they allowed themselves to be undermined and then, when the worst had happened, rushed in blind haste to the defence. The Right were reading their lesson by the hullabaloo over the film *All Quiet on the Western Front* and the Left by the far more serious case of Schattendorf.

On 30 January 1927, five weeks before the 'Arsenal affair' almost set light to the political powder barrel, an ominous incident occurred in the village of Schattendorf in Burgenland, but the warning passed largely unheeded. Like the province and the country the village was divided into hostile political camps, on the one side the League of War Veterans [*Frontkämpfer*] and on the other the members of the Republican *Schutzbund*. But in Schattendorf feelings ran even deeper than that, for at the time of Béla Kun's soviet dictatorship the village had belonged to Hungary. Though they had now been Austrians for some time, the villagers could not forget the bloody days of terror. Anyone who at that time had made his peace with Béla Kun's supporters was still looked upon as a bolshevist; anyone on the other side was branded as a Horthy adherent and white terrorist. In this situation the *Frontkämpfer* were automatically labelled as right-wingers and the members of the *Schutzbund* as the Left.

The Schattendorf *Frontkämpfer* had arranged a regional rally for Sunday 30 January; as usual it included a parade. There was nothing unusual in this. Meetings and processions of all colours were being held up and down the country every Sunday. Unlike Wiener-Neustadt, neither side regarded Schattendorf as a political stronghold in which the appearance of the other would have been regarded on principle as provocation. Unfortunately the local *Schutzbund* decided to hold a meeting on the same Sunday, equally preceded by a parade; it was to be held at the usual *Schutzbund* meeting place, one of the two adjacent and competing village inns, the other being the headquarters of the *Frontkämpfer*.

There was a clash and the *Frontkämpfer* had the worst of it. The *Schutzbund* marched to the Tscharmann Inn, the *Frontkämpfer* headquarters, and some of them forced their way in with provocative cries. It has been said that there was shooting but there is no proof. In any case the die was cast when rumours spread that shooting had already taken place at the railway station. Three youngsters, including the innkeeper's two sons, rushed in panic up to the first floor where rifles were kept in case the place should be attacked. They shot blindly down into the street. One war-disabled ex-soldier and an eight-year-old boy were killed and five other people wounded.

As so often in the past, the gunmen had started a trail of disaster greater than they could ever have imagined in their wildest dreams. The fire smouldered on, and on 15 July 1927, when the tragedy of Schattendorf was almost forgotten, the flames burst from the Palace of Justice in Vienna. They were fanned partly by irrational hatred but also by the highly rational determination of men who recognised no leadership, particularly not that of the Social Democrats, to whom the will of the majority and rights of the minority meant nothing, and who thought that the great moment had come when the dictatorship of the proletariat could at last be set up.

This was Austria's first experience of insurrection's bloody reality since the communist disturbances of April 1919 in Vienna and the sporadic lootings of December 1921.

The occasion was the acquittal by a Vienna court of the accused in the Schattendorf affair. The jury consisted of eleven men and one woman; they chose as their foreman a little Floridsdorf official. The three peasant lads were accused of public disturbance of the peace, the court suggesting to the jury that an alternative might be intent to do grievous bodily harm. The defence pleaded the right of self-defence. In contrast to the situation in Germany since the 1924 revision of the law, the jury had only to decide on the question of guilt or innocence. After a three-hour absence they produced a verdict of 'not guilty'.

Undoubtedly this was one of the many questionable acquittals by a jury. Whatever may have been the intentions of their writers, a series of press articles let loose the storm. There was a wildcat general strike which no one had prepared or ordered and demonstrations which no one wanted or had instigated.

The raging mob, soon reinforced by professional agitators, turned on the Palace of Justice, the seat of the Supreme Court, although it had nothing to do with the jury's verdict and was physically separate from the Court of penal jurisdiction. Military assistance was applied for but refused in order to avoid further exciting the mob. It would probably have saved many casualties, as the history of old Austria had frequently proved. Seitz the Burgomaster, General Körner, Dr Julius Deutsch and Otto Glöckel, all Social Democrat leaders, made every effort at least to get the fire brigade through to the burning Palace of Justice where a police detachment was surrounded. They had no success. Finally resistance was broken by rifle fire from massed police forces. The tragic balance sheet showed 84 dead.

Had the revolt succeeded, it would undoubtedly have meant

the end of the democratic regime. As soon as it had been suppressed, the opposition lined up behind the demonstrators in protesting against 'police brutality' and authorised a transport strike, initially without time limit. Two days later it was called off, however, an outcome for which the *Heimwehr* was largely responsible, at least in the western provinces. The opposition also demanded the government's resignation but Chancellor Seipel replied that he saw no reason for this and that he was only prepared to negotiate once the transport strike had been ended. This was essential, he said, in order to allow deputies from the provinces to travel to Vienna for the session of the National Diet.

Reactions to these events were clearly largely influenced by the political views of those involved. Undoubtedly, however, sins of commission or omission played a large part in the tragic course of events. The violent language used in leading articles, though later characterised as a safety valve, in fact brought the pot to boiling point and sparked off the explosion.

The refusal to call for military assistance proved to be a boomerang. On the other hand failure to provide the Vienna police with resources such as water cannon, tear gas and the like probably contributed materially to the use of firearms and perhaps there was too much shooting anyway. However this may be, the fact remains that, as a result of a chain of unwanted circumstances, 'the government held the Social Democrat Party responsible for the uncontrolled course of events and the Party held the government responsible for bloody repression'.[13]

Julius Deutsch records that at a combined conference of the Party leaders and the national Trades Union Commission held on the evening of this unhappy day it was stated that 'in the morning we lost control of the masses and in the afternoon the Police President lost control of the police'. During the discussion on future policy at this meeting many representatives urged that the struggle now unintentionally begun should be fought through to the end, in other words 'instead of haphazard fortuitous clashes between police and workers a struggle for the ultimate decision should be initiated'. The majority of the senior representatives, however, rejected this proposal and contented themselves with calling a twenty-four-hour general strike and an indefinite railway strike.

It was soon to prove that 15 July 1927 had opened a new period of Austrian history. The Republic's first decade had ended in flames. In the second decade the tune was to be called, not by internal policy, but by foreign policy. As the direct result of 15 July Czechoslovakia, Hungary and even Italy had mobilised for a possible invasion.

There was vast excitement on either side. The extremists in both camps regarded any backing down as suicidal – as well it might have been. As a result the National Diet was, for all practical purposes, paralysed. Among the bourgeoisie discontent with the party system grew and the extra-parliamentary forces grouped around the two opposing radical poles swelled considerably.

Italy and Hungary on one side and Czechoslovakia and Jugoslavia on the other began to show interest in the potential Austrian trouble-spot and to take sides in accordance with their own external political interests. The rapid rise of the *Heimwehr* following the events of July 1927 had caused its leaders, Steidle in particular, to establish contact both with Hungary and Italy, since neither Rome nor Budapest considered anything other than a right-wing government in Austria to be compatible with their concept of Central Europe. A left-wing or even a coalition government in Vienna might well line up with the Little Entente, Czechoslovakia in particular, and in Budapest's view this would be contrary to Hungary's revisionist policy; the immediate result might well be the formation of an economic bloc which would inevitably be opposed to Hungarian and Italian interests. It was further argued that close ties between Austria, Hungary and Italy, only to be anticipated from a right-wing government in Austria, would reduce the danger of an Anschluss, the German government of the time (1928) having its eye elsewhere so far as internal politics were concerned. In the spring of 1928 Mussolini told Bethlen, the Hungarian Minister-President, that he was willing to provide financial aid for the Austrian *Heimwehr* and that it should be channelled through Hungary.

We know from Starhemberg's memoirs that Mussolini also

made considerable sums available to the *Heimwehr* in later years, when it was principally occupied in dealing with the National-Socialist terror.[14] If the *Heimwehr*, however, were arming themselves with assistance from abroad, the situation was no different in the case of their opponents, the Republican *Schutzbund*.

In the early years both sides had obtained their weapons from demobilisation stocks, at first openly, then in secret. The Arsenal affair had been eloquent proof of that. After July 1927 the secret accumulation of weapons continued, each side assuming that the other was preparing to attack, fearing an assault and being determined to forestall it. Julius Deutsch says:

> 'Once one had succeeded, despite all the difficulties, in setting up a military organisation and training it as well as one might under the circumstances, one was faced with the great overriding problem of weapons. How could one [illegally!] obtain arms for tens of thousands of *Schutzbund* members?'[15]

Josef Buttinger gives a graphic description of the tense situation leading up to 12 February 1934: at that time the *Heimwehr* had concentrated in the provincial capitals and was threatening to overthrow the elected provincial governments by force; along the Danube Czech rifles and ammunition were moving into Austria to replenish the *Schutzbund*'s caches of arms.[16]

On 28 February 1934 Police Headquarters in Vienna issued a comprehensive report dealing with the case of a large number of persons accused of treason and contravention of the law on explosives; the report gave details of the large-scale arms traffic from Czechoslovakia up to January 1934. Czech weapons were not purchased direct from Vienna but via the Communist International in Zürich; purchases ran to several million schillings. The Economic Section of Police Headquarters also discovered that bonds to the value of 1,800,000 schillings had been deposited with Edi Fimmen, Head of the International Transport Workers Union who lived in Amsterdam, via Berthold König, a member of the National Diet and Head of the Trade Union and Legal Aid Association for Austrian railway personnel. Fimmen and other leading personalities of the International had frequently visited Vienna to negotiate with *Schutzbund* officials.[17]

Nevertheless up to 27 January 1932 when the bourgeois coalition collapsed and Dr Karl Buresch formed his second cabinet, the government had an adequate parliamentary majority and was therefore strong enough to prevent more serious collisions and further bloodshed.

Meanwhile, however, Austria had been very severely hit by the world economic crisis. The *Creditanstalt* collapsed on 13 May 1931 and was kept afloat only by large-scale government backing. The currency was once more in danger and a new League of Nations loan was essential for the support of the schilling. This necessitated agreement from France.

Externally, however, the scene for the foreseeable future had been set by the unhappy Customs Union Plan of March 1931. Even for those Austrians who believed in the Anschluss, the question was now closed for as far ahead as one could see; it was not even a long-term aim. The great coalition finally fell when the Greater-German Party left it over the question of the Lausanne loan and the foreign political obligations coupled with it. This is largely to be explained by the fact that ominous storm signals had meanwhile become visible from Germany: at the Reichstag elections in September 1930 the NSDAP with 107 seats became the second strongest party after the Social Democrats with 142. (In July 1932 the NSDAP became the strongest party with 230 seats. In November 1932 it was still the strongest with 196 seats followed by the Social Democrats with 121 and the Communists with 100.)

The collapse of the coalition and therewith the disappearance of a parliamentary majority led to open and serious crisis. At first sight there were only two possible solutions: an attempt to form a major coalition including the Social Democrats and coupled with a general reduction of arms at home, or fresh elections.

The significance for Europe, in other words the external implications, of possible consolidation of the position in Austria was now clearly recognised abroad. This was evidenced by Italy's increasing interest in Austrian developments, also by the generally friendly attitude of the Bank of England under Montagu Norman and Sir Otto Niemeyer.[18] Most important of all, however, was the policy of France. Tardieu, the French Prime Minister, came forward with his plan for a Danube economic federation, under which Austria, Hungary and the three countries of the Little Entente would form a common market through a system of preferential tariffs. The plan was obviously the French counter-proposal to the Austro-German customs union vetoed in the previous year.

In March 1932, however, this plan foundered, primarily on objections from Italy and Germany who were at one in their aversion to French hegemony in the Danube area. In addition in October 1931 the so-called Harzburg Front had been formed in Germany, bringing together the Nazis, the German Nationals and the *Stahlhelm* in a political alliance. On the German side, there-fore, the Tardieu plan was met with the ominous battle-cry 'Harzburg or Habsburg'.

All efforts by the Christian Socials to form a coalition with the Social Democrats proved fruitless. Seipel had opened negotiations in June 1931, proposing a 'government of concentration' (Seipel-Bauer) but he had failed. Karl Renner later declared that the negotiations with Seipel on 18 June 1931 were symptomatic and represented the highspot of tragedy in the history of Austrian democracy. Franz Winkler, the ex-Vice-Chancellor and leader of the *Landbund*, wrote that the Social Democrat attitude in rejecting the offer had been quite incomprehensibly dogmatic.[19] A further feeler on the possibility of a coalition with the Left, made by Buresch in October 1931, was also doomed to fail-ure.

In the eyes of Otto Bauer, the dogmatist of Austrian social democracy – and on this subject he was generally in opposition to Karl Renner – a renewal of the coalition was not a subject for discussion at any time. This was not so much a question of principle; he simply considered that in the Austrian situation of the time it was a political impossibility. In his view it would bring no advantage to the working class; they would merely be faced with the necessity of participating in inevitable and un-

popular measures and in the final analysis would simply be assist-
ing to keep the bourgeois social order in being.

Mutual disarmament, which was seriously discussed at the time
of the Buresch cabinet, also proved unattainable; perhaps the
political price demanded was too high or perhaps the government
lacked authority both inside and outside parliament to take really
decisive measures. In any case the plan for internal disarmament
was dropped for the foreseeable future along with that for a
'government of concentration'.

So fresh elections were the only way out of the dilemma. The
next elections for the National Diet were not due until autumn
1934 but provincial elections were held in Vienna, Lower Austria
and Salzburg on 24 April 1932. The Vienna result was the most
significant. Even before the campaign a violent assault by supporters of the Hitler Movement was expected; in the event the
Christian Socials lost 49,000 votes, the Social Democrats 20,000,
the Greater-Germans were practically annihilated and the NSDAP
under their *Gauleiter* Leopold entered the Vienna Provincial
Council with fifteen deputies.

The result administered a shock to the government. With the
National-Socialist break-through a new opponent had appeared,
and he was more than just a new piece on the political chessboard.
This was a revolutionary movement directed from outside the
frontiers and it threatened not only the existing parties and
political system but the very existence of the State itself. It has
been said that the NSDAP would never have obtained a majority
by normal methods. This may be true. . . . If so, there was every
reason not to postpone the new elections for which there was so
much clamour.

But, in all probability, the result would have been a repetition
of events in Germany in 1932; there the voters were called to the
polls twice within four months and the cause neither of democracy nor of the nation was served thereby.

However this may be, the Buresch government, despite rather
than because of the narrowness of its base, answered the demand
for new elections with a decided No. They were naturally
concerned over the highly precarious economic and financial situa-

tion but the real reason was anxiety at the approach of the brown-shirted avalanche. Franz Winkler, Vice-Chancellor at the time, says:

> 'The tempestuous new National-Socialist opposition had won an electoral victory by democratic means. This was the starting point of a tragic crisis which intensified with every link in the chain of misfortune. After the 24 April elections the Social Democrats put down a motion in parliament calling for dissolution of the National Diet and the calling of fresh elections – Otto Bauer describes this fateful decision by his party as "left-wing deviationism". The motion was supported by the Greater German Peoples Party and the government was highly embarrassed since it could not muster an adequate majority to oppose it. The balance was held by the hitherto insignificant *Heimwehr* representation in parliament. To give time for the Christian Socials to negotiate with the *Heimwehr*, Chancellor Buresch resigned on 13 May 1932, thereby automatically blocking a vote on the floor of the House on the motion for dissolution.'[20]

[*The author was Minister of Justice in the Buresch government – Translator.*]

The new Chancellor was Engelbert Dollfuss, a member neither of the *Heimwehr* nor of any other defence formation. He had been Minister of Agriculture in the Buresch government and was a recognised agrarian expert who had made a name for himself at international conferences. As a member of the Lower Austrian Peasants League he was a Christian Social but, though a great admirer of Seipel personally, had not been afraid to cross swords with him in the past on matters of opinion. He had been an officer in a *Kaiserschützen* Regiment (Tyrol Rifles) and so felt himself in sympathy with the war generation. He took a lively interest in the anxieties and ambitions of the younger academics. He was a master of man management, intelligent, honest and a sworn enemy of all intrigue, appreciated and respected by friend and foe alike. In particular, like most Lower Austrians, he was on good terms with the Social Democrats. His outstanding quality was perhaps a highly developed sensitivity which would never allow him to forget anything which he thought unjust, unlawful or underhand.

In Dollfuss' view his first and most urgent tasks were to lead Austria out of the economic slump and obtain a new League of Nations loan to stabilise the precarious currency. But before that he was faced with the problem of finding a parliamentary majority.

Coalition with the Social Democrats seemed out of the question. It ran counter to the general trend shown in the 24 April elections and paralleled in Germany in the *Landtag* elections in Prussia, Württemberg and Bavaria; in addition the Left, perhaps blinded by their relatively good showing at the local elections and in spite of the apparently desperate situation, showed no more inclination than hitherto to assume responsibility with all its attendant risks. The Greater-Germans flatly declined to cooperate since, like Buresch, Dollfuss would make no concessions to the 'nationalist' viewpoint in the matter of the League of Nations loan.

Apart from the *Landbund*, therefore, if Dollfuss was to assemble a majority, however painfully narrow, he had no alternative but to include the *Heimwehr* bloc in the government; it was represented in the cabinet by the Minister of Trade, Dr Guido Jakoncig. Dollfuss' support in the National Diet therefore consisted of 66 Christian Socials, 9 members of the *Landbund* and 8 representatives of the *Heimwehr* bloc of whom two had nationalist leanings. This meant that he had a majority of one.

Obviously, in these circumstances and in view of the difficult problems which had to be solved, such a parliamentary situation could not be expected to work long-term. Understandably, therefore, everyone regarded the Dollfuss cabinet as merely another provisional arrangement. Everyone that is – except Dollfuss. He had undertaken to deal with the crisis and until he had done so he would neither call new elections nor resign.

He journeyed off to Lausanne and came back with agreement to a twenty-year loan of 300 million gold schillings. To this, however, the lenders had attached a condition: until repayment, in other words until 1952, Austria was to give up all thought of the Anschluss or a customs union with Germany. Compared to the 1922 Geneva agreement, this meant that the ban on the Anschluss was extended by a further ten years, although in theory it was open to Austria to repay the loan any time after 1942.

The Social Democrats and Greater-Germans violently opposed the ban on the Anschluss – just at the moment when Hitler was clearly girding his loins for the final struggle for power in Germany. In the National Diet Dollfuss just scraped through by a single vote and even that was in doubt up to the last moment. As it so happened, just at this time two members of the House were on their deathbeds, both historic personalities whose names were coupled with a programme. One was Seipel who died on 2 August 1932 and whose vote would have gone to the government coalition; the other was Schober (died 19 August) who belonged to the opposition. The deciding session of the Diet took place on 17 August. Seipel was already dead, his replacement had been sworn in and with his vote Dollfuss won.

But he was not yet home and dry; the motion had to come before the Federal Council [*Bundesrat*] and in this the government was in a hopeless minority as a result of the provincial elections in April. As was to be expected, the *Bundesrat* objected and so, in accordance with the constitution, the National Diet had to take up the question once more.

The same scenario was re-enacted. Meanwhile, however, Schober had died. His replacement somewhat unexpectedly voted with the government and so on 23 August 1932 the last hurdle was surmounted by 82 votes to 80.

For Dollfuss the battle lines were now finally drawn. So they were also for Theo Habicht, the German 'Inspector of the Austrian NSDAP', who had been doing business for Hitler in Vienna ever since 1931. The stake was Austria versus the Anschluss and in the last analysis everything which followed stemmed from this antithesis.

Dollfuss was well aware of the danger and, despite many warnings, continued on his perilous way trusting to some change in the international climate. He could not choose his path himself but was driven on to it by force of circumstances. Nevertheless he pursued it, not in a spirit of adventurism, but as part of his duty to Austria.

Dollfuss could have set his sights on becoming Hitler's *Reichsstatthalter* [Reich Regent] in Austria, although in 1932 there was officially no such thing; he would then have had no need to eliminate parliament since he would have been assured of a majority whether there had been new elections or not. In all probability the tragic events of 12 February 1934 would never have happened, nor the equally tragic *putsch* in the July. As we now know, however, the Second World War would not have been avoided; we should have become a sort of second Danzig. Whether there would now be an independent neutral Austria – that is the question.

On 30 January 1933 Hitler seized power in Germany and, as a result, a solution – any solution – to Austria's internal problems took on the character of a foreign policy decision. Hitler's views and intentions regarding Austria were known from *Mein Kampf*; speaking during the Vienna electoral campaign in April 1932, Goebbels had left no doubt on the subject. Hitler had laid down policy towards Austria at a cabinet meeting on 26 May 1933.[21] He maintained that, by trying to implant in people's minds the idea of Austria rather than Germany as their home country, the Austrian government was playing a dangerous game. The six million Germans in Austria ran the risk of being 'turned into Swiss'. At this same meeting the Thousand-mark Blockade of Austria was decided upon; when von Papen, the Vice-Chancellor, the Foreign Minister and the Minister of Economics objected, Hitler countered with: 'The struggle will be over by this summer.' The Austrian Nazi press said likewise and the other German propaganda media added their voices in support of this story. Even at this stage Hitler calculated that the Little Entente and Italy might intervene in the Austrian question but felt sure that he could come to some agreement with Italy.

Twelve weeks earlier, on 4 March 1933, Dollfuss had temporarily put an end to the parliamentary regime and so relieved himself of anxiety about the single precarious vote on which his majority depended. Buttinger says that he made use of 'the flimsiest of all pretexts known to the history of *coups d'état*'.[22] Franz Winkler, on the other hand, who was at this time a member of the government, says: 'It was not the government's fault that the National Diet did not function and new elections were not due until 1934.'[23]

The resignation of the President and both Vice-Presidents of the National Diet was utilised as a pretext to declare any further sitting of the House illegal. There can be no argument about that. At first sight, therefore, there would seem to be grounds for political criticism, particularly since all subsequent internal political measures can be traced back to this 4 March 1933. This was the beginning of 'Austro-fascist dictatorship' (Gulick's description) or of the 'inevitable transitional solution which for a time had even certain dictatorial aspects' (Ender's description), depending on the ideological viewpoint from which you look at it. It is also true that Dollfuss was determined not to call fresh elections. After 30 January 1933, and in view of Austria's probable susceptibility to German developments, this would have been far too risky if straightforward adherence to the German Nazi Party was to be avoided in the longer or shorter term – and behind the Nazi Party stood the German government.

Dollfuss' decision was based, not on a lack of self-confidence, but on the sober conclusion that genuinely free elections were a technical impossibility in Austria at the time and in the circumstances. The fact that, despite courageous resistance over the Enabling Law, the mighty German Social Democrat Party together with its trade union movement and the *Reichsbanner*[24] had been swept away like a house of cards shortly after 30 January 1933 had not failed to make its impression in Austria as everywhere else.

Dollfuss had by no means engineered what has been called parliament's 'self-dissolution'. He was as surprised by it as the rest of us who attended the session of 4 March 1933. The agenda included a question of no special significance from the opposition to the government concerning disciplinary action taken by the Railway Board against employees involved in a recent short protest strike. During the discussion such a procedural imbroglio developed that Renner, the President of the Diet, and his two deputies Dr Ramek, a Christian Social, and Dr Straffner, a

Greater-German, all felt themselves compelled to lay down their offices in turn. The assembly broke up in disorder.

The government drew its conclusions. It made clear that this was a parliamentary not a national crisis. For Dollfuss the main obstacle to the salvation of Austria, and therefore to the task he had set himself, seemed to have disappeared. Nevertheless, for a long time he had no intention of eliminating parliament permanently; he merely wished to seize this opportunity of carrying out the long overdue reform of its standing orders.[25]

The fourth of March 1933 opened a new phase in Austrian history, the last preceding the Anschluss. Next day, at the last elections for the German Reichstag, the NSDAP was returned as the strongest party with 43·9 per cent of the votes and 288 seats out of 647. Shortly thereafter Hitler showed how democracy could be turned into totalitarianism without a formal change of constitution.

In his memorandum dated 11 July 1936 and entitled 'For the internal pacification of Austria' Captain Leopold, the Austrian Nazi *Gauleiter*, declared that the decisive reason for the rising of July 1934 had been the complete exclusion of the National-Socialist movement from any legal activity; government measures in violation of the constitution had forced it to turn to illegality.[26] Of this there can be no question up to 4 March 1933. Theo Habicht, the NSDAP Inspector appointed by the Reich, however, had been in Vienna since the summer of 1931 setting up his network. In October 1932 a whole series of Nazi outrages took place in Vienna University which eventually had to be closed. The first tear gas attacks on Jewish chain-stores occurred at Christmas that year. The main Nazi offensive against Austria opened shortly after Hitler's seizure of power and intensified after the Reichstag elections of 5 March 1933. On 27 May 1933 the Thousand-mark Blockade was declared with catastrophic economic consequences for Austria and with the avowed object of forcing her to her knees and popularising the idea of the Anschluss. Throughout the spring of 1933 the Nazis used every form of terrorism including bombs and explosives culminating in the hand-grenade outrage at Krems on 19 June which led to the banning of the Party. Official government records for the months June–August 1933 show eleven serious bomb attacks, four murders and numerous finds of explosives. And all the time the Nazi press was repeating that Austria's existence was to be reckoned only in weeks or months.

The 'government measures in violation of the constitution' of which *Gauleiter* Leopold complained, were designed to protect the State, its population and its property against illegal action hiding behind a façade of legality, and this could not be dealt with by normal methods. And why? Because this illegal action was first instigated and financed, then acclaimed and defended from across the frontier.[27] None of the Austrian government's emergency measures based on the wartime enabling law of 1917 (which Leopold explicitly mentions) were issued until the 'cold war' had broken out and the Nazi offensive was in full swing. They were defensive, not provocative.

On the dissolution of the Nazi Party in Austria the Nazi deputies were removed from their seats in provincial and municipal chambers – and the left-wing opposition raised no objection. On the other side, however, under pressure of the internal political situation the Republican *Schutzbund*[28] was disbanded on 31 March 1933 and the Communist Party on 26 May. The *Schutzbund* continued to exist underground and when it rose in February 1934, measures were then taken against the Social Democrat Party.

It is not surprising that the effort to preserve at least the ostensible continuance of the rule of law looks somewhat different today from what it did thirty-five years ago. In those days the word 'revolution' was on everyone's lips; the difference was that some – both on the Right and the Left – thought it desirable and talked about it much more than was wise; others – both on the Right and the Left – regarded it as inevitable and were determined to direct it if and when it happened; there was a third, smaller, section which believed in the possibility of bringing about the necessary changes by mutual agreement. All were agreed, however, that things could not go on as they were.

That the parliamentary crisis of 4 March 1933 was not a national crisis is correct. Equally, however, it is incorrect to regard the genuine national crisis born of the civil war psychosis of 1933–4 as a purely governmental one. It may be argued that the national crisis could have been solved by the Christian Socials and Social Democrats together and that, had they been willing to unite in common defence against Hitler, they would have been representing the wishes of a large majority of the Austrian people. But such thinking is purely academic, for an increasing and militant majority of the people was opposed to such a solution; emergency legislation would therefore have been necessary in any case. More important still, Austria's external political situation made a coalition solution impossible. Any idea of relying for support on the Western Powers and the Little Entente instead of Italy was impractical, for it left out of account the fact that at this time and for some years to come Italy was tied to the so-called Stresa Powers, primarily France in other words – and the French attitude was unequivocal. The menacing shadow of the Third Reich was therefore not to be countered by an exclusively Western orientation.

If the Anschluss with Hitler's Reich with all its implications was to be avoided, the way did not lie via the Left, even if either side had been disposed to follow it – which in fact neither were. This is not to say that some tacit agreement in principle was out of the question, but the price demanded would have been so high that neither the Dollfuss regime nor any other in its position could have conceded it and still retained the other essential partners in the coalition and the necessary foreign support.

It was clearly in Austria's interest to reach some agreement with Germany if at all possible and if it could be done without sacrificing essentials. If for no other reason, Germany had the whip hand economically; if Austria was to survive, the economic war could not be prolonged indefinitely. The more severely the Austrian economy was hit by the German boycott, the easier it became for Nazi propaganda to make its impact, particularly in the western provinces; there traditionally conservative sections of the population were affected, such as the peasants and those who lived off trade and tourism together with all their employees and workers. On the other hand a sell-out to Germany, particularly in the years 1933 to 1935 would have been a breach of international agreements (Geneva and Lausanne) with all the inevitable repercussions. People had not forgotten the cancellation of credits at the time of the Customs Union plan. The Powers would have made a political *démarche* which might easily have led to a repetition of the Austrian situation of 1919–20 and this, with the public mood as explosive as it was, would have produced serious and incalculable consequences. How crippling was Hitler's Thousand-mark Blockade is shown by the fact that in 1932 60 per cent of Tyrol's tourists were Germans and the same was true of Vorarlberg, Salzburg and Carinthia.

All this gave Dollfuss to think that a real State emergency existed. This enemy was bent on eliminating not merely the Austrian government, but the State of Austria as an entity. He could not be fought with police methods alone. Had Dollfuss veered left, he would have closed both avenues still open to him, one leading to Germany, the other to Italy. Had his overtures to the Left succeeded, he would have been rewarded by friendly leading articles in the London, Paris, Prague and New York press; but there it would have ended, until the articles were later discovered by some student of history who would have constructed hypotheses thereon.

So Dollfuss decided to try to break out into the open by exploring both avenues simultaneously. The most obvious was to try to achieve some *détente* with Germany by negotiation and so re-establish normal neighbourly relations between the two countries. Some agreement must be contrived to relieve the Austrian people and economy from the growing German pressure and the dangers of open enmity with the Third Reich.

How serious Dollfuss was in this intention is shown by the fact that he proposed to meet Hitler personally. The first hint of the possibility of such a meeting came via contacts between agricultural experts. On the Austrian side Dollfuss used Dr Leo Müller, Director of the Lower Austrian Chamber of Agriculture, to make the necessary soundings. On the German side the contact was Dr Kanzler of the Green Front in Munich who was probably also acting for the Reich Food Organisation [*Reichsnährstand*] and whom Dollfuss knew personally. Dollfuss was told that Hitler would expect an Austrian plenipotentiary in Munich on 31 October 1933 for discussion without commitment but that the strictest secrecy must be observed. Accordingly on the afternoon of 30 October I was commissioned by the Chancellor to take the overnight train to Munich together with Dr Müller and meet Hitler, as agreed, on the next morning.

For a loyal Austrian a train journey from Vienna to Munich in the autumn of 1933 was like a foray into enemy territory. All our secrecy precautions were nullified by the fact that one of the heads of mission accredited to Vienna happened to be travelling in the same sleeping car on his way to Paris. Munich Main Station was decked with swastika flags – banned in Austria; for an Austrian their effect was forbidding; Munich, once so familiar, had become foreign. Agreement was not going to be easy here.

A liaison officer from the Reich Food Organisation took me by car to his apartment in Schwabing. Once there all arrangements would be made, he said. After a long wait an inconspicuous Party functionary in civilian clothes appeared; he was quite polite but apparently totally uninformed, not particularly interested, cold and condescendingly distant, though not arrogant. He was Dr Himmler, he told me, and asked what I wanted in Munich. . . . No, there must be some misunderstanding; the Führer was not even in Munich. . . . He would, however, take me to Rudolf Hess's private house on condition that strict secrecy was observed on both sides.

Himmler was not yet the ogre he became later. Nevertheless he was known as head of the SS and of the Bavarian Gestapo. As was the case later there was nothing in his appearance, talk or behaviour to betray the fanatic; one's first impression was of a very ordinary lower middle class person who deliberately avoided meaningful discussion and laid down the law politely but uncompromisingly. During the drive to Hess's villa, therefore, there was no real conversation.

Rudolf Hess, though outwardly calm, forthcoming and conciliatory, was far more akin to the fanatical ideologist; his eyes particularly gave this impression. Once again there were expressions of astonishment over my visit to Munich which was apparently entirely unexpected, then enquiry about my authority to negotiate. Finally, when I had explained Austria's position stressing her interest in good neighbourly relations, came the German conditions: immediate permission for the flying of the swastika flag, lifting of the ban on the Party, cessation of press polemics, fresh parliamentary elections. This was followed by a lengthy monologue about the iniquity of the peace *diktat*, denial of the right of national self-determination, the injustice of the League of Nations regime backed by Britain and France and the Führer's determination to protect German honour and ensure that Germany's just claims were met. The unspoken conclusion to this disquisition was that a change in the Central European *status quo* was essential.

In Austria we had already seen the powerful political influence on the younger generation of the idealistic and highly nationalistic doctrine of Othmar Spann, the Vienna sociologist and philosopher. Rudolf Hess belonged to the influential geopolitical school of Karl Haushofer in Munich which laid stress on power politics and the right of a people to greater *lebensraum*. In 1933 both Spann's and Haushofer's doctrines could be summed up in the one word Anschluss.

My talk with Rudolf Hess was therefore entirely unproductive. It was clear, moreover, that the German authorities were not prepared to negotiate unless Theo Habicht, their *Gauleiter* who had been expelled from Austria, was present. Habicht was a German citizen and a member of the Reichstag; quite apart, therefore, from the fact that he had organised bomb attacks and other outrages, international custom barred him from political activity in Austria. One of our conditions for negotiation was his complete exclusion from any political function in the country.

My meeting with Hess lasted an hour and Himmler then escorted me to the airport. He regretted that no result had been achieved this time and expressed the hope that our next meeting would take place under friendlier auspices. His hope was not fulfilled. The next (and last) time I saw Himmler was on 12 December 1938 when, as Head of Security of the Greater German Reich, he inspected the room in which I was confined in Vienna.

On that occasion he remarked that I should have remembered our Munich meeting in October 1933 and not forgotten that I was a 'German'.[29]

After the failure of this first attempt, advised by our German intermediary Dr Kanzler, Dollfuss deputed Ambassador Hornbostel, Head of the Political Department in the Foreign Ministry, to take further soundings in Berlin on 30 November and 1 December 1933. Martin Bormann accompanied Hess, who made a point of insisting that this was an Austrian initiative and stated that:

1. The German side must know for whom Dollfuss was speaking
2. Austria must recognise that the conflict with the Reich was a consequence of the persecution of National-Socialists by the Federal government
3. It must be clearly stated whether Austria was merely desirous of improving her foreign relations, without at the same time having any intention of altering her internal policy
4. Clarification must be given of the Austrian Chancellor's relationship to Starhemberg who had recently been highly insulting to the Reich Chancellor.

Ambassador Hornbostel's soundings in Berlin were therefore equally fruitless[30] and the German avenue for the moment seemed closed.

The NSDAP was thereupon charged by Hitler to deal with the 'Austrian question' and proceeded to try and bring the Dollfuss regime down by other means; the chief planner, armed with plenary powers by Hitler, was Habicht.[31] His principal assistants were Rudolf Weydenhammer, a German industrialist and bank director, Dr Otto Wächter, Fridolin Glass and, more important than all, Dr Anton Rintelen, who had been Austrian Minister in Rome since May 1933. Weydenhammer admitted that during the first six months of 1934 he visited Rome more than a dozen times to discuss with Rintelen a change of Austrian government by *coup d'état*.[32]

Ever since Bethlen's visit at Easter 1932 Mussolini had been determined that Austria should belong to the Italian sphere of influence; he was prepared to go a long way to maintain Austrian independence. This, of course, presupposed a right-wing government in Vienna unlikely to veer into the anti-Italian camp. Personal contacts with Austria were initially maintained primarily through Starhemberg. In 1933 Dollfuss met Mussolini three times, first in April when he visited Rome, then in June when the Concordat was signed and finally in August at Riccione. The published exchange of letters between Mussolini and Dollfuss shows that Mussolini promised Austria the full support of Italy in the struggle for her independence, particularly in the economic field. According to information given to the Hungarian Chargé d'Affaires in Rome after the Riccione meeting by Fulvio Suvich, the ex-State Secretary, Mussolini had urged Dollfuss to act quickly and energetically on three matters: constitutional reform, the build-up of the Fatherland Front, and the struggle against Marxism.[33]

Adolf Schärf has published an Italian draft of the points to be put to Dollfuss when he visited Riccione:

'1. This third visit to Italy, being more hurried and sensational than its predecessors, must not leave matters at their present dead centre. It must signal the start of a new development in Austrian internal and external policy. Otherwise the journey will have been purposeless and therefore detrimental.

2. On return to Vienna Dollfuss must announce a major political speech for the early days of September, in other words before the planned *putsch*. A number of preparatory measures should be taken to raise the morale of the Austrians such as:

(a) Reinforcement of the government by the inclusion of new men such as Steidle and Starhemberg to remove the present impression that the government consists merely of left-overs from the old regime.

(b) Combination of all forces and fronts into a single national front with the motto: Independence and renewal of Austria.

(c) The government should be markedly dictatorial.

(d) A government commissar should be appointed for the Vienna municipality.

(e) Large-scale propaganda.'[34]

Dollfuss did not accept this programme *in toto* and modified various points to suit himself. On the internal political question for instance, the official Austrian record of the Dollfuss–Mussolini conversations on 19 and 20 August says:

'Mussolini tried to pressurise the Chancellor to make greater use of the *Heimwehr* but the Chancellor successfully avoided giving any undertaking. Mussolini recommended that constitutional reform on a corporative basis should be complete by the end of September, also that a major political speech should be made as soon as possible with the theme: "Independence of Austria externally, renewal of Austria internally." . . . Mussolini also urged that the various patriotic fronts be merged under the exclusive leadership of the Chancellor.'[35]

Dollfuss did in fact make the suggested speech on 11 September in the Trabrennplatz during the Catholic Congress and the celebrations of the 250th anniversary of the defeat of the Turks before Vienna. It contained no mention of a *putsch* and Dollfuss had actually never thought of such a thing. The appointment of a government commissar for Vienna was postponed for six months and made only during the emergency of February 1934. Dollfuss then nominated his own candidate and not one from the *Heimwehr* as expected.[36]

There is no mention in the published exchange of letters of any Italian pressure on Dollfuss to use force against the Social Democrats or of any readiness on his part to do so. It is also untrue that Fulvio Suvich, the Italian State Secretary for Foreign Affairs, urged this on Dollfuss or that he ganged up with Fey against Dollfuss, as has sometimes been stated. There is no evidence for any of these intrigues and Suvich explicitly says that he remembers nothing of them and can produce documentary evidence to support this.[37] Dollfuss never gave up hope of coming to some peaceful agreement with his Marxist opponents, calculating on the weakness of the Social Democrat position in Austria and the neighbouring countries as a result of general international developments.

How, then, did the tragedy of 12 February 1934 come about?

Naturally each side has its own views on the causes, the course of events and their effects; each can point to undoubted facts, as they have every right to do. Nevertheless, despite variations of political phraseology and differing shades of emphasis, accounts of events and the conclusions drawn largely agree.[38]

Certain basic facts are indisputable and can be interpreted only one way: The Socialist Party leadership did not want the revolt of 12 February 1934 nor did it order its outbreak in Linz. On 14 October 1933 the Party Congress had decided that in certain circumstances they would proceed to armed action against the government combined with a general strike. This was to happen in the event of any of the following:

1. Proscription of the Social Democrat Party
2. Occupation of Vienna Town Hall
3. A fascist *putsch*
4. Suspension of the constitution[39]

(According to Karwinsky's notes No. 3 read: Dissolution of the trades unions.)

None of these things had happened when the revolt broke out.

The occasion was a weapons search ordered by the police in the Hotel Schiff, the Social Democrat Party headquarters in Linz. This was violently resisted in spite of the fact that during the night 11–12 February Richard Bernaschek, the Social Democrat Party Secretary and *Schutzbund* leader in Upper Austria, had received a coded telegram from Otto Bauer in Vienna saying that, should the proposed search take place, nothing was to be done. Large-scale searches had taken place before – in the Ottakring workers' hostel in 1932, in Schwechat, in Simmering, in the Arsenal, etc. None had led to serious consequences and there was nothing to differentiate the Linz search from its predecessors.

On receipt of the news from Linz, however, the Social Democrat Party leadership in Vienna gave the agreed signal for a general strike and an armed rising by the *Schutzbund*. The decision was not made without argument; opinions were divided; in particular, Berthold König, the leader of the Railwaymen's Union, warned against calling a general strike saying that there was no certainty that his people would conform.[40] The call to strike was not generally obeyed and so the rising seemed doomed to failure.

The first casualty was Police Inspector Josef Schiel who was shot in Simmering by a member of the *Schutzbund* whom he had asked to show his papers.

On the evening of 14 February Dollfuss broadcast an appeal to those still resisting to lay down their arms by midday on 15 February, promising them an amnesty. This was unsuccessful; the *Schutzbund*, entrenched in great blocks of flats and other buildings such as the Ottakring workers' hostel, continued to resist and infantry attacks were repulsed with heavy losses. The military commander thereupon called up artillery to put a quick end to the fighting. This did, in fact, spare both attackers and defenders further casualties and cut the struggle short – one of Dollfuss's primary objects. Colonel-General Schönburg-Hartenstein, the military commander and Secretary of State for National Defence, subsequently stated that use of artillery was the only way of ending the fighting and avoiding further casualties. The final tragic figures were: on the government side 105 dead and 319 wounded, civilians, in so far as numbers could be established, 137 dead and nearly 400 wounded.

Opinions will always differ about the possibility, given the situation, of avoiding this national disaster – for such it was. The real causes are to be sought not in the events of 1932 and 1933 but much earlier. Obviously for any government faced with a revolt, the only alternatives are to fight or to capitulate. In this case, had the government capitulated and the rising been successful, democracy would not have revived nor would Austria as a state have continued to exist. This being so, armed action was no way to protect the existing constitution.

Franz Winkler, the ex-Vice-Chancellor, calls the events of February 1934 unique in the history of revolutions:

> 'The red revolt was something unique in the history of revolutionary action. Rebels and revolutionaries man the barricades . . . in order to overturn existing constitutions and change existing circumstances. The *Schutzbund* rebels of 12 February 1934, however, manned the barricades to defend the constitution then in force.'[41]

Gordon Brook-Shepherd says:

'The Right Wing provoked violence, but without thinking of civil war; the Left reacted reluctantly with their long-prepared *defensive* putsch and thus made civil war unavoidable.'[42]

It should be remembered in this connection that it has not been possible so far to arrive at a generally acceptable definition of aggression in international law and the main reason is the difference of opinion about the so-called preventive or pre-emptive attack. It may be launched for defensive purposes but it is still an attack which makes defence by the recipient legitimate. Winkler's revolutionaries fighting for purposes other than a change in existing circumstances are as rare as Shepherd's counter-revolutionaries whose *putsch* is defensive only.

Up to 12 February 1934, and indeed as far as 12 March 1938, the Social Democrats were divided into two groups: those who believed in evolution and advised moderation, and the activists for whom moderation was the betrayal of an ideal. Any genuine revolutionary fights for his ideal, of the virtue of which he is convinced and which he is prepared to enforce and defend. The members of the Republican *Schutzbund* were activists convinced that the government's challenge meant the end of any hope of establishing the dictatorship of the proletariat. After the February rising this and nothing else would satisfy the revolutionary socialists.[43] The battle was fought, not for re-establishment of the bourgeois democratic republic, but for the dictatorship of the proletariat. In their eyes the existing constitution was worn out and dilapidated; it had proved ineffective. Something new must be put in its place. On this both halves of the Social Democrat movement were at one – also that the previous situation could not somehow be re-established by fire and sword.

In the ultimate issue the contestants were divided by two irreconcilable notions, the international on one side and the national on the other. Austria's mortal danger was that the space between 'National' and 'Socialism' might be filled by a hyphen and lead to an unholy alliance. In 1934 she escaped only by a hair's breadth.

Argument about the objects of the rising is not a mere question of semantics. The 'wherefore' matters more than the 'why'. The contestants must be given credit for being revolutionaries not nihilists.

The leaders must have realised from the outset that prospects of success were almost non-existent, if for no other reason than because of the external situation. Without help from outside the enterprise was doomed to failure, but foreign aid carried with it the threat of war and so the chances of it being provided were small in the extreme. *Mutatis mutandis* the parallel to March 1938 is close. The leadership had good and cogent reason for its decision to 'go down with honour'.

To the men on the barricades of those February days it was soon clear that they had no hope of success. They showed a courage which evoked the admiration of their opponents. On the government side, however, the overriding factors were anxiety both about foreign intervention and the attitude of Germany. The Hungarian Foreign Ministry's official published documents, for instance, include a report dated 15 February from von Mackensen, the German Minister in Budapest, to the German Foreign Ministry to the effect that as a result of the 12 February news from Vienna the leader of an organisation known as Hungary Awake was planning to march into Burgenland with 9,000 men on the night 13–14 February; the news from Vienna on 13 February caused the plan to be called off but the intention remained.[44] Ever since 30 December 1933 Italian headquarters had been prepared for 'Plan Piano K(34)' visualising partial mobilisation in northern Italy and a move of Italian troops into Austria with the primary object of relieving Austrian troops in the event of a rising.

Any development of the rising into full-scale civil war, therefore, carried with it great dangers and these could be countered only by the quickest possible end to the fighting. For this reason martial law was declared and remained in force until 21 February. Of the considerable number of death sentences pronounced by military courts, nine were carried out. Severe though they seemed when looked at individually, they were indispensable in cases where the declaration of martial law failed to achieve its object, an immediate laying down of arms.

It is, of course, true that weighty decisions taken under the special circumstances of the present have weighty implications for the future. Churchill's comment is universally valid: 'The only place where no grass can grow is on graves beneath a gallows.'

That there was no real or prolonged civil war was primarily due to the fact that the vast majority of workers and trades unions, particularly the railwaymen, did not obey the strike call.

The revolt of 12 February 1934 provided the occasion for the proscription of the Social Democrat Party so urgently demanded by Mussolini. Ostensibly the Republican *Schutzbund* was an integral part of the Party and was undoubtedly so regarded. As subsequently emerged, it had received its orders from the Party leadership. In this it differed significantly from the *Heimwehr* which did not form part of the Christian Social or any other Party and was frequently in opposition to them. In the government the *Heimwehr* was represented as one of the partners in the coalition.

As always with such explosive happenings there were certain atrocities on both sides in February 1934; they are equally inexcusable, whatever their origin.

At Christmas 1935 an amnesty was declared and of the 1,521 Social Democrat rebels in prison 1,505 were released.

The differences of opinion about the causes, purposes and effects of 12 February 1934 will lose their bitterness only with the passing of the generation concerned; that will not be long now. Then it will be easier to agree that (in Dostoyevsky's words) 'all our quarrels and dissensions stem from errors of the mind, not of the heart'.

BETWEEN HAMMER AND ANVIL

Our anxiety lest the Nazi activists continue or even intensify their campaign of terrorism during the bloody days of February had proved unfounded. The trend of the German press, inspired by the Propaganda Ministry, was definitely hostile and tendentious, but over the German radio Theo Habicht had declared an armistice to last till 28 February and this was observed.

Berlin decided initially to wait and see how matters developed in Austria. From his Rome observation post Dollfuss's opponent, Dr Rintelen, was counting on Fey seizing power. This, he reckoned, would lead to the break-up of the government coalition and he, Rintelen, would then move into the Ballhausplatz as the saviour in a crisis. The Christian Socials would accept him as one of themselves and he was also in favour with the *Heimwehr* since his days with the Styrian *Heimatschutz*, now disbanded and swallowed up by the Nazis; in view of the increasingly open rivalry between Fey and Starhemberg he might perhaps have been considered the obvious solution. He liked to think that both in Rome and Berlin his position was unassailable, though in both cases he was over-optimistic; in fact no one trusted him, although Berlin was ready to give him a try. At heart Rintelen had long since swung over into the Anschluss camp, accepting National-Socialism without formally belonging to the Movement. In recent years he had become firmly convinced that he was the leader whom Austria needed. To friends of Dollfuss his main criticism was the loss of the German market for Styrian apples.[1]

However this may be, a planned invitation to Fey, then Vice-Chancellor, for personal discussions in Berlin was called off. A memorandum dated April 1934 by Bernhard von Bülow, the State Secretary, on 'further political handling of the Austrian question' states that contact with the Austrian government should be postponed until the situation in Vienna was clearer and one could tell with whom to deal.[2]

Berlin, therefore, still thought that far-reaching personnel changes in the Austrian government were possible. In Rome, on the other hand, people were quite clear, despite the dubious activities of the Austrian Ambassador. For this there were two reasons: in the first place, when Fey presented his bill, Starhemberg came down on the side of Dollfuss; Starhemberg declared himself in favour of the *Heimwehr* combining with the other self-defence formations under the umbrella of the Fatherland Front. This brought him into conflict with Fey and Neustädter-Stürmer who still visualised formation of a *Heimwehr* government. The decision was made at a meeting held on 6 March 1934 in Dollfuss's apartment in the Stallburggasse, Vienna. The Chancellor presided and at the round table were Starhemberg, Fey and Neustädter-Stürmer on the one side and on the other Dr Buresch, Fritz Stockinger, the Minister of Trade, Dr Karl Stepan, the newly-appointed Secretary-General of the Fatherland Front, and myself.[3]

The second reason for Italian support was that Mussolini had known Dollfuss personally since 1933 and trusted him. Dollfuss had convinced the Duce that there could be no question of a fascist regime on the Italian model in Austria; Mussolini had not therefore pressed him to run the country entirely through the *Heimwehr* militia, aping Italian fascism. 'Fascism is not suitable for export,' he had said, 'it is Italian.'[4]

As early as 17 January 1934 Dollfuss had informed the German government through Tauschitz, the Austrian Ambassador in Berlin, that Austria must seriously consider proceeding with her complaint to the League of Nations unless 'an early end was put to the activity by German National-Socialists against Austria and the regime in power'. The German government's reply denied that there was any conflict between the two countries and described existing tension as being due to 'the Austrian government's opposition to an historic movement of the German people'. The

Austrian *démarche* and the German reply were published and repeated by the entire world press, but the Germans adhered to
their totally untenable viewpoint that an Austro-German conflict
was not an international matter but a purely internal disagreement
'among the German people'. The first hint by Hitler that he might
abandon this standpoint came in his Reichstag speech of 21 May
1935 as a result of foreign pressure.[5] He formally renounced it
when the 11 July 1936 agreement was concluded.

In view of the totally unsatisfactory, and indeed provocative,
reply from Berlin, the Austrian cabinet decided on 5 February
1934 to take their case to the League Council. Italy was unhappy
about this and argued that Germany was no longer a member of
the League. Britain and France too advised against it, since they
considered (rightly) that condemnation of Germany by the
League would have no practical effect and they were more interested in avoiding a further loss of prestige by the League.

Austria had confidentially supplied the three Great Powers
with evidence of German interference in contravention of international law. On 17 February the Powers issued a concerted
declaration recognising the justice of Austria's complaint and
stressing their unanimity regarding maintenance of Austria's independence and integrity in accordance with the treaties in force.
In addition all three Powers, Great Britain, France and Italy, in
practically identical notes assured Austria that their determination
to preserve her independence and integrity had not altered and
that they would therefore support her energetically in front of the
League Council. All Austrian missions abroad were so informed
by circular dated 6 March 1934.[6]

On 17 March 1934 Dollfuss, Gömbös and Mussolini met in
Rome and signed the Rome Protocols [see below]. In July 1933,
on the way back from a visit to Berlin, Gömbös had met Dollfuss
in Vienna. Dollfuss, I remember, was slightly disappointed with
his Hungarian opposite number; he had told Gömbös flatly that
his visit to Germany without prior coordination with his Austrian
ally and at the very moment when Austro-German tension was
increasing, might adversely affect Austro-Hungarian relations.
Austria knew that Hungary was canvassing the Third Reich for

support for her revisionist policy – all the more eagerly because Italy was as hostile to the Little Entente, Czechoslovakia in particular, as was Hungary. Gömbös reassured the Chancellor; he had been concerned only to expand Hungary's vital economic relations with Germany.

Verbally both sides emphasised their readiness to work closely together both economically and politically; Austria was as interested as Hungary in maintaining friendship with Italy. Both wished to be on friendly terms with Germany, always provided that their full independence was preserved. Dollfuss informed Mussolini of his talk with Gömbös by letter dated 22 July 1933.[7]

When I met Gömbös in Budapest early in August 1934 after becoming Chancellor he referred at once to his talk with the late Chancellor Dollfuss. Of his own accord he reiterated the principles of Hungarian policy towards Austria, explained his attitude to Germany and told me that, in her own interests, Hungary fully supported Austrian independence. He asked how the Habsburg question stood in Austria; on 24 April 1934 Archduke Eugen had returned to Austria, a fact exploited in various quarters to accuse Austria of secretly pursuing a restoration policy. Horthy in particular was alarmed. Since Hungary had allowed Archduke Josef to stay in Budapest, Dollfuss had felt that Austria could hardly refuse the same right to her Archduke Eugen. In addition the protocol department of the Hungarian Foreign Ministry was proposing to leave cards in Archduke Josef's palace. I was therefore able to reply to Gömbös that the restoration question was not actual in Austria; I also assured him that, in view of our specially friendly relations, nothing would be done on this subject without prior agreement with Hungary. Gömbös seemed fully satisfied with my answer.

As we have already seen (Chapter 3), by the end of 1933 the Italian government was making preparations for possible military action in defence of Austria. Early in 1934 Colonel Lothar Rendulic, Austrian Military Attaché in Paris, told his Hungarian colleague that 'an agreement existed between the Italian government and the Dollfuss government; should National-Socialism gain ground or if, as a result of a German attack on German-

Austria [*sic*], there should be fighting during which the Dollfuss government was forced to give up parts of German-Austria, that government would withdraw to the Italian frontier with its loyal troops and Italy, which would meanwhile have made preparations, would hasten to its aid. The French government was in agreement with Italy on this subject and had urged the Czechoslovak and Jugoslav governments to remain neutral in this event. The Czechoslovak government had agreed but the Jugoslavs had stated that, if Italy intervened, they would do likewise.'[8]

Three Italo-Austro-Hungarian protocols were signed in Rome on 17 March 1934, one political and two economic. In the political protocol agreement was recorded on close collaboration and mutual understanding 'in order to work together in accordance with existing treaties of friendship to promote genuine collaboration between the states of Europe and in particular between Italy, Austria and Hungary in the conviction that thereby conditions for wider collaboration with other states will be created'.[9] The minutes of the discussions show that the 'conditions' referred primarily to Germany and that German recognition of Austria's independence both internally and externally was essential. The relevant section of the minutes reads as follows:

'The core of the political problem was the relationship between Austria and Germany. In this connection it was stated that the interests of peace and of a liberal policy would be served if this relationship were to improve and lead to mutual understanding between Austria and Germany. The Austrian Chancellor stated that he had no objection to this as an aim; the prerequisite for cooperation with Germany, however, was a guarantee of German recognition of Austria's independence both externally and internally.

The Hungarian Prime Minister referred to the necessity for friendship and cooperation between Italy, Germany, Austria and Hungary; he stressed that, in the matter of revision, his country required German support north of the Danube [in Slovakia – author].

The Head of the Italian government agreed with and took note of these statements.'

Para three of the minutes dealt with the Habsburg question:

'On the Habsburg question the Chancellor stated that the problem of a restoration was not actual in Austria. As far as Italy was concerned it was settled in a negative sense. Hungary's viewpoint was known. It was stressed that the question concerned all three countries. The Head of the Italian government advised the Chancellor to postpone to a later date even the return of the Emperor Karl's ashes to Vienna.'

According to para seven of the minutes, in answer to a question Mussolini said that 'both the atmosphere and nature of Franco-Italian relations had recently improved'.[10] Six months later they deteriorated again, however, when Louis Barthou, the French Foreign Minister, and King Alexander of Jugoslavia were murdered in Marseilles on 9 October 1934.

The Rome Protocols set the stage. Their purpose had nothing to do with 12 February 1934 but everything to do with the Thousand-mark Blockade. Not too much was to be hoped from them apart from economic aid in emergency, which did in fact materialise. Italy alone could offer some compensation for the loss of the German market in timber and cattle – for economic and geographical not political reasons. Only creation of jobs could help the unemployed.

The Anschluss was held up as the solution to the problem – but that was a price which Austria would never willingly pay and could not pay if she was to avoid invasion and partition.

This attempt to join Germany's potential friends and secure ourselves that way was at least more promising than handing Germany the argument that we had gone over to her potential enemies. That could only have done them harm and us no good.

Berlin, however, regarded these political agreements as unmistakably directed against Germany, although this was true only in so far as she was not prepared to leave Austria alone. In fact all the signatories to the Protocols had hoped that Germany would be prepared to cooperate both economically and politically in the Danube area. Berlin, however, made representations in Budapest, admittedly with some caution at first, protesting against Hungarian adherence to an Austro-Italian agreement 'unmistakably directed against Germany'; it was not compatible with the 'close friendly relationship' between Germany and Hungary.

The German Foreign Ministry was therefore prepared to label an international agreement recognising, though not guaranteeing, Austrian independence as an unfriendly act on the part of Hungary. Von Hassell, the German Ambassador in Rome, reported that the Rome Protocols had given Austria a new and conspicuous pledge of her independence.[11]

The Protocol States met again in Rome in March 1936 when three supplementary protocols were signed; representatives met in Vienna in November 1936 and the last meeting took place in Budapest from 10 to 12 January 1938.

Meanwhile the fatal year 1934 ran its course. It had begun with a flare-up in Paris and a devastating catastrophe in Vienna. Its trail of blood led through the Third Reich's St Bartholomew's Night on 30 June[12] and outrage and upheaval in the most diverse parts of the world to the Marseilles assassination on 9 October. In the midst of it all came 25 July in Austria.

Everywhere the motives were the same or similar. People turned to force in order to eliminate a regime which they accused of oppression, or to precipitate a public reckoning or to enforce some national demand. In every case one man or a few men decided to act 'in the name and in the interests of all' without stopping to think whether they had any legitimate right to do so. They therefore did exactly that of which they were accusing their victims – the Croat assassins when they shot the Serbian King Alexander; Hitler when he despatched his alleged rivals, Röhm and Gregor Strasser, and liquidated shadows of the past, von Kahr and General Schleicher; Hitler when he gave the green light for the elimination of his only declared opponent at the time, Engelbert Dollfuss.

There is no more to be said about either the background or the story of 25 July 1934. Once more, as on 12 February, the first victim, during the attack on the Vienna RAVAG broadcasting studio, was a police officer, Inspector Fluch. Shortly thereafter, just after 1.0 p.m., Dollfuss was shot down by Planetta in the Federal Chancellery. The Austrian government's 'Brown Book', compiled from official sources by Walter Adam of the Federal Commissariat for Internal Affairs and published in 1934, states that Otto Planetta fired two shots, both of which hit Dollfuss. It estimates the time of the Chancellor's death as about 3.45 p.m.[13]

The President then telephoned entrusting me with provisional conduct of the government. In the name of the cabinet I accordingly dictated to General Zehner, the State Secretary for Defence, an ultimatum with a time limit to the rebels in the Federal Chancellery. It included this:

'If no loss of life has been caused among the imprisoned ministers, the government declares that it will guarantee the rebels free exit and safe-conduct across the frontier. Once the time limit [15 minutes] has expired, the forces of the State will be sent into action.'[14]

This ultimatum was taken to the Ballhausplatz about 5.30 p.m. by Minister Neustädter-Stürmer and General Zehner personally. When it was drafted, no one in the government knew, and could not know, that the Chancellor was already dead. It must have been about 4.30 when Seydel, the Police President, accompanied by Franz Kamba, a police official who, as it later proved, was an accomplice of the conspirators, arrived with the news that the Chancellor had been slightly wounded. Later, about 5.0 p.m., came a telephone call from Fey in answer to an enquiry by Neustädter-Stürmer saying that the Chancellor's wound was 'somewhat severe'.

In addition to the official Austrian Brown Book we now have the report of the so-called Historical Commission of the *Reichsführer-SS*, completed on 27 January 1939. Its object was to collect material for a possible People's Court trial and it differs in important respects from the Austrian official account.[15]

Heydrich's covering note to Himmler on the 'Investigation of the events connected with the rising of 25 July 1934 in Austria' stated that of the important problems one remained to be cleared up – who fired the second shot at Dollfuss. For this an X-ray examination of Dollfuss's body would have been necessary. Special steps should be taken, the note continues, against those responsible for breaking the promise of safe-conduct given to the National-Socialists (pp. 53 *et seq.*).

By a strange coincidence the American press and public are still puzzling over the 'second shot' which murdered President Kennedy. There too the hunt for a supposed second assassin has remained fruitless – presumably because in neither case was there any such person. Under interrogation Planetta did not altogether deny that he might 'inadvertently have fired a second shot' (pp. 90 *et seq.* of the SS report); he did, however, deny any intention to kill:

'. . . I came in some form of bodily contact with this person [Dollfuss whom he had not yet recognised], whether because he knocked against me or whether I knocked against him as I raised my revolver, I do not know. As a result of this bodily contact a shot was fired from my revolver . . .' (pp. 90 *et seq.*).

Other eyewitnesses, however, tell a different story.

About 6 p.m. Dr Kemptner brought the news of the Chancellor's death to the cabinet in the Defence Ministry on the Stubenring; by this time Neustädter-Stürmer and Zehner had already left for the Ballhausplatz. Neustädter-Stürmer confirms that when he handed over the ultimatum, he did not know that Dollfuss was dead. He was told only later by Fey. On receipt of Kemptner's information, about 6.30 p.m., I and the rest of the government moved to the Ballhausplatz. Dollfuss's death, of course, completely altered the situation and made it impossible to keep the conditional promise of safe-conduct.

Moreover, once the *putsch* had failed, the Third Reich quickly disowned its people. On 26 July a government communiqué stated that 'the German government has . . . ordered that, should the rebels cross the German frontier, they are to be arrested forthwith . . .'.[16] On the same day Lieutenant-General Muff, the German Military Attaché, reported to the *Reichswehr* Ministry: 'I had known for a long time that the National-Socialists were considering the idea of, and had also made certain preparations for, a raid by an SA formation disguised in Federal army and police uniforms on the government during a cabinet meeting.' The report continues that the venture could have succeeded only had there been a popular rising or had the army intervened on the rebels' side; he, Muff, had invariably reported that the government was firmly in control of the armed forces.[17]

On 24 January the Hungarian Military Attaché in Paris had reported to his Chief of Staff that Colonel Rendulic, his Austrian colleague, had said that 'the advance and eventual victory of National-Socialism in German-Austria could no longer be stopped'. He thought that 'Dollfuss, Fey and others would probably lose their lives as a result of their political attitude. In his opinion there can be no question of overt incorporation of German-Austria into Germany at the present time. From this he concludes that German-Austria will be turned into a National-Socialist state, ostensibly retaining its independence – provisionally – whereas in fact it will be entirely under German direction.'[18]

This was the whole problem both before and after 25 July 1934 – to prevent Austria being turned into a National-Socialist state and an appendage of the Third Reich with all the inevitable consequences.

After the failure of the revolt in Vienna, fighting with rebels broke out in the provinces, principally Carinthia, Styria, Salzburg and Upper Austria. It lasted until 28 July. Nazi fugitives received much aid and comfort from Jugoslavia, Belgrade's main object being to emphasise its anti-Italian attitude. Both Belgrade and Berlin were well aware that Italy was genuinely prepared to help us if necessary. At the time we were only too thankful that this was so. The fact that help was not required seemed to be the one bright spot in the midst of our misfortunes.

In many countries, but particularly in Austria, 1934 was a year of force and upheaval, violence and reprisals. The *Heimwehr* was shouting for a *coup d'état*; Dollfuss replied with a call for unity based on a new governmental and social order.[19] The Social Democrat Party demanded new elections; admittedly the situation was difficult, but it failed to realise that it was thereby playing the game of its fascist enemy, whose threat came far more from beyond the frontiers than from within. So far as the Nazis were concerned, Dr Otto Gustav Wächter, later a State Commissar and one of the prime movers of the July *putsch*, admitted that they were determined to 'break the tyranny' of the Dollfuss government because 'by yet another breach of the constitution' it had ordered the death sentence for the mere possession of explosives.[20]

[*The author succeeded Dollfuss as Chancellor of Austria in July 1934 - Translator.*]

The clearest indication of the existing state of tension was the fact that immediately on nomination of the new government written instructions were drawn up in agreement with the President providing for automatic succession in the event of elimination of the President, the Chancellor and the Vice-Chancellor. Dr Skubl, the newly-appointed Police President of Vienna, was to take over the government and, after obtaining his agreement, he was so notified in writing. Should Skubl also be prevented from acting, his place was to be taken by the State Secretary, Hans Hammerstein-Equord, who was also given written instructions. In the new cabinet Starhemberg remained Vice-Chancellor; Fey became Minister of the Interior but responsibility for the Security Service was allotted to the Vice-Chancellor, for which purpose Hammerstein-Equord, lately Director of Security in Upper Austria, was attached to him.

There was little difficulty in bringing together the ex-Christian Social members of the cabinet in spite of their differing backgrounds and interests; the problem was to get those members of the cabinet who belonged to the *Heimwehr* to work together, the primary cause of the trouble being the long-standing rivalry and mutual distrust between Starhemberg and Fey. There was no real difference between them so far as their basic attitude to Austria was concerned. Fey's Vienna *Heimwehr* had always followed an Austrian traditionalist line apart from a short flirtation with Berlin and Budapest immediately after February 1934, when ambitious plans led to some false hopes being roused and vice-versa. Starhemberg too had been a firm and unequivocal Austrian patriot ever since September 1931.

As a result of 25 July 1934 there was a Fey crisis. A number of constructions could be placed on his behaviour during the occupation of the Federal Chancellery by the rebels and so inevitably the wildest rumours began to circulate, not without assistance from circles who had no wish to see the situation in Austria consolidate. Before submitting my cabinet proposals to the President I had a long private discussion with Fey; it was very frank and we did not mince words. I came away with the definite conviction that the rumours about Fey were unfounded. He had been neither directly nor indirectly involved in the *putsch* which had hit him, like the rest of us, out of the blue. Admittedly on that tragic 25 July he had been the first to get news of the *putschists'* suspicious preparations and, for some reason or other, had underestimated its importance; in any case he did not pass it on as quickly as he should have. Although he himself strenuously denied any deliberate delay, the theory that, even if only subconsciously, he may have toyed with the idea of mobilising the Vienna *Heimwehr* and then appearing as the saviour cannot be totally disproved. He was not, however, responsible for public security at the time.

Even authors who are critical of Fey and rely on the so-called Weydenhammer Report, have come to the conclusion that the suspicion of collusion between Fey and the Nazi *putschists* is unfounded. Brook-Shepherd, for instance, says:

> 'It can be said with virtual certainty that Fey had no previous knowledge whatsoever of the Nazi revolt and that he was not therefore in any sense a deliberate traitor. The Nazis themselves have unconsciously cleared him of this suspicion . . . the written instructions sent from Germany to organise the "nation-wide Nazi uprising" on the 25th prove that Fey was regarded as being just as great a danger to Hitler's plans as Dollfuss.'[21]

Nevertheless it was obvious that his continuance in the government could be shortlived only. With the government reshuffle of 17 October 1935 he was dropped from the cabinet and became Chairman of the Danube Steamship Company. He remained leader of the Vienna *Heimwehr*, however, so his quarrel with Starhemberg continued. Shortly after the Anschluss Fey, his wife and his son, a cadet at the Wiener-Neustadt Military Academy, all committed suicide.

Two closely interconnected reasons led to the government reshuffle of 17 October 1935: in the first place tension between Starhemberg and Fey had visibly increased; secondly, and far more important, insoluble differences of opinion arose with Neustädter-Stürmer (then Minister for Social Welfare) who came out clearly on the side of Fey and against Starhemberg. These differences stemmed from Neustädter-Stürmer's clearly fascist ideas; these brought him into sharp conflict with the Trades Union League which he urged should be dissolved and replaced by syndicates on the fascist model. In addition he was obviously increasingly opposed to the policy of Richard Schmitz, the Burgomaster of Vienna and ex-Vice-Chancellor, who was doing his best to heal the wounds of 12 February 1934. During the argument I reminded Neustädter-Stürmer that the State was basically authoritarian in character and that it was the Chancellor's prerogative to lay down the general lines of policy; he replied that in fact there was no authoritarian leadership and that people were simply trying to cling to the principles of the old party-run State. It was impossible to reach agreement with him about the Trades Union League or get him to work with Schmitz on urgent matters of social policy. On 17 October 1935, therefore, Dr Josef Dobretsberger, a university professor, was appointed Minister for Social Affairs. He remained until 14 May 1936 when he was replaced by Dr Josef Resch who had already run the Ministry under Seipel. Resch was there until March 1938.

From May 1935 there existed within the Fatherland Front the *Soziale Arbeitsgemeinschaft* [Social Study Group – SAG] which maintained close contact with the Trades Union League. It represented an attempt to form a political workers' movement alongside the organisation based primarily on economic interests. Guido Zernatto says in his book:

'The SAG developed slowly but surely. Thousands of discussion evenings were held when the workers were given the opportunity to express their political thoughts and desires and make acquaintance with the spirit of the new State. We knew that both the revolutionary socialists and the communists were continually trying to use the SAG as a tool for their illegal activity. On occasions they succeeded. In general, however, it must be said that we achieved our object – to bring the mass of the workers into closer contact with the political organisation. . . .

Only a small proportion of SAG agents came from the former Christian trades unions; by the turn of the year 1937–8 the majority were from the ranks of ex-Social Democrat workers and employees. Given peaceful development in 1938 government policy would undoubtedly have come down more firmly on the side of the workers. Working-class representation in many local government organisations was too small; in the cultural organisations many aspects would have been handed over to the workers to run themselves. The plans were ready. All we lacked was time and tranquillity.'[22]

The SAG's forerunner and to a certain extent its founder was the Workers' Action Committee under Dr Karl Ernst Winter, a Vienna historian and political philosopher, who was also the founder and editor of the *Wiener Politischen Blätter*; he was a personal friend of Dollfuss from his regimental days in the First World War. After the events of February 1934 Dollfuss, who had a high opinion of him, commissioned him to win over the left-wing workers to genuine collaboration with the new State. Winter accordingly master-minded the ex-Social Democrat press through the *Vorwärts* publishing concern. The Workers' Action Committee was formed in July 1934 as a specifically workers' circle inside the Fatherland Front.[23]

Dr Winter was regarded as a left-wing conservative; even in his young days, out of pure Christian idealism he had worked on and stuck to the principle: 'Whenever there is a top dog, be on the side of the under-dog.' His committee operated until the early summer of 1936. That it finally failed was due primarily to deliberate infiltration by left-wing extremists determined to prevent any reconciliation with the government – in contrast to the moderate non-revolutionary Social Democrats. On 1 August 1934 the combined Central Action Committee of the Socialists and Communists passed a resolution including this: 'For us, anything but the most ruthless revolutionary class struggle until the fall of fascism and the establishment of the dictatorship of the proletariat is out of the question.'[24]

Disturbances therefore occurred at Winter's meetings and discussion evenings together with attempts to discredit both him personally and his efforts, sincerely meant though they were. A headline in the third issue of the illegal propaganda leaflet *Revolution* described Winter as 'a court jester of fascism'; the accompanying article referred to him as 'a creature of Dollfuss, bought with honours, money and influence'.[25]

Joseph Buttinger, alias Gustav Richter, spokesman of the Central Committee of Revolutionary Socialists, says that Winter's efforts soon came to grief 'despite their apostolic zeal'. His meetings were banned after the police were called in on several occasions owing to the disorderly behaviour of the audience. Buttinger says 'the network of organisers never got beyond a pitifully small band of impotent renegades and a few well-meaning fools'.[26]

In October Winter was relieved as Vice-Burgomaster of Vienna, though he retained his position in the *Vorwärts* concern. The reason was that he had given a number of lectures abroad which were susceptible to misinterpretation and exploitation not only by the opponents of the regime but also by those of Austria – which he certainly never intended.

The Trades Union League under Johann Staud, formerly Secretary-General of the Christian Trades Unions, was far more successful. After a slow start membership rose from a bare 150,000 in June 1934 to 261,000 by the end of that year. Entry was entirely voluntary; the benefits accruing from the collective agreements freshly negotiated by the League applied equally to members and non-members.[27]

Spring 1937 seemed to offer a further opening for collaboration with the Left via the Trades Union League. Dr Renner advocated an end to the boycott of the League by ex-officials of the Free Trades Unions and pleaded for the idea of legal cooperation. This, not illegal action, he said, offered socialist workers their only prospect of success. Staud seized on the idea and was supported by responsible opinion both inside and outside the Trades Union League. People were ready to make far-reaching concessions – Johann Böhm (well-known union leader in the Second Austrian Republic), for instance, was to resume leadership of the Building Workers, Union. He gave his agreement but immediately withdrew it when a storm of protest from the Brno *émigrés* and the Central Committee of Revolutionary Socialists brought the whole idea to an abrupt end. A resolution by the leaders of the (illegal) underground trades unions branded as a traitor anyone who accepted a paid post in the Trades Union League. Negotiations were not formally broken off and were resumed in November 1937. They had not produced any result, however, before the Germans moved in.[28]

On 12 May 1936 von Papen sent Hitler a secret report dealing with the disagreements between the Freedom League under Staud and the *Heimwehr*; it refers to a German subsidy to the Freedom League and the 'intimate relationship' of the League and its leader Staud to the German Embassy.[29] What von Papen could not know, and did not need to know, was that Staud was in permanent contact with me and kept me informed in detail of his visits to the German Embassy. The same was true of the Czech Embassy's efforts to bring political influence to bear on the Trades Union League. Johann Staud's loyalty and patriotism cost him his life in Flossenbürg concentration camp.

No single factor was responsible for the failure to come to some accommodation with the Left before it was too late. One side had the brakes on while the other yielded to the pressure of extremists who regarded any agreement as compromising to their ideal of militant resistance and refused all reconciliation with 'the establishment'.

The widely held view that the government sought to gain contact with the Left only when the supreme emergency was upon them, in other words on 3 March 1938, is both an over-simplification and a distortion. It takes account of only one side of the coin; the other shows that continuous negotiations were undertaken, and on government initiative through the competent agencies, the spokesman of the Trades Union League, the State Secretary (later Minister) for Labour Law and Labour Protection, Hans Rott, and the SAG leaders in the Fatherland Front. I myself, with the knowledge of all these people, had occasional contact with Alois Köhler, a communist metalworker from Floridsdorf, described by Buttinger as 'a man who legally played along with the conciliators, and illegally with the communists'.[30]

Within the Left, as well as within the National-Socialist opposition, there were two opposing groups: those prepared to cooperate and the irreconcilable enemies bent on illegality and subterranean plotting. The old conflict between the 'evolutionary' socialists (Karl Renner) and the 'revolutionary' (the left wing) was still alive. The evolutionists, without in the least sacrificing their political beliefs, preached legal participation in the Trades Union League on purely pragmatic grounds; the revolutionaries went the whole hog, in other words they were working to bring down the hated Austrian regime. In doing so they made themselves willy-nilly the natural allies of their National-Socialist opponents.

Once more the revolutionaries, supported by the Brno *émigrés*, gained the upper hand. They formed a central Action Committee including an unacknowledged communist minority; its declared aim was the overthrow of the regime. They accordingly opposed any compromise with the government and labelled 'collaborators' as traitors to the working class. It should, nevertheless, be recorded that, looked at from the government point of view, the revolutionary socialists, whatever their reasons, kept themselves within perfectly tolerable, even 'decent', bounds compared to the sabotage activities of the Nazis. At the time we were under the impression that the number of ex-*Schutzbund* members who had joined the Freedom League had forced the revolutionaries to lower their sights; the same was true of the influx into the Trades Union League into which there was no question of compulsory entry. Some may have joined purely in the expectation of benefits but there would be nothing extraordinary in that; trades unions, after all, exist to obtain some advantage for their members.

The declared long-term aim of the revolutionary socialists was identical with that of the former Republican *Schutzbund*, the dictatorship of the proletariat. The immediate aim, however, was the unconditional reconstitution of the Social Democrat Party and its re-establishment in all its old rights.[31] Insistence on this doomed to failure all attempts at mediation. What is possible is not invariably right; equally what is right is not always possible.

All parties had been suspended, thus removing from the Third Reich any excuse to demand relaxation of the ban on the NSDAP. Re-establishment of the Social Democrat Party would in practice have meant reintroduction of parliamentary democracy. Would that have been the only proper course? Theoretically perhaps. In practice it would have produced a common front of Germany, Italy and Hungary against Austria. Again theoretically, it was open to us to change our foreign policy and rely on France and the Little Entente. But, quite apart from economic considerations, the Little Entente was in a state of collapse and France was tied to Britain who had long ago stated that she had no intention of undertaking active commitments in Central Europe.[32] In fact, therefore, it was not possible to turn the wheel back and smooth the path for any party to return to the surface at this time. All negotiations were therefore bound to fail. The Berchtesgaden Agreement proved that we did not lack the will to come to an understanding.

In the first place, when the government was reshuffled for the last time on 15 February 1938, Adolf Watzek, an ex-Social Democrat official of the Free Trades Unions, was included as State Secretary for Labour Protection; secondly the amnesty was extended beyond the limits demanded by the Berchtesgaden Agreement. Under Point 4 of that Agreement an amnesty was to be declared 'for all persons punished by the courts or the police for National-Socialist activity'.[33] In fact, however, the amnesty of 16 February 1938 declared '. . . immunity for all acts punishable by the courts committed in the service of a political party or from political motives, provided that the person concerned is resident in Austria at the time of the proclamation of this decision'.[34] It therefore applied to Social Democrats and communists too. Arnold Toynbee says:

'The most masterly touch in Herr Hitler's uncanny manipulation of the Austrian body politic from his wizard's cave at Berchtesgaden was his insistence upon a general amnesty which would benefit the Austrian Social Democrats as well as the Austrian Nazis.'[35]

Gulick, on the other hand, states that nothing in the Berchtesgaden demands indicates that the amnesty was to be extended to non-National-Socialists. In fact this was done deliberately and was by no means welcome to the Nazis; it was generally hailed as an invitation to the Left to clear up their long-outstanding differences with the government in so far as this was possible. In any case as at 1 January 1937 there were only sixty-nine socialists and communists in prison for political offences and even this figure was later reduced.[36] At the end of December 1937 the detainees of all sorts in Wöllersdorf detention camp totalled 105.[37]

On 3 March 1938 a discussion took place in the Federal Chancellery with the Action Committee of the workers' organisations (hitherto illegal); its spokesman was Friedrich Hillgeist with Alois Köhler for the communists. The meeting lasted four hours. The Committee put forward a four-point programme including the following demands:

1. The right of workers to avow their socialist convictions and to enjoy the same rights of political activity as the Nazis
2. Free elections in the Trades Union League
3. Permission to publish a daily newspaper
4. Guarantees of improved social legislation.[38]

This at least broke the ice in that there was no mention of re-constituting the Party or overthrowing the regime. A negotiating committee was set up, represented on the government side by Staud, as Director of the Trades Union League, and Rott, the Minister. Owing to disagreements about responsibilities on the other side meaningful discussions did not resume until 8 March but this was not the government's fault. Some positive conclusion would undoubtedly have emerged but there was not time and, even had it done so, it would not have altered the ultimate out-come. Nevertheless as regards the proposed plebiscite on 13 March the attitude of the Central Committee of Revolutionary Socialists was that: 'The 13th of March was not their day of settling with the Austro-fascists; it was the day to show their hatred of Hitler. Therefore they had to vote "Yes" on Sunday the 13th. A yes-vote is not cast for Schuschnigg and his authoritarian regime but against Hitler and *Gleichschaltung*.'[39] This was as much as anyone had a right to expect.

A further fact worth mentioning is that according to Buttinger, who as Gustav Richter was then Chairman of the Combined Action Committee of Revolutionary Socialists, during their discussions the communist minority had not invariably approved the revolutionaries' tactics and at an early stage had urged that opportunities be kept open for legal activity inside the Trades Union League.[40]

The government has frequently been criticised for failing to submit the new constitution to a plebiscite and in retrospect this criticism is undoubtedly well-founded both legally and politically.[41] Unquestionably, however, during the period preceding 25 July 1934 no plebiscite was possible owing to the increasing wave of Nazi terrorism. Later a number of important considerations weighed against it: that it would be better to see out the transitional period and hold the plebiscite immediately before the entry into force of the constitution – this would have put it in 1938; the attitude of Mussolini who had already advised against it when the question came up in 1934;[42] the fact that we should ostensibly have been giving way to the reiterated demand from Berlin; the real and considerable threat posed by German propaganda and the 'flexible mark'. All these may be extenuating circumstances but they are no real excuse. Whatever one may think of plebiscites, in this case the failure to hold one was an undoubted weakness. In August 1934 a plebiscite would have been meaningful and probably successful. But it would have made no difference to the course of events.

The next major domestic development came on 14 May 1936 when Starhemberg resigned as Vice-Chancellor. The reason was his famous telegram sent to Mussolini on the capture of Addis Ababa; it read as follows:

'Conscious of fascist solidarity and following with intense interest the destiny of fascist Italy I heartily congratulate Your Excellency in the name of all those fighting for the fascist ideal and in my own name on the glorious and magnificent victory of Italian arms over barbarism, on the victory of the fascist spirit over democratic insincerity and hypocrisy and on the victory of the fascist spirit of self-sacrifice and disciplined determination over demagogic mendacity. Long live the resolute leader of victorious fascist Italy; long live the victory of the fascist concept in the world.'[43]

The Foreign Minister apparently knew of the despatch of this telegram. I was not informed and, like the public, learnt of it only through a handout from the *Heimwehr* press office. Inquiry showed that it had been issued, not through the official press agency, but through the *Heimwehr* press office. The text was given to the Vienna press at the same time as the official press agency if not earlier. All this happened about 11.0 p.m. so that no ban on its publication was possible.[44]

The Austrian authorities hardly needed the anticipated angry protest from the British Embassy to convince them that action to repair this *faux pas* was indispensable. It could only be the government's resignation. But this, of course, implied the possibility of a change of Chancellor and a change of regime on the President's authority. In view of the attitude of the Western Powers, however, it was clear that at least the Vice-Chancellor and Foreign Minister must go.

The Italian reaction was less definite. An *aide memoire* of Mussolini's dated 15 May 1936 shows that he appreciated the necessity for some change in the Austrian cabinet. Colonel Liebitzky, the Austrian Military Attaché in Rome, reported Mussolini as saying that, in the event of differences between the head of government and his deputy, the latter must give way. The *aide memoire* of 15 May states that Mussolini was still prepared to support my policy; it stresses the importance of efforts to combine all the volunteer formations into a militia closely connected to the army; finally it remarks that, as things were, the *Heimwehr* would still have adequate representation in the new cabinet.[45]

In *Heimwehr* circles anger and indignation reigned, particularly seeing that all the circumstances could not be made public. Leaflets, some of which may have been masquerading under false colours, gave vent in violent language to *Heimwehr* discontent.[46] On the government side everything was done to make clear that this was merely a change of personnel made necessary in the circumstances.

If discontent on the part of the *Heimwehr* was unavoidable, the same was true of their partners in the coalition; the *Heimwehr* claim to a monopoly was a thorn in their flesh. As might be expected, each side demanded severe retribution for any slip on the part of the other – the majority of 'slips' were verbal only. In any case retribution was called for only against the other side and neither would permit any criticism of itself. In a coalition differences of opinion are the rule rather than the exception. It is this which differentiates it from dictatorship which, in its various forms, was frequently talked of in Austria at the time but never became a reality. Even after the *Heimwehr* had left the government on 3 November 1936 the Chancellor could still be removed at any time and the regime was based on a transitional constitution only. Austria was not the only country where, during the 1930s, disagreements on the most diverse subjects arose between people supposedly of the same way of thinking. The Austrian methods of dealing with them certainly had nothing in common with those in vogue in the dictatorships of the time.

As early as April 1935 steps had been announced to bring the armed volunteer formations under central control when universal military service was introduced. Finally on 10 October 1936 all the volunteer formations were disbanded and the Front Militia formed under command of Lieutenant-General Ludwig Hülgerth, who joined the government as Vice-Chancellor on 3 November 1936. This change, inevitable sooner or later, was occasioned by the increasingly explosive situation inside the *Heimwehr*, or rather between its leaders and their supporters. The Vienna *Heimwehr* had demanded the appointment of Fey as federal leader and the removal of Starhemberg; some settlement was urgently necessary. On 30 September Starhemberg expelled Fey and his adherents, including Lahr, the Vice-Burgomaster of Vienna. Thereupon a revolt by the Vienna *Heimwehr* seemed imminent. On 7 October Fey called a press conference and made a savage attack on Starhemberg. Gulick refers to 'a challenge to a duel which, however, was not followed up by either side',[47] but I know nothing of this. On the same day, however, Starhemberg made a somewhat threatening speech to *Heimwehr* members, including the remark that he and his companions would probably next meet in Wöllersdorf.[48]

For some days confusion reigned. Telegrams came in from the

Heimwehr in Upper Styria and Carinthia asking for Fey to be appointed to command the militia as well as the Vienna *Heimwehr*. Nevertheless the disbandment of the volunteer formations proceeded smoothly and there were no incidents. That some personal feelings should be hurt was neither avoidable nor surprising. The Army Command, however, found the development and organisation of the militia entirely satisfactory.

There was, of course, one major worry: if the ex-*Heimwehr* members were too deeply disillusioned, support for the government would be even narrower. On the other hand, the Left might become less antagonistic and there might be a better prospect of domestic peace under the umbrella of the Fatherland Front.

But it was now the end of 1936 and the storm signals had been hoisted. The world situation had altered radically – and this had been nothing to do with us nor had we been able to bring any influence to bear. In 1933 political alignments had apparently been so firm that Badoglio, the Italian Chief of Staff, had concluded an agreement with Gamelin, his French opposite number, allowing French troops to move through Italian territory in the event of a German attack. At that time, in other words, Paris and Rome were still prepared to work together to preserve the *status quo* and the League of Nations system.[49] In July 1934 Rome, Paris and London were agreed that politically the murder of Dollfuss could be laid at the door of the Third Reich. And they were right – no doubt about it. On 7 August Grandi, the Italian Ambassador in London, had reported that British public opinion thought the same.[50] On 6 September 1934 at the opening of the fifth *Fiera di Levante* in Bari Mussolini had said in his impulsive way: 'Thirty centuries of history allow us to regard with supreme indulgence certain doctrines taught beyond the Alps by the descendants of people who were wholly illiterate when Caesar, Virgil and Augustus flourished in Rome.'[51]

By 1934, however, Mussolini was bent on the Abyssinian campaign; that much was clear from a conversation I had with him during my first official visit to Florence on 21 August 1934. There was no doubt that at that time he disliked Hitler both politically and personally. Never one to mince words and in semi-journalese, he made no secret of the fact that he thought the Nazi racial doctrine barbaric and incompatible with Latin humanist ideas. A revolution, he said, had to have its adventurers; fascism had got rid of them once he had come to power, but Nazism had promoted them to leading positions; therein lay the difference. . . . An expanded presence in East Africa was the Italian nation's 'historic right' and an expression of its cultural mission. In the interest of everybody he must act quickly and bring the enterprise to a successful conclusion within about a year so that he could then once more devote himself entirely to European problems. He did not anticipate any opposition from England; Italy was at one with France and the Germans would need another four years before they counted. . . . No, he did not believe in permanent peace but until 1938 we had time; by that time Austria must be domestically consolidated and mobilised, for then we must reckon on warlike complications.[52]

Shortly before these four years were up Mussolini paid a state visit to Berlin (25–29 September 1937). On 30 September Neurath, the German Foreign Minister, announced the results in a circular telegram to all German missions abroad:

'Italy will not be impeded by Germany in the Mediterranean, whereas, on the other hand, the German special interest in Austria will not be impaired by Italy. However it is entirely correct that, as Mussolini publicly stated, the Rome-Berlin Axis is not directed against other countries and that therefore nothing was discussed or agreed upon which Austria could consider dangerous or infringing upon her independence.'[53]

This is typical of the way in which the Wilhelmstrasse dealt with the Austrian question at this time. The second sentence contradicts the first and is clearly intended as a talking point for representatives abroad.

The world had changed. The murder in Marseilles on 9 October 1934 of King Alexander of Jugoslavia and Louis Barthou, the French Foreign Minister, introduced a note of tension, though temporary only, into the hitherto untroubled French-Italian relationship. The murderer belonged to the Croat Ustachi movement, whose leader, Ante Pavelic, had sought asylum in Italy as a political refugee. The activist members of the Croat revolutionary freedom movement were trained and equipped in Hungary. When the French government demanded the extradition of Pavelic as suspected leader of the conspiracy, Mussolini agreed for political reasons; the Italian courts, however, refused to hand him over citing the general principles of international law. An anti-Italian campaign developed in the French press, although officially the relations of the two countries remained undisturbed.

Italian support for the Croat Ustachis had not been directed against Jugoslavia where the regime had been entirely acceptable to Italy ever since King Alexander's *coup d'état* on 5 January 1929; the object was rather to block any increase of German influence in the country, particularly among the Croats.[54] Göring's famous hunting trips and economic agreements were all part of the German game. The political object was clear: by detaching Jugoslavia to destroy the Little Entente and so weaken France; this would be the first step towards freedom of manœuvre for Germany in Central Europe.

German wooing of Jugoslavia was more successful than the Italian. The Third Reich made good use of the bogy of a Habsburg restoration in Austria with the grotesque result that Germans, including Nazi 'freedom fighters' from Carinthia and southern Styria, found refuge and at times an enthusiastic welcome in Jugoslavia, where everything Austrian remained suspect.

The Abyssinian adventure did not go as smoothly as Mussolini had anticipated either militarily (there were supply difficulties) or politically, and the Third Reich exploited the situation to break out of her previous diplomatic isolation. After the failure of the Hoare-Laval plan[55] and the imposition of League sanctions, ineffective though they were, Mussolini was forced to contemplate the possibility that Italy might be the one to be isolated and he turned increasingly towards Germany. As a result the Stresa front, formed in April 1935 and vital both to Austria and European peace, collapsed; its place was taken by the Rome-Berlin Axis. The League of Nations was hopelessly compromised; Germany had left it in 1933 and in 1937 Italy followed her example.

To cap all this, in July 1936 the Spanish Civil War broke out and this forged a further link between Germany and Italy additional to that of the Axis, the background to which was primarily ideological. Italian policy during these years was largely determined by Mussolini's personal susceptibilities; he saw his position as Europe's leader-writer threatened, primarily by the policy of England. The Western Powers' unexpectedly sharp reaction to Italian aggression in Africa caused him to execute a 180-degree turn and revise his ideas on the Nazi system, notwithstanding the fact that Western opposition had been limited to words, notes and minor gestures; notoriously there had been no mention of an oil embargo, though this would at least have forced Italy to negotiate.

In 1936, therefore, Italy opted for Germany; neither Rome nor Berlin regarded their alliance as more than a marriage of convenience; Mussolini distrusted Hitler and never overcame his unadmitted but pronounced Germanophobia. Hitler did admire the founder of fascism but he never really understood Italy or the Italians. With their help, however, he now set out to blow Germany's 'encirclement' skyhigh and break the fetters of Versailles.

The weakest links in the fetters seemed to him to be Czechoslovakia and Austria. On Czechoslovakia Mussolini was easily talked round since he was considerably influenced by the anti-Czech attitude of Hungary. The case of Austria was very different. Her disappearance would bring the Germans to the Brenner, Italy's northern frontier; moreover there would then be no stopping German hegemony in Central Europe. The new Roman Empire would be compelled to renounce its *limes*.

For Austria, relations with her Hungarian neighbour, the third partner in the Rome Protocols, were of special importance. Hungary's interest in her connection with Austria was primarily economic. For Hungary Austria's independence was of value politically only so long as it could be maintained in agreement with Germany. In view of her revisionist policy, aimed primarily at Czechoslovakia, Hungary was determined to keep in line with Berlin in all circumstances. Clearly, therefore, Hungary was keenly interested in 'the normalisation of Austro-German relations' because only then could she maintain 'that independence from Rome on which she laid so much stress, the Protocols notwithstanding'.[56]

Early in the summer of 1936 Sir Austen Chamberlain arrived in Vienna on a fact-finding mission; his next port of call was Prague. We – and Berlin too for that matter – took his journey as a demonstration of continuing British interest in the maintenance of existing frontiers in Central Europe, now already threatened. A year before (11 March 1935) Clement Attlee, leader of the Labour opposition in the House of Commons, had passionately opposed rearmament on the ground that it violated the principles of the League of Nations. Sir Austen, now an elder statesman of international repute as the ex-Foreign Secretary of the Locarno period (1925), was an equally convinced supporter of the League and of the concept of peace through world law; he had not, however, lost his sense of realities.

Personally Sir Austen was captivating – angular features, eyeglass in eye (as typical in his case as Lord Derby's grey top hat or his step-brother Neville's umbrella), courteous in expression, impeccable manners; he was very well briefed and both his ideas and his comments were far more definite than anything we had heard during our state visit to London in 1935 from the then leaders Ramsay MacDonald, Stanley Baldwin and Sir John Simon. Of course, much had changed in the last year; the clouds on the horizon were increasingly threatening.

No, said Sir Austen, let no one count on direct British action in Central Europe. Britain was watching developments with great concern, however, and would do everything in her power to stabilise the situation in the framework of the existing pact system. As the most immediately threatened areas, Vienna and Prague must do all they could to avoid giving their dangerous neighbour any pretext for aggression.

Basically these ideas were the same as those we had heard two years earlier in Geneva from Louis Barthou, then French Foreign Minister; shortly before his murder he had been making great efforts to arrange a mutual assistance pact between France and

Soviet Russia to compensate in some degree for the absence of an 'Eastern Locarno'. As a first step in this direction he had contrived to secure acceptance of Soviet Russia into the League. With his eye on the Little Entente (Prague–Belgrade–Bucharest) which was vital to his concept, he had advised us: '*ne restaurez pas les Habsbourg*' – a warning hardly necessary in the circumstances. Anthony Eden, who was also a realist, later wrote: 'I was convinced that the League of Nations must gain from wider membership, whatever our views about Soviet policy. The League could not survive as a club; it might as a forum.'

Paul Reynaud also put forward similar ideas in Vienna; he was one of those French statesmen like Edouard Herriot and Pierre Laval who, though of differing political backgrounds, showed much sympathy for the Austrian position. Pacificism, of which there was plenty in Paris and London, he said, was crying for a disarmament conference; this was worthy of respect and in principle desirable; in view of the warlike noises from beyond the Rhine, however, it would be madness to rely upon it. So far as I know, Paul Reynaud's address in Vienna was the first occasion when he produced his description of the French, so often quoted and still apt today: 'a man who wears his heart on his left side but carries his briefcase in his right hand'. By this striking phrase he was in fact trying to counter the widespread anxiety about possible effects of a French Popular Front on the Third Reich activists.

At this time the West was still working on the assumption that the primary responsibility for action to maintain the Central European *status quo* lay with Italy. It was an open secret that among leading Italians the ex-Austrians, the former 'irredentists', saw the danger far more clearly and were far less susceptible to German propaganda than the others such as Count Ciano and later even Mussolini. So long as Suvich, who had been born in Trieste, was guiding Italian foreign policy, there was no danger of a breach with the West; he would have nothing to do with the Rome-Berlin Axis. This was the line followed, on his instructions, by the Italian diplomatic representatives in Vienna, first being the Minister Gabriele Preziosi, an explosive southerner, with his mercurial press attaché Eugenio Morreale; Senator Francesco Salata, who needed no instructions from Suvich, later succeeded them; he was a calmer but no less pertinacious character, had been born in ex-Austrian Istria and spent many years in Vienna as Head of the Italian Cultural Institute; he was finally removed, having become *persona non grata* with Berlin.

Relations with Czechoslovakia were different although considerable contact on the personal level continued between the two countries even after 1918. Until Milan Hodza took over as Minister-President in Prague the atmosphere was decidedly cool, primarily because the Czechs were represented in Vienna by Zdenko Fierlinger who was later to play a considerable part in the communist take-over in Czechoslovakia in 1948 and has been prominent since. As an ex-serviceman of World War I he had little time for Austria and was notorious for his partisan views and influence on domestic Austrian matters. Gabriel Puaux, the French Ambassador in Vienna and a true friend of Austria, says in his memoirs that on the morning of 12 February 1934, before the Vienna riots had begun, Fierlinger telephoned to tell him 'in triumphant tones' that a general strike had just been decided on. The general strike did not happen, but the deep wounds opened at that time could be of benefit only to one man – Hitler.

Meanwhile, on 7 March 1936, Hitler had unilaterally denounced the Locarno treaties by reoccupying the Rhineland. The operation was risky of course, but it succeeded. France and England registered angry protests but obviously with no intention of following them up; Italy applauded discreetly.

From 21 to 23 March 1936 a conference of the three Rome Protocol Powers took place in Rome. Gömbös, the Hungarian Minister-President, and Kanya, his Foreign Minister, proposed that the pact be broadened by the addition of Germany and, if possible, of Poland as well. Germany herself had never considered joining since this would have been contrary to her policy *vis-à-vis* Austria.[57] Questioned by the others, particularly the Hungarians, I stated:

'I do not consider a bilateral agreement between Vienna and Berlin to be possible since I see no prospect, if left to herself, of Austria reaching a satisfactory settlement with Germany. Austria will never adopt an anti-German policy and will not participate in any possible sanctions against Germany in connection with the reoccupation of the Rhineland. I have made this known to the German government through von Papen, their Ambassador in Vienna. On the other hand I refuse to accept German interference in Austrian domestic policy under any circumstances. I therefore consider there to be no prospect for direct Austro-German negotiations seeing that the Berlin government has recently manifested an extraordinarily unfriendly attitude towards us. . . . In my view genuine reconciliation between Germany and Austria is possible only on the basis of multilateral treaties. . . . As a result of the recently concluded trade agreement our differences with Czechoslovakia have been narrowed. Austrian relations with Jugoslavia, on the other hand, are subject to a certain tension at the present time, primarily because the irredentist movement among the Slovene population of southern Carinthia is supported from Jugoslavia; in addition Austrian Nazis living in Jugoslavia are given much assistance by the government. Despite all this the Austrian government is prepared for closer relations with Jugoslavia for the reason that, until the Austro-German problem is satisfactorily solved, Austria must keep open the possibility of friendly discussions both with Czechoslovakia and Jugoslavia – Rumania is less important.'[58]

It was obvious that the Stresa front was gradually and silently dissolving. Austria was therefore forced to look for some other backing for her policy of maintaining her independence; the most promising possibility was an approach to the Little Entente leading to an expansion of the Rome Protocols and thence to the formation of a genuine Central European bloc.

In Vienna we knew that Czechoslovakia shared our anxieties and that Milan Hodza had it in mind to initiate an approach to Budapest and Rome. The increasingly obvious German revisionist intentions had therefore brought about a complete reversal of the policy formerly adopted by the President, Eduard Benes, who, as we had noted with astonishment in Vienna, had said: 'Rather the Anschluss than the Habsburgs.' Much water had flowed under the bridges of the Danube and the Moldau since then and, in the light of the international situation, a multilateral agreement between the Central European powers was in fact the best, and perhaps the only, method of guaranteeing the *status quo* in the Danube basin.

The first contact was made in January 1936 with a semi-official Austrian visit to Prague. President Benes received me in his official suite in the Hradchin and the atmosphere during our interview was most harmonious. Like Austria, he said, Czechoslovakia was vitally interested in peaceful and friendly relations with our great German neighbour. Failing this, we both faced the possibility of intervention by force and must therefore protect ourselves. He was honestly trying to deal with the Sudeten German problem and to find a satisfactory solution on the basis of protection for a national minority. He was very anxious to reach some friendly settlement with Hungary and would welcome Austrian mediation in Budapest.

Milan Hodza, the Minister-President, who was a Slovak and had been a Slovak Deputy in the Budapest parliament under the monarchy as well as one of the advisers to the heir to the throne, Archduke Franz Ferdinand, laid special stress on an agreement with Hungary; he asked me to tell Budapest that Czechoslovakia was prepared for frontier rectifications.

A few months later Hodza paid an official return visit to Vienna. We established very good personal relations leading to a regular exchange of views, initially pursued in my Vienna apartment. We both did our best to keep these contacts as secret as possible to avoid otherwise inevitable sniping from Berlin and Budapest and even also from Rome.

In the autumn of 1937, when the situation was obviously deteriorating, Hodza suggested a meeting on a country road between Bratislava and Vienna; for technical reasons this plan was abandoned and the meeting took place late one evening in late September in a blacked-out hotel room in Baden near Vienna. We took all possible security precautions and avoided any publicity. The subject of our discussion was the clear threat both to Austria and Czechoslovakia from the Third Reich's aggressive policy. As was to be expected, Berlin soon came to know of the

Baden meeting through indiscretions originating both in Vienna and Prague. Only much later did it emerge that the squad of selected detectives permanently in attendance on me included a German agent named Z (immediately after 12 March 1938 he was posted to Gestapo headquarters Vienna); he was in contact both with the proscribed Nazi Party and the German Embassy. Von Stein, the German Chargé d'Affaires, was therefore able to render an initial report to Berlin on the Baden meeting on 30 September; on 7 October this was followed by more detailed comments on the principles of the Austrian government's foreign policy:

'With respect to the meeting in Baden between Schuschnigg and Hodza, my informant received his information not only here but also from Prague. The Vienna conversation began with economic questions, but later the Federal Chancellor, anxious about Austria's independence, also pleaded for a political *rapprochement* of the Little Entente with Austria and Hungary. In Prague M. Hodza expressed great satisfaction regarding his conversation with Schuschnigg, who on this occasion not only spoke of the necessity of close economic cooperation of the countries of the Little Entente with Austria and Hungary, but also lent a very willing ear to Hodza's wish that at Budapest he support an improvement in relations with the Little Entente. . . .

It is clear from all this that the Schuschnigg government continues, as in the past, to travel along several tracks. Fine words and many a phrase feigning sympathy for Germanism cannot conceal that fact. The strengthening of German-Italian relations, instead of inducing Herr Schuschnigg to adopt the line of the Berlin-Rome Axis, has rather added to his apprehensions concerning what is most important to him, Austria's independence. Being of Slovene ancestry and from the pro-Habsburg military caste and educated by the clergy, he does not find it too difficult to pursue rather openly a policy of security directed against the Reich, since he is connected with all the forces working against the Reich here. It is also well known that, besides the Vatican and France, Czechoslovakia too is one of these forces.'[59]

Savage opposition from the Third Reich was not the only reason for the failure of all attempts to reach a broader-based agreement in Central Europe to preserve the *status quo* and thus the peace. They also met with resistance from Hungary. Budapest let it be known in no uncertain terms that Hungary was interested in frontier rectifications only if they included Bratislava. Called Poszony in Magyar, it was the ancient capital of Slovakia and the Hungarian kings had once been crowned there. Obviously, however, a concession of this magnitude was quite out of the question for Czechoslovakia and this demand from Hungary frustrated all attempts to bring the states of the Danube basin together. To make matters worse, Budapest had informed both Rome and Berlin of Austria's confidential moves, thereby sowing distrust in Rome and giving Berlin a fresh handle for its anti-Austrian campaign. For a time, however, Benes's and Hodza's policy on the Sudeten German question seemed to be bearing fruit. As early as 1936 a Sudeten German delegation presented itself to me in Vienna for confidential talks. It included Dr Frank, the Sudeten German political leader. At that time the Sudeten Germans evidently did not know that Germany was opposed to any agreement on the subject; they were much in favour of Hodza's conciliatory policy and showed full understanding for that of Austria.

Mussolini, however, gave us clearly to understand that, in view of the general situation and the Italian commitment in Africa, he regarded an improvement of Austro-German relations as urgently necessary; Vienna should make direct contact with Berlin; this would be an effective extension of the function of the Rome Protocols and offer the best possible international guarantee of Austrian independence. We were therefore forced to rethink our policy and so embarked on the road which led to the agreement with the German Reich of 11 July 1936.

Politically Austria was now isolated. The order of priority of Italian interests had changed; support from Hungary was lukewarm; Britain's interest was purely platonic and so France was paralysed; the League of Nations no longer counted. In addition, however, it was the domestic and economic situation which led Austria to risk one more attempt to reach direct agreement with Germany. If multilateral guarantees were unobtainable the only solution lay in a bilateral agreement. This mere fact, however, implied a diplomatic victory for the Third Reich which, for obvious reasons, insisted in dealing only in bilateral treaties. In January 1934, for instance, Germany had signed a ten-year non-aggression pact with Poland, ostensibly settling all her differences with that country.

The first indication that Germany was thinking of regularising her relations with Austria by means of an agreement is to be found in a memorandum of 9 April 1934 written by Bernhard von Bülow, State Secretary in the German Foreign Ministry. It was drafted in preparation for 'a possible meeting between the Reich Chancellor and Mussolini' and contains all the important points of the subsequent plan; in particular it refers to the fact that at the time 'a military solution to the Austrian question along German lines', in other words Anschluss or at least *Gleichschaltung*, was not possible owing to the international situation. Any international ties between Austria and other states, however, were to be avoided, in particular 'recognition of the basic concept of the Geneva Protocol of 1922' which Benes had recently described as Austria's Magna Charta.[60] At the time Hitler was unimpressed by this memorandum. At a conference on 10 April with Neurath, Blomberg, von Bülow and Ambassador Hassell preparatory to a possible visit to Italy he said that he was totally disinterested in Austria both politically and economically; he had no intention of raising the Thousand-mark Blockade because it helped southern German tourist traffic among other things; he was ready to write off Austria for years and 'hand her over to economic fertilisation by Italy'. Austria's prospects were as hopeless as those of reviving the ports of Trieste and Fiume. But he had no intention of telling Mussolini this in so many words, still less of giving him anything in writing.[61]

The first formal draft of an agreement was handed over by Ambassador von Papen on 11 July 1935; the first time that he indicated that Hitler was ready to negotiate was on 9 September 1935. Further feelers produced no result until March 1936.[62] Not until this point, on my return from the Rome conference, was serious consideration given to an agreement based on the draft originally handed over by von Papen and the Austrian counter-proposals. My visit to Rocca delle Caminate in June 1936 provided the first opportunity for a detailed discussion of a *modus vivendi* with Germany in accordance with the duty to consult laid down in the Rome Protocols. Mussolini started by emphasising that Italy's attitude to Austria was completely unchanged and that she was still interested in supporting Austrian efforts to preserve her independence. He added, however, that in view of Italian commitments elsewhere, Austria must now stand on her own feet in the world – 'it will be easier for Italy to help Austria if both Italy and Austria are on good terms with Germany'.

We then discussed in detail the paragraphs of the proposed agreement which Mussolini welcomed as the only possible solution in the circumstances. Germany, he said in his analysis of the draft, would undertake not to interfere in Austrian domestic affairs and would explicitly recognise Austrian sovereignty and independence. This implied that the German-directed NSDAP-Hitler-movement would disappear as a political factor in Austria. A further German contribution to the normalisation of relations, Mussolini said, would be the ending of the economic boycott and the raising of the Thousand-mark Blockade. The Austrian *quid pro quo* would be an undertaking not to adopt any anti-German attitude in foreign policy; internal political polemics in both states should be stopped. All these points were in fact contained in Papen's original 1935 draft.

Clearly there were likely to be difficulties in the implementation of any *modus vivendi* arrived at; it was also clear that Hitler would observe the agreement only so long as it suited his own external political aims; inevitably also the domestic Austrian battle against National-Socialism would be made more difficult; the truce, even if observed by the other side, would be to the disadvantage of our own Movement. The question was whether the price Austria was prepared to pay was worth it. Our answer, after weighing all the pros and cons, was in the affirmative, since Germany had the whip hand and Austria had no alternative. In his testimony at the Schmidt trial Ambassador Hornbostel aptly explained the motives which caused Austria to conclude the July 1936 agreement:

'If National-Socialism had not been in power in Germany this agreement would have marked a step forward, for the pacification of Europe in particular. It was clear to me that this agreement was meaningful only if the Third Reich was thought to be capable of keeping its word. On this, however, we were doubtful. We gained confidence, however, from the agreement between Poland and Germany, for this seemed to guarantee peace for ten years between the chauvinist Poles and the fanatical frontier Germans. We were not convinced of the dependability of the July agreement. We realised that Italy would lower her guard on the Brenner. The attitude of other countries was not such as to permit us to count on their active intervention in support of our independence. The Abyssinian adventure and the chauvinism reigning in Europe made us realise that in the last resort we must rely on our own resources.

There were varying opinions about the July agreement but I worked on it with a good conscience because there was no alternative. It was the only way of providing some legal basis for our relations with Germany and the only solution offering some prospect of putting an end to the intolerable terror in the country.'[63]

Counsel then asked: 'In the light of your knowledge what would the situation have been without the July agreement? What difference would there have been in practice?' Hornbostel replied: 'I have often cudgelled my brains over that. The July experiment (25 July 1934) would have been repeated only a little later and with considerably greater savagery.' Counsel: 'Supposing the agreement had not been concluded?' Hornbostel: 'Then the catastrophe would have occurred long before 1938.'[64]

The majority of Austrians involved in the negotiations leading to the agreement of 11 July 1936 regarded it as a necessary evil in the circumstances. No one thought that it would cause Hitler to desist from further insistence on the incorporation of Austria. We estimated the validity of the agreement at two years; it was to be hoped that, during this time, the Powers would not give way to further illusions about the dangerous nature of Berlin's policy and would once more coalesce in the Stresa front.[65] The object and purport of the agreement were outlined to the heads of all Austrian missions abroad in a circular dated 8 July 1936.[66]

The text of the 11 July protocol is as follows:

'Convinced of contributing to the general progress in Europe toward the maintenance of peace, and

Believing that the manifold reciprocal interests of the two German States might thereby best be served, the Governments of the German Reich and of the Federal State of Austria have decided to restore their relations to normality and friendship.

Therefore the following declaration is made:

1. In accordance with the statements made by the Führer and Chancellor on May 21, 1935, the Government of the German Reich recognises the full sovereignty of the Federal State of Austria.

2. Each of the two Governments regards the internal political structure of the other country, including the question of Austrian National-Socialism, as an internal affair of the other country, which it will influence neither directly nor indirectly.

3. The Austrian Government will in general, and particularly with regard to the German Reich, maintain a policy based always on the principle that Austria acknowledges herself to be a German State. This shall not affect the Rome Protocols of 1934 and the Supplementary Protocols of 1936, nor the relations of Austria to Italy and Hungary as parties to the protocols.

In consideration of the fact that the *détente* desired by both sides can only be achieved if certain preliminary conditions are provided by the Governments of both countries, the Government of the Reich and the Austrian Government will, in a series of individual measures, create the basic conditions necessary.'

The official Austrian comment on this was:

'. . . Text of the German Chancellor's statement referred to in the official communiqué is as follows: "Germany has neither the intention nor the desire to interfere in internal Austrian affairs, to annex or incorporate Austria." . . . At the same time the agreement . . . finally makes clear that both Austria and the German Reich recognise and respect each other's internal political situation and that, with particular reference to National-Socialism in Austria, there will be no further direct or indirect interference or influence. This statement constitutes a considerable contribution to Austria's security and independence and a valuable contribution to the maintenance of peace in Europe.

In future, as generally in the past, Austria's foreign policy will take account of the peaceful aims of the German Reich's foreign policy. . . . Reports on the agreement therefore lay particular emphasis on the fact that peace between the two states has been reached on the basis of full equality of status and complete respect for the other's internal arrangements. A situation has therefore been achieved for which Chancellor Dollfuss and his successor have continuously striven.

It goes without saying that the position of the Fatherland Front as the sole instrument for the direction of political public opinion in Austria, is unaffected by this agreement. The President has today appointed Dr Edmund Glaise-Horstenau, the Director of War Archives, to be Minister without Portfolio. At the same time the President has nominated as State Secretary Dr Guido Schmidt,[67] the Deputy Director of the Cabinet, and placed him at the disposal of the Chancellor for the direction of foreign policy matters.[68]

Instructions to the directing agencies of the Fatherland Front said:

'1. The normalisation of relations between Vienna and Berlin, including unconditional recognition of Austrian independence and non-interference in our domestic affairs, is a direct continuation of the policy of Dollfuss.

2. Illegal propaganda, whether open or clandestine, will be investigated and punished according to the same principles as hitherto. . . .

3. Austria's overall policy is still based on the maintenance of her independence. There must therefore be no Anschluss propaganda. . . . Fears will undoubtedly be expressed that the agreement will not be observed by the other side. We must wait and see how the agreement works out in practice. Austria would, however, have assumed an intolerable responsibility, had she rejected such a peace offer.'[69]

A supplementary 'Gentlemen's Agreement' laid down detailed regulations dealing, among other things, with treatment of the other country's nationals; as regards the press, the agreement was that:

'Both parties shall influence their respective press to the end that it refrain from exerting any political influence on conditions in the other country and limit its objective criticism of conditions in the other country to an extent not offensive to public opinion in the other country. This obligation also applies to the *émigré* press in both countries.'

To further the political *détente* consideration was to be given to a reduction of the prohibitions on the import of press material. The extremist Nazi press such as the *Völkischer Beobachter*, the *Stürmer*, etc. were still banned, but permission was given forthwith for the entry of five German newspapers, one of which was definitely a Party organ – the *Essener National-Zeitung*, regarded as Göring's mouthpiece. Five Austrian newspapers were cleared for Germany, the *Wiener Zeitung*, the *Neues Wiener Journal*, the *Volkszeitung*, the *Grazer Tagespost* and the *Linzer Tagespost*.

Of particular importance to Austria were the economic provisions which were intended to normalise economic and tourist traffic in both directions by 'putting aside considerations of Party policy'. As a result the Thousand-mark Blockade and economic discrimination against Austria ended.

The touchstone of the agreement, however, was the Austrian government statement on domestic policy. This was contained in Point IX of the 'Gentlemen's Agreement' and was as follows:

'The Federal Chancellor declares that he is prepared:
(a) to grant a far-reaching political amnesty, from which persons who have committed serious public crimes shall be excluded. . . .
(b) for the purpose of promoting a real pacification, to appoint at the appropriate moment, contemplated for the near future, representatives of the so-called "National Opposition in Austria" to participate in political responsibility; they shall be men who enjoy the personal confidence of the Federal Chancellor and whose selection he reserves to himself. It is agreed in this connection that persons trusted by the Federal Chancellor shall be charged with the task of arranging, in accordance with a plan worked out with the Federal Chancellor, for the internal pacification of the National Opposition and for its participation in the shaping of the political will in Austria.'[70]

Such were the provisions of the agreement, the alleged non-observance of which was to give rise to so much argument in years to come and to confirm which the invitation to Berchtesgaden was issued in February 1938. It included an assurance that no demands would be made outside the terms of the agreement.

The agreement came as a surprise to the Austrian public but it was initially hailed, both in Austria and by the world at large, as putting an end to a nightmare. The Austrian militant National-Socialists, however, thought very differently. At first they felt that they had been betrayed and sold down the river and they attacked with every means in their power. One of their problems was that the old underground leaders, now amnestied, insisted on returning to their previous posts, which their younger successors had no intention of relinquishing. Captain Leopold, the ex-National Leader, for instance, was released after twenty-six months in confinement and divested his Party heirs of their functions in short order. The quarrel had to be settled by the German Party and government authorities. This showed the Austrian Nazis, however, that they had lost nothing; they were told to abide by the letter of the agreement, but soon saw that basically nothing had changed. They still received their instructions from the Reich as before.[71]

Ambassador von Papen regarded the agreement as his personal achievement and was very pleased with it. Initially he tried to ensure that it was loyally observed but soon ran into difficulties with the Austrian Nazis (primarily Leopold and In der Maur) which led to a temporary breach of relations between them.[72]

As early as 23 July 1936 Papen was able to report to Berlin that, as a result of the agreement, a total of 17,045 persons had benefited from the amnesty; this included 12,618 held for minor offences whose cases were quashed; of a total of 46 sentenced to life imprisonment 13 were amnestied initially; 213 of those still held would probably have their sentences reduced soon. Papen's report stressed the far-reaching nature of the amnesty.[73]

The position was well summarised by Hornbostel, the responsible officer in the Foreign Ministry, on 12 July 1936:

'It is not possible today to estimate the value of the *modus vivendi* suggested by Germany and now achieved. This depends on whether and how the agreement can and will be observed in practice, i.e. whether on the German side it is regarded and used as the final end to the tragic conflicts of 1933–1936 or merely as a stage in the plan to absorb Austria which remains unchanged, though modified tactically. The motives of the rulers in Berlin now seem clear: removal of a point of disagreement between Berlin and Rome, reinforcement of the Reich's diplomatic position *vis-à-vis* the Western Powers and the League, removal (or at least greater hope of removal) of the danger of collective security pacts in Central Europe, effective proof that Germany is "peace-loving" – to be used as necessary in replying to the British questionnaire. In view of the vague nature of the agreements, however, they do not prejudice Germany's long-term aim to incorporate Austria one day, which certainly remains unchanged.'[74]

One year later Papen found himself defending the agreement to an impatient Hitler. His report stressed its political effects, both present and future, and pointed out that it had been concluded with three objects:

1. To exclude Austria to a great extent from international discussion
2. To wreck the growing efforts towards a restoration of the Habsburgs
3. To pave the way for the exertion of a spiritual influence on Austria by the Reich in order to prevent the creation of an indigenous Austrian culture.

The agreement, he said, had largely achieved these objects since, in the first place, Austrian efforts to obtain an international guarantee had failed and, secondly, the restoration question had been shelved.[75]

That was hardly the original intention.

Meanwhile, however, von Stein had arrived as Counsellor at the German Embassy; he was a Party man and his reports to Berlin bear eloquent testimony to the fact that he was anti everything Austrian and non-National-Socialist. They were largely written behind the back of his Ambassador. In fact Stein did his utmost to torpedo, not only his master, but the agreement as well.[76]

There are many accounts testifying convincingly to the difficulties which arose in implementing the agreement and the reasons
for them. Max Hoffinger, for instance, Head of the German Desk
in the Political Department of the Austrian Foreign Ministry,
confirms that we did everything to counter violations of the
agreement by the Reich. Protests were sent either via von Papen
or direct to our Ambassador (Tauschitz) in Berlin. The German
authorities answered with complaints of their own, in the vast
majority of cases unfounded. At the Schmidt trial Hoffinger said:

> 'The Germans started from the standpoint that the 11 July agree-
> ment was only a stage which should be put behind us as soon as
> possible. On our side, however, the agreement represented *the utmost
> limit of concessions*. People in the Reich frequently complained because,
> in certain cases, we had failed to go further than the agreement.'[77]

Ambassador Hornbostel laid emphasis on the hopes of an improvement in both internal and political relations resulting from
the agreement. If Hitler had negotiated in bad faith, he said, then
the agreement was no more than a scrap of paper from the outset;
it did no more than demonstrate Austria's desire for peace. Had
Hitler been more reliable, it might have been possible to arrive
at a semi-tolerable settlement with this as a basis. At the Schmidt
trial he said:

> 'Domestically the Chancellor needed as calm a period as possible
> in order to pursue economic consolidation. He believed that an im-
> provement in the economic situation might relieve the pressure
> from the illegal National-Socialist movement. Internally, therefore,
> he required the longest possible breathing space. . . . Externally we
> placed our hopes on the favourable impression the agreement would
> make abroad. . . . In fact there was general applause, not only from
> friends but also from neutrals – even Prague agreed warmly. The
> long-term repercussions could not be reduced to paper.'[78]

No one was in any doubt why the other side wanted the agreement or what their motives were. *We* knew what Hitler was after
and *he* knew why we needed the agreement; he required external
tranquillity and we primarily required economic progress. Two

years for the validity of the treaty turned out, as it so happened, to be an overestimation by four months but this was primarily due to developments in Italo-British relations which could hardly have been foreseen.

Economically the agreement produced much, if not all, of what could have been expected of it. Professor Wilhelm Taucher, who was Trade Minister at the time, regarded reduction of unemployment as his most important task and here the negotiations for a trade treaty with Germany, opened as a result of the Agreement, played a vital part. Germany's interest was to obtain raw materials from Austria, whereas we laid stress on increased exports of manufactured and semi-manufactured goods. In fact considerable progress was achieved; export quotas of processed products were noticeably increased and an additional blast furnace was put into service at Donawitz – a notable success. At the Schmidt trial Taucher said:

> 'In 1936–1937 the volume both of export and import trade increased. While I was Minister the volume of external trade rose by half a milliard schilling [five milliard at the present rate of exchange]. Economically the country was on the upgrade; of that there is no doubt.'[79]

In 1936–7 exports rose by 28 to 55 per cent compared to 1933. Taking 1929 as the basic year (index 100) the production index rose to 104, having fallen to 62 in the crisis year 1933. Between 1933 and 1937 the value of, for example, the Austrian film production rose by 50 per cent.[80]

On the economic side, therefore, the July agreement did achieve a proportion of what was expected of it; on the political side, however, although major acts of terrorism ceased, it made the Austrian position more difficult rather than the reverse.

On 11 July 1936 von Hassell, the German Ambassador in Rome, reported to the Berlin Foreign Ministry on a conversation with Mussolini. It had dealt primarily with *de jure* recognition of the Italian conquest of Abyssinia, but Mussolini had seized the opportunity of expressing his lively satisfaction over the Austro-German agreement because it would 'bring to an end the unhappy situation of Austria as a football of foreign interests and, above all, would finally remove the last and only mortgage on German-Italian relations. He had energetically pressed Schuschnigg last time along these lines, starting from the viewpoint that Austria was a German State which must move parallel to the Great German Reich. . . . He had urgently exhorted Schuschnigg, who had declared himself a monarchist, just as he was himself, to let this question rest at present.'[81]

Perhaps the Duce was thinking of Seipel's remark that there could be no Central European settlement in which Germany did not participate as the leading Central European state; in other words, that lasting peace in Central Europe was not possible without or in opposition to Germany.

The question was: what sort of Germany were we dealing with? This was made clear by a whole series of diplomatic reports to Berlin from the German Embassy in Vienna on the results of 11 July 1936 and by recorded statements from the competent Berlin authorities. On 16 July Papen reported to Hitler that he considered his short-term mission to re-establish 'normal and friendly relations', undertaken on 26 July 1934, to be at an end; signature of the 11 July agreement had been the decisive step in this direction. Knowing how hard the decision had been for Hitler from many points of view, he said, he regarded it as a statesmanlike act of the first order. The report ended with thanks to the Führer.[82]

As early as August 1936 the Austrian Foreign Ministry learnt that Theo Habicht was once more busying himself with the Austrian question; a note by Günther Altenburg of the German Foreign Ministry records that Wilhelm Stuckart, State Secretary of the Reich Ministry of the Interior, had summoned Habicht to tell him what demands should, in his view, be put to the Austrian government in furtherance of the agreement. Habicht was, of course, only too willing to comply.[83] Another note from Altenburg dated 22 September 1936 says that developments in the Party in Austria had recently been less than encouraging. In spite of objections from other Party members, Captain Leopold had installed as his deputy Franz Schattenfroh who had been voted down because of a racially questionable marriage contracted two years earlier. The German Party would try to get Leopold to compromise.[84]

An office minute by Altenburg of October 1936, commenting on information from Lieutenant-General Wolfgang Muff, German Military Attaché in Vienna, is illuminating. Glaise-Horstenau, the Austrian Minister, had made some very pessimistic remarks to Muff regarding developments in Austria:

> 'They desired, of course, to obtain as much as possible for Austria from the agreement of 11 July, especially in the economic field, but were not inclined to make concessions in the field of domestic policy. There were objections to negotiating with the Reich on the points established in the Gentlemen's Agreement, such as the press, cultural questions, exiles and amnesty. Under such circumstances Minister von Glaise-Horstenau wondered whether there was any further use for him to remain in office; he would, however, not give up his position until he was expressly authorised or directed to do so by the Reich. . . . General Muff remarked further that . . . it was becoming more and more apparent that General Zehner was an opponent of the Third Reich . . . Hornbostel had apparently been clever enough to consolidate his position in the Austrian Chancellery.'[85]

It was indicated to Glaise-Horstenau by the Reich that his continuance in office was desired.

Towards the end of the year the atmosphere deteriorated visibly. In November 1936 Schmidt had gone to Berlin for personal discussions and these had produced a few firm agreements concerning (for instance) the rights of German nationals resident in Austria and their associations; under certain conditions they were allowed to wear the Party badge, give the Hitler salute and hoist the German flag. These perfectly normal rules had to be explicitly laid down since experience had shown that one could not rely on Germans observing the normal code of conduct towards a host country. Admittedly there were Germans who had no wish to flout international good manners but they were practically compelled to do so since they were at all times under the supervision of some Party agency. Some of these regulations were by no means strictly covered by the agreement, as is shown in a minute dated 7 October 1936 by Ernst von Weizsäcker, Director in the German Foreign Ministry and later State Secretary, concerning the formation of a Party organisation in Austria by and under the foreign organisation of the NSDAP.[86]

How intent the Germans were on extracting further political concessions from Austria is shown by the confidential guidance from the Berlin Foreign Ministry to the German Ambassador in Vienna preparatory to Schmidt's visit to Berlin on 5 November 1936. It includes this:

'We are primarily concerned with conducting the economic and political discussions in such a manner as to contribute indirectly towards furthering the . . . conversations regarding the political execution of the July 11 agreement. We do not, however, consider it expedient to express this purpose to the Austrian government or even to let it be too clearly recognised through the manner of our tactical procedure. . . . During the negotiations a renewed aggravation of the domestic situation in Austria and in consequence of her relations with the Reich might occur. In either of these two cases it will be possible for us to handle matters in a dilatory fashion and thus indirectly let the Austrian government know that we are not disposed to render performance in advance in the field of commercial policy . . . if political developments do not assume the shape we may rightfully expect from the Agreement of July 11.'[87]

From the turn of the year 1936–7 tension increased still further. On 18 December 1936 the German consulate in Graz reported, according to a confidential communication from the Foreign Organisation of the NSDAP, that, as stated by 'a reliable source in the illegal Austrian Party' the Federal Chancellor had instructed that 'the communist party in Austria is to be kept under surveillance but not treated too harshly, whereas Austrian National-Socialists are to be punished most severely on the slightest occasion. Directives given by the Minister Glaise-Horstenau are to be . . . disregarded and not acted upon'.[88] There was not a word of truth in this, as the consulate could easily have found out.

During 1937 many of the reports both from Papen and his Counsellor, von Stein, referred to the desirability of bringing about a change of government in Austria: 'The strengthening of German-Italian relations, instead of inducing Herr Schuschnigg to adopt the line of the Berlin-Rome Axis, has rather added to his apprehensions concerning what is most important to him, Austria's independence.'[89] In a report of 1 September 1937 to von Neurath, Papen once more raised the question of a cabinet change in Austria, referring to the 'Chancellor of the Customs Union' (Dr Ender) as a candidate since he 'does not hold to the "Austrian ideology" so fanatically as the present Chancellor'.[90] This shows, incidentally, that von Papen had completely misjudged Dr Ender as a man, a politician and an Austrian. On 10 August 1937 von Neurath, the German Foreign Minister, urged the resumption of talks on the customs union; he remarked that in his view the Austrian government was at variance with the policy desired by the majority of Austrians and emphasised his impression that, on the part of Vienna, the goodwill necessary to implement the agreement was lacking. An Austro-German settlement was, therefore, unlikely to come about as a result of the agreement.[91] And what if, in fact, 'the Austrian government had been at variance with the policy desired by the majority of Austrians'? At times that is possible with any government and under any system. In time the situation adjusts itself one way or the other.

In fact, of course, the majority of Austrians would have preferred to postpone Anschluss with the Third Reich as long as possible, if for no other reason than because no one was prepared to take the risk of war. The agreement stipulated that Austrian foreign policy would be conducted in accord with the *peaceful* aims of the Third Reich's foreign policy; that was the clearly established limit of our readiness to collaborate.

It is of interest that on 28 May 1937, only a few months before von Neurath's remark about the Austrian government being at variance with the wishes of the majority of Austrians, the Hungarian Minister in Vienna had reported as follows on a conversation with von Papen, his German colleague:

'Finally Papen referred to Czechoslovakia, the partition of which figured among the German government's plans. He added: "Czechoslovakia cannot remain; I also think that, if the international situation is favourable, a far-reaching decision will have to be taken in respect of Austria."

Should the international situation be such that the Germans would risk making an active move against Austria, we [Hungary] should, in my humble opinion, make preparations to ensure that this led not to the annexation but the partition of Austria. We should therefore start now a diplomatic manœuvre to ensure that, should this happen, we can re-establish our western frontier and bargain the Bacska for southern Carinthia.[92] [*In a Hungarian-Yugoslav agreement – Author.*]

Such an international situation with all its possible consequences the majority of the Austrian people certainly did not want, but it could hardly be referred to in public. In the Ballhausplatz, of course, we had to deal with problems like this and, with our very restricted resources, we were doing our best to prevent a whole people, our people, from vanishing into obscurity. Perhaps there was a certain similarity between this agreement on 11 July and the old German *Bund*; basically it was probably not a bad one; it merely presupposed something now out of date – honesty and good faith.

Difficulties of interpretation are liable to arise in the interpretation of any agreement. We in Austria undoubtedly had justification for complaint, but it may well be that Germany also felt that we were dilatory in implementing certain clauses, particularly as concerned the thorny subject of internal pacification. When all is said and done, the real reason for all the difficulties was that Germany tacitly had an entirely different conception of the object of the agreement from that of Austria. For us it was the maintenance and for Germany the elimination of Austria as an entity. Many in German Party circles liked to think that they could appeal direct to the people over the Austrian government's head and so take over the government themselves.

On the Austrian side two important assumptions, thought to be valid, proved to be inaccurate. In the first place there turned out to be no such thing in the country as a 'national opposition' of any consequence prepared to divorce itself from National-Socialism. Secondly, the idea that it might be possible to sever the connections between the Austrian and German NSDAP and terminate the Austrian Nazis' allegiance to Hitler proved to be utopian. A serious attempt was made, for instance, to persuade Heinrich Srbik, the university professor and ex-Minister of Education, and Egbert Mannlicher, later President of the Senate, to join the government and so pave the way for further co-responsibility on the part of the national opposition – but in vain. Impossible political demands were made – fortunately for all those involved, as it subsequently proved. The only 'national' representative we could obtain was Glaise-Horstenau, joined in summer 1937 by Seyss-Inquart, not as a member of the government but as Councillor of State. Neither of these two appointments produced much satisfaction either in Austria or in Germany, although there was no doubt at the time that Glaise-Horstenau was a solid 'national'. It must be admitted, however, that, as Minister without Portfolio, he had a certain justification for feeling that he had been demoted.

The Austrian Nazis soon recovered from their initial shock of surprise at the conclusion of the agreement. The amnesty clause was fulfilled punctually and liberally; as a result, despite occasional doubts, the Party comrades took courage once more; they still received their instructions from the Reich and the German Embassy in Vienna and they now made full use of their right to hold 'peaceful' mass demonstrations, the object of which was unmistakable. The radicals resumed their activities with the object of torpedoing any attempts at reconciliation either at home or with Germany, killing any disposition to compromise and 'going the whole hog'. It should be remembered, too, that Hitler had in fact no liking for the July agreement. Von Papen says in his Memoirs:

'When I returned to the Embassy after signing the agreement, I telephoned Hitler to advise him of its completion. His reaction astonished me. Instead of expressing his gratification at the result of nearly two years' hard work on my part, he broke into a flood of abuse. I had misled him, he said, into making exaggerated concessions in return for purely platonic undertakings by the Austrian government. The whole thing was a trap. . . . He was in one of those hysterical rages which I had experienced before, though never on the telephone. . . . I wondered what could have caused this sudden change of mind. Some of the Party leaders . . . must have criticised him for making too many concessions.'[93]

This explains also why all the more promising attempts to come to some settlement invariably failed. Among them was the formation of a German Peoples League [*Deutscher Volksbund*] under the patronage of Neustädter-Stürmer and Glaise-Horstenau. Signatures were canvassed but the enterprise had hardly started when Captain Leopold, the illegal Nazi leader, came out in public against it, describing it as a camouflage manœuvre and so compromising it hopelessly.[94]

The next attempt was the formation of the so-called Committee of Seven with sub-committees in the provinces; its task was to persuade 'national' circles to cooperate with the Fatherland Front. The Committee originally consisted of Leopold, Tavs and Jury for the National-Socialists and, among others, Dr Oswald Menghin, the university professor, and Wolsegger, ex-Director of the Provincial Office in Klagenfurt. It set up an office in the Teinfaltstrasse, Vienna, which later became the headquarters of the illegal Nazi Party in Austria; Tavs ran the office, the titular head of which was Leopold. The non-Nazi members soon resigned. Our final effort was the organisation of the so-called *Volkspolitische* Offices within the Fatherland Front under the overall direction of Seyss-Inquart.

The occasional Nazi acts of terrorism, deliberately aimed at propaganda effect both at home and abroad, led to countermeasures. We also attempted to explain our attitude at public meetings and interviews which were then seized upon by Germany as unfriendly acts and breaches of the agreement. Among these was a speech I made at Klagenfurt on 26 November 1936 which was intended as an unequivocal retort to the preceding illegal actions. In it I enumerated three enemies of the Fatherland movement and therefore of the existence of the State:

1. Communism, which presented, however, no serious danger
2. Nazism – I said: 'The National-Socialists in Austria, and no one else, confront us as enemies'
3. Defeatism in our own ranks.[95]

Von Stein, the German Counsellor, reported the speech in detail to Berlin on 27 November and it was blown up into an 'incident' leading to postponement of the planned return visit to Vienna by the German Foreign Minister.[96] Similarly, early in January 1938 I gave an interview to the *Daily Telegraph* correspondent in Vienna during which I said that 'between Austria and Nazism there was a gulf and that the government was decidedly in favour of maintenance of the *status quo* and against the Anschluss'. The *Daily Telegraph*'s Berlin correspondent thereupon reported that 'Ambassador von Papen had been instructed to seek clarification of the interview from the Austrian government. Berlin official circles seem to regard this as the most disturbing incident in Austro-German relations since the conclusion of the July 1936 agreement.' These incidents show that Germany did not regard herself as bound by the clauses which laid down that the National-Socialist Party in Austria was a purely domestic Austrian matter in which there would be no interference.

Differences of view on this subject were also prominent in discussions with Glaise-Horstenau and later Seyss-Inquart. They are well illustrated in a letter I wrote to Glaise-Horstenau on 31 May 1937, of which the following are extracts:

'. . . Looking objectively at the history of recent years one must admit that until National-Socialism seized power in Germany, laid claim to total authority and equated National-Socialism with Germanism, Austria had placed no obstacles in the way of relations with Germany and had even tolerated the strident Anschluss propaganda. In particular the "volksdeutsche" concept was to a large extent the very basis of my predecessor's political policy and he sought conflict neither with Germany nor with National-Socialism. As you well know, the course of events led him to work on an entirely different plane. It cannot be denied that the revival of a broadly-based Austrian patriotism is the reaction to the intemperance of National-Socialist propaganda. There is no real truth in the assertion that the suppression of and subsequent ban on National-Socialism is due to efforts by the other parties to prevent National-Socialism in Austria seizing power legally. There is no need for me to repeat that the ban was preceded by a whole series of bloody crimes, started well before July 1934, beginning with gang murder and ending with a hand grenade attack on innocent sportsmen; the ban had to be imposed not only to protect the population but in the interests of decency, honour, loyalty, faith, authority and self-respect. The propaganda principle enunciated in Hitler's book *Mein Kampf* is that it must be intemperate and, even when right is on the side of the enemy, must not give an impression of objectivity; its sole purpose is to hammer some theme into the masses until the vast majority of the waverers and the uncertain are carried along by it. Acceptance of this principle would imply submission, submission to appointed or self-appointed leaders who possess neither the breadth of intellect nor other qualities to justify letting them loose on the Austrian people. The fact that not everyone on the other side is an angel and that there have unfortunately been a number of excesses must be regarded as a circumstance to be encountered anywhere in the world in similar cases and under similar conditions. . . .

We have proved that we are serious in trying to direct Austria's foreign policy along German lines. I need not emphasise that my desire is not only *détente* at home but also the best possible relations with Germany under the circumstances. My task is made more difficult by the well-known fact that still (and today has given further proof) Germany implants and fosters among leading National-Socialists ideas which can only lead us astray. It has been abundantly proved that neither German nor Austrian National-Socialists really want peace; their heads are filled with the out-dated idea of power. In addition every terrorist act so far has provoked a reaction from Austrian radicalism, thereby destroying any long-term prospects of creating the psychological atmosphere necessary for peace. . . . The picture is always the same. One side calls out the demonstrators, organises and directs them; intervention by the security forces is thereby provoked as intended; the cry then goes round that the German population is being prevented from giving a friendly welcome to German visitors – this scenario needs no further comment. To prevent a repetition there is unfortunately only one method – to ensure that such affairs cannot take place at all. . . .

Whatever can sensibly be done to consolidate the 11 July agreement without breaking too many bones, will be done. You know how far I would have been prepared to go to correlate and merge things Austrian and German. Today I know full well that my ideas were impracticable and unrealistic. We must therefore look for new ways. As far as I am concerned only one thing is certain: at the present time and under my responsibility there can be no question of National-Socialist participation in government in Austria. For a country which has lived through July 1934, the road to political co-operation and responsibility must be restarted from the beginning. That has always been my view, as you will remember. There are three reasons for this: the first is ideological; the second is based on political practicalities – genuine political recognition of the May 1934 constitution and the demand for a coalition with National-Socialism (for this is what it amounts to) are incompatible and the idea that Austria is peopled entirely or almost entirely by National-Socialists is obviously false; for my third reason – and it is by no means the least – I advise you to read Reich Minister Goebbels' last speech and to read it in full. Under these circumstances – and I must say this to you clearly and unequivocally – there can be only one answer, a *non possum*.

I have not altered my view that Germany, even the Germany of today, stands to gain far more from Austria if she could make up her mind to leave this country in peace. Remember Bismarck who said that the Bavarian was a being halfway between man and Austrian. Please make such use of this letter as you wish. My purpose has been to set down certain basic thoughts in more definite language than is possible in conversation. Please do not think that I am like old Taaffe, who certainly had more presence and more scope than we humble people have today; his remark about "muddling through", however, had a deeper significance than the superficial thinkers of his time believed. The point now is not to muddle along but to gain time. Even the Thirty Years War came to an end one day. May Austria emerge unscathed from whatever must inexorably come. That would be some compensation for the unjust verdict of world history, from the consequences of which we are now suffering.'[97]

In June 1937 I exchanged letters with Dr Seyss-Inquart. They show the basis of the agreements intended to lead to legal participation by the National-Socialists in the Fatherland Front. They are reproduced below and require no further comment:

'to Dr Arthur Seyss-Inquart
   Vienna.   Vienna, 16 June 1937.

Dear Doctor,
   Now that the proposed *Volkspolitische* Office in the Secretariat-

General of the Fatherland Front has been set up and Dr Walter Pembaur has been appointed, I think it would be useful to look for ways in which legal participation by additional national circles in the spirit of the 11 July 1936 agreement and the discussions of February this year would be possible on a broader basis than has been the case hitherto. I therefore revert to our verbal discussions of last week and ask, my dear Doctor, for your cooperation. I believe you agree with me that such collaboration is possible only on the basis of mutual and acknowledged confidence. In my case this basic condition is not met in so far as the leading personalities of the representative committee [the Committee of Seven] are concerned; I think, therefore, that under the circumstances, any further attempt to reach our goal via this Committee is useless. I say this because the conditions laid down in the memorandum of agreement of February this year, in particular those concerning the activity and status of the illegal movement, have not been observed.

If I can count on your readiness to cooperate, I shall propose to the President that you be nominated to the Council of State and this, I assume, would publicly legitimise your political activity. I take it for granted that, in this case you would become a full member of the Fatherland Front, so as to create a situation which would be clear and indisputable to all the world. There need, of course, be no announcement on the subject. Finally I would ask you to hold yourself ready to participate in the forthcoming negotiations in the inter-state Commission. In accordance with the agreement of July 1936 the Commission itself is to be manned by Foreign Ministry officials on both sides.

With all my esteem, Yours sincerely, Schuschnigg.'

'Vienna, 21 June 1937.

Dear Chancellor,

When you asked for my cooperation on the 16th of this month, I sent an immediate and very short reply since all important matters involved had been settled by our recent conversations and rapid action seemed best calculated to eliminate the possibility of "talking at cross purposes". May I thank you again for the proof of your confidence which you have given me, for my nomination to the Council of State and in particular for the special task with which you have entrusted me. Having thus concluded the, so to speak, personal introduction to our work together, I would like, my dear Chancellor, to reiterate briefly my ideas on the way in which the situation should and must develop; this will also illustrate the principles which I hope to follow in the task allotted to me. . . .

You rightly point out that our collaboration must be based on mutual and acknowledged confidence. I need not say that I regard this as the first prerequisite for my task, which would otherwise be insoluble, and that, as far as I am concerned, this basis exists already. In view of the task you have given me I infer with gratitude that you too, my dear Chancellor, regard this prerequisite as fulfilled as far as working with me is concerned.

This confidence must rest primarily on two things: personal aptitude for confidential relationships and agreement on actual practical aims. In so far as the first is concerned, I can tell you that I have been able to gather men around me who have given me their complete confidence and to whom I feel equally committed; the inevitable differences of opinion, albeit only on tactics, are never to affect our solidarity. I believe, therefore, that personally I am able to give and inspire confidence. As far as actual aims are concerned, I would point to the results of our frequent and prolonged discussions. . . . A decisive factor in the continuance of this work, however, is the question whether it will be possible to maintain active non-interference, in other words whether it will be possible for the Reich Chancellor actively to prevent any persons or agencies whatsoever from interfering. Were this so, it would reduce the problem of the status and activities of the illegal movement to more or less manageable proportions. The effect on national circles of such clarification would be to alert them to the possibility that judgement can be freely exercised uninfluenced by subversive anti-state tendencies. Referring to National Socialism in this context, I would say that, unless we are to disregard the basic connotation of those words, it cannot be looked upon as a *"Weltanschauung"* but only as a political approach to actualities. National-Socialism provides no answer to the problem of the cosmos or relationship to God. Any attempt to do so might lead to a dialectic of physiological materialism as a counterpart to the Marxist dialectic of historical materialism. I do not believe, moreover, that any serious National-Socialist really thinks that the entire universe was created in order that the German people, as its most perfect manifestation, might form its centrepiece and that that is why everything exists. If, however, we acknowledge that race [*Volkstum*] is the god-given cornerstone of mankind and, as a result, decide to use our energies in the service of the organic racial community, formed according to the laws of nature, then the acknowledgement can be regarded as national and the decision as socialist. We may thus perhaps have discovered a practical form of words to describe the political attitude of all those circles whose political views are not dictated by some definite creed – and today this must include the majority of Germans and westerners. Race [*Volkstum*], therefore, becomes a special, if not the highest, criterion of values and the principles and ideals which spring from recognition of this fact should be followed or striven for in the community of our people. The concept of the "Reich", therefore, does not imply some imperialistic urge for expansion but a moral obligation.

There exists, however, a faction which obsequiously follows every political development in the Reich and which is both the source of and channel for interference; this must be regarded as illegal since it contravenes the concept of Austrian independence. This attitude leads to dependence on the political will and decisions of forces outside Austria and eventually to a semi-dependent status – the "Eighth *Gau* policy" with its system of inspectors. A clear distinction must be drawn, however, between those who support this view and the present national opposition which desires to participate responsibly in the formation of the political will. . . . In addition to all this, there remains the question of active non-interference from outside. Without this none of our efforts can succeed. By active non-interference I mean a relationship in which all the manifold indissoluble ties which spring from community of race would be under control of persons who, on the basis of the 11 July agreement, enjoy the confidence of both parties; on objection being raised by these persons, official agencies, and more especially the Party, would immediately suspend all relations leading to the intrusion of outside influence in the form of instructions or seeking to reduce the influence of those acting responsibly on the basis of the 11 July agreement. If this can be achieved, the way will be open for genuine broad-based pacification at home and for the exercise of all those plenary powers which I outlined in my "address" to the leaders of the Front and which are essential to the fulfilment of these tasks.

The agreement of 11 July sets out clearly the basis for our political activity:

1. Recognition of Austria's independence and a promise of non-interference implicit in the declaration that Austrian National-Socialism is an Austrian affair.

2. Acknowledgement that Austria is a German state.

In my view it is no accident nor a mere matter of drafting that independence should be placed first; under present circumstances this is a premise on which all activity in the overall German sense must be based. The acknowledgement that Austria is a German state, however, does not imply that she occupies some special position in the German community; it means that she must be worked into that community and, for national circles in Austria, this is prerequisite to their acceptance of the state and its independence. If this is to happen, however, it implies that Austria's forces and potentialities must be employed on the side of the German Reich and therefore indirectly on the side of National-Socialism as practised in that country. This can only be done, however, if internal independence is unquestioned. National circles are not interested in scoring successes for the Party or the movement in Austria; their interest lies in ensuring that Austria will stand shoulder to shoulder with the Reich in the struggle of the German race as a whole for its *lebensraum*. It will obviously be of advantage if Austrian influence is brought to bear on the means and methods employed in this struggle.

I believe that the active non-interference which I desire can be brought about if Austria's cooperation with the Reich is assured. In a recent conversation with Dr Schacht he indicated that this was a perfectly practical possibility. I understand that Blomberg too could be persuaded and this will undoubtedly be Neurath's view in any case. I therefore feel that I must urge once more that these personalities and these circles should be won over to support this point of view. At the moment the general situation would seem to favour this solution since the persons I have mentioned are the leading figures as far as the Reich's external relations are concerned. I also think that the next few weeks and months will provide the basis for important and far-reaching decisions. These may extend to a decision by the Reich Chancellor, in his capacity as *Party leader*, to support non-interference in the sense described above, provided that, in his capacity as Head of State, he receives every assistance from Austria. The result would be that the men who stand surety for Austria and protect her from interference would be the same as those whom the Reich would regard as protagonists of an all-German policy, Austrian independence being maintained nevertheless. We have already taken a step in this direction with the formation of the bilateral committees and for this purpose I have gladly made myself available to cooperate.

I assume that the new law for the preservation of order will be promulgated within the next few days and I urge that all those sentenced by the courts prior to 11 July 1936 be now amnestied.

In this letter, together with my address to the leaders of the Front, I have taken the liberty, my dear Chancellor, of summarising the principles and immediate purposes of my activity. I repeat, as at the beginning of this letter, my suggestion for further personal discussions and, with the expression of my highest regard,

I remain,

Yours sincerely . . .'[98] [signed Seyss-Inquart]

This exchange of letters with Seyss-Inquart highlights the political and psychological obstacles which made it difficult for us to work together or establish relations of confidence; for a time Seyss-Inquart thought of resigning. Admittedly he had nothing to do with the *putschists* and was not yet a radical, fully committed Hitler disciple; basically, however, his idea of the all-German concept was incompatible with Austrian independence. As his letter shows, he visualised a sort of satellite relationship, with Austria being carried along in Germany's wake for good or ill. In fact Austria's acknowledgement that she was 'a German state' meant no more and no less than that she would not range herself *against* Germany – by participating in an anti-German alliance, for instance, or 'encirclement plans' and the like. This by no means implied, however, that we must join in or even approve all Germany's adventures. This difference of interpretation was glaringly illustrated when Hitler tried to pillory Austria for remaining in the League of Nations, saying that this was an anti-German 'extravagance' and a breach of the agreement. Austria's attachment to the principles of the League was as firm as her rejection of German racial theory, though this did not prevent her emphasising that the vast majority of her population was German.

In autumn 1937 Guido Schmidt, State Secretary for External Affairs, represented me at the League meeting in Geneva. On my instructions he contacted both the French and British representatives (Italy and Germany were no longer members of the League by this time) to explain to them personally how extremely difficult Austria's position had become. On his return to Vienna

Schmidt told me of a private meeting he had had with Sir Robert Vansittart, then Permanent Under-Secretary of the Foreign Office, who became Chief Diplomatic Adviser to His Majesty's Government at the beginning of 1938. Schmidt had explained the Austrian position and particularly the importance of Italian support under existing treaties in view of the increasingly serious conflict with Germany; it was vital for Austria, he had said, that the Italo-British disagreement be settled as soon as possible and the Stresa front re-established; Austria would continue to exist only if the Western Powers showed renewed interest in Central Europe and concentrated less on Africa (Ethiopia).

In this conversation with Vansittart Schmidt had been following his instructions closely. Shortly afterwards Francesco Salata, the Italian Minister in Vienna, told me in confidence that, according to reliable information available in Rome, while in Geneva Schmidt had made insulting remarks to Vansittart about Italian policy in general and Mussolini in particular; the Italian government therefore recommended Schmidt's dismissal from the Foreign Ministry. I replied that there must be some misunderstanding and there was no valid reason for Schmidt's dismissal. Salata promised to pass on my views to Rome. Thereupon Philippo Anfuso, the Italian Foreign Ministry's Head of Protocol, appeared in Vienna and, on behalf of his government, showed me a photostat copy of a report by Vansittart to Anthony Eden, then Secretary of State for Foreign Affairs. This reported in detail on the conversation with Schmidt in Geneva and referred, among other things, to 'Mussolini's totally incomprehensible adventurist policy'. On instructions from Ciano Anfuso reiterated the demand for Schmidt's dismissal. When I questioned the authenticity of the report, Anfuso replied that there was no doubt of the genuineness of the document which had been obtained by a most reliable agent. On behalf of his government, however, he swore me to secrecy *vis-à-vis* both Schmidt and London. I replied that, in spite of what he had told me, I adhered to my previous opinion; I emphasised that there must be some misunderstanding which would be difficult to clear up in view of the ban of secrecy. It was agreed that the case would be further investigated.

When I next met Ciano in Budapest in January 1938 the matter was discussed again, with Schmidt present. Ciano maintained that there was no question of the reliability of his agents in London and that very considerable sums of money were involved, for which reason he could not agree to further enquiries in London. There the matter rested, both Schmidt and I assuring him that there must have been some misunderstanding on the part of Vansittart.

The incident does at least show that, in view of the increasing danger of the situation, Austria was making every effort to re-establish the Stresa front; this, we thought, was the only solution to a situation which was becoming increasingly critical for Britain as well as for world peace, in view of the Third Reich's aggressive attitude.

In Vienna we did what we could to reduce our differences with Germany and work with her as far as possible; these efforts had produced no concrete result, however, when in January 1938 the discovery by the police of the so-called Tavs Plan created a new situation. Preparations for violent upheaval were clearly afoot; Seyss-Inquart was holding himself aloof.

On 22 January 1938 Dr Leopold Tavs had given an interview to Roman Fajans, the political correspondent of the Slovak newspaper *Slovanský hlas*; in it he had said: 'We shall observe the agreement of 11 July 1936; so long as the Anschluss would provoke armed conflict in Europe, there can be no further question of it. Under no circumstances do we want an explosion. We are leaving these matters to be settled by time.'

Asked whether there was direct contact and an intimate connection between the Austrian and German Nazis, Tavs replied: 'The relationship between us and Hitler's Chancellery is one of complete trust and one-hundred-per-cent obedience. This being so, orders and formal instructions are unnecessary; friendly advice and hints suffice. We all understand each other very well, even without orders.' This passage, which appeared in the interview as published, was denied by Tavs.

During the same month (January 1938) the so-called Action Programme 1938 was seized by the Vienna police among Dr Tavs' papers in his house. It read as follows:

'Schuschnigg's interview in the *Daily Mail* brings into the open facts which have long been clear to any thinking person. Schuschnigg does not want to fulfil the agreement of 11 July 1936; fulfilment of the agreement must therefore be enforced without or in opposition to Schuschnigg.

European situation:

Italy is firmly bent on friendship with Germany. The Little Entente is isolated. France is in the midst of a severe internal crisis and is incapable of attacking outside her frontiers. Russia is in chaos. England is tied down in the Far East, the Middle East, India and the Mediterranean. She did not even march when the Rhineland was reoccupied although the Rhine is England's frontier. Circumstances being different, she is even less likely to march to the Danube. The German Reich therefore has freedom of action. The Party must hold itself ready for the plebiscite.

1. In an article in *Deutsche Diplomatische Korrespondenz* the German Reich describes the NSDAP-Hitler-Movement in Austria and its leader Captain Josef Leopold as a conservative and constructive factor for law and order in Central European policy, which the German people neither can nor will dispense with.

2. By a *démarche* including a time limit the German Reich will demand complete fulfilment by the Austrian government of the agreement of 11 July 1936 in so far as that government is able and willing to do so. Should there be a demand for the resignation of the government and the appointment of a Chancellor able and willing to fulfil bilateral agreements, diplomatic discussions on the subject will be initiated with the other partner in the Axis.

3. Should the Federal government fail to satisfy the demand of the other party to the agreement of 11 July 1936, four air force formations and all available Panzer divisions will be moved into the area Ulm-Passau-Salzburg-Munich-Pfronten-Buchloe. Italy and Jugoslavia will be urged to take similar measures.

4. After the necessary preparation a final *démarche* will be made with a four-week time limit.

5. Transitional governments and the Federal Chancellor, whoever he may be, must undertake to give full freedom to the NSDAP-Hitler-Movement in Austria and adopt a liberal attitude in the plebiscite [*sic*], the questions in which shall be freely agreed with the other party to the 11 July 1936 agreement; to facilitate agreement the list of Ministers will be drawn up in conjunction with the leader of

the National-Socialist opposition.

6. The national opposition candidates for the transitional cabinet
are . . .

The general rule to be followed by provincial governors is that for
the duration of the provisional cabinet, in other words until a plebiscite has taken place, every agency will be composed half of National-
Socialists and half of other participants; the chairman must be a
National-Socialist.

7. No blame will attach to any member of the Fatherland Front
or to any official for past fulfilment of his duty as a member or for
exercising his legal function, nor will he suffer any disadvantages.
To signify the personal position of Captain Josef Leopold, the Reich
Chancellor will be asked to decree that, while resident on Reich
territory, he will occupy the position and have the official preroga-
tives of a *Reichsleiter* directly subordinate to the Führer; he will deal
direct with the Minister responsible for internal Austrian questions,
Minister-President Hermann Göring.'[99]

In addition to this 'action programme' other drafts were found
showing that an armed insurrection in the country was planned
to provoke intervention by Germany to re-establish order. Krüger,
the *Essener National-Zeitung* correspondent, reported that the
German Embassy was most uneasy over Tavs' arrest; a proper
mess had been uncovered in the Teinfaltstrasse (Nazi Party headquarters); he wondered whether the government would finally
move in and clean it up; the Embassy would be most relieved if
it did. Krüger's informant had the impression that the Embassy
had every reason to assume that most incriminating material had
been found in the Teinfaltstrasse and that the gentlemen in the
Embassy knew all about it.[100]

The Austrian government drew the conclusion that, if the
previous policy was to be pursued, further contact with Germany
was essential in order to eliminate those influences which were
obviously bent on doing away with the 11 July 1936 agreement.
It would also be necessary to insist on the removal from Austria
of the illegal Nazi leaders, Leopold and Tavs.

So the ground was prepared for the subsequent discussions with
von Papen, the German Ambassador, at the conclusion of which
came the invitation to Berchtesgaden.

5

PARTING OF THE WAYS

The Berchtesgaden encounter was our final effort to bring a continuously deteriorating situation under control.

By the summer of 1937, if not earlier, resumption of extremist
propaganda and terrorism by the Nazis had aggravated the situation in Austria, and it was not helped by the external situation;
all the Great Powers were preoccupied over the Abyssinian question and the Spanish Civil War, the Third Reich thereby being
presented with an opportunity for unilateral action.

Our first attempt to reduce tension and gain time by personal
contact and discussion culminated in November 1937 in a hunting
invitation to Göring; rightly or wrongly it was thought that he
was the most open to reason and the least insistent on radical
solutions and would therefore not be averse to talking.

My own personal contacts with leaders of the Third Reich
could be counted on the fingers of one hand. Apart from my
brief meeting in Munich with Rudolf Hess and Heinrich Himmler
in October 1933 (see Chapter 3), I knew Konstantin von Neurath,
the Foreign Minister, from his official visit in February 1937; I
had, of course, had considerable official business with Ambassador von Papen but my social contacts with him had been restricted to the essential civilities; I had met Göring once, at the funeral
of Gömbös, the Hungarian Minister-President.

There were differing views about Göring. One knew, of course,
from the accounts of various diplomats of his predilection for
dressing up and wearing jewellery; Guido Schmidt had visited
Karinhall in 1937 and returned with the story of a young lion
lying under the table.[1] More ominous was the fact that in Göring's

hunting lodge on the Schorfheide Schmidt had seen a map of Germany on which the Austro-German frontier did not appear. Equally ominous was an incident which took place during a visit by certain Austrian industrialists to Berlin in the autumn of 1937, when Göring had told them bluntly that Austria must join the Reich soon or the Germans would march in. Diplomatic protests were invariably answered by lies, evasions and excuses. In short, it was difficult to make sense of Göring.

When von Neurath paid his official visit to Vienna in 1937 I protested to him energetically about the totally inadmissible statements and threats issuing from responsible German government and Party authorities, Göring in particular. His answer was that no one took Göring or the Party people seriously; only criminals played with that sort of fire; there was no question of armed action against Austria and we must not be intimidated by Göring's silly chatter.

In casual conversation Frau von Papen, the wife of the German Ambassador, was equally, if not more, critical of the Reich's Party dignitaries. As a rule it is neither customary nor desirable to refer to impromptu remarks by the wife of an Ambassador. It was generally known in Vienna, however, that Frau von Papen, who was otherwise very reserved and highly respected even by opponents of her husband's policy, was outspoken about the Third Reich, particularly the anti-church movement. She did not mince her words about the press campaign of vilification nor about Gestapo methods; no doubt her personal memories of 30 June 1934 had something to do with it; small wonder that she had not a good word to say, particularly about Göring and Goebbels, and that she was anything but optimistic about developments in Germany.

However incalculable he might be, however, Göring had at least kept his *Luftwaffe* free from corrupting Party influences. It was also well known that he was at loggerheads with the SS, Himmler and Goebbels; moreover he had summarily rejected the revolutionary tendencies of the Austrian National-Socialists – 'If they don't toe the line, I'll have their heads off'.

In Vienna, therefore, we drew the conclusion (wrongly as it

turned out) that Göring and the *Wehrmacht* would not be persuaded into some violent adventure against Austria. In the highly
inflammable situation of autumn 1937, therefore, I thought that
an attempt to discuss personally with Göring offered the best
prospects.

The invitation was for a hunting expedition in the Tyrol to be
followed by a meeting in Innsbruck; the initial reception was
friendly. Personally I did not go hunting nor did I like political
hunting parties; to Göring, however, they formed an important
adjunct to his political and economic activities, as had been proved
in Hungary, Jugoslavia and Poland. No sooner, however, had his
tentative acceptance of the invitation become known and news of
it had filtered into the press than the Austrian Nazi activists
started an opposition campaign; they were, after all, averse to any
conciliatory move and wanted the opposite of *détente*. Shortly
thereafter came a refusal from Göring; it was couched in friendly
terms and gave as the reason that the time was not yet ripe for
such contacts; a meeting would be purposeless, he said, unless
there could emerge from it some tangible results leading to a final
solution of the outstanding problems in relationships between
Austria and the German Reich; one tangible result, for instance,
would be a customs and currency union. . . . In no circumstances
could this even be considered.[2]

So the attempt to clear up the situation by means of personal
contact failed. It will be remembered that in late 1933, during the
first period of conflict with Austrian National-Socialism, Dollfuss
had also considered the possibility of pacification by means of
personal contact with Hitler.[3]

As before, Austria's main interest lay in reaffirmation and confirmation of the basic principles contained in the July 1936
agreement. In so far as words meant anything, they were clear.
In the event, however, as with many international political
agreements (the Yalta agreement was a later example), the two
parties had placed a totally different interpretation on the text.
Yet in this case both parties spoke German; there were therefore
none of the usual difficulties of accurate translation or other problems of a semantic nature. The text of the agreement explicitly

referred to non-interference and the absence of any intention on the part of the German Reich to impose the Anschluss, basing itself on an official declaration by Hitler of May 1935. The Austrian concession had been a declaration that Austrian foreign policy would be conducted in conformity with the 'peaceful aims' of German foreign policy; the reason for our emphasis on the peaceful aspect was obvious. We could not, of course, expect that a mere agreement would change Hitler's determination to have the Anschluss. In the last analysis, like everything else which both Vienna and Berlin said and did at this period, this was a struggle for time – in view of the rapidly changing international situation. What was not in the agreement and could not be, was the tacit German assumption that the Anschluss must come 'by hook or by crook', even without further action on Germany's part; in Austria's view the Anschluss was out of the question whether by 'hook' or by 'crook'.

Externally Germany was not so sure of herself in 1936 as in 1938; she had not yet completely emerged from her isolation. For Hitler, therefore, postponement of a solution to the Austrian question was a necessary tactical move; he probably gave it a two-year time limit even then. For Austria, however, it had been even more important to gain time since it had looked as if there might be an Italo-British *détente* over both Abyssinia and Spain and this could have led to the formation of a genuine Stresa front, without which there was no binding agreement upon the Powers to maintain the *status quo* in Europe.[4]

On the Austrian side we could and did justifiably complain that Germany had never taken her non-interference obligation seriously. The illegal Nazis were still directed, encouraged and financed from the Reich; the Austrian Legion was still in existence in Germany and the German press had taken little notice of the agreement on a press truce.

From the other side the German government and the Nazi Party complained that Austria was being dilatory in fulfilling the agreement because the promised inclusion of persons from the national opposition in positions of political responsibility had been implemented either not at all or inadequately. The agreement, however, had explicitly laid down that these people must enjoy the confidence of the Federal Chancellor and were to be nominated by him. In any case Glaise-Horstenau, an undisputed 'national' though not a National-Socialist, had been a member of the cabinet ever since the July agreement; as part of the government reshuffle of 3 November 1936 Neustädter-Stürmer had been appointed Minister of Security (he remained so until 20 March 1937) and, although again not a National-Socialist, by background he was a *Heimwehr* man and his subsequent political career shows that he was definitely among the 'nationals'.[5]

Before the July 1936 agreement the strongest argument, apart from the economic, in favour of an attempt to settle matters by treaty was the fact that all agreements with the Austrian Nazis aimed at a cessation of terrorism had remained purposeless and fruitless unless approved by the German leaders. In the increased tension of 1937-8 exactly the same reasoning led to a renewed attempt at direct contact with the German authorities as the sole method of possibly achieving some *détente*.

In a conversation in December 1937 von Papen threw out a vague suggestion about a possible personal discussion between Hitler and myself. He had already expressed equally vague ideas on other occasions, for instance during the Austrian state visit to Paris in February 1935 when he had remarked that a visit to Berlin too would not be out of place. This first feeler in December 1937, however, produced nothing, since Austrian ideas had no hope of acceptance in Berlin; they included dissolution of the illegal Nazi Party and fulfilment of all those obligations which, in the Austrian view, were still outstanding from the July 1936 agreement. Meanwhile in January 1938 the so-called Tavs Plan, already referred to, became known in Austria.

Another plan also existed, unknown to the Austrian government, the so-called Keppler Plan. Instead of the Tavs Plan's revolutionary methods this visualised a 'peaceful development' by means of diplomatic blackmail, in other words ultimata would be presented which would force the Austrian government to make concessions turning Austria into a second Danzig with all the inevitable consequences.

On 7 and 26 January von Papen once more reverted to the possibility of a personal meeting and discussion with Hitler; on 7 February he transmitted the formal verbal invitation. This, we thought, must be accepted subject to certain conditions, since it seemed the only remaining method of reaching a peaceful solution to the increasingly serious conflict. The Austrian conditions were: first, that the invitation must be seen to come from the German side; second, that the 11 July 1936 agreement should again be confirmed; third, that in accordance with diplomatic usage an agenda should be agreed beforehand; fourth, that the form of the customary press communiqué should be agreed beforehand; finally, that strict secrecy be guaranteed. On these conditions the invitation to Berchtesgaden was accepted, but before the final decision had been made there came a remarkable interlude.

On 4 February 1938 von Papen was suddenly relieved of his post as Ambassador to Vienna, no reason being given. Rumour had it that Berlin had decided to replace him by an out-and-out Party man; *Gauleiter* Bürckel's name was mentioned. The manner of Papen's sudden recall had apparently been very discourteous but before the background had even become known in Vienna, Papen reappeared from Berchtesgaden whither he had gone to enquire. His dismissal had apparently been cancelled on the understanding that our Berchtesgaden meeting took place. He explained that Hitler had assured him personally that any discussion would be confined to the difficulties of both sides in carrying out the agreement of 1936; he had been explicitly instructed to say that Hitler's interest lay in the renewal, reinforcement and perpetuation of the July 1936 agreement and that *no new demands would be made*; it was agreed that the final communiqué should expressly refer to the continuance of the 1936 agreement. Finally the Ambassador added that he had been commissioned by Hitler to say that, *whatever the course of the negotiations, in no case would they alter Austro-German relations to the disadvantage of Austria nor lead to any aggravation of the Austrian situation.* At the worst, von Papen said, all that could happen was that no progress would be made and everything would remain as it was. He added as his personal opinion that this was a particularly favourable moment for the removal of all difficulties and the achievement of a genuine settlement: Hitler was in a difficult position at home; the changes of senior personnel in the *Wehrmacht* had created serious problems; Hitler needed a period of calm abroad and would probably never again be ready to make concessions such as he would now think useful and necessary. The date agreed for the meeting was 12 February; an Austrian suggestion for a fortnight's postponement was turned down on the grounds that Hitler was due to make a speech to the Reichstag on the state of the nation later in the month.[6]

So the die was cast. The invitation to Berchtesgaden for 12 February was accepted because we felt that we could not risk being reproached by international, and particularly British, opinion for having brushed aside a conciliatory gesture by Germany.

The fact that we took such precautions to avoid any public announcement about the meeting, in order to prevent any premature international shock reaction, shows how different the climate of the day was from that now regarded as customary and normal. Only the diplomatic representatives of friendly Great Powers and of the Holy See were informed.

To evaluate the Berchtesgaden discussion and situate it correctly in the context of events which were to lead to the Anschluss four weeks later, four important aspects must be considered:

1. Hitler's motives and aims together with the role (of secondary importance) of his representative in Vienna, Ambassador von Papen
2. The Austrian motive in going to Berchtesgaden and the equally secondary role played by Seyss-Inquart
3. The course and outcome of the discussion
4. The prospects of fulfilment and the risks of non-acceptance of the Berchtesgaden protocol together with the ostensible publicity ban.

Until well into January 1938 Hitler had been stressing his peaceful intentions in conversations with official foreign visitors. In London in particular the view was prevalent that there would be no *fait accompli* or act of force in Europe. Nevertheless, after the visit to Berlin by Stoyadinovich, the Jugoslav Minister-President, early in 1938 there were certain warning signs indicating that Hitler might be planning imminent action against Austria.[7] In the light of our information in Vienna we had to assume that, whatever happened, Jugoslavia would side with Germany. As early as June 1937 Stoyadinovich had spoken of the threat of an Anschluss, adding, however, that 'in view of the consequent dangers to peace, he would hope to postpone this moment as long as possible'.[8]

Hitler's story, together with current talk about Austria in Berlin, revolved round the well-worn theme, welcomed in Belgrade and Bucharest and at least accepted in London, that any attempt at a Habsburg restoration in Austria would lead to immediate military invasion and a German occupation of Vienna within twenty-four hours.[9] As early as 30 January 1935 von Papen had reported to Hitler:

> 'Finally I would mention that Sir Walford Selby, my British colleague, yesterday visited M. Nastasiyevich [Jugoslav Minister in Vienna]; in the course of a discussion about the funeral of King George which took place today, Selby said that the British government was determined under no circumstances to countenance a restoration of the Habsburgs.'[10]

The restoration question had been artificially blown up by Berlin for years. It obviously served to keep the Little Entente, primarily Jugoslavia and Rumania, in line with Germany and cast suspicion on Austria as the troublemaker in the eyes of Paris and London. Hence the remark, half joking and half serious, by Louis Barthou, the French Foreign Minister, in Geneva in September 1934: '*Ne restaurez pas les Habsbourgs*.'[11] The question of our alleged intention to restore the Habsburgs runs like a scarlet thread through German anti-Austrian propaganda and through German diplomatic reports right up to 1938. That it was entirely untrue and that the subject was at no time even under discussion must have been perfectly well known in Berlin. Yet even the code word for the military invasion of Austria was 'Operation Otto'.

When Hitler, following Papen's suggestion on 5 February,

issued his invitation for a meeting in the next few days,[12] he had as yet no defined idea how his plans for Austria were to be carried out. He was simply determined that the Austrian question should be solved in the near future according to his standard 'by hook or by crook' formula. Hitler was, of course, a man who worked on intuitive decisions; how and when he would act were seldom decided beforehand; matters were left to develop with his apparatus of power guiding events in the direction he wished. When the nation and its interests were at stake (and with these he identified himself) legal or other scruples were of no account.

Hitler's views on Austria were known. He was in no doubt that Germany had a right to Austria and that Austrians wanted the Anschluss; he found confirmation of this belief in the continuous pressure from Austrian Nazi *émigrés* and from many of his extremist supporters in Austria including businessmen like Meindl, ex-managing director of the Steyr Works, ex-officers like General Alfred Krauss, intellectuals like Professor Gleispach and others. Although Nazi action in Austria frequently upset his foreign policy plans and was ill-timed, he invariably described any Austrian government measures against Nazi violations of the law as discrimination and persecution of Germans; the ban on the use of 'Heil Hitler', for instance, he considered incompatible with the honour of the German people and the dignity of a Great Power.

In Hitler's eyes, however, the military requirement to eliminate Austria and Czechoslovakia was far more important than these racio-political questions. He had to 'remove any threat from that flank, should we have to move westwards. . . . From the politico-military point of view the incorporation of these two states into Germany would constitute a considerable relief since frontiers would be better and shorter. . . . It would carry with it an increase of food resources sufficient to feed five to six million people, always provided that some two million were deported from Czechoslovakia and one million from Austria.' In addition it would enable some twelve additional divisions to be formed, reckoning one division per million inhabitants.[13] Hitler expected war in the Mediterranean and this would tie the hands of France and

England; it might even happen as early as summer 1938; he was determined to exploit this situation, he said, to settle the Czech and Austrian questions. 'The German problem can only be solved by force and this can never be without risk. . . . It was his unalterable decision to solve the German *lebensraum* problem by 1943 to 1945 at the latest. . . . After this period a change unfavourable to Germany was to be anticipated.'[14]

The above are extracts from what have come to be known as the Hossbach Minutes recording a discussion in the Reich Chancellery on 10 November 1937. There were present, among others, von Neurath, the Foreign Minister, and Generals Blomberg and Fritsch, all of whom raised serious objections to Hitler's views; but he took no notice.

In January 1938 the well-known affair of his marriage forced Field Marshal Blomberg to resign as *Wehrmacht* Minister. At the same time Heydrich and the Gestapo began their campaign against Colonel-General von Fritsch, the Commander-in-Chief of the Army, accusing him of homosexual practices on the basis of forged documents. The case against von Fritsch dragged on into the spring and ended with an acquittal. Meanwhile, however, both Blomberg and Fritsch had drawn the consequences and on 4 February 1938 far-reaching personnel changes took place in the higher posts of the *Wehrmacht* and the Reich government; Hitler assumed supreme command of the entire *Wehrmacht* and appointed General Wilhelm Keitel Chief of OKW [*Oberkommando der Wehrmacht* – High Command of the Armed Forces]. These changes and their accompaniments, particularly the attempted slander of Fritsch and the well-known critical attitude of Colonel-General Ludwig Beck, the Chief of the General Staff, led to an internal crisis liable to cause Hitler and his National-Socialist Party serious difficulties. Some spectacular foreign policy success was therefore all the more attractive in order to divert attention from the internal problems. Von Papen's suggestion of 5 February, which seemed to offer a solution to the Austrian question, therefore came at a good moment.

Admittedly the conditions were renewed recognition of Austrian sovereignty and a renewed promise of non-interference in her internal affairs. As the case of Poland was later to show, however – and as his domestic promises after the seizure of power had already shown – Hitler regarded himself as bound by agreements only so long as they were to his advantage. In Austria's case his primary object was non-violent seizure of power after the pattern of 30 January 1933; for external reasons the use of force was only to be considered in the most extreme emergency. He therefore set out to extract such wide concessions from Austria that she would in practice become a satellite state, to which he was willing initially to allow the external trappings of sovereignty; naturally at the same time he wished to see National-Socialism rehabilitated in Austria, though he was entirely indifferent to the personalities involved. Hitler was determined that Austria should become a second Danzig; subsequent developments and the details of the full Anschluss would then emerge automatically.

Turning now to von Papen: having accepted the post of diplomatic representative of the Third Reich in Vienna after the murder of Dollfuss in July 1934, he was necessarily bound by Hitler's directives. He was certainly no dyed-in-the-wool Party man nor a supporter of revolution and he attempted to restrain the renewal of terrorism which he thought would postpone achievement of his ultimate objective. And this, for him as for the Wilhelmstrasse and Hitler, was the Anschluss or, in official terminology, 'the ultimate solution of the Austrian question'. All his activity was therefore directed towards prompting this solution by evolutionary methods. Basically no senior German diplomat would have done otherwise at this time. The question remains, however, how far the German diplomatic representatives in Vienna confined themselves to the normal duties of their office which, in accordance with international law, excluded interference in the internal affairs of their host country, party politics in particular. On this an objective judgement can be made in the light of the Embassy's pre-1938 reports, now available.[15]

Austrian acceptance of the invitation to Berchtesgaden was based on the assumption that, at this point in time, renewal of the July 1936 agreement was in the German interest too. Even a comparatively short breathing space (in Hungary people were thinking of six months)[16] would get us through the danger period. We had, of course, little hope of military support; according to reports available in Vienna, however, we could count on a determined diplomatic *démarche* by the Great Powers, particularly when England and Italy had settled their differences – and Mussolini had told us that Grandi, the Italian Ambassador in London, was conducting negotiations which had every prospect of success within a fortnight. Settlement of Italo-British difficulties might radically change the external situation, particularly since it was known that France would undertake no obligations without British backing. From the Austrian point of view, therefore, as in July 1936, everything turned on the possibility of bridging the gap and gaining some respite, at least for the immediately succeeding weeks and months.

In Vienna we knew about the Tavs Plan.[17] This, prepared by the Austrian Nazi activists supported by German Party agencies, visualised revolutionary developments – provocation of incidents leading to large-scale intervention by the Austrian authorities and probably the creation of new national martyrs. In this way the German government would have been given some semi-legal reason for military intervention under pretext of protecting German interests threatened in Austria; from there everything would have gone according to the prearranged plan. We were determined to prevent such a development. We realised that this time matters would not stop short at an attempted advance across the frontier by the Austrian Legion and that the overall external position was considerably more unfavourable to Austria than it had been four years earlier.

It was also clear that a flood of protests about Austrian shortcomings in fulfilling the July 1936 agreement were to be expected from the German side. Austria had in fact done all in her power to fulfil both the letter and spirit of the agreement. It was true that we had not been able to achieve the measure of domestic pacification visualised, but the reason was that, as so often happens, different interpretations had been placed on the provisions of the agreement and the deciding factor was not what the agreement said but what it did not say. On these unspoken differences there was still a yawning gap between Austrian and National-Socialist ideas. The Austrians had concluded the agreement in order to guarantee Austrian sovereignty permanently or at least long term; the Germans and the Nazis had regarded it from the outset as a mere short-term transitional solution; they had never abandoned their purpose to impose the Anschluss at the first available opportunity and using every possible method.

People are quite right to point out that we ought not to have allowed ourselves to be deceived over this fundamental German attitude. We were not deceived; we did, however, assume that however much the other side may have wanted to achieve their aim and been prepared to use any method to do so, it was just not possible in the foreseeable future. In practice it proved that the shelving of the Tavs Plan and the expulsion from Austria of its protagonists, Tavs and Leopold, achieved nothing, although at the time it seemed that this could be counted as a tangible victory.

The Keppler Plan, which replaced it, visualised a gradual escalation of political demands culminating in an avalanche which would quickly sweep away all the tiresome clutter of treaty commitments and obligations in order to create an entirely new situation and force Austria into the status of a satellite. As we shall see, only three weeks after the conclusion of the Berchtesgaden agreement Keppler personally presented an enlarged programme of requirements which had to be bluntly and totally rejected.

To our complete surprise and in defiance of all agreements we were first confronted with the Keppler programme on our arrival in Berchtesgaden; it was in effect a copybook pattern of indirect aggression, of which history provides many examples both earlier and later. Its purpose was to impose the Anschluss either by subterfuge or openly, events since 1933 having shown that other methods were ineffective; the decision had been made to shelve the idea of military intervention provoked by some stage-managed revolt on the lines of the Tavs Plan; among Austrian Nazis views on these tactics were very divided, particularly between the Seyss-Inquart group and the illegal SS. Rivalry between the SS and SA undoubtedly played a considerable role in Austria as well as Germany.

Wilhelm Keppler was proprietor of a small industrial concern in west Germany. Even before the seizure of power he had been one of Hitler's immediate entourage as economic adviser; in 1933 he had entered the Reich Chancellery as commissioner for the Four Year Plan directly subordinate to Hitler, and was later taken on by Göring in the same capacity; in June 1937 he was given special responsibility for Austria and from then on maintained close contact with the Austrian Nazis. He was opposed to revolutionary methods and their protagonists; his permanent contact was Dr Seyss-Inquart.

Von Papen – not without reason – felt that the intrusion of this 'irresponsible emissary' from Party circles was a hindrance to him in his job as Ambassador.[18] In fact Keppler, who was made State Secretary in the Reich Ministry of the Interior and given senior SS rank in 1938, did his best to exert a moderating influence on the Austrian Nazis. On the other hand he had clearly been commissioned to accelerate the evolutionary process and find a solution of his own conforming to Hitler's time scale and political plans.

In view of Seyss-Inquart's responsibilities it was not only understandable but opportune that he should keep in close contact with Keppler. It was in the interests of both to block the various private channels of communication in use between the Austrian Nazis and Party or government authorities in the Reich, which were continuously leading to contretemps. It soon proved, however, that Keppler was not a *bona fide* intermediary between Austria and Hitler; he was there simply to engineer the Anschluss and pave the way for a 'peaceful' seizure of power by National-Socialism in Austria, just as he had done in Germany prior to 30 January 1933.

Initially Seyss-Inquart both acted and thought entirely along the lines of his task as agreed with me; in other words he accepted the principle of Austrian independence and the current Austrian constitution which ruled out any reactivation of the National-Socialist Party. The problem was to avert the danger of renewed terrorism, to exorcise the myth of a 'war of liberation' and to persuade the national opposition, now the majority of moderate

National-Socialists analogous to the old Pan-German Party and the *Landbund*, to collaborate in a common Austrian front. The intention was that this should lead to the organisation of ideological and political groups within the Fatherland Front, the concept of Austria being their common denominator; within the overall organisation there would therefore have been special desks: the Social Labour Community, to attract ex-Social Democrats, the 'tradition' desk to concentrate the former Christian Socials and Conservatives, and the *Volkspolitische* desk to attract the 'Nationals' under the leadership of Seyss-Inquart.

It soon became apparent, however, that Seyss-Inquart could succeed only if he had the backing of the German Nazi Party and government authorities, a fact which, in view of the actual ratio of power, could not be overlooked. Inevitably, therefore, he was brought into contact both with the German Ambassador and Keppler. An already obscure situation was further complicated by the facts that von Papen and Keppler were pulling in different directions and that a special Nazi Party representative was located in the Embassy in the person of von Stein, the Counsellor.

Unfortunately Seyss-Inquart had never told us of his confidential discussions with Keppler; worse still, he had never admitted that, without authorisation, he had been passing to Keppler the gist of all negotiations in the Ballhausplatz and the headquarters of the Fatherland Front. Von Papen says that the transmission by Seyss-Inquart to Keppler of the highly confidential *Punktationen* (see below) prepared for the Berchtesgaden discussion was a gross breach of confidence; he was quite right.[19]

Seyss-Inquart knew that he had made many enemies among the Party extremists and so he thought to cover himself via Keppler; he omitted, however, to tell his Austrian friends. Papen too was never informed either by Seyss-Inquart or Keppler. As a result two channels were functioning: on the one hand the normal diplomatic method of preparation by which, according to international usage, conditions for the meeting were agreed and which we in Austria regarded as authoritative; on the other hand, and independently thereof, the agreements made between Keppler and Seyss-Inquart, in other words the programme of demands

formulated by the German Nazi Party representative (the Keppler
Plan), of which we in Austria knew nothing. Had we known –
had we known even of the insistent demand for the nomination
of Seyss-Inquart as Minister of the Interior and Minister of
Security – the 12 February 1938 meeting in Berchtesgaden would
never have happened, for the Keppler programme was completely inconsistent with the agreed preliminary conditions for
the talks. In the witness box at the Schmidt trial Seyss-Inquart
maintained that he had not been briefed about Hitler's list of
demands; he had told some of his friends, certainly Dr Rainer, of
the substance of the agreements with Zernatto and Dr Schuschnigg on 'the activity of the national opposition and the invitation
to it to collaborate' (the *Punktationen* in other words); 'it was a
safe assumption that the others, or rather Dr Rainer, would inform the Reich'.[20]

There is therefore an apparent conflict between Seyss-Inquart's
evidence and the proven fact that he was in continuous contact
with Keppler and was therefore undoubtedly familiar with the
outline of the Keppler Plan. The explanation may be that he left
the detailed work on the list of demands to his staff, Dr Rainer and
Globocnik, and, although he knew of it, did not express an
opinion on it. It is quite possible, indeed probable, that he deliberately avoided tying his hands too soon in order to safeguard his
role as mediator, which in all good faith he was still hoping to
carry out.

The *Punktationen* represented the extreme limit of concession
to which the Austrian government was prepared to go in order
to meet the German complaint that it was not fulfilling its obligations under the 11 July 1936 agreement and, in view of the
strained political situation, to reach some firm settlement. The
Austrian Foreign Ministry had already told von Papen that 'if the
proposed discussion would lead to any positive result, thought
might be given, now that the Teinfaltstrasse office has been closed,
to an Austrian proposal for Germany to accept into exile the most
heavily compromised leaders, Tavs, Leopold and In der Maur.
This would be proof positive that the methods employed by these
gentlemen are not approved in the highest quarters of the Reich.'[21]

The *Punktationen* agreed with Seyss-Inquart were based on the July 1936 agreement and provided for the following:

(a) All communications of a political nature issuing from Germany and destined for Austria, apart from those passing through the official diplomatic channel, to be routed exclusively through Councillor of State Seyss-Inquart. All contacts between the Reich and illegal Austrian agencies to cease.

(b) From the outset particular difficulty has been encountered in fulfilling Point IXb[22] of the Gentlemen's Agreement of 11 July 1936; this was at the root of all our differences and we had never succeeded in reaching an agreed interpretation. Considering it objectively and in retrospect it must be admitted that the German criticism, based on the text of the agreement, was not totally unjustified nor the Austrian rebuttal totally justified. The Austrian case was based on a strict grammatical interpretation, in other words upon the letter of the text; Germany, on the other hand, based her case upon the logical implications of the text and these pointed to a general line of policy known in Austria and contrary to the Austrian viewpoint.

The measures which the Austrian government had taken or had genuinely tried to take between 11 July 1936 and the end of 1937 to fulfil Point IX were numerous, but they were found unsatisfactory and inadequate by Germany. Accordingly, in the *Punktationen* an attempt was made to find a solution tolerable to both sides. It was agreed between Zernatto and Seyss-Inquart that 'an adequate number of members of the Fatherland Front of "national" background would be appointed to the various government and local government bodies – Council of State [*Staatsrat*], Provincial Councils [*Landesrat*], District Councils [*Landtag*] and Parish Councils [*Gemeindetag*]. Suitable persons should later be worked into the senior positions.'

There was no mention of appointments to the Federal government. The entire agreement revolved largely round the person of Dr Seyss-Inquart; he was prepared to issue a public statement unequivocally renouncing all illegal activity and professing readiness for peaceful cooperation; as the sole spokesman for the Austrian Nazis in dealings with the Reich, he was also prepared to forbid all illegal contacts.

Had things worked out as planned, Seyss-Inquart might later have become a member of the Federal government; our idea was that he should be Minister of Justice. I once discussed the subject with him privately, immediately before 12 February. He did not seem averse to the idea and we had agreed that the appointment could take place only after a successful outcome to the talks.

As things now stood, Seyss-Inquart's cooperation could not be either meaningful or effective unless he was recognised as sole spokesman by the Austrian Nazis and their associates, the pro-Anschluss German Austrians, and also accepted as such by the Reich government and Nazi Party. This was by no means assured since he was opposed by the Austrian Nazi émigrés and by the influential group around Heydrich. Göring was not interested in personalities, Himmler had not yet come out into the open and, so far as one knew, Hitler had not yet said his last word. Everything therefore depended on our capacity to master the hitherto unsolved problem of incorporating the 'national opposition' into the Fatherland Front without shaking it to its very foundations and without giving the Nazi Party a handle to reactivate itself in camouflaged form.

The only possibility seemed to be the old idea of ideological compartmentation, National-Socialists, Socialists, Conservatives, Legitimists all being permitted to pursue their national, social and political ideas provided that they accepted the basic concept of an independent Austrian Fatherland. In the days of parliamentary democracy, after all, coalitions had found sufficient common ground to work together on this basis. Once the State and its flag could be acknowledged without question, the state of emergency could be ended, the way would be open for reforms and changes agreed in peaceful discussion, and the safety valves could be opened before internal pressure built up to danger point once more. The international situation had changed of course, but the political geography had not and so there was still tension in Central Europe. The immediate objective was to safeguard the existence of Austria for the present, the more important to avoid mortgaging her future. Here lay the danger of being mesmerised by the increased internal difficulties which would inevitably follow our attempt at political conciliation, and of an understandable failure to see the wood for our own beloved trees. From the Austrian point of view, however, it was clear that there were certain limits beyond which, for reasons of self-preservation, we could not go and which were not even open to discussion. The floodgates could not be opened, for instance, directly or indirectly to the Nazi Party programme and for this reason block entry of Nazi organisations, formations or associations into the Fatherland Front was invariably refused; as with people of all other shades of political opinion, we insisted on individual applications.

When the Austrian delegation left for Berchtesgaden we seemed to have reached agreement in broad terms. When I told Seyss-Inquart on 11 February about our forthcoming journey, he obviously knew of it already. There was nothing peculiar about that, however, in spite of our strict secrecy precautions; quite apart from the German diplomatic representatives in Vienna, the number of those in the know was unavoidably considerable.

What we did not know was that full details of the preliminary negotiations and of the *Punktationen* had been passed to Keppler. We also did not know that late in January Dr Rainer and Globocnik (subsequently *Gauleiter* of Vienna), both close associates of Seyss-Inquart, had gone to Berlin to present the demands of the Austrian Nazis; remarkably enough these included the appointment of Seyss-Inquart as Minister of the Interior with responsibility for Security.[23] But above all we did not know how large the list of demands was nor that they were all 'minimum demands'. The draft was found only after the war among Seyss-Inquart's papers.

Neither Seyss-Inquart nor Keppler ever referred to this document – and for good reason; it would have meant the end of the plan for a meeting with Hitler and the end of all attempts at conciliation. Under the heading 'Proposals' it set out with brutal clarity how the 'evolutionists' among Austrian Nazis proposed to solve the Austrian question. The end result would have been no different from that of the 'revolutionaries'; the only differences lay in the tactics and in the personalities who would have earned their national laurels for services in the 'liberation' of Austria. In detail the 'Proposals' demanded a general unconditional amnesty with full restitution for all injuries suffered, including repayment of fines and legal costs and cancellation of sentences; in addition it demanded, among other things, complete freedom for 'racio-political activity' as it existed prior to 1933, in other words; unrestricted Anschluss propaganda, resurrection of a high-pressure national and National-Socialist press, a plebiscite 'for or against pacification', a free plebiscite on the form of the State and on the Anschluss, a ban on the Jewish press and a series of measures amounting to anti-semitism both in principle and in practice. Point 16 of the 'Proposals' said: 'With the achievement of these conditions or shortly thereafter the assumption of full responsibility will be possible through entry into the government. The objectives must be . . . the Vice-Chancellorship, Minister of the Interior, one State Secretary in the Foreign Ministry (Dr Schmidt being appointed Foreign Minister), the Ministries of Justice, Trade, Social questions and Health'. In conclusion these proposals were described as minimum requirements for the achievement of pacification.

It is barely credible that Seyss-Inquart should not have known of these proposals. The fact remains that before our arrival in the Berghof the other side knew of the secret agreed *Punktationen*; Seyss-Inquart had also already received the much more far-reaching demands of the Austrian Nazis; he could therefore base his case on proposals which had come to him from Austrians. Guido Zernatto's account of a dinner we had together in the Grand Hotel in Vienna on 9 February is as follows:

'Dr Schuschnigg was . . . not looking forward to the proposed talks. He explained what he thought on the subject and expressed the opinion that probably no one would get what he wanted from these discussions. The inflexible opponents of any agreement with Germany would accuse him of betraying the Austrian programme in its entirety; national circles would be discontented with any concessions he made to them. I particularly remember the Chancellor saying that ecclesiastical circles would undoubtedly come out in opposition to any agreement.'[24]

So, on the evening of 11 February, we – that is to say, myself, Guido Schmidt, Lieutenant-Colonel Bartl and Hamberger, my detective – left for Berchtesgaden.

The setting for the meeting in the Berghof, part conventional and part highly unusual, is of little consequence; in any case changes of atmosphere were deliberately engineered. Everything was designed to lend weight to the 'hook or crook' principle.

As a surprise effect three Generals were present – Wilhelm Keitel, Chief of OKW, Walter von Reichenau, the Military District Commander in Munich and recently appointed Commander of the Group Headquarters Leipzig, and Hugo Sperrle, *Luftwaffe* Commander in Bavaria and ex-Commander of the Condor Legion in Spain. They were present as part of the bluff, as we now know from Jodl's diary and other accounts. Also present were Joachim von Ribbentrop, the Foreign Minister, who knew nothing about Austria, and Otto Dietrich, the Reich Press Chief, who knew little; von Papen was also there; he, of course, knew what it was all about but had not been informed of the details. Finally there was Dr Kajetan Mühlmann, the art historian and an Austrian Nazi of moderate leanings, he kept out of sight and we did not know that he was there but, as later emerged, he kept the other side informed, with the connivance of Seyss-Inquart and perhaps also that of Guido Zernatto. The latter might have considered him a suitable antidote to possible pressure from Christian extremists.

Above all, there was Adolf Hitler, the Führer and Reich Chancellor, swastika armband on his brown SA tunic, determined to solve the Austrian question on 12 February 1936 'by hook or by crook'.

What sort of a person was Hitler? I have been asked this question times out of number, particularly in the USA, but for someone who has seen Hitler only once in his life it is difficult to answer. Passing judgement on men who are out of the ordinary is always a problematical exercise, particularly when their scale of values can be judged by no normal standards. Stalin has sometimes been compared to Peter the Great. Hitler and Stalin had much in common so far as their political ideas were concerned, particularly in their complete identification of their views with the interests of the nation; they therefore felt themselves bound by none of the accepted legal or moral limitations. The superman has a heart and mind like anyone else, but when he begins to think he becomes inhuman, a machine, a computer. In addition, to any well-read conservative Austrian, Hitler's concept of history was the inevitable end product of extremist Pan-german education. In the liberal periods of the Empire this had been tolerated in the name of freedom of opinion and the basic constitutional rights, although in essence it was anti-humanist.

Undoubtedly Hitler was obsessed by his germanic mission; his obsession had developed into racial mania. Millions had been carried away by his faith and by his successes, which in February 1938 were already considerable; further millions were prepared to follow him as long as the sun shone. Against this the 'voice of conscience' was powerless, though it was still to be heard particularly from the churches and from beyond the frontiers. Internal resistance seemed little better than a forlorn hope; its voice was muffled - or stifled by blood and tears. People knew about Dachau and Oranienburg - new expressions with a very definite meaning to which the horrified world was apparently already becoming accustomed. No one liked to talk about them; they preferred to enthuse about 1936 and the Olympic Games in Berlin. . . .

Much of this was known to us when we went to Berchtesgaden; we were prepared for many things; there were other things, however, which we did not know and could not foresee. Neither the Austrians nor later the Czechs, Hungarians or Poles were in a position to convince the man who faced them of the risk of his 'hook or crook' solution. How was one to say to Hitler

that since ancient times there had never been a nationalist prophet
of force who had not shipwrecked on the iron laws of history,
however spectacular his successes? How, if one hoped for some
reasonable result, was one to say this on 12 February 1938 and in
German with an Austrian accent? It might perhaps have been said
in English. Yet after a visit to the Berghof in 1936, Lloyd George,
the British Liberal leader and ex-Prime Minister of the First
World War, had greeted his daughter Megan with 'Heil Hitler',
adding 'for he really is a great man'.[25] Insignificant though it was,
we were not to know of this incident. Speaking in the House of
Commons in July of that year and after energetically defending
the territorial integrity of Abyssinia, Lloyd George had declared
that 'whatever government was in power, the British people
would never go to war again for an Austrian quarrel'.[26] We were
soon to learn from Hitler that, in the very room where we were,
he had recently given a British diplomat his views on the Austrian
question – and no objection had been raised. 'You have nothing
to hope for from England,' Hitler said. We did not believe him.

We now know from the memoirs of Schmidt, Hitler's interpreter, that on 19 November 1937 Hitler had in fact had a long discussion with Lord Halifax (who became Secretary of State for
Foreign Affairs on 25 February 1938). The question of Austria
had been raised and Hitler had declared that the Austrian Anschluss was imperative and had been urgently desired by the Austrian
people ever since 1919. Nor could the Czechs be allowed any
longer to oppress the Sudeten Germans. . . . Halifax replied that
England was ready to consider any solution provided that it was
not based on force. 'That also applies to Austria.'[27]

Anthony Eden says in his memoirs that he was 'not eager' about
Halifax's proposed trip but 'saw no sufficient reason to oppose it'.
Primarily he wished to avoid any impression that the British
government was not interested in a meeting with Hitler and
Neville Chamberlain, the Prime Minister, had shown marked
interest. At the request of the Foreign Office the German Foreign
Ministry had made available the notes taken by the interpreter
during the Berghof meeting. These showed that Lord Halifax
had referred to 'possible alterations in the European order which

might be destined to come about with the passage of time. Among these questions were Danzig, Austria and Czechoslovakia. England was interested to see that any alterations should come through the course of peaceful evolution and that methods should be avoided which might cause far-reaching disturbances, which neither the Chancellor nor other countries desired. . . . Hitler had replied that a settlement with Austria and Czechoslovakia could be reached, given a reasonable attitude. He hoped that the recent agreement with Austria (11 July 1936) would lead to a removal of all difficulties. . . . Czechoslovakia . . . only needed to treat the Sudeten Germans well and they would be entirely happy.' Anthony Eden comments: 'We now know that a fortnight before this interview, Hitler had secretly announced to his Foreign Minister, War Minister and his Chiefs of Staff his plans for subjugating Austria and Czechoslovakia as a first step towards conquering more territory for Germany in Europe' (the Hossbach Minutes of 5 November 1937). Eden was not pleased with Halifax's report and 'wished that Halifax had warned Hitler more strongly against intervention in Central Europe. "Alterations through the course of peaceful evolution" meant one thing to Halifax and probably something quite different to Hitler. . . . As I had feared, Lord Halifax's visit was without positive results. . . . Hitler had offered no guarantee about his policy in Central Europe'.[28] Exactly this, however, was what British foreign policy was striving for as long as it was under Anthony Eden's direction; it was also what we wanted in Austria.

On 12 February 1938 Eden was still Foreign Minister in London, but he was succeeded by Lord Halifax on 25 February.

Such was the background to our talks in the Berghof.

We took the night train from Vienna to Salzburg and thence continued by car to Berchtesgaden, only some fifteen miles away. Ambassador von Papen joined us at the frontier and mentioned casually that the three Generals 'happened' to be in the Berghof. From Berchtesgaden we went up to the Berghof by half-track vehicle. The Berghof was exactly as one imagined it from numerous pictures; it was tastefully, not ostentatiously, arranged; there were many flowers; on the walls were heads by Lenbach and a particularly beautiful Madonna by Dürer – pictures one had already seen elsewhere.

The military chorus appeared only when we arrived, at lunch and when we left, apart from the dramatic five minutes in late afternoon when our refusal to accept Hitler's demands unconditionally caused him to break off the negotiations and ostentatiously summon General Keitel. Keitel later told the Nuremberg court that this was merely an insignificant intimidation manœuvre.

However this may be, it changed nothing – neither Hitler's determination to solve the Austrian problem nor the Austrian refusal voluntarily to renounce her existence as a state and accept satellite status for the time being. Emil Hacha, the Czechoslovak President, was to receive the same treatment in 1939 and Nikolaus Horthy, the Hungarian Regent, in 1944; even Neville Chamberlain did little better in Godesberg, though the civilities were somewhat better preserved. This was diplomacy by intimidation and brandishing power, aimed not to deceive but to blackmail. Hitler wanted to march and in every case he put his desire into practice sooner or later – in Austria's case 'later' was four weeks.

The general impression in the Berghof was unmistakable; every decision was Hitler's alone; neither diplomats nor military were allowed to argue; they did as they were told. We heard practically nothing from Hitler's entourage that day except 'That is for the Führer to decide' and 'Yes, my Führer'.

For the first part of the discussion Hitler and I were alone; for the second, in the afternoon, others were present. The struggle, for such it was, lasted some ten hours in all. The details, now well known and frequently described, are of little practical significance.[29] Hitler frequently spoke very loud, though he never bellowed; I spoke quietly, though not in a whisper. There were tense moments, particularly after some clash, but they passed as quickly as they had come. After two hours in the morning neither side had yielded an inch and neither had convinced the other; we had talked primarily basic principles and background, Hitler on the offensive all the time; it was certainly not what, in diplomatic language, is called a *tour d'horizon*.

Hitler opened with a general attack on the 'un-German history' of old Austria and on contemporary Austrian policy in particular. He referred to persecution of Germans, meaning the measures taken in Austria against National-Socialism and its practices. He condemned Austria for remaining a member of the League of Nations, saying that this showed an unfriendly attitude towards the German nation. Then came violent criticism of the Austrian frontier defences, although these had been started along all our frontiers, in other words facing all neighbouring states. He made a special point of the alleged British agreement with his plans for Austria (Lord Halifax's visit, though the name was not mentioned), of France's impotence and of the firm Italo-German friendship.

The encounter had begun at 11.0 a.m. and by 1.0 p.m. – lunch-time – none of Hitler's concrete demands had been mentioned, probably because at this point he did not yet know them himself. When I asked him: 'Herr *Reichskanzler*, what exactly are your wishes?' he replied: 'That we can discuss this afternoon.'[30]

This had been preceded by a curious invitation which 'out of deep personal conviction and as a political duty' I had politely but firmly declined: 'I am giving you the unique opportunity, Herr Schuschnigg, of having your name recorded on the roll of great Germans' (Göring, Hess, Frick and von Epp were cited as examples); 'that would be an honourable deed and everything could be settled. I am well aware that due regard must be paid to certain Austrian peculiarities.' Hitler's views, as already expressed, made it clear that what he really meant was satellite status for Austria and a camouflaged Anschluss.

Once more, therefore, it was clear that all previous arguments, whether from the Austrian or the German side, against such a solution had made not the smallest impression. In political speeches after the Anschluss Hitler repeatedly referred to the 'unique opportunity' he had given me.

Peculiar though the 'offer' was, it was followed by something even more extraordinary: 'I am well aware that your friend, the Jesuit Muckermann, one of the bitterest enemies of the German people, is in Vienna, plotting to assassinate me – and with your knowledge and your government's assistance.'[31] To this monstrous accusation, apparently made in all seriousness, the basis of which was a complete mystery to me, I could only reply: 'Austria does not use assassination as an instrument of policy.'

By 1.0 p.m. only one thing was clear – Hitler was determined to settle the Austrian question that very day. 'By hook or by crook' was the tenor of the discussion; 'how' was of secondary interest. If it could be done peacefully, so much the better; if not, he would order his troops to march. 'Do you want to turn Austria into a second Spain?' and then a veiled threat of air attack on Vienna: 'Don't forget that Munich is only one hour's flying time from Vienna.'

It was hardly surprising that, during the lunch which now followed, this threat was buzzing in my ears and that I found it difficult to adjust myself to the perfectly normal atmosphere of the lunchtable. Hitler had changed completely and never let fall a word to indicate the tension of the last few moments. He talked of the advantages of motorisation and of the autobahns, of the great building projects about to be started or nearing completion. In Hamburg, for instance, plans were in hand for the largest bridge in the world; skyscrapers would mushroom; sea travellers from the West would see that they could produce bigger and better buildings in Germany than in the United States. Then he turned to more personal questions: he had refused the Reich President's salary, for instance; it was a pittance compared to the obligations he had to meet; he could not accept all the houses and land offered him by public agencies and private owners because he could not afford to maintain them; he found it hard to refuse the love and affection shown him by the Germans; he needed no police escort – he had one only to check the enthusiasm of people who thronged round him, in the interests of their own safety. . . . Undoubtedly all this was said in complete seriousness. Hitler believed what he said, in particular that he *was* Germany; he also believed that he had a historic claim to Austria and that his mission before history was to make that claim good.

Of all that Hitler said during these ten hours nothing was more significant than a remark he let fall after the agreement had been drafted, in other words shortly before our departure: 'It would be completely irresponsible and unjustifiable before history if an instrument like the German *Wehrmacht* were not used.'

It has been said that Hitler's military threats on 12 February 1938 were sheer bluff. Knowing what we do today, however, it seems probable, indeed almost certain, that any rupture of negotiations would have triggered off military action by Germany – with all its unforeseeable and uncontrollable consequences for Austria. In the first place, Hitler was a man of sudden intuitive decisions and he was perfectly capable of issuing the order to march on 12 February, even though he had no intention of doing so on 10 February. Plans for 'Operation Otto' had been prepared long before. The presence of generals in the Obersalzberg, and especially these particular generals, was a good gambit but it might also have had its practical uses. In his famous diary General Jodl refers to the 'severe political and military pressure' to which the Austrians were subjected in the Berghof. Dr Kajetan Mühlmann stated in evidence that during the negotiations in Hitler's study on the afternoon of 12 February he had himself heard Ribbentrop report our stubborn refusal to appoint Seyss-Inquart Minister in charge of Security. To this Hitler had replied: 'Tell Schuschnigg that, if he does not accept this demand, I shall march this very moment.' Later, when we asked for three days to think matters over, he said: 'What does he want three days for? I really don't want to give them to him. . . . All right then. I don't like it; I would much rather have marched. Gentlemen, I will have one last try; let him have his three days.'[32]

The three days' grace after signature of the protocol was demanded for constitutional reasons and was finally conceded. The protocol followed the general lines of Keppler's draft and was presented for immediate signature late in the afternoon. It provided for the following:

1. A commitment to prior consultation on questions of foreign policy of common concern to both countries.
2. Recognition that National-Socialism was compatible with Austrian conditions, 'provided that National-Socialists

recognise and adhere to the Austrian Constitution in carrying out their ideas'. No measures to be taken, therefore, which would in effect outlaw the National-Socialist movement within the meaning of the above aims. Further expansion of the *'Volkspolitische* Offices'. This form of words was intended to facilitate block adherence of National-Socialist organisations to the Fatherland Front.

3. Appointment of Seyss-Inquart as Minister of the Interior with responsibility for security. Seyss-Inquart to have the right and duty to issue the measures required under Para 2.

4. A general amnesty for all persons punished by the courts or the police for National-Socialist activity. Persons whose further stay in Austria appeared detrimental to relations between the two countries to transfer residence to the Reich by agreement between the two governments. This meant that Leopold and Tavs, who were opposed to the policy of Seyss-Inquart and his friends, could transfer to the Reich. Germany did in fact accept them.

5. Revocation of measures taken in the fields of pensions, annuities, public welfare, and education, especially the withholding or reduction of benefits because of National-Socialist activities. Full restitution to be made.

6. Elimination of all economic discrimination against National-Socialists.

7. Execution of the press truce agreed upon by means of the replacement of Minister Ludwig and Federal Commissioner Colonel Adam.

8. Reciprocal military relations to be assured by the following measures:
   (a) Appointment of Minister Glaise-Horstenau as Minister of the Armed Forces.
   (b) A systematic exchange of officers (the figure was set at approximately 100).
   (c) Regular General Staff discussions.
   (d) Systematic cultivation of comradely and professional relations.

9. All discrimination against National-Socialists, especially as

affected acceptance into the army and completion of military service, to be stopped. Past discriminatory action to be cancelled.

10. Preparations to be made for the assimilation of the Austrian to the German economic system. For this purpose Dr Fischböck to be appointed Minister of Finance.

11. Recognition by the Reich government that Seyss-Inquart was solely responsible for the question of inclusion of National-Socialists under Para 2. The Reich government to take measures to prevent interference in the internal affairs of Austria by German Party agencies. In case of differences of opinion concerning the interpretation of Para 2, negotiations to be conducted exclusively through Seyss-Inquart.

Here then was Hitler's list of concrete demands. It was handed to us in the first instance by Ribbentrop who told us that it must be accepted or rejected *en bloc*. Even the most cursory glance showed that it bore no relation to the *Punktationen*, at least in so far as the vital Para 2 was concerned. Apart from this the *Punktationen* had made no mention of the appointment of Seyss-Inquart as Minister of the Interior with responsibility for security nor of the other personnel changes. Equally the list bore no relation to the suggestions made in the correspondence with Göring during the previous autumn, apart from a customs and currency union which at that time had been agreed to be impossible.

No mention was made of the conditions agreed beforehand through diplomatic channels – that no new demands would be made and that, whatever the outcome of the talks, Austria's position would be no worse than before. The Berchtesgaden meeting was the first case of departure from the normal diplomatic rules and customs. The era of sabre-rattling in its most extreme form was with us. Contrary to our original agreement even the communiqué issued at the conclusion of the meeting did not reaffirm the July agreement and consequently included no renewed recognition of Austrian independence. This came only in Hitler's Reichstag speech of 20 February – with the ominous addendum that the Reich was assuming the protection of the ten million Germans on its frontiers.

It is true that we did succeed in moderating the Keppler draft in certain important points and that in this von Papen acted as a helpful mediator. What is not true is that, from the Austrian point of view, this process produced any marked or decisive improvement in the document as a whole.[33]

The differences between the final protocol and the original list of demands were as follows:

1. The original time limit (18 February) applied only to the appointment of Seyss-Inquart and the vital internal provisions about admission of National-Socialists to the Fatherland Front, the amnesty, etc.

2. The provisions about coordination of foreign policy were redrafted. Instead of the obligation to consult, these provided for 'a diplomatic exchange of views' as a result of which Austria world 'on request give moral, diplomatic and press support . . . to the extent that circumstances permit'.

3. The passage about 'compatibility of National-Socialism with Austrian conditions' and 'recognition of National-Socialism by Austria' was dropped and replaced by a clause admitting individual National-Socialists to the Fatherland Front and other Austrian organisations on certain conditions. This accorded with existing Austrian practice in the interests of pacification.

4. *Émigrés* were excepted from the general amnesty.

5. The stipulation that Minister Ludwig and Federal Commissioner Colonel Adam be removed was dropped. Instead we agreed to appoint to the Press Service Dr Wilhelm Wolf, a civil servant of national and catholic background.

6. No change was made in the post of Minister of the Armed Forces. General Zehner, who had been severely criticised by the Reich, remained in office. Instead the replacement of Lieutenant General Jansa by General Beyer as Chief of the General Staff was proposed. Though Jansa was a most efficient officer whose loss would be felt, from our point of

view the change was comparatively easy to agree to, since he was in any case due to retire shortly for reasons of age. He had already been notified in January.

7. The number of exchange officers envisaged was reduced to fifty.

8. The appointment of Dr Fischböck to the cabinet was dropped and he was merely to be given 'a leading post' in the financial administration. An 'intensification of commerce' between the two economies was also agreed.[34]

This last requirement, however intrinsically desirable as an objective, created serious difficulties because of the fundamental differences between the two currency systems. For us to abandon the freely convertible hard-currency schilling and adapt ourselves to the German monetary and price system would have bound us to Germany in a common market; we should lose our connections with the rest of the world, however, and so our other markets. This was in fact a surreptitious demand for a customs and currency union, a favourite idea of Göring's and Keppler's. It would have been tantamount to surrender on Austria's part and would have carried with it the odium of a unilateral breach of international agreements.

So the day in the Berghof ended with the signature of the final protocol which now, according to the constitution, had to be presented to the Federal President for implementation. Our original agreement had stipulated that there would be an agreed final communiqué but all that the outside world was given was a short paragraph dictated by Hitler himself:

'The Federal Chancellor, Dr Schuschnigg, accompanied by the Austrian State Secretary for Foreign Affairs, Dr Guido Schmidt, and the German Ambassador, von Papen, paid a visit today to the Führer and Chancellor at the Obersalzberg, at the latter's invitation, in the presence of Foreign Minister von Ribbentrop. This unofficial meeting was the result of a mutual desire to talk over all questions pertaining to relations between the German Reich and Austria.'[35]

The result, of course, was increased uncertainty in Austria, reach-

ing panic proportions during the next few days. On 14 February
we drafted a communiqué in Vienna and it was handed to von
Papen for transmission to Berlin. It ran as follows:

'At the conference which took place between Federal Chancellor
Dr Schuschnigg and the German Chancellor on February 12 at the
Obersalzberg near Berchtesgaden, all questions concerning relations
between Austria and the German Reich were discussed in detail with
the object of finding ways to eliminate the difficulties which have
arisen in connection with the application of the Agreement of July
11, 1936. It was agreed that the principles of the Agreement and the
mutual desire for its full implementation are to be maintained. To
this end measures were agreed upon by both sides, which are to
guarantee the smooth execution of the Agreement and thus such
close and friendly relations between the two German States as befit
the interests of the German race [*Volkstum*].'[36]

The phraseology of official communiqués, particularly in critical
situations, is usually general and sometimes deliberately obscure.
The text proposed admittedly did not say much and was non-
committal but, reading between the lines, it emphasised the important points from the Austrian point of view: continuance of
the July 1936 agreement with its provisions for recognition and
non-interference: the fact that the February agreement was based
on that of 1936 and was intended to supplement, not replace it,
with all the legal consequences of this clear differentiation. In his
report von Papen recommended acceptance of the Austrian draft
but suggested that the last sentence contain specific reference to
the 'long common history' of the two states. The text was
accepted and, as proposed, was published simultaneously in
Vienna and Berlin on the evening of 15 February.

The extent of the desire for 'close and friendly relations' is
shown by the fact that the day before (14 February) at 7.30 p.m.
Hitler approved a proposal by General Keitel that neither the
army nor the air force should make any real military preparations; instead 'false but credible information should be spread . . .
creating the impression that detailed military preparations were
being undertaken against Austria'.[37]

Hitler was not interested in the details of the agreements. To him 'recognition of sovereignty' and 'non-interference' were simply empty ideas, the hair-splitting of the weaker side who could see no other means of saving his skin than reliance on the recognised rules of international negotiation and the recognised practices of international law. His counterpart to these was a precipitate decision to reach a solution 'by hook or by crook'. In a relaxed mood when it was all over Hitler had said that Austro-German relations were now settled for the next five years; after that the world would look very different anyway. Asked what he thought were the possibilities of keeping the peace, he replied that if his advice were followed, peace would be assured, but if it were not – and there followed the remark about the irresponsibility of failing to use an instrument like the German *Wehrmacht*.

It is idle to speculate what else might have occurred on 12 February 1938 or before or after. Months later, when I was in solitary confinement in the Hotel Metropol, Vienna, a young SS sentry, from Carinthia to judge by his accent, asked me whether I recognised him. He had presented arms to me as I drove into the Berghof on 12 February. On our way up from Berchtesgaden we had noticed a crowd of curious faces at the windows of the SS barracks; they had all been Austrians, my young guard said. If this was true, it was indeed a curious coincidence.

'Two years ago, when we marched into the Rhineland with a couple of battalions, I was acting against the views of my advisers and taking a great risk. If France had marched then, we should have had to withdraw. But now France has left it too late.'[38] Thus Hitler during the first part of our talks to emphasise his conviction that he now had a free hand and that Austria could not count on international support. We now had to draw such conclusions as were possible or inevitable from this hard fact.

One course would have been to abandon our efforts at agreement and break off negotiations as fruitless. The second course, the one which Hitler wanted, was to surrender, in other words agree to an admitted or unadmitted Anschluss. This would have been tantamount to an invitation to National-Socialism to overrun Austria.

Had we broken off negotiations, in all probability the immediate consequence would have been a Nazi seizure of power by force, and in existing circumstances this would have had unforeseeable consequences from more than one point of view. Politically surrender would have led to the same result but it would have implied a breach of international law by Austria which might have prejudiced her future position, should times change.

The only remaining course was to try to save what we could from the wreck and on this we had to take a final decision in Vienna within three days. Of course it had all turned out differently from what we had expected. We had relied on prior agreements, of the validity of which there should have been no doubt under established international custom. There is also no reason to doubt that Hitler had failed to put von Papen in the picture; the latter had certainly not approved the general procedure and precipitate goings-on. On the other hand he had been assiduous in his efforts to bring about an Austrian Anschluss by evolutionary methods and in a secret report to the Reich Chancellery as late as the end of 1937 had recommended 'subjecting the Federal Chancellor to the strongest possible pressure'.[39]

The methods used against Austria later proved effective in the cases of Czechoslovakia, Poland and Hungary and for a time also against Britain and the USSR, although both had had their warnings.

The start of all this was Hitler's decision, taken in January 1938, to 'enforce the right of self-determination' for six and a half million Germans in Austria 'during the course of this year' and 'by hook or by crook'. How the Anschluss was to take place was left open; what was not was the determination to strike a decisive blow against the existence of Austria as an independent state.[40]

On 12 February 1938 we knew nothing of all this. It does, however, show what 'negotiating' with Hitler was like and illustrates what sort of a man he was and what his intentions were. The list of demands drawn up by Keppler with Globocnik and Dr Friedrich Rainer (both Austrians) was never intended to lead to a settlement with Austria but to the incorporation of Austria into the German Reich under National-Socialist leadership. It may well be that, in contrast to the revolutionaries, Leopold and Tavs, and in contrast to Hitler himself, Keppler and his associates hoped to achieve their aim without a military invasion. Rainer said in the witness box at Nuremberg: 'With this agreement the Nazi Party had won a legal foothold in the government which could be used to paralyse the governmental system when the planned revolution came.'[41] Elsewhere he said: 'It is true that the 11 July 1936 agreement did not produce the results we wished; had it done so the further meeting on 12 February in Berchtesgaden would not have been necessary. In my opinion the Reich observed the 11 July 1936 agreement and I would not dispute that in the case of Austria either.'[42]

Dr Kajetan Mühlmann, Seyss-Inquart's contact man, said that he went to Berchtesgaden on 12 February 1938 on Seyss's instructions (and possibly with the knowledge of Zernatto) to ensure 'that no one tried to upset things at the last moment; we feared that Leopold and his people might try. Such intrigues were the reason why neither the July nor the February agreements could last'.[43]

In retrospect the day at Berchtesgaden was a copybook example of strict adherence to the theory that the end justifies the means, so long decried as 'jesuitical'. Since the days of Machiavelli this principle has never been more consistently followed than in the period of the twentieth-century totalitarian ideologies. Once more it was proved that, though it can at times lead to apparently spectacular successes, against the canvas of history they are short-lived. This does not alter the fact that we were the first of a long list of people who had to try to deal with the new shock therapy.

Was, therefore, Berchtesgaden really the beginning of the end or the end of the beginning (to use a famous Churchillian phrase),[44] in a process starting with Hitler's seizure of power in January 1933?

The preliminary agreements which led to acceptance of the invitation to Berchtesgaden and which were in fact a condition of the meeting, had clearly been broken. Indirectly at least, von Papen's memoirs confirm that the talks were to take place on the basis of the July agreement and with the explicit purpose of reinforcing it.[45] In his speech to the Reichstag of 20 February 1938, in which he dealt with the Berchtesgaden agreement among other things, Hitler referred to 'fulfilling the spirit of the agreement of 11 July 1936'.[46] In fact we were confronted in Berchtesgaden with interference in our internal political affairs in its crudest form: we were expected to accept a named member of the cabinet with authority over public security; we were told to take certain administrative measures, such as the amnesty, within a prescribed time limit – and all this under the blackmailer's pressure of a threat of military invasion. We weighed the pros and cons but it was eventually this threat which decided us to sign, although we temporised by stipulating that under the constitution the agreement must be approved by the President.

An undated report by Veesenmayer of SD headquarters, probably destined for Keppler and written either on or immediately before 12 February 1938 says:

'The following appointments are conceded in principle: Interior together with Public Security (Seyss-Inquart) and Finance. The Federal Chancellor, however, pointed to the recent acts of violence ... he is of the opinion that it is not possible to proceed with the appointments at this time ... he wants to wait till 20 March. ... Seyss-Inquart urgently requests you to see to it that the Federal Chancellor is definitely committed to make the ministerial appointments before 20 February ... since otherwise ... domestic disorder will not only disturb the diplomatic agreements of the Führer but will also supply the Federal Chancellor with a plausible pretext for not honouring his commitments. As regards the removal of the *Landesleitung* in Austria [acceptance into the Reich of Leopold, Tavs and others] ... we are convinced of the unavoidable necessity of these measures. Nevertheless we must urgently request you to keep this from the public, as the Federal Chancellor is anxious to make the removal of the *Landesleitung* by the Führer appear as though the Führer was abandoning the movement.'[47]

All other available documents – Seyss-Inquart's evidence, Papen's reports, the so-called *Punktationen* and the record of the Berchtesgaden talks – prove conclusively that no mention was ever made of any agreements concluded before 12 February. The personnel changes demanded came as a complete surprise to the Austrian negotiators; hence the well-known course of events during the Berghof encounter.

The report quoted above, however, indicates clearly who was really calling the tune on the German side both before and after 12 February; it was not the illegal *Landesleitung* (Leopold) nor Seyss-Inquart, but Veesenmayer of the SD and Keppler, the 'Party Commissioner for Austria'.

Numerous reports from the Austrian Consul-General in Munich, both before 12 February and during the period 13 February–11 March confirm that Austria was subject to an immediate military threat at this time.[48]

On 13 February I reported to the President. Then followed exhaustive talks and discussions with leading figures in politics and industry. No one was under illusions as to the significance of Hitler's demands.

There seemed to be three alternatives:

1. The Chancellor to resign and the President to form a new government which would not be bound by the Berchtesgaden agreement.
2. Abide by the agreement but appoint a new Chancellor.
3. Abide by the agreement and keep the existing government in office.

After exhaustive discussion of the pros and cons the President decided for the third course. Accordingly we now had to address ourselves to three urgent tasks: immediate implementation of the agreed personnel changes; preparation and implementation of the agreed political amnesty; provision of information both at home and abroad taking account of the fact that we had decided to abide by the agreement.

By 15 February, in other words within the time limit, Austria had without exception carried out everything contained in the Berchtesgaden Protocol. The only obligation, so far as membership of the cabinet was concerned, was the appointment of Seyss-Inquart as Minister of the Interior with responsibility for public security. In view of previous developments and the agreement, Glaise-Horstenau's position in the cabinet was confirmed.

In addition, to underline the broad-based nature of the cabinet, on our own initiative we appointed Professor Ludwig Adamovich Minister of Justice, Julius Raab Minister of Trade and Adolf Watzek State Secretary in the Ministry of Social Affairs with responsibility for the legal protection of workers and employees. The previous State Secretary for Security, the Police President Michael Skubl, was seconded to the new Minister of Security and nominated Inspector-General of Security Forces.

Seyss-Inquart accepted all these appointments, in particular that of Skubl, noting that the new Minister of Justice was a legitimist, the new Minister of Trade a Christian Social and the new State Secretary in the Ministry of Social Affairs a Social Democrat. The amnesty too was carried out, and more liberally than the Berchtesgaden agreement provided; it was made applicable to all political offences and therefore included Social Democrats and communists under arrest or held responsible for illegal activity. The amnesty therefore provided for cancellation of sentences, in some cases conditional, in others unconditional, for all crimes committed before 15 February 1938 in the service of a political party or from political motives, provided the person concerned was resident in Austria at the time of the announcement of this decision. Police court sentences were also included in the amnesty in accordance with the agreement. The National-Socialists objected to this lenient policy on the part of the government; they saw no advantage in extension of the amnesty beyond their own people.[49]

So assembly positions were occupied for the final political battle.

6

TO THE BRINK

'By the spring of 1938 German military and economic preparations had reached the point where Hitler was prepared to make his first move towards world conquest, which was the reconstitution of the Great German Reich. The first step was taken on 12 March 1938 when German troops invaded Austria and the Republic became a German province.'[1]

'How easy it would have been then (1937) to create a relationship with the German Reich similar to that of Bavaria between 1871 and 1918 – full governmental and administrative autonomy and an independent parliament. Only foreign policy and military command in wartime need have been matters of common concern.' (From the so-called Papen Memorandum of 3 May 1945.)[2]

In a note on his farewell visit to me on 26 February 1938 von Papen said:

'I then turned the conversation to the widely held opinion that he [the Chancellor] had acted under "brutal pressure" in Berchtesgaden. After all, I had been present myself and had been able to ascertain that he had always and at every point possessed complete freedom of decision. The Chancellor replied that he had actually been exposed to strong moral pressure; he could not deny that. He had made notes on his conversation with the Führer which bore this out. I reminded him of the fact that, despite this conversation, he had not seen his way clear to make any concessions and I asked him whether he would have been willing to grant the concessions he did make late at night without pressure. His reply was: "Frankly, no." It seems important to me to record this. . . .'[3]

These three quotations illustrate clearly what the Berchtesgaden agreement was really about and why it could not last; paradoxical though it may sound, this is so in spite of the fact that both sides, Austria certainly, intended to abide by the letter of the agreement. In Hitler's eyes it was a foregone conclusion, as inevitable as a law of nature, that in some form or another the Austrians would force through the Anschluss from within, even against the will of their government; how it happened was to him unimportant; only one thing mattered – Anschluss now, in other words in spring 1938; everything else would work itself out. He was not really interested in the 'liberation' of Austria; he viewed the Anschluss from the standpoint of a wide-ranging geo-political concept, the hegemony of the German race in the framework of his vision of a future European order.[4]

Even National-Socialism as a political ideology, and the National-Socialists both in Germany and Austria were means to an end – nothing more. This explains why, as a general rule and particularly in Austria, the idealists thrown up by the Movement did not do so well as the careerists for whom the brown shirt represented neither one extreme nor the other in the political spectrum of their careers.

By this time, however, National-Socialism in Austria implied unconditional Hitler discipleship;[5] in spite of internal personal rivalries this went far deeper than we were prepared to admit at the time. The Austrian Nazi Party had become a Hitler movement. Growing recognition of this political fact largely explains the readiness of the Ballhausplatz to try its luck with the agreements of 11 July 1936 and 12 February 1938.

Left to himself Hitler would have liked to settle the Austrian 'problem' as he conceived it on the model of his seizure of power in January 1933, in other words without the overt use of force. Should this prove impossible, however, he was ready to use military force, taking care, so far as might be, to preserve external appearances.

For the sake of these external appearances Hitler was initially prepared to make concessions. They were welcomed by conservative nationalist opinion in leading German military, diplomatic and economic circles which were basically averse to Nazi methods and the political philosophy underlying them. In so far as Austria was concerned, this was evidenced in the emphasis laid by von Papen on the evolutionary theory as opposed to the view of the Party activists that only revolution, in other words the use of force, could win the day. In fact it proved that the objective, the elimination of an independent Austria, could be attained only by revolutionary methods, in other words illegally. To this extent Leopold, Tavs and Frauenfeld, the revolutionary law-breakers, were right and the apostles of evolution (von Papen, Glaise-Horstenau and, prior to the 12 March 1938 upheaval, even Seyss-Inquart, Neubacher and their allies) were wrong. They were wrong, however, only for seven bitter fateful years. It is idle to speculate what might have happened if the evolution theory had been successfully pursued and a solution on the lines of von Papen's[6] adopted; even in that case there would have had to have been a change of system in Austria and for as far ahead as could be foreseen this could not have taken place without the use of force. What von Papen had in mind was clearly a Bismarck-type solution leaving Austria in a relationship to the Reich similar to that of the South German states after 1866 and 1871.

The concept of a Central European empire which many conservative, educated and loyal Austrians discussed after 1918, though admittedly in hazy outline only, was later labelled as utopian romancing with an undercurrent of nationalism. This does it an injustice. In fact it was conceived as a conscious defence against Pan-Germanism, holding out the hope of supra-national integration in Central Europe and basically by no means so unrealistic. It stood in direct contrast to the ideas of the Third Reich with its racial intolerance and national arrogance. Quite apart from all this, however, as the Third Reich's short history proves only too abundantly, a 'federal' solution on Bismarckian lines would have conflicted on principle with Nazi centralism; it could no more have been accepted than could an autonomous administratively independent Austrian entity after Austria's 'home-coming' in 1938. Neither the free will of the people nor the right of self-determination nor even the consent of a majority of convinced National-Socialists can be cited as justification for the obliteration of Austria after 1938.

Clearly, therefore, not even Hitler's minimum demand, a camouflaged incorporation into the Reich, could be a subject of discussion. The concessions eventually made in Berchtesgaden and then exploited to enforce this demand, were in fact extracted under pressure. In this one can only agree with von Papen: 'It seems important to me to record this. . . .'

The pressure was primarily of a military nature. The gravity of the situation was confirmed by a report dated 24 February 1938 from Dr Ludwig Jordan, the Austrian Consul-General in Munich:

'During the last week I have received reports from various sources that during the Berchtesgaden meeting German forces were on the frontier and ready to move. These reports were apparently belied by the fact that about this time pre-arranged field firing exercises were taking place in the area Reichenhall-Laufen. Now, however, I hear from various reliable people that on the twelfth of the month preparations for military action were actually under way in Upper Bavaria; two independent sources have told me, for instance, that 200 military aircraft were ready to take off from the new airfield at Bad Aibling. . . . I am further assured that mile-long columns of mechanised troops (tanks and artillery) were parked on the autobahn near Traunstein.'[7]

Report dated 21 January 1938:

'Yesterday Mr D. St Clair Gainer, the British Consul-General here, told me the following:

1. A few days ago he had been visited by the secretary to Mosley, the British fascist leader, who had attended the recent National-Socialist leaders' rally in Sonthofen and had also been in Austria. Captain Leopold had told him that in the spring the NSDAP in Austria would take armed action with the support of Germany. He [Leopold] believed that some *Wehrmacht* units would be used against the Federal government. Before this the Austrian Legion, now in the Godesberg area, would be moved up to the frontier. . . . Captain Leopold had originally been afraid that, when the NSDAP seized power in Austria as expected, he would not be placed at the head of the government. He had subsequently received the necessary assur-

ances, however, from the Reich Chancellor. Mr Gainer takes this information very seriously. He had immediately informed the British Embassy in Berlin.

2. Yesterday evening, from an entirely reliable source, I learnt the following in amplification of the above: In a private conversation a Party functionary belonging to Hitler's entourage said that there would be "a move against Austria" in the spring. Unless the Federal Chancellor "came to his senses" he would share the fate of the late Chancellor Dollfuss.'[8]

Alarming reports about imminent action against Austria had been arriving from our Consul-General in Munich ever since the autumn of 1937. They culminated with one dated 8 February 1938, only a few days before the Berchtesgaden meeting, saying that all foreign policy rumours in Munich revolved around Austria and that there was talk about a 'spring action'. The latest personnel changes in the German army (the dismissal of von Blomberg and von Fritsch) and in the foreign service (the dismissal of von Neurath and of Ambassadors von Papen and von Hassell) were generally regarded as signs that Germany was swinging away from the 11 July 1936 policy.[9]

As was subsequently proved, Jordan's reports from Munich and those of Stephan Tauschitz, the Austrian Minister in Berlin, were entirely correct and factual. Leopold, the ex-*Landesleiter* (illegal) for Austria, was thoroughly indiscreet and frequently committed himself to paper which then fell into the hands of the Austrian police. Even before the Anschluss he was severely dressed down by Hitler who had told him that he was liable to create grave foreign policy difficulties; on this particular occasion he, Hitler, had managed to control the situation.[10] The fact that after 11 March 1938 Dr Jordan was called to account and victimised by the authorities merely for doing his duty shows what 'evolutionary development' meant in practice.

Hitler's view of the Berchtesgaden talks is shown by the confidential record of an interview between the Führer and Sir Nevile Henderson, the British Ambassador in Berlin. This took place on 3 March 1938, at a time when Austria had fulfilled all her undertakings under the Berchtesgaden Protocol and Hitler could not yet say that he was faced with a new situation owing to Austria's 'breach of the agreement' because of the plebiscite. The record says:

'. . . while in London he [the Ambassador] had, upon orders of his Government, examined all questions resulting from the Halifax visit to Germany [November 1937] in conversations with Prime Minister Chamberlain and other interested Cabinet members. In this connection he stressed the importance of German collaboration in the pacification of Europe, to which he had already referred in previous conversations with Herr von Neurath and Herr von Ribbentrop. This pacification could be furthered by limitation of armaments and by appeasement in Czechoslovakia and Austria. In this connection the British Ambassador read the following instructions, which he later presented in writing:

"In our view appeasement would be dependent, amongst other things, on the measures taken to inspire confidence in Austria and Czechoslovakia. His Majesty's Government at present cannot estimate the effect of the recent arrangement between Germany and Austria which must depend upon the manner in which the several undertakings of arrangements made are implemented by the two parties to them. They are therefore at present doubtful as to the effects which these arrangements are likely to have on the situation in Central Europe and cannot conceal from themselves that recent events have aroused apprehension in many quarters which must inevitably render more difficult the negotiation of a general settlement." '

After a sharp attack on the 'inflammatory campaign' in the British press Hitler replied:

'Concerning Central Europe it should be noted that Germany would not tolerate any interference by third powers in the settlement of her relations with kindred countries or with countries having large German elements in their population, just as Germany would never think of interfering in the settlement of relations between England and Ireland. It was a question of preventing the continuance or renewal of an injustice to millions of Germans. In this attempt at a settlement Germany would have to declare most seriously that she was not willing to be influenced in any way by other parties in

this settlement. It was impossible that freedom of nations and democratic rights should always be described as elements of the European
order, but the very opposite be maintained when it came to improving the lot of the Germans in Austria. There a government which
(unlike the German Government) had not been formed in a legal
manner and which was supported by only 15 per cent of the population, had suppressed the rest of the Germans. This was an intolerable
situation in the long run and if England continued to resist German
attempts to achieve a just and reasonable settlement, then the time
would come when one would have to fight. If he, the Führer, en-
deavoured – as he had done in Berchtesgaden – to get some relief for
the oppressed Germans peacefully, and Paris and London not only
watched his efforts with scepticism but even instructed their diplomats to obstruct this peaceful attempt [here the British Ambassador
interrupted to say that England had never done that], they were
rendering very poor service to the cause of peace. Ultimately the
people themselves in Austria must be consulted and the Germans in
Czechoslovakia must be granted their rightful autonomy in cultural
and other matters in order to obtain a satisfactory solution there. This
was the simplest application of that right of self-determination of
nations which had played such an important part in Wilson's
Fourteen Points. The present state of affairs at any rate was impossible
in the long run; it would lead to an explosion and in order to avoid
this, the Agreements of Berchtesgaden had been concluded. It might
be added that the difficulties could be considered eliminated, if the
Austrian Government fulfilled its obligations. But, as he had said in
his Reichstag speech, whoever proceeded by force against reason and
justice would invite violence.

To a question by the British Ambassador whether Germany
demanded a plebiscite in Austria, the Führer replied that she would
demand that by evolutionary means the legitimate interests of the
Germans in Austria be secured and that there be an end to oppression.
. . . The conversation then turned to Central European problems
again. In reply to the remark by the British Ambassador that for
Chamberlain to achieve anything Germany would also have to
make some contribution in this matter, the Führer replied that his
contribution to these problems consisted of the Berchtesgaden
Agreement with Austria; but he must emphasise very strongly that
once Germans were fired upon in Austria or in Czechoslovakia, the
German Reich would intervene. He, the Führer, had had to talk a good

deal in his political career, and therefore some circles perhaps believed that his words need not always be taken too seriously. But whoever considered his utterances concerning Central European questions mere rhetoric would be very cruelly disappointed. *If internal explosions occurred in Austria or in Czechoslovakia, Germany would not remain neutral, but would act with lightning speed.* Therefore it was false if certain diplomats or members of the Vienna Government stated that they need have no fear and need not be very careful about the fulfilment of their obligations.

In this connection Foreign Minister von Ribbentrop referred to the dramatic conversation between the British Minister in Vienna [Michael Palairet] and Herr von Papen, during which the Minister had complained with great animation about the pressure which Germany had allegedly exerted on Austria. The only Berchtesgaden pressure had consisted in calling Austria's attention to certain dangers and suggesting a solution for them. If the British Minister had protested in such a dramatic manner to Herr von Papen, one can imagine how he must have spoken to Austrian Foreign Minister Schmidt. The British Ambassador pointed out *that these statements by the Minister did not necessarily represent the opinion of the British Government and declared that he, Sir Nevile Henderson, had himself often advocated the Anschluss. . . .*

The British Ambassador recapitulated the German views concerning Austria and Czechoslovakia by stating that, if the Germans in these countries were further oppressed, an explosion would occur, while if full equality was granted, no conflict was to be expected. . .'[11]

In a letter to von Ribbentrop dated 4 March 1938 Sir Nevile Henderson commented on the record prepared by Schmidt, the interpreter, and transmitted to the Embassy that it contained 'one quite incorrect statement'; he had never spoken in favour of the Anschluss; he had sometimes expressed personal views which might not have been entirely in accordance with those of his government.[12]

Anthony Eden, who was in charge of British foreign policy until 20 February 1938 and had recommended Henderson for the Berlin post, later commented:

'It was an international misfortune that we should have been represented in Berlin at this time by a man who, so far from warning the Nazis, was constantly making excuses for them, often in their company. . . . He grew to see himself as the man predestined to make peace with the Nazis. Sincerely believing this to be possible, he came to regard me, and others at the Foreign Office who shared my opinions, as obstacles to his purpose. More than once in the next months, I had to warn him against the recurring habit of interpreting my instructions in a fashion too friendly to the Nazis. Lord Halifax was to suffer the same experience later more intensely than I could have tolerated. Henderson's confidence in Nazi good intentions and his support of their claims in Austria and Czechoslovakia accelerated events which it was his duty to retard. Despite all this Hitler felt an increasing antipathy towards him.'[13]

The conversation with Henderson quoted above shows that, as so often before, Hitler's views on Austria were based on the alleged oppression and persecution of the Austrian National-Socialists or, in the current over-simplified jargon, Germans in Austria. Nevertheless, almost in the same breath, he had just recognised the Austrian constitution and taken note that it did not permit political parties, not even the NSDAP. From the outset 'persecution' had consisted solely of the punishment of terrorist activities and the suppression and punishment of sabotage. In addition, since 1933 legal proceedings had been taken against propaganda for the Hitler movement and pro-Anschluss demonstrations clearly directed against the existence of the State.

How organised activity directed against the independence of Austria could be said to be consistent with the 'German peace' – here lay the insoluble contradiction.

The Berchtesgaden agreement never even mentioned whether a political movement directed against Austrian independence was admissible or not. The subject was not even discussed since this would not have been compatible with an attempt to establish normal friendly relations between the two countries. Hitler's statements to the British Ambassador on 3 March prove that, though it was never admitted, the views of the two sides were as diametrically and irreconcilably opposed as in the spring of 1933 when Hitler thought that he could force his Austrian opponent to his knees with the Thousand-mark Blockade. It showed that everything which had happened since, and in particular the attempted settlement under the July 1936 agreement, was merely a postponement necessitated by the international situation, but that the ultimate objective remained unchanged.

After 12 February 1938 the great question-mark was whether Hitler would regard the Berchtesgaden agreement as a temporarily satisfactory basis for Austro-German relations in the light of his overall foreign policy or whether it was merely a springboard. If the first alternative came true, judging by previous experience, Austria could count on some two years of peaceful development during which to consolidate her economic and internal political position. One of the main reasons for the recent extremism on the part of all those who had been committed to a National-Socialist takeover ever since 1933 was undoubtedly fear of stabilisation in Austria.[14] Should the second alternative be true the last, somewhat faint, hope lay in an early change in the international situation; London and Rome, for instance, might perhaps reach agreement on the Abyssinian and Spanish problems, but to be of use this would have to come in a matter of weeks after 12 February.

We could not of course guess Hitler's timetable; even with our present-day knowledge it is not entirely clear. One thing is certain: for him the Austrian Anschluss was a foregone conclusion – and in the foreseeable future; in his view conditions for it must be created during 1938; the quicker and more unobtrusively the better.

In accordance with our agreement, in his Reichstag speech of 20 February 1938 Hitler referred to the 'spirit of . . . 11 July'.[15] He had thereby confirmed afresh his recognition of the independence of sovereign Austria and its constitution, also the obligation not to interfere in internal Austrian affairs. By 26 February, however, in the presence of Ribbentrop and Keppler he was telling Leopold and his friends after their enforced departure from Austria in accordance with the Berchtesgaden agreement that the Berchtesgaden Protocol 'was so far-reaching that, if completely carried out, the Austrian problem would be solved automatically'. He did not now desire a solution by violent means.[16]

Early in March Hitler interviewed one of the leading Austrian

Nazis who had been expelled into Germany and was now asking either for something to do or permission to return to Austria. But Hitler counselled patience, saying that he himself would shortly be in Vienna and then everything would solve itself.

Here lay the great difference between the views of the two sides: verbally the Germans recognised Austrian independence and denied any intention of annexing the country; they were, however, convinced that of her own free will and by her own exertions Austria would bring about the Anschluss from within; they therefore considered themselves entitled to accelerate this internal Austrian development and expected the Austrian government to give them a free hand in the name of national freedom. On the Austrian side we were concerned to assert our internationally recognised independence and, by ending the cold war overtly conducted ever since Hitler's seizure of power in Germany until 11 July 1936, to eliminate the blatant threat posed by Germany. For this vital assurance, and for this alone, Austria was prepared to pay a considerable political price. To this extent it is correct to say that differing political interpretations were placed upon an international agreement which, as usual, favoured the stronger side.

The case of the non-interference undertaking, however, was a different matter. Without this the entire agreement was worthless and meaningless to Austria from the outset. By February 1938 Hitler had realised that the Austrian problem would not be solved in his favour in the foreseeable future without large-scale direct or indirect intervention. Nevertheless he undertook not to interfere.

To this it may be objected that, despite all denials and assurances, the Austrian negotiators were well aware that, in the light of the overall situation and of experience, the scale of German intervention in National-Socialist – or in Hitler's terminology German – affairs was dependent solely on the international outlook. This was fully understood in other European quarters. Winston Churchill's comment on the Austrian passages in Hitler's Reichstag speech of 20 February, for instance, was: 'One can hardly find a more perfect specimen of humbug and hypocrisy for British and American benefit. . . . What is astounding is that it should have been regarded with anything but scorn by men and women of intelligence in any free country.'[17]

On my return to Vienna from Berchtesgaden on 13 February it would of course have been possible to sound the alarm in public, over the radio for instance. This would, however, have produced exactly the situation which we had gone to Berchtesgaden to avoid. I thought then, and I still think, that this would have been tantamount to submission, in other words the result would have been to produce exactly that which happened a bare month later, when the Austrian plebiscite was announced. On 13 February however, there was no knowing what Hitler's short-term plans were nor that he was then prepared to go the whole hog. We should thus have played the only trump remaining in our hand and made it easy for our opponent to preserve appearances and present Austria to the world as the guilty party. Diplomatic *démarches* in Berlin, and that is all there would have been, would have helped us as little then as they did later.

Naturally, however, some information to the outer world was required. It had to be factual and avoid spreading alarm as long as possible in order not to provoke economic panic in Austria.

The normal detailed briefing of Austrian representatives abroad was, therefore, impractical; in the first place the provisions of the Berchtesgaden agreement had to be implemented; secondly, on 13 and 14 February the decision had to be taken in Vienna whether to accept or reject it. The remodelled cabinet was sworn in on the evening of the 14th. On the 15th Austrian representatives abroad were informed by cipher telegram of this fact and of the further measures envisaged. German diplomatic missions were informed by the Reich Foreign Ministry on the 16th.

The Vienna circular telegram of 15 February (Z.51.601–13) read as follows:

'The conversations held between the Federal Chancellor and the Reich Chancellor in Berchtesgaden were extraordinarily difficult; there were sharp disagreements owing to increased demands from the Germans and the pressure with which their fulfilment was sought. Only after many hours of negotiations was a basis of agreement found. Its main provisions are: recognition by the Germans of the continued validity of the 11 July 1936 agreement and explicit re-affirmation of the pledge of non-interference in internal Austrian affairs. On his side the Federal Chancellor declared himself ready to promote the internal pacification of Austria by certain measures introduced in a spirit of generous reconciliation. . . . Without concealing the difficulty of the negotiations you should emphasise in any conversation that no change in the 11 July agreement has been made; also that pursuit of pacification in Austria in no sense implies renunciation of or departure from the previous principles of the Federal Government. As before, it adheres firmly to the inviolability of Austrian independence, to the constitution and to the unchallenged position of the Fatherland Front.'

Another circular telegram of the same day (Z.51.616) set out the measures agreed and concluded:

'The essential today is to reduce the understandable nervousness both at home and abroad: this is also vital for the normal development of our relations with the Reich on the basis of adherence to the principles of the July agreement. . . . Will you therefore please regard references in the previous telegram to difficulties connected with the Berchtesgaden conversations as for your personal information only. In all conversations emphasis should be placed on the necessity for calm and on our confidence in the normal development of our relations with the Reich which have now been clarified by the Berchtesgaden discussions.[18]

Scrambled telephone conversations were also held with Prague, London and Paris and additional information forwarded by letter.[19]

The object of these instructions to Austrian representatives abroad was the avoidance of possible complications; in addition, for practical reasons, the main emphasis was laid on the provision of information on a personal basis to the representatives of the great powers in Vienna. This seemed to be the quickest, most secure and (an important point in this case) more discreet method of informing the interested powers. Whatever may have been said later, that this precise information found its mark is proved by the special interest later shown by the German SD and Gestapo in discovering how Paris and London in particular were so fully informed of the details of the conversations immediately after 12 February. Washington too was kept abreast of the threatening developments in Central Europe through its overseas representatives. In December 1948 a number of secret diplomatic reports were published in the American press in somewhat dramatic circumstances.[20]

Whittaker Chambers, a former communist courier, then editor of *Time* magazine, stated to the Un-American Activities Committee of Congress that secret documents of a political nature had been passed to him by Alger Hiss when the latter was a senior State Department official. Hiss was then President of the Carnegie Foundation and had been Secretary-General of the San Francisco Conference in 1945. He denied the accusation and notified the Justice Department in Washington which charged the New York Grand Jury with the investigation. In his private apartment Chambers thereupon handed over to a representative of the Congressional Committee microfilms of the State Department secret documents which he had prepared from the originals and kept ever since 1938. He said that these had been given him by officials of the State Department, one of whom was Alger Hiss. His wife had typed copies from the originals. Her typewriter was later found. Alger Hiss denied under oath having handed over the documents but was convicted of perjury by the court. A member of the Un-American Activities Committee, the Representative for California, Richard M. Nixon, undertook to forward to the New York Grand Jury the documents in evidence, as demanded by the Federal Attorney.[21]

Among the so-called Chambers papers were three diplomatic reports on the Austrian situation of February 1938. In December 1948 these were released by the State Department and published by the Chairman of the parliamentary Investigating Committee. They consisted first of a summary report from the US Consul-General in Vienna dated 13 February 1938 and transmitted to Washington by telegram (parts of it are incorrect); second, a further report from the Consul-General dated 15 February; third, a report from the US Ambassador in Paris dated 16 February. They read as follows:[22]

'Secretary of State, Washington   Vienna
(Received 3.50 p.m. 13 Feb.)   13 February 1938

Reports from reliable source indicate that Hitler made unacceptable demands and that Austrian Government is now formulating
counter-proposals. Government inaccessible to diplomatic corps.
Even French Minister, who was promised appointment, has been
unable to see Schmidt. It seems possible that Hitler is seeking foreign
political triumph at the expense of Austria to redress adverse effect of
Party crisis.

Innsbruck correspondent of an American news agency reports
Ribbentrop passed through today en route to Italy. Rumors from
several sources alleged that Schuschnigg had long telephone conversations with Mussolini before proceeding to Berchtesgaden. Small
Heimwehr demonstration this afternoon for Starhemberg. Austrian
legitimists reported discouraged over probable course of events.

John C. Wiley
Consul-General'

'Rush   Vienna
Secretary of State, Washington   15 February 1938.
(Received 12.32 p.m. 15 Feb.)
My telegram February 15, 9.0 p.m.

Dined last night at a large dinner given by Schmidt with Chancellor Schuschnigg, Seyss-Inquart, members of government and diplomatic corps. Atmosphere most oppressive. To French Minister
Schuschnigg described visit to Berchtesgaden as the most horrible
day of his life. He says that Hitler is undoubtedly a madman with a
mission and in complete control of Germany. Hitler openly told him
of his desire to annex Austria and declared that he could march into
Austria with much greater ease and infinitely less danger than he
incurred in remilitarisation of the Rhineland. Schuschnigg admits
that appointment of Seyss-Inquart is highly dangerous but states that
he will make it in order to avert the "worst". In respect of Italy
Schuschnigg declared that he can count only on moral, not material,
support.

Schuschnigg is attempting to make best of bad situation and was
in a long and friendly conversation with Seyss-Inquart. Hornbostel
is in utter despair and states openly that there is nothing left for him
to do but to leave Foreign Office.

Italian Minister claims that he was informed of Berchtesgaden meeting only on the eleventh and denied that Italy took any initiative in the matter. He telegraphed full information to Mussolini. Latter, however, is engaged in winter sports and up to last night Ghigi had no information that his messages had reached the Duce. Italian Minister gives anxious impression.

Papal Nuncio admits that Seyss-Inquart may be good Catholic but fears, nevertheless, that it is the beginning of the end.

French Minister, who has been here five years, states that this is the most critical moment since July 1934. "It is not the end. It is the moment before the end." In his opinion Austria can only be saved by immediate reconciliation of France and England with Italy and energetic joint action. Ender, author of May constitution, made identical remark this morning.

In my opinion Austria's situation is most unfortunate and menacing. If Seyss-Inquart is loyal his appointment would not be a solution. If he is disloyal it is a catastrophe. Germany probably plans gradual Danzigification and to outmanœuvre any unsupported efforts Schuschnigg may make. Seyss-Inquart can at best only retard this process.

Repeated by telegraph to Paris, London, Berlin and Rome.

Wiley.'

'Secretary of State, Washington   Paris
(Received 3.47 p.m.)   16 February 1938
Strictly confidential for the Secretary.

The Austrian Minister just read to me a telegram which he received this morning from Schuschnigg. It indicated that Schuschnigg had by no means given up hope of maintaining Austrian independence. Schuschnigg had confidence that Seyss-Inquart, although a Pan-German, would not work in an underhand manner for the introduction of Nazis into the regime.

Amnesty would be extended at once not only to Nazis but also to Social Democrats. This amnesty would, however, not include those who had emigrated from Austria, thus excluding from the country all those Austrian Nazis who are now in Germany.

The right to conduct political propaganda would be extended not only to the Nazis, but also to the monarchists and Social Democrats. Those Nazis who had been excluded from office and pensions because of their political opinions, would have their pensions restored but would not be given their former offices.

The position of Schuschnigg was, I gathered, the following: that he would continue to struggle for Austrian independence; that he believed this independence could be maintained in the long run only if there should be reconciliation between England, France and Italy; that he considered recognition of Ethiopia essential for any such reconciliation, since the Italians were genuinely convinced that the British at some future date would attempt to drive the Italians out of Ethiopia, which would mean the collapse of the fascist regime in Italy.

Section Two: Schuschnigg felt that the actions which he was about to take would produce a temporary breathing period but in the end would prove to be just as unsatisfactory to Hitler as his actions which followed the accord of July 1936. He expected therefore that at some future date Germany would attempt again to repeat the Berchtesgaden coup and would mobilise, if necessary, on the Austrian frontier. He would make no further concessions. He could not attempt to fight Germany alone and, if faced by German mobilisation, would have to resign.

The question of Austrian existence as an independent state therefore depended on the possibility that, before Hitler again should become sufficiently irritated to mobilise on the Austrian frontier, there might be reconciliation between England, France and Italy and an agreement between those states to support Austrian independence. The Austrian Minister added that he believed that extension of amnesty to the Social Democrats would add greatly to the strength of Schuschnigg's regime, as the Social Democrats would be the strongest opponents of a gradual nazification of Austria. In contradiction of the opinions expressed above with regard to Seyss-Inquart, I was told this morning by a gentleman who says he knows Seyss-Inquart intimately that the latter is a hundred-per-cent Nazi by conviction, although a devout Catholic, and that he will insert Nazis gradually into all vital posts and strike for a decision in a few months.

William C. Bullitt
Ambassador.'

From our point of view there was clearly no object in presenting Berlin with the opportunity to say that parliamentary debates in other countries (Paris 25 February, London 16 and 17 February) had been instigated by Austria. We should merely have put ourselves in the wrong *vis-à-vis* not only Hitler but also our own 'nationals' whom we still hoped to win over to the cause of

Austria; we should have squandered our last, admittedly faint, hope of self-preservation without gaining anything. Had there been any prospect of armed intervention against the Anschluss by the Powers, as might have happened up to 1935, there would have been no Berchtesgaden agreement. Since, however, as everybody knew, there was no such prospect, oratory, parliamentary questions and resolutions could do us little good, as was clearly demonstrated right up to the outbreak of World War II and not in Austria's case alone.

We had done what we could for peace. Peace was the whole basis of our existence. Now it was up to others to do their bit and appreciate the future correctly. The stake was not Austria alone but the maintenance of the European order. Naturally, anything which might be said or done to mobilise world public opinion and the world's conscience could not but be of assistance to us; we concealed nothing and we suppressed nothing; but beyond that our hands were tied so long as no one more powerful was willing to register a genuine veto in Berlin.[23]

On 16 February I briefed Gabriel Puaux, the French Minister in Vienna, in detail; he had already been given an outline by the Foreign Ministry. On 17 February he reported to Paris:

> 'It is the duty of the French and British governments to speak frankly to Mussolini before it is too late. No defence of Austrian independence can be arranged without Italy. Whatever *démarches* the French and British governments may make in Berlin, they would neither impress Hitler nor help the Austrian patriots, unless Italy was openly and genuinely associated with them.'

On 21 February he telegraphed to Paris:

> 'In the light of Hitler's statements, as divulged to me by the Federal Chancellor, no honest person in Paris or London can be under any further illusions about the possibility of a settlement with Germany unless he is prepared to pay the price of the subjugation of all Europe to the will of the Führer. The moment has come when all who are threatened must combine to preserve peace.'

This telegram also refers to the urgent necessity of participation by Italy. On 22 February Puaux telegraphed again:

'I had assumed that we would have six to eight months respite. I fear I was too optimistic. The threat is perhaps far more imminent. Europe has no time to lose in organising the defence of Vienna.'[24]

There is no truth whatsoever in the supposition (by von Papen among others in his Memoirs) that Puaux advised me to hold a plebiscite or exerted any influence on developments in Austria.

German accounts confirm that we had good reason for our anxiety to avoid panic and that most serious economic difficulties were looming. A situation report on Austria dated 18 February 7.0 p.m. and signed by Veesenmayer says:

'According to the latest advices, Schuschnigg is under heavy pressure from both the Jews and, especially, the Catholics. The Jews are attacking mainly through the stock exchange, to exert pressure on the currency. Since February 17 1938 there has been an extraordinarily heavy flight of capital, which led to a substantial drop in Austrian securities in Switzerland and London, as well as in other foreign countries. Schilling notes are being taken over the border illegally in large quantities, so that they have not been quoted since last night. This development is for the time being not unfavourable to the Reich, but great care will have to be taken lest the undermining of the Austrian currency, and thus also of the economy, goes too far. This is now probably only a matter of days.

From the Catholic side, the Nuncio yesterday afternoon made a very sharp attack on Schuschnigg.'[25]

According to notes made by Erich Kordt of the Berlin Foreign Ministry von Papen had already telephoned on 15 February:

'There was considerable agitation in Vienna because of the political and economic consequences of the German-Austrian Agreements. Vienna at the moment resembled an ant hill. Quite a few Jews were preparing to emigrate. The stock exchange was agitated and the banks were under heavy pressure. Besides, Prague was doing its bit to add to the confusion, spreading rumors that Austria had decided on large-scale rearmament with German aid.'[26]

All our efforts were therefore directed towards the avoidance of inordinate alarm with all its consequences; otherwise the spread of panic, of which there were already signs and the consequences of which could not have been more serious, could hardly have been stopped. Our argument was that there were still good grounds for hoping that Austria could maintain her position, at least for the foreseeable future, in spite of the ever-increasing pressure from within and still more from without.

Mussolini had explicitly stated – and after his visit to Germany in September 1937 – that Italy's attitude to the Austrian question was basically unchanged.[27] He had welcomed the Berchtesgaden meeting and, after it was over, had sent Senator Salata, the former Italian Minister in Austria, to Vienna with the message that he thought the conclusion of the agreement entirely right; for Austria the point was to gain time, he said; even if there should be difficulties in the provinces – he meant primarily Graz – the vital thing was to keep control in Vienna until the international situation changed; Ambassador Grandi was negotiating in London and there was every hope that a successful conclusion could be reached in about a fortnight; this would create an entirely new situation for Austria. . . . When Dr Emil Liebitzky, the Austrian Military Attaché, was instructed to tell Mussolini of Austrian anxieties about possible German intentions to use force, he replied indignantly: 'That the Germans will not do; we have Göring's word of honour.'[28]

In fact Italo-British negotiations had been going on in earnest for some time in order to settle their conflicts about Abyssinia and Spain. On 22 November 1937 von Weizsäcker, then Director in the German Foreign Ministry, informed von Hassell, the German Ambassador in Rome, of two letters sent by Ciano to Eden in February proposing an overall Anglo-Italian settlement; it was to cover Spain and the Mediterranean and include cessation of anti-British propaganda from Radio Bari; the Italian condition was de jure recognition of the conquest of Abyssinia; 'far-reaching commitments to Germany, which would otherwise be within the realm of possibility, would not be made, in case England agreed'.[29]

Negotiations between Dino Grandi, the Italian Ambassador in London, and Anthony Eden began on 10 February 1938. Recognition of Italy's position in Abyssinia, the Spanish question and anti-British radio propaganda were on the agenda, as were the implications of an Anglo-Italian agreement on the overall European situation. Anthony Eden says that at the end he had 'a faint feeling of confidence that Mussolini might possibly want the talks between us to succeed'.[30]

On 16 February, after the Berchtesgaden meeting therefore, Eden arranged a meeting between Grandi, Chamberlain and himself at which the Austrian question was to be discussed. Grandi had meanwhile proposed official negotiations but was met with marked mistrust on the part of the British. Eden comments that about this time he had become convinced by secret reports that Hitler was intending to liquidate Austria – with Mussolini's tacit agreement. He therefore thought negotiations in Rome inopportune at this time; 'it would be humiliating for us to be talking there when Hitler marched into Vienna and while Mussolini was reinforcing his troops in Spain and asking for recognition of his Abyssinian empire'.[31] On 17 February Chamberlain received a message from Ciano via his sister-in-law, Sir Austen's widow, who lived in Rome. It urged conclusion of the negotiations – 'Today an agreement will be easy but things are happening in Europe which will make it impossible tomorrow.'[32]

On 18 February there followed the talk between Grandi, Chamberlain and Eden. According to information available to the Berlin Foreign Ministry Chamberlain opened the discussion by asking Grandi about Austria but he refused to discuss it.[33] According to Eden's notes, approved by Chamberlain, discussion did in fact open with the Austrian question. The Prime Minister referred to the widely held view that there was some agreement between Italy and Germany about Austria. This was energetically denied by Grandi. Italy was not surprised by developments, he said, but they were certainly not the result of some pact between Italy and Germany. If nothing could be done to stop these developments, this was the result of the changed relationship between the Stresa Powers. When the Prime Minister objected that all was not yet lost in Austria, Grandi replied that we were perhaps at the end of the Third Act out of four. Italy was now in the position of having Germany on the Brenner and she could not risk finding herself alone confronting two potentially hostile Great Powers, Germany and Great Britain. If it proved impossible to create better relations with Great Britain, Italy would have to move closer to Germany; this would be a final decision; it had not yet been taken but there was not much time left.

Asked what effect the opening of negotiations in Rome, as proposed by Italy, would have on the Austrian problem, Grandi replied that it was very difficult to answer this question, although it might encourage people in Austria. Asked further whether the Italian government would be prepared to participate in an exchange of views on Austria with the Stresa Powers (Great Britain and France), he gave an evasive reply, saying that he had no instructions on the subject. The rest of the discussion dealt primarily with the question of intervention in Spain. From Grandi's attitude Eden concluded that there was no future in opening negotiations in Rome in the circumstances. Chamberlain, however, took the opposite view and was in principle ready to come to an understanding with Italy at the price of recognition of the Italian empire in Abyssinia and a compromise in the Mediterranean.[34]

Comparison of British and Italian sources leads to the supposition (it cannot be more) that at this period Mussolini really did intend to use the Rome negotiations in some way or other to reconstitute the so-called Stresa front. On 22 February, however, differences inside the British cabinet led to Eden's resignation. Ever since becoming Prime Minister Chamberlain had been pressing for an understanding with Italy; to reconstitute the Stresa front he was prepared to pay the price of recognition of the Italian conquest of Abyssinia and a Mediterranean agreement. His obvious purpose was to maintain the *status quo* in Europe and avoid dangerous upheavals with all their incalculable consequences. Prospects of these efforts succeeding in the early months of 1938, however, were, to say the least, problematical, primarily because Chamberlain's policy had no worthwhile military backing.[35]

Eden was deeply mistrustful of Mussolini, whom he accused of having broken various agreements over the Spanish question; he was working for a genuine League of Nations regime as guarantor of conventional relations under international law. Neither he nor Chamberlain was prepared to sacrifice Austria in principle but, in view of the state of British armaments and his own fundamentally peaceful policy, Chamberlain would have no truck with any possibility of military intervention. It may therefore be assumed that Mussolini was serious about these negotiations, thinking that he could get a *quid pro quo*. In fact Great Britain gave *de jure* recognition to the Italian conquest of Abyssinia on 16 April 1938 – two months too late for Central Europe.

It is quite possible, indeed probable, that had Anglo-Italian negotiations produced some positive result before 20 February, Hitler would at least have postponed action against Austria; his entire concept was based on the inevitability of conflict between the Western Powers and therefore on the impossibility of re-establishment of the Stresa front.[36] This view of Mussolini's attitude is apparently contradicted by certain entries in Ciano's diary recording utterances by Mussolini during the crisis period. Though their authenticity is not in doubt, they are probably to be accounted for by the temperament of the Italian Dictator who was not always to be taken literally and was subject to sudden changes of mood.[37]

A report dated 25 February 1938 from von Plessen, the German Chargé d'Affaires in Rome, shows clearly that Germany had acted without prior agreement with Italy and that Italy by no means welcomed the situation created by the blatant German efforts to annex Austria from the beginning of 1938. The report deals with Italian reactions to Hitler's Reichstag speech of 20 February and describes the frame of mind in the Palazzo Venezia (Mussolini's office) and Palazzo Chigi (the Italian Foreign Ministry); it says:

'In my opinion there is no doubt that Italy is not entirely pleased with recent developments in the Austrian question. In the press and in the Foreign Ministry, to be sure, it is emphasised that they are entirely satisfied with the result of the meeting at Berchtesgaden. However this cannot conceal the true frame of mind. Whether she likes it or not, Italy will perhaps finally become reconciled to something which, as she has been aware for a long time, she cannot change. But she certainly does not like the course of events. This fact appears to me particularly worth noting at a time when Anglo-Italian relations are entering a new stage.'

Von Plessen attached a memorandum dated 24 February which he said originated from a reliable informant:

'Although the Führer's Reichstag speech as a whole was received with sympathy and understanding in official Italian circles and although particularly the statements regarding the collaboration of the two revolutions and the appreciation of Mussolini caused great satisfaction, the impression prevails here that German-Italian co-operation should, in the opinion of Germany, be confined to the stand against Moscow and Geneva. Announcement of a considerably more far-reaching cooperation would have been desirable. . . . Above all, however, a confirmation of Austria's independence is missed. Hitler had spoken only of supplementing the Agreements of July 11 1936. The impression prevails here that the Berchtesgaden Agreement is the result of sudden pressure which may substantially change the character of the Agreement of July 11. Germany, moreover, had not previously consulted Italy, as had been agreed upon. If Berlin should continue to use this method, it would no longer be possible to speak of cooperation, and the danger would arise that the respective political lines would diverge. They also claim to know in the Palazzo Chigi that the British Government, and particularly Chamberlain personally, are very much concerned about the Berchtesgaden Agreement and the procedure that was used in regard to Austria. According to the opinion here there is the danger that, just when the prospects for an understanding between England, Italy and Germany have considerably improved, German policy in regard to Austria is furnishing very effective and disturbing arguments to the counter-propaganda of Eden and the Quai d'Orsay. . . . Italy . . . fears that German policy in regard to Austria tends to precipitate and accelerate matters too much. In Italian opinion this would necessarily result in disturbing the existing balance, also upsetting the state of the rest of Europe in a manner which cannot as yet be foreseen.

Germany wished . . . to retain her freedom of action and did not feel sufficiently strong as yet to decide matters in Europe by force of arms in the immediate future. If, however, an alliance and war were to be ruled out, no other solution remains but cooperation, or at least another attempt at cooperation, with the Western Powers excluding Soviet Russia. But if this attempt is to be made, then, in order to avoid violent clashes and conflicts in the near future, the Austrian question must not be precipitated. Anxiety is felt here in this respect, however, because further German surprises are not considered impossible but, on the contrary, are feared.'[38]

Barely five weeks separated 12 February from 11 March 1938. Even after the first week it was clear that the only hope of saving Austria lay in the field of foreign policy; only an early Anglo-Italian settlement and the resulting possibility of re-establishing the European Powers' *status quo* policy could guarantee that future developments would be peaceful. In comparison the immediate problem was of minor proportions; the results of the First World War had been devastating, the results of a second would be crushing.

Admittedly there were many in Austria who felt that the only salvation lay in union with Germany, largely as a result of their traumatic experiences of 1919 and subsequent years. A generation had grown up under the influence of unrestrained Anschluss propaganda; in so far as Austria was referred to as their country at all, either at school or at home, the historical picture of it which children were given was a deliberately distorted one. The short-sightedness of the victor Powers and the successor states had had much to do with this process; the result was that people took refuge in a National-Socialist dream-world.

On the other hand there was an equal number who, both sentimentally and rationally, were and wished to remain Austrians. Their picture of Central Europe included a new Austria but with her old historic mission; they considered the Anschluss to be detrimental to Austrian, German and European interests alike; they therefore opposed all Anschluss talk as illusory and were as passionate in their rejection as were the others in their glorification of it as the only possible solution. Admittedly the 'Austrians', who preferred to call themselves Tyrolese, Upper Austrians, Viennese and so forth, were often at first just as dissatisfied with the new political system as were the others who either simply wished to attach to it the label 'German' or demolish it altogether. The red-white-red flag was hoisted in 1932 and that was just ten years too late.

This does not mean that the German-speaking Austrians who for simplicity's sake may be termed conservatives, were anti-German, although in the argument between shoes and jackboots hard words flew back and forth from time to time. The anti-Anschluss Austrians who were committed heart and soul to the independence of their country without necessarily meandering off into ideas about restoration, were by no means anti-German and had no wish to be. Historically, geographically and economically they would make common cause with Germany in the service of Europe, peace, progress and culture – but they would not become German property.[39]

The situation had altered with the victory of National-Socialism in Germany. This had brought with it a claim to totalitarian political authority without regard for national frontiers. With the proclamation of nationality as a law of nature was coupled the call to national revolution and this was held to justify the use of new revolutionary methods to enforce compliance with the claim. The creeping crisis in Austria and in Europe originated from the identification of 'German' with 'National-Socialist'.

Hitler, an Austrian by birth, proclaimed that the two were identical for evermore and was followed with enthusiasm by the mass of people for whom he was a prophet promising them a future in a Promised Land; with every success, ostensible or genuine, his star seemed to shine brighter. To his opponents, however, he was nothing but a fleeting comet, an episode in German history, not its fulfilment.

In reality the tragedy of 1945 sprang from this identification of Hitler with the fulfilment of German history; in 1938 that tragedy was only a presentiment; it could not be foreseen. Those who believed in Austria fought with all their might against the equation both of Germanism with National-Socialism and Hitler with German history. Many who initially favoured the Anschluss and thought the swastika not too high a price to pay for the achievement of their national goal realised their mistake soon enough. Despite all the jubilation – and many later alibis to prove why one had been on the wrong side for a time – one thing is certain: no one wanted what happened in March 1938 and afterwards and no one had foreseen it.

It is of course true that after 12 February 1938 Austria was autonomous only within limits. The Minister responsible for public security owed his office to Hitler and, were he to resign, Hitler would have a free hand. On my recommendation, however, he was a member of the Council of State, though not of the government; he had certain obligations towards Austria too. Much was clearly going to depend on how he could and would tackle his admittedly difficult job.

Before 12 February Seyss-Inquart undoubtedly knew more than he admitted; for some time, and without reporting the fact, he had been in close touch with Keppler, the German Nazi Party's Commissioner for Austria. Nevertheless, so far as one could tell, there was much that initially he did not know, which explains the difference in his attitude before and after. Like the Austrian government, he too had welcomed as a relief the removal of Captain Leopold and his group of Nazi leaders, the revolutionaries in other words. According to his lights he was an evolutionist. The antipathy between the two wings of the Austrian Nazi Party was in fact greater than we knew.

Leopold had been nominated *Landesleiter* of the illegal Austrian Nazi Party by Hitler and remained so even after 11 July 1936. In a long letter to Hitler from Krems on 22 August 1937 he had complained bitterly about Seyss-Inquart and von Papen and asked for an interview so that he could explain verbally; significantly he referred in this letter to the fact that, during his last visit on 3 May 1937, Hitler had explicitly authorised him to report 'if anyone in Austria was incommoding him in his work'.[40] Meanwhile Keppler had been appointed Nazi Party Commissioner for Austria and had got in touch with Seyss-Inquart and his staff, including Anton Reinthaller, Franz Langoth, Friedrich Rainer and Odilo Globocnik.[41] The interview Leopold asked for did not take place.

By this time Leopold was at odds with von Papen too. On 8

September 1937 he wrote again to Hitler accusing Keppler of ignorance of Austrian conditions and obviously aiming to have him removed and eliminate the influence of Germans in Austrian Party affairs. Leopold also complained about Seyss-Inquart's staff and said that he would have to expel Globocnik for behaviour injurious to the Party. This was all the more remarkable in that, as we found in February and March 1938, Globocnik was a revolutionary like Leopold and, when in Germany, had urged military intervention in Austria – presumably without Seyss-Inquart's knowledge. Captain Fritz Wiedemann, Hitler's aide, passed Leopold's letter to Keppler, who returned it on 3 November with a request for an interview with Hitler to discuss the Austrian question. On 30 September 1937 Leopold journeyed to Berlin and again asked for an interview with Hitler which was refused on Keppler's advice.[42] On 1 October 1937 in a memorandum entitled 'Some Thoughts' Leopold repeated his criticisms of Keppler and Seyss-Inquart, stressing that the latter had no official Party position; he was merely Schuschnigg's go-between for relations between the Austrian Nazis and the government.[43]

In fact Seyss-Inquart's position had been confirmed by a report from von Papen to Hitler dated 14 July 1937 which, as Papen himself said, was intended to give Seyss a good start. This was unknown to Leopold. In the summer of 1937 these tactical manœuvrings and personal intrigues led to a complete breach between the Leopold group and the German Embassy.[44] In addition Leopold complained about 'intrigues' by Eduard Frauenfeld, the ex-*Gauleiter* who had fled to the Reich in 1934, and his friends outside the country.

A letter of 10 February 1938 from Keppler to Ribbentrop shows that, even as late as this, Leopold was still trying to assert himself as the Nazi Leader in Austria and opposing Keppler and Seyss-Inquart. The letter accuses the Austrian Nazis of being 'engaged almost exclusively in illegal activities' in spite of the Führer's repeated instructions 'that we should do less illegal fighting and shift our work to more lawful activities'. (This continuation of illegal activity after 11 July 1936 and the refusal to 'shift to more lawful activities' was one of the main and repeated points of complaint by Austria against the Reich for non-observance of the agreement.) The letter continues that Leopold had evidently got wind of the forthcoming negotiations (in Berchtesgaden) and had organised big demonstrations in the last week. As a result 400 men had been arrested two days before and some 400 Hitler Youth expelled from school; the Hitler Youth 'evidently in accordance with Leopold's wishes, also began rioting, etc., which led to a great many expulsions from school'. Lauterbacher, executive officer to the Reich Youth Leader, was also said to be 'not at all pleased with these developments' and to be willing to put an end to these abuses, 'for it serves no useful purpose and is not in accordance with the Führer's wishes if arrests are made and misery inflicted on the Party members in Austria on such a scale, without any commensurate success'.[45]

After 12 February even larger-scale violence was planned; with the assistance of members of the former leadership released under the amnesty the revolutionaries did their best to torpedo the agreement – obviously to prove that they alone were able to solve the Austrian problem.[46]

Relations between the potential Nazi leaders in Austria were therefore very strained, primarily for personal rather than objective reasons. Leopold was counting on being appointed Chancellor in the event of a Nazi seizure of power and was bitterly disappointed when he found himself to all intents and purposes empty-handed in March 1938. Even from his bitterest enemies, however, he is entitled to some respect for his behaviour after 1939: he volunteered for active service and fell commanding a battalion fighting for the cause in which he had believed.

From the Austrian point of view the quarrels inside the Nazi leadership had their advantages. The police were often able to act on the basis of information supplied by the various sections of the Nazi movement to incriminate each other; much that was denounced by Germany as 'nationalist persecution' stemmed from denunciations from within their own ranks.

In the longer term, however, these internal disagreements carried with them serious dangers. They were liable to accelerate Hitler's decision to intervene in Austria on a large scale 'to re-establish order'; moreover they were grist to the mill of those authorities in Berlin who thought that, after incorporation, Austria should be under purely German administration. Early in 1938, for instance, a meeting was held in Gestapo headquarters in the Prinz-Albrecht-Strasse, Berlin, in preparation for a 'seizure of power' in Austria and the question of the return of Austrian public officials who had fled to Germany was discussed. Heydrich, who was in the chair, was emphatic that German officials only should be employed in Austria.[47]

Veesenmayer's situation report of 18 February referred to above,[48] in addition to false rumours and exaggerations, contains much that is accurate; it says:

'On the basis of a detailed and comprehensive 4-day observation, it must be stated that the break-through succeeded absolutely and is much deeper than is assumed in many quarters in the Reich. After the Powers had left Schuschnigg in the lurch, he immediately saw his former supports partly fall away, partly quarrel among themselves, and fight furiously over the succession to the Chancellorship. In legitimist circles chaos prevails; all hope has been abandoned. In Jewish circles the conviction prevails that it is now only a matter of time until Austria is politically and economically united with the Reich. The collapse is so complete that, *if an acceleration of developments fits into the Führer's foreign policy, a number of decisive positions can be captured within the succeeding weeks by means of definite pressure on the part of the Reich.* Of great importance is the imminent removal of President Kienböck of the National Bank, who, as an avowed friend of the Jews, not only tolerates the present catastrophic policy of the Jews, but even promotes it. . . . The position of the illegal Party has become extremely critical. I succeeded through level-headed intermediaries in getting Herr Leopold to leave for the Reich on February 18 1938, and he arrived in Berlin on the morning of February 19, stopping at the Hotel Fürstenhof. On February 17 another very unfortunate circular was issued by the Party, a copy of which has already been transmitted. *In addition telephone messages from Vienna today disclose that activities on a rather large scale are planned by the illegal Party.* According to a communication just received, Dr Tavs, who was released yesterday, gave instructions to smash all windows in the German Legation this evening. One of the most important persons in the entourage of Captain Leopold, Herr Rüdiger, an engineer, had the presumption to assert to some business executives whom he had called to a meeting that even the Führer had no right to meddle in Austrian affairs.

It is further planned to provoke the Minister of Security, Seyss-Inquart, into further arrests and then brand him as a traitor to the National cause. Under these circumstances Leopold's presence here became dangerous and something had to be done. On the other hand it would have been intolerable for the movement if he had had to be sent to the Reich by force; therefore his departure yesterday in the manner stated was perhaps the only solution as regards time and manner. Our reliable Party people and the SS have strict instructions to prevent, as far as possible, any demonstrations and it is to be hoped that they will succeed.'

Nevertheless, as viewed from the Ballhausplatz, apart from the inevitable irritations things proceeded in a more or less orderly fashion up to 20 February. On 17 February Seyss-Inquart visited Hitler in Berlin and reported on his return. According to his own evidence he said that

'he intended to take his stand on the basis of a free independent Austria, in other words to respect the legal constitution, to avoid any violence and to guide Austria to a free expression of opinion. In no circumstances did he wish to play the role of Trojan Horse in a new *Kulturkampf*. His adherence to the government must constitute a guarantee that neither of the two parties to the agreement would abandon evolution and seek to impose a solution by force.'[49]

During his first week as a member of the cabinet it seemed that Seyss-Inquart was both willing and able to control his own people. Inevitably there was a marked feeling of uncertainty and depression in Fatherland Front circles. The illegal Nazis, however, were no better off; they felt at first that they had been sacrificed by Hitler and saw their dream of German intervention disappear – and on this their leaders had based all their hopes. As four years before in Germany, the mass of SA men in Austria – and Leopold's illegal organisation had been primarily SA – were deeply disillusioned; they felt that they had been outmanœuvred by a small group of SS intellectuals, the know-alls.

Hitler's Reichstag speech of 20 February, however, set events in a new perspective and things began to move again; hope revived among Austrian National-Socialists. In spite of some standard friendly phrases about Austria indicating respect for Austrian independence, the speech culminated in an unmistakable threat: the German people was no longer willing to tolerate oppression of ten million Germans on its borders. (There were seven million Austrians and three million Sudeten-Germans.) This could mean only Austria and Czechoslovakia. Admittedly Hitler had referred to 'the spirit of the agreement of 11 July 1936' with Austria – and that had stipulated non-interference.

It soon became known, however, that a few days after the Berchtesgaden agreement Hitler had appointed the Austrian ex-Major Hubert Klausner to be *Landesleiter* (illegal) of the Austrian NSDAP; a *Gauleiter* (also illegal) had been appointed for each province; Globocnik and Rainer of Seyss-Inquart's staff had been nominated executives in the headquarters of the new organisation. In short Hitler had reactivated the National-Socialist Party in Austria.

On 26 February Hitler himself summoned Keppler, Leopold and the ex-members of the illegal Austrian Party leadership and, according to a note by Keppler, told them that 'Seyss-Inquart did not enter into consideration as Party leader and had, besides, already rejected this position'. There could be only two solutions for Austria, he said, force or evolution; he wished the evolutionary course to be taken whether or not the possibility of success could be foreseen today; the Protocol signed by Schuschnigg was so far-reaching that, if completely carried out, the Austrian problem would be solved automatically; he did not desire a solution by violent means now, if it could be in any way avoided since 'the danger for us in the field of foreign policy became less each year and our military power greater each year'. The note ends with the statement: 'The Führer informed the gentlemen that he had entrusted the Austrian problem to me' (Keppler).[50]

The Berchtesgaden agreement had laid down that Seyss-Inquart should be the sole authority for relations with the Reich, but he now found himself completely by-passed. It had been explicitly agreed that the illegal organisation should be disbanded, but now Seyss-Inquart was confronted with a new illegal leadership presenting new demands over and above what had been agreed and carried out.

So the new tactics gradually became clear: Seyss-Inquart was nothing but a figure-head; his role was to play the loyal partner in the cabinet, but the tiller had been wrenched out of his hand. On the bridge now stood Dr Keppler supported by Dr Veesenmayer. Klausner, the new *Landesleiter*, had little say in matters, but the executive officers, Globocnik and Rainer, now set about deliberately radicalising the reorganised Party over the head of Seyss-Inquart.[51]

It soon became obvious what was meant by 'evolution': mobilisation of the mob, open provocation of political opponents, mass meetings, rallies and, to cap it all, a 'German Day in Austria'. Should there be incidents, as was almost inevitable, so much the better; every clash would produce fresh national martyrs; the executive would be forced to intervene; the alarm would be sounded – and then all preparations were made to call for immediate military assistance from the Third Reich. . . . But for the moment we had not yet reached that stage.

On 21 February the Austrian cabinet met for the last time before the Anschluss; harmony reigned. Measures were decided on to revive the economy, primarily in the fields of building and tourism; the result was an employment programme, agreed unanimously, visualising the expenditure of some three milliard schillings (at today's rate of exchange).[52] Göring later described this as a ridiculous drop in the ocean. It was also unlikely to satisfy Keppler who even before 12 February was visualising considerably more far-reaching objectives, as his letter to Ribbentrop of the 10th showed. In his eyes the main obstacle was Austria's monetary policy as directed by Dr Kienböck, President of the National Bank; in his view this needed fundamental alteration; revival of the Austrian economy and trade would, he considered, be child's play once the currency barrier between Germany and Austria had disappeared.[53]

On 24 February, twelve days after the Berchtesgaden agreement and four days after Hitler's Reichstag speech, I appeared before the Federal Diet. The formal reason was to present the newly-formed government, the real reason to make clear Austria's position both at home and abroad in unmistakable language; I intended to counter the Nazi erosion tactics with a firm statement that no further concessions were forthcoming since they would be incompatible with maintenance of an independent Austria and in open contravention of the recently concluded Berchtesgaden agreement. The vital sentence was: 'We knew that we could go, and did go, up to that boundary line beyond which appear, clearly and unequivocally the words "Thus far and no further".'

Towards the end of the month events began to move fast. Graz was obviously planned as the centre of unrest; there Dr Dadieu, head of the *Volkspolitische* Office for Styria, called for open revolt. New demands were being made continuously. Pressure for full legalisation of the Nazi Party and its formations with their uniforms, badges and typical propaganda ritual increased in violence; the reaction of non-Nazi Austrians accordingly became fiercer. It was now quite clear that Germany had no intention of abiding by the provisions of the Berchtesgaden agreement; by no possible stretch of the imagination could a revocation of the ban on the Nazi Party be read into it. On the contrary it was explicitly laid down that the individual National-Socialist, like the individual Social Democrat or anyone else, would be accepted into the Fatherland Front if he was prepared to accept its principles. It was now clear that a calculated attempt was being made to force the Austrian government to resign by increasing the pressure; with the assistance of possible transitional regimes it was then planned to bring about *Gleichschaltung* in the end. In 1938, as at any other time, this would have meant the end of Austria. Keppler would have got the raw materials he needed for his Four Year Plan; in view of the German currency situation currency equalisation alone would have turned Austria into a dependency of the Third Reich; Hitler would get his additional divisions which he wanted for his future plans (see the Hossbach Minutes). All this is not mere supposition; documentary proof of these tactics now exists.

Seyss-Inquart declared openly that he could do nothing in face of the 'dynamic of the Party'; he had hauled down his flag. Papen had packed up and left Vienna on the evening of 26 February.[54] In his letter to Ribbentrop of 28 February Keppler enclosed a memorandum as follows:

'Dr Seyss-Inquart today sent me the following report on the situation from Reichenhall:

"In Austria, among the people, things have become fairly quiet. The Party is maintaining discipline. It was especially encouraging during the last few days to note to what an unexpected degree Labor has come over to our side. Even in the Alpine Mining Company, where the board of directors assumed 70 per cent to be communists, some two-thirds of the workmen are said to have marched on our side. Meanwhile strong efforts to sabotage the Agreement are being made in Vienna by foreign countries, particularly by Soviet Russia, France, England and Italy. Besides Prince Colonna, Salata, the former Minister to Vienna, has arrived in Vienna. Furthermore, Schuschnigg on the day of his speech (February 24) had a long talk with the Duce.

The Government, by-passing Dr Seyss-Inquart, is also doing everything it can to sabotage the Agreement. Thus instructions have been issued to officials by various provincial governments forbidding participation in National-Socialist activities. Also attempts are being made on the part of the Marxists, with Government support, to marshal Labor against the Agreement. The work of obtaining signatures, in particular, is continuing. It has, moreover, been definitely established that Catholics and Marxists, perhaps to a certain extent in agreement with the Government, have distributed arms to the workers." '[55]

Whether this report originated with Seyss-Inquart it is not possible to say. In any case it is full of inaccuracies. Things were by no means 'fairly quiet' in Austria, although at this time the Nazi Party was still obeying the orders of its leaders; neither on the day of my speech nor before nor after did I talk to the Duce; there was no question of the distribution of arms to workers, at least at this time.

Other countries too were following the dangerous developments in Austria with close attention. On 23 February von Neurath, in his capacity as President of the Secret Cabinet Council, noted that François-Poncet, the French Ambassador in Berlin, had referred to Austria saying that: 'France could not acquiesce in our brushing aside Austria's independence, which was guaranteed by international treaties.' Von Neurath had replied that the case of Austria was entirely a bilateral matter. It was not correct to say that the Austrian question was subject to an international settlement. The only agreement was that of Stresa, but this was no longer in force since Italy was not now a party to it and in any case it was not binding on third parties.[56] On 1 March Graf Welczeck, the German Ambassador in Paris, reported that Flandin, ex-Foreign Minister of France, had said to him: 'If we proceeded gradually with respect to the Austrians and without offending against form, we could achieve very much in the way of "coordination" without any objections; what mattered was the procedure. But a formal Anschluss had to be avoided under any circumstances.'[57]

Before this, on 21 February, Yvon Delbos, the French Foreign Minister, had said at a press conference that 'faithful to the principle of collective security' France 'could not disinterest herself in the fate of Austria'. Paris had in fact suggested to London that a strong combined protest should be made, but owing to Eden's resignation on 20 February the proposal remained unanswered. On 25 February a long debate on French foreign policy took place in the French Chamber, when much play was made with my speech of the previous day; the general sense of the debate was that action was now necessary. Delbos described Austrian independence as an essential factor in the European balance.[58]

On 7 March Major-General Jahn, our Military Attaché in Paris, arrived in Vienna bringing a note from Vollgruber, our Minister there, about a long talk he had had with Alexis Saint-Léger, Secretary-General of the French Foreign Ministry. It said:

> 'The existence of Czechoslovakia and the independence of Austria are among the dispositions in Europe which the French government considers vital to the interests of France. Leading authorities in France are convinced that, sooner or later, Germany will attempt another

coup against the independence of Austria and that, should this succeed, it will then be Czechoslovakia's turn. At present France seems in principle prepared to draw the sword if necessary in defence of either of these two positions. In practice, however, she must ensure that this extreme step takes place only under the most favourable conditions, which of course entails ensuring the participation of England. If England were ready, if necessary, to defend Austrian independence by force of arms, France too would go to war for it; if this is not so, however, failing a change in the Italian attitude meanwhile, France would await the rape of Czechoslovakia since, in the view of authoritative French circles, this must drag England into war. Since, however, France hopes that war might perhaps somehow be avoided if it is possible to persuade Germany of the seriousness of the situation which would ensue from a rape of Austria, she will first make further efforts to get England to take an active interest in the Austrian *status quo*. Hope that such efforts may succeed persists, based, in the first place, upon a favourable outcome to the long drawn out Anglo-Italian negotiations and secondly upon a possible early return of Mr Eden when the effects of the Anglo-Italian negotiations are seen. . . .

England may, of course, decide to take an active interest in Austrian independence, in which case the rape of Austria would present France with a favourable opportunity to strike; alternatively England may still hold back but a fresh coup might force France to consider drawing the sword in the hope that the turmoil of events would drag England in. In either case, however, France would only draw the sword if the case of rape were clear, in other words if the Austrian government itself considered that it had been assaulted, if the Austrian people reacted against this assault and if German propaganda had not succeeded in convincing French public opinion that the only genuine Austrians in Austria were the government and one or two diplomats.'[59]

On 17 February Oliver Sargent, the Deputy Under-Secretary of State in the Foreign Office, told Woermann, the German Chargé d'Affaires, that the idea of a joint *démarche* had been rejected by the British cabinet.[60] On 16 February, after contacting Georg Franckenstein, the Austrian Minister in London, Eden gave an evasive reply to a question in the House. This was what we wanted and Franckenstein was acting on our instructions. In the first week after Berchtesgaden we still hoped to prevent a panic mood, particularly in London and, if the facts had come out into the open, this would have been inevitable. The steep fall of Austrian securities on the London stock market gave an alarming impression.[61]

During another debate in the House on 22 February, overshadowed by Eden's resignation, the only positive declaration of support for Austria came from Winston Churchill: 'If it were possible for Italy to discharge her duty in aiding Great Britain and France in defending the integrity and independence of Austria, for the sake of that I would go as far as any man in making concessions.'[62] To a question from Arthur Henderson on 2 March Chamberlain replied:

> 'There was nothing to convey the impression that he himself [the Austrian Chancellor] considered that the independence of his country had been yielded up to another country. . . . It still remains to be seen what the practical effect of the agreement might turn out to be. In this connection I may say that His Majesty's Government obviously cannot disinterest themselves in events in Central Europe. . . . It is at present too early for His Majesty's Government to estimate the effect of the recent arrangements between Germany and Austria. . . . I am glad to note from the speech made by the German Chancellor on 20 February that these arrangements are to be considered as an extension to the framework of the Austro-German agreement on 11 July 1936. That agreement . . . provided among other things for the recognition by the German Government of the full sovereignty of the Federal State of Austria. There, I think, we must leave the matter for the present but His Majesty's Government will continue to watch what goes on in Austria with the closest possible attention and interest.'[63]

During the time between Eden's resignation on 20 February and Chamberlain's statement in the House on 2 March, however, things had moved noticeably in Austria. Naturally during these critical weeks we followed with the utmost satisfaction anything said, written or planned in support of Austria, particularly in Paris and London; from the end of the month we waited impatiently. The clearer it became that Germany regarded the Berchtesgaden agreement merely as a springboard (in other words from about the last week of February), the more obvious it was that only some energetic joint step by the Great Powers could preserve the *status quo* in Europe and with it Austria's independence. Today we know that it is doubtful whether such a step, if in the form of a diplomatic *démarche*, would have stopped developments but it would probably have delayed them, thereby offering everybody, Germany included, an opportunity of adopting positions more favourable to progress in the immediate future.

As I have already said Vienna had two alternatives:

1. To sound the alarm as loudly as possible immediately after Berchtesgaden. This would have entailed a breach with Germany and this we could not risk in view of the international situation, the vital interests of our own people and their mood at the time.

2. To do everything humanly possible to fulfil the agreement, to place Germany obviously in the wrong if she broke it and to gain time. The Rome-Berlin Axis was vulnerable, Hitler only human and not without opposition, and the Nazi leaders were not Germany.

It was, of course, important that governments, primarily those in Rome, London and Paris, should know what had really gone on. They were told in detail only a few days after Berchtesgaden and so were in a position to draw their own conclusions. Rome we informed direct and Paris and London were briefed by their diplomatic representatives in Vienna. In addition, as we knew in Vienna, the Foreign Office in London had received full information without any action on our part through its own secret service in Germany.[64]

It is true that we asked for assistance or advice neither from London nor from Paris; it is also true that Austrian representatives were instructed to express the hope that the agreements reached with Hitler would be fulfilled. Could we have done anything else if we did not wish to make it easy for Hitler to accuse Austria of breach of the agreement from the outset? In addition, experience had shown that communications from Vienna to foreign countries were not invariably watertight and we therefore had to assume that any steps we took would immediately become known to Berlin.[65] Anyone who has the fire-raiser in his house usually has difficulties in getting into touch with the police and the fire brigade.

Reduced to its simplest terms, the situation was this: Either the Western Powers shared Aristide Briand's view *L'Anschluss c'est la guerre*; in that case they would act without awaiting any steps by Austria which they could hardly expect in the circumstances; they had, after all, acted between 1919 and 1931 not only without Austria but against her will. Alternatively they were prepared for concessions as in the preceding years (witness the Anglo-German Naval Agreement of 1935); in that case an Austrian request would not have affected the ultimate issue and would merely have impaired Austria's position and that of her people.

In the West opinion on future European developments had been divided for years. As early as spring 1935 Sir Eric Phipps, the British Ambassador in Berlin and previously Minister in Vienna, had forecast that Hitler would go to war later. At the same period André François-Poncet, his French colleague, estimated that 'war would break out, should there be disturbances in Austria or Danzig giving Hitler the opportunity to intervene'. In November 1936 President Roosevelt suggested an international conference in view of the threat to world peace, openly expressing his mistrust of Hitler. During a private stay in Berlin in mid-December 1937 Flandin, the French ex-Prime Minister, talked to Neurath and Goebbels and came away convinced that Germany would move into Austria before the next three months were up. François-Poncet records that, talking to Sir Nevile Henderson, the British Ambassador, Flandin laid him a bet: 'The Englishman says: "We're moving towards peace", the Frenchman: "It's the calm before the storm"; who is right?'[66] Finally, since Germany's openly declared rearmament in 1935, it was by no means clear whether and how London, Paris and Washington (there was as yet no question of Moscow in this connection) would react to a threat of war.

All this is not said to shift the burden of responsibility on to other shoulders. The European order of 1938 stood or fell by the concept of collective security; in this Anthony Eden was entirely right. In view of the international conflict of interests, however, this principle could be acted upon only if an order of priority of those interests were agreed – but that is another story. The vital fact was that in 1938 neither Britain nor France felt strong enough to oppose the expansionism of a rearmed Third Reich by force, if necessary. But all this was nothing like so obvious at the beginning of March 1938 as it is today.

The pace of events in Austria made a decision urgent; every day might bring the internal explosion which we feared and which the Nazis were doing everything in their power to provoke. We just succeeded in postponing the planned 'German Day'. The turning point was a visit to Vienna by Dr Keppler on 4 and 5 March. On his own admission he had come to present fresh demands; in fact they included everything which he had originally proposed or which Globocnik and Rainer had suggested to him via Veesenmayer but which we had managed to delete from the Berchtesgaden agreement.

Keppler was a long-standing Party member and an *SS-Gruppenführer*; officially he was now an Under-Secretary of State in the Foreign Ministry; he had long been one of Hitler's immediate entourage; in January 1933 he had accompanied Hitler to the famous and momentous luncheon party in von Schröder's house in Cologne.[67] Keppler had been Hitler's Party Commissioner for Austria since mid-1937. At this time there were three more or less independent channels of communication between Germany and Austria: first there was Keppler, the *eminence grise* on Austrian questions, who used Veesenmayer as his staff officer; secondly there was the official channel through Ambassador von Papen; finally there was Otto von Stein, an enthusiastic friend and supporter of the NSDAP to which he had belonged since 1928, and a confidant of Captain Leopold.[68]

Outwardly Keppler was pleasant and not at all the arrogant Nazi of the type of von Stein; he bore no relation to the various sorts of SS boor whose acquaintance we were soon to make in the Vienna Gestapo headquarters and the concentration camps. Even the SS were not all cast in one mould.

Keppler's main interest was economic. He knew little about Austria and merely regarded it as a natural economic appendage of Germany. For him the Anschluss was an economic imperative, as practically all Austrians had thought about 1920 and later. He took no account of the fact that Austria had meanwhile found her place in the world economy and that, despite setbacks, depressions and the world economic crisis she could show a highly promising upward trend economically; he equally brushed aside the undeniable fact that his favourite scheme of a currency union meant the abandonment of the Austrian schilling, a hard and stable currency, and that the price of Austria's adherence to the German market would be her exclusion from world markets. Austrian production figures had in fact risen remarkably since 1929 in all important fields – steel, petroleum, cereals, potatoes, sugar, milk, meat; the railways had at last been put in order and the tourist trade was rising. Keppler remained imperturbably friendly but simply impervious to all this. His conclusion was that any sensible Austrian, and not the Nazis only, must be longing for the Anschluss for economic reasons – and an economic Anschluss was not possible without a political one. The Führer's wish at the time was for an evolutionary development; in other words he wished to roll up Austria from within, if possible without any apparent German involvement. Keppler thought that the time had come to accelerate this process.

At first sight Keppler's reasoning seemed convincing on one point: the figures of unemployed in Austria, though slowly falling, were a serious factor influencing both the economy and the general popular mood. Even including those not on public assistance, however, they never reached the heights which later propaganda ascribed to them; the monthly average during 1937 was 321,000 against a peak of 406,000 registered unemployed in 1933 and 350,000 in 1936.[69] The forecast that the Anschluss and a currency union would quickly eliminate the unemployment problem was correct – but at a price (not realised at the time) of absorption into a deceptive 'economic boom' inspired and directed by a political ideology which was set on autarchy and armaments and determined to challenge the world.

On 4 March Keppler presented himself to Schmidt, the Foreign Minister, in Vienna and put forward his new political demands; he also protested about alleged unsatisfactory fulfilment of various provisions in the Berchtesgaden agreement. Schmidt told him that the new demands lacked all justification and referred him to me.[70]

At 5.45 p.m. on 5 March I received Keppler in my house. The interview lasted some forty minutes. According to Keppler's notes it 'began tempestuously but concluded in an entirely conciliatory manner'; he continues that he 'had the impression that Schuschnigg will by no means submit to force but that, if treated sensibly, he will come along to a great extent, if this is made possible for him without loss of prestige. We can rely on his loyalty as regards the Berchtesgaden agreements.'[71] In fact I had the definite feeling that Keppler was acting on instructions and, in his urbane way, was presenting the bill for my statement on 24 February – 'Thus far and no further'. He now demanded everything which had been laboriously eliminated from the original list in Berchtesgaden on 12 February, in other words everything on which he was specially keen: immediate appointment of Dr Hans Fischböck, the bank director and Nazi economic expert, as Minister of Economics, raising of the number of exchange officers from fifty to the hundred originally demanded, immediate cancellation of the ban on German newspapers including the *Völkischer Beobachter*, far-reaching economic measures including the introduction of strict currency control to prevent the flight of capital. His main demand, however, was, in his own words, 'the elimination of the illegal movement by the formal legalisation of National-Socialism'. This was the point in the original so-called Keppler programme which had not been agreed in Berchtesgaden; it could not be agreed, for it was in clear contravention of the explicit recognition of the Austrian constitution.

I flatly rejected all these demands and referred Keppler to the wording of the Berchtesgaden agreement, saying that it was quite impossible for us to go beyond it. At the end Hitler himself had said in so many words that, if the agreed provisions were fulfilled, our quarrel was at an end and it was quite incomprehensible to me how anyone could come along, barely four weeks later, with a fresh set of demands. There then followed a discussion on the Austrian standpoint in the struggle ever since 1933; I stated that cooperation with Austrian National-Socialism was possible only on the basis of recognition of Austrian independence long term and of the current constitution which forbade the formation of political parties; I pointed out that we had previously been able to work with the Pan-Germans and had not demanded that they should renounce their basic views on the German question, in other words their national ideology. The interview ended inconclusively but I had the definite impression that the boats were now burnt, although Keppler took note of my rejection with polite sorrow and neither hectored nor threatened.

The next, and last, occasion on which I met Dr Keppler was late in the evening of 11 March in the Federal Chancellery after I had resigned. He was apparently as unruffled as ever and said: 'Now you see, a few days ago you made a scene over a few minor requests I put to you. You would have done better to give way.' He then asked if there was anything he could do for me personally.[72]

Keppler's object in Vienna on 4 and 5 March was obviously to get things moving; this emerges clearly from his memorandum written on return to Berlin on 6 March; extracts are as follows:

'In Austria the Party is now in fine shape. . . . Leopold is hardly mentioned any more. In particular there is satisfaction wherever one goes at the fact that the road for further progress is now clearly outlined. . . . Graz has progressed most; it is estimated that about 80 per cent of the population has professed National-Socialism. In other parts of the country they are jealous because it has not yet been possible to prove that the percentage of National-Socialism there is of corresponding importance. At present we are inclined to apply the brakes to the movement, in order to wring more and more concessions from Schuschnigg. It seems the prime necessity, for the time being, to secure for the future further possibilities of organising legally and for that reason to forgo a parade or two.

This coming Sunday, on the occasion of Heroes' Memorial Day, great National-Socialist celebrations and parades will take place. It has further been promised that a "German Day" for all of Austria will soon take place, with great National-Socialist parades. . . .

"Heil Hitler" and the Hitler salute are permitted and the negotiations regarding permission for a National-Socialist badge with a swastika look quite favourable. While stamped swastikas are not yet officially approved, they are tolerated everywhere. . . .

Dr Seyss-Inquart makes use of the SA and SS to a great extent, even in his official tasks; with their help he brought about orderly conditions again within a very short time in Graz, where it was generally feared that the movement would get out of hand, and he emphasised to Schuschnigg that this was only possible by utilising the old organisations and leaders, as a result of the discipline which prevailed there. . . .

On the basis of all my impressions I believe that *the Party is again ready for action and, as a disciplined body, can be used in the political game* and that Dr Seyss-Inquart will to a great extent be successful in obtaining the possibility of organising legally.

There is no more material for flags and no brown cloth to be had in Austria. The factories have large orders for more.

In Graz extensive fraternisation has taken place with the military and the police, who took a very correct attitude everywhere. It is to be hoped that after further fraternising and after the incorporation of exchange officers, the use of the military and the police against the Party will no longer be possible. Apparently there is also a great influx from Labor, although the Communists and the trade unions and radicals from the Fatherland Front are endeavouring to mobilise a popular front. . . .

In the opposition camp there are many who are now discovering long-standing National-Socialist convictions and are seeking to join. On the other hand, many are coming forward who previously found it impossible to show their colours freely.'[73]

Against this background, both internal and external, we were clearly facing a 'bend or break' situation.

Hence the decision to hold the plebiscite.

ACROSS THE RUBICON

A plebiscite was first seriously considered in late February 1938 in view of general developments in Austria and the international situation; the decision was finally and irrevocably taken on 4 March. We did so primarily because we were convinced that a hard-core minority of Nazi activists was preparing armed insurrection in the near future. Peaceful assimilation of Austria to Germany, which the majority of Nazis wanted, would lead to the Anschluss sooner or later; on that everyone was agreed.

Despite the agreements of 11 July 1936 and Berchtesgaden, Hitler's policy aimed at and calculated on this assimilation from within, in other words without visible German involvement; Germany did everything she could to promote it. We could not be unaware of this in Austria – and we were not. Consequently there could never be a genuine relaxation of tension; our diplomatic relations were reduced to a continuous stream of reciprocal remonstrances.

So long as international guarantees (Peace Treaties, League of Nations Covenant) held good or there was reason to assume that they would not break down completely, Austria's situation was serious but not hopeless. In February 1938 no one either in Vienna or the Western capitals realised that it had in fact become both serious and hopeless by the end of 1937 – any more than Berlin realised on the outbreak of war that what looked like a walk-over at first was in reality hopeless from the outset because of the immensity of the German war aims.[1]

In his treatise on the *Historical Course of Events in Austria* Walter Goldinger says:

'Berlin was disinclined to allot him [Seyss-Inquart] more than the role of a recipient of orders. Of course people there were calculating on a slow development. Schuschnigg was to be allowed a transitional period and then would come full re-establishment of the National-Socialist Party; after that it would only be a question of time before it asserted its claim to total authority.'[2]

This is true. Precisely for this reason we were driven to the plebiscite plan which Goldinger, Taylor, David Hoggan and others consider as the 'first error in the unequal struggle' and 'shortsighted'.[3]

As it turned out, the planned plebiscite triggered off German action on 11 March. Hitler shelved his plan to deal with the Austrian question by automatic evolution[4] and decided on invasion; Austria therefore forfeited the transitional period allotted to her pending assertion of Austrian National-Socialism's claim to total authority. Today, however, we know that the Third Reich was determined to absorb Austria in the immediate future. There were good reasons for fearing so at the time.

Naturally we had no intention of provoking Hitler to action. Instead we were clinging to the letter and spirit of the agreement and defending it against sabotage on the part of the illegal Party. As in the months following the July agreement, however, this sabotage was deliberate; Veesenmayer's situation report of 18 February 1938 refers to 'activities on a rather large scale' being planned.[5] That our purpose was to defend the Berchtesgaden agreement (which had been fully observed on the Austrian side) is proved by the fact that we seriously considered including affirmation of it in the plebiscite formula to ensure that it had broad-based support. Our errors, of course, lay in the failure to foresee Hitler's reaction and in underestimation of the difference of interpretation of the agreement between Berlin and Vienna.

Lack of foresight and its resulting errors led too many Austrians to rejoice and too many Germans to be dazzled after 12 March 1938. For the same reason the British deluded themselves, the Italians miscalculated and the Americans were too late in discovering what was at stake for them. Even those whose forecast was correct, however, did not always draw the right conclusions, as the examples of the French and the Russians show. In the period 1933 to 1939 Austria was definitely not the only country where short-sighted reactions were the rule – and they reacted on each other.

This does not alter the fact that, looked at in isolation and in retrospect the decision to hold a plebiscite was based on false premises. Nevertheless its sequel, unforeseen though it was, was the lesser of two evils for Austria. Had we remained inactive, the alternative would have been 'evolution' indirectly supported from the Reich and, as it proved, Austria was in no position to stop this without the use of force, the Berchtesgaden agreement notwithstanding. In that case the assimilation of Austria would ostensibly have been a voluntary process, as Hitler wanted, with all its possible consequences for the fate of Austria after 1945.

The plebiscite, it was thought, would clarify the situation both internally and externally and put an end to Germany's double game. Austrian National-Socialism, after all, had been declared an internal Austrian matter and non-interference had been agreed. This was binding upon the official German representative in Austria (von Papen until 26 February); it was equally binding upon his Counsellor von Stein, who had in fact been sent to keep an eye on his master, and whose reports prove that he interfered with all his might and did his best to stoke the fire;[6] it was also binding upon Keppler and Veesenmayer, who had been specially commissioned to make the actual preparations for the Anschluss.

Another course would simply have been to allow the opposing camps to come to blows, which we feared might happen any day from the end of February onwards; we should then have had to use the security forces and this we could have done even in Graz. But we should then have been playing the enemy's game; he was doing all he could to create a situation which would produce an appeal for aid from across the frontier and thus provide the cue for German armed intervention. There was no doubt that the Third Reich was searching for some semi-legal face-saving pretext for action to cover itself under international law. There was purpose behind the German propaganda story of 11 March about 'bloody riots' in Austria; it was even repeated in the operational report of the German Eighth Army, the formation detailed for the invasion.[7]

The plebiscite could achieve its purpose only if it demonstrated the unequivocal determination of the Austrians to cling to the independence of their country – and it must do so immediately, before German counter-propaganda could produce any major effect. Its primary aim was to unite all non-National-Socialist Austrians under the national colours. At the same time we hoped to persuade all those National-Socialists who were opposed to illegal disruptive action either to cooperate or at least to sympathise with us; we were, after all, issuing a call to everybody to abide by the Berchtesgaden agreement and so observe the 'German peace'. Contrary to subsequent statements there was no obligation to consult; the agreement provided only that 'The Austrian government will from time to time enter into a diplomatic exchange of views on questions of foreign policy of common concern to both countries'.[8] It could scarcely be maintained that the determination of one party to the agreement to remain alive, as expressed through a plebiscite, necessitated an exchange of views with the other party.

The formula we chose was one to which every Austrian could subscribe and which in no way contravened the Austro-German agreement:

> 'For a free and a German Austria, an independent and a social Austria, a Christian and a united Austria; for peace and employment and for the equality of all who stand for their people and their nation.'

The Germans knew perfectly well that this was the basis on which we had negotiated in Berchtesgaden and that we were not to be dissuaded. They might have had their reservations about the long-term interpretation. A bare four weeks, however, could hardly be called long term.

'Equality' was included in the formula to guard against any totalitarian tendencies, from whatever quarter they might appear. It never entered our heads that the efforts of the Fatherland Front to preserve the existence of the State could be classified as totalitarian, although it must be admitted that legalistically there might have been some grounds for the charge.

The President gave unqualified approval to the proposal to hold a plebiscite.[9] The question was not brought to the cabinet in order to guarantee the essential secrecy during the few days of preparation; we knew that Seyss-Inquart was in close touch with Keppler and Glaise-Horstenau with General Muff, the German Military Attaché, and von Stein, the German Counsellor. The latter, who was now Chargé d'Affaires, had reported to the German Foreign Ministry on 22 October 1937:

'Minister von Glaise-Horstenau called on me today and said confidentially that in the last few days he had obtained a shocking insight into the Federal Chancellor's political mentality. The Federal Chancellor had stated that, from the point of view of foreign as well as domestic policy, National-Socialism was the enemy of peaceful development in Austria. The July Agreement had not fulfilled his expectations: the establishment of relatively close cooperation with the Reich in foreign affairs and the maintenance of absolute freedom to pursue an entirely independent Austrian – meaning Clerical and Legitimist – policy in domestic affairs. The Federal Chancellor had then stated with relative frankness that after his disappointing experience with the Agreement of 11 July 1936, although he did not wish to turn against the Reich in his foreign policy, he would work for closer ties between Austria and the Succession States of the Danube monarchy, including Poland; such an orientation of foreign policy, independent of the Reich, would also help him in his struggle against the National-Socialist movement at home. When Minister von Glaise-Horstenau had expressed grave misgivings about the Federal Chancellor's plans, he had been told that the new policy contemplated would by no means be directed against the Reich; perhaps after the formation of such a confederation, it might even be easier to arrive at a compromise with the Reich along the lines of the pre-war situation. Herr von Glaise-Horstenau added that, as Berlin was well aware, he was not clinging to his post and would rather resign from it today than tomorrow. I asked him to carry on for the sake of the cause; only in that way might he still exert some influence on the course of events and at least keep us informed of possible developments.'[10]

Knowing Rome's sensitivity to any approach by Austria to the Successor States, the Berlin Foreign Ministry hastened to transmit this report to von Hassell, their Ambassador in Rome, 'for communication of contents to Mussolini'.[11]

I was confident that all members of the cabinet apart from Glaise-Horstenau and probably also Seyss-Inquart would observe the pledge of secrecy; as we shall see, I personally told Seyss-Inquart of the project on the evening of 8 March. Glaise-Horstenau was not in Austria at the time.

In fact the possibility and advisability of a referendum had already been discussed on various occasions. There would have been an opportunity both before and after the murder of Dollfuss, but opposition both at home and abroad had scotched the plan. During our state visit to London in February 1935 Sir John Simon, then Foreign Secretary, had enquired about the possibility of a plebiscite. As on other occasions, we had replied that Austria would approach this problem of her own volition and without external pressure. In Berchtesgaden Hitler had talked of a referendum, but under conditions which, to use Göring's words, would have turned it into an official and legal 'farce'. Finally on 3 March 1938 Hitler had said to Henderson, the British Ambassador:

> 'Ultimately the people themselves in Austria must be consulted. . . . This was the simplest application of that right of self-determination of nations which had played such an important part in Wilson's Fourteen Points. The present state of affairs at any rate was impossible in the long run; it would lead to an explosion. . . .'

When the Ambassador asked whether Germany demanded a plebiscite in Austria, Hitler replied that:

> 'she would demand that by evolutionary means the legitimate interests of the Germans in Austria be secured and that there be an end to oppression.'[12]

The defenders of Austrian independence can hardly be blamed for drafting a positive plebiscite formula rather than a negative one on Hitler's lines. It must, however, be admitted that, all things considered, an earlier plebiscite, say between 1934 and 1936, would have been better and less risky; the obstacles at that time were internal rather than external and these, as it proved, disappeared once it became clear that a real state of emergency existed. In fact the decision to hold a plebiscite was an act of desperation, taken under extreme pressure – in a situation, in other words, which we had always been trying to avoid.

The question of constitutionality was answered by the experts in the Federal Chancellor's office. The plebiscite was based on Article 93 of the constitution, giving the Federal Chancellor the right to lay down broad lines of policy. Germany had explicitly agreed to respect the Austrian constitution. Quite apart from the recent agreement, non-interference by foreign states in constitutional matters is one of the most elementary rules of international law; any conflict of opinion on the constitutional aspect, therefore, could be only a domestic Austrian matter. This was emphasised in Chamberlain's protest against the German arguments when he referred to the indisputable right of any sovereign state to hold a plebiscite on its own territory free from foreign interference.[13]

Clearly the proposed plebiscite represented one last attempt to bring some order into the turbulent state of affairs instigated from outside; it was also the only SOS signal open to us which perhaps might alert the world. I do not deny that, because of the lack of time and the peculiar circumstances, errors were made; they may be explicable but they are not excusable. Two of them in particular were to have far-reaching consequences:

1. The voting rules and conditions initially laid down;
2. The betrayal of the plan and premature notification to Berlin.

In so far as my memory and the available documents allow me to reconstruct a timetable of events, preparations proceeded as follows: The question of a plebiscite was raised from several quarters at the first conference of provincial leaders of the Fatherland Front following 12 February – probably about 18 February; the object was primarily to counter the already apparent discouragement among our own supporters, which it was feared might spread. No decision was taken at this time, however.

Several important voices stressed the necessity of demonstrating to the world, Germany and our own people the untruth of the story that a majority of Austrians were longing to join the National-Socialist Reich. In fact we were confident of our majority with the possible exceptions of Graz and parts of Carinthia. Even Seyss-Inquart agreed with me in this and subsequent events proved that there was another who did so – Hitler. In the long run, however, we felt that we simply could not stand up to the effects of the Anschluss propaganda deliberately and persistently directed at us from the Third Reich with all the resources of its superior technique; that we knew its content to be contrary to all fact, was immaterial.

Guido Zernatto, the Secretary-General of the Fatherland Front, was commissioned to clarify the legal position and then initiate preparations for the plebiscite. Among my political advisers he was the only one to voice some doubts in the early stages. There was no point in contacting the Nazi side too early since in these days and weeks it was quite impossible to tell who among them was calling the tune. On the other hand I had arranged contacts with the illegal Left (see Chapter 4). The subsequent suspicion that the plebiscite decision had been taken on foreign advice, particularly that of Puaux, the French Minister, is entirely without foundation.[14]

As the internal situation became more turbulent and threatening, particularly when Seyss-Inquart admitted that he could no longer control his own people, the decision to take the risk hardened; the turning point was Keppler's visit to Vienna on 4 March and his new list of demands.

The plebiscite formula was drawn up on the justifiable assumption that there was nothing in it which any Austrian National-Socialist could not sign if he wished to be accepted into the Fatherland Front. The Berchtesgaden agreement had said:

'The Federal Chancellor states that the Austrian National-Socialists shall in principle have opportunity for legal activity within the framework of the Fatherland Front and all other Austrian organisations. This activity shall take place on an equal footing with all other groups, and in accordance with the constitution. Dr Seyss-Inquart has the right and the duty to see to it that the activity of the National-Socialists can develop along the lines indicated above, and to take appropriate measures for this purpose.'[15]

Final instructions to Zernatto to prepare the plebiscite for 13 March were issued on the 6th, the day after my interview with Keppler. For obvious reasons the strictest secrecy was prescribed; anything tending to further disturbance was to be avoided.

On the evening of 6 March a restricted meeting to prepare the organisational details was held in the headquarters of the Fatherland Front under the chairmanship of Zernatto. On the 7th there was a conference of provincial leaders of the Fatherland Front at which I was present. I briefed them in detail on the plan for the plebiscite and the formula, and they gave their agreement.[16]

On the evening of Tuesday, 8 March, twenty-four hours before the official announcement of the plebiscite was to be made in Innsbruck, I told Seyss-Inquart of the plan, obtaining his word of honour to keep the matter secret until the announcement. I had the distinct impression that up to this point secrecy had been preserved.

This was not so, however – and it was no fault of Seyss-Inquart's. So far as one can tell, as early as the evening of 7 March, two days before the announcement therefore, Berlin knew of the draft of a poster intended for display at 7 a.m. on Thursday 10 March and of the discussion on arrangements for the plebiscite. It has been said[17] that Zernatto's secretary passed the transcript of her shorthand to the Nazis, but whether this is so or whether some other employee of the Fatherland Front betrayed the secret, it is not possible to say. The fact remains that some six weeks later Karl Wolff, Head of the *Reichsführer-SS* Personal Staff and the later *Waffen-SS* General, sent 'the original of the girl's report on the Schuschnigg plebiscite' with a covering letter dated 25 April 1938 to Ernst Kaltenbrunner, then commanding SS *Oberabschnitt* [Region] Danube in Vienna. In 1945 both the letter and the report were found in the files of SS headquarters by the American occupation authorities. The report is in manuscript and ends with a note 'This evening's meeting held by Secretary-General Fatherland Front. Good wishes' and an initial. The note and report are not in the same handwriting. Though the report is not dated it can only refer to the evening meeting of Sunday, 6 March. A special channel was available for urgent communications from Vienna to Germany: reports went by courier to Salzburg, where the German Frontier Commissar, an *SS-Untersturmführer* [Lieutenant] of Bavarian origin, was in teleprinter communication with Gestapo headquarters in Berlin; a secret report leaving Vienna by courier in the evening, therefore, was in the hands of the Gestapo the next morning and in urgent cases they were passed to Hitler via Himmler.

Hitler had therefore gained at least one day, probably two, for the preparation of his counterstroke. In fact in the first week of March Dr Humbert Pifrader, Head of the Austrian Department of the Gestapo in Berlin, noted that, following the arrival of an important document, accelerated action against Austria must be reckoned with.[18]

The leakage of these notes gave the other side some timely and dangerous ammunition. It was particularly dangerous because both the poster and the proposed arrangements were only in provisional draft, hurriedly prepared and by no means approved. The draft of the proclamation, for instance, referred to a 'popular vote' whereas in the final version as issued on 9 March and in my Innsbruck speech the word 'plebiscite' was used.[19] Owing to the constitutional aspect, already referred to, the difference was of importance.

The draft which was leaked dealt with arrangements for the plebiscite and ran as follows:

'Polling stations if possible to be the same as those for the 1930 elections or 1932 local elections, set up in the same way if possible. Twice as many "Yes" voting papers as there are voters in each district. "Yes" voting papers only. Blank paper to be held ready, however, for any who might wish to vote "No". Such persons must cut their voting papers out of the blank sheets available. Security of the proceedings in each station: at least two men, in mufti and unarmed, to maintain law and order. Anyone disturbing or hindering the voting or influencing people against it [!] to be removed from the station forthwith. If necessary they should be handed over to the competent government agency, the gendarmerie or police. Two stewards in front of the station. Two officials for communications between the station and the Fatherland Front Recruiting Office or other localities. Provincial Governors to determine times of opening and closing. Closure by 5.0 p.m. at latest. Documents: Fatherland Front membership card, identity card, or certificate of citizenship and registration form. In cities the latter two only. Those who vote "No" must undertake in writing to observe above regulations. No additions to voting paper – otherwise invalid; blank papers count as "Yes" votes. If "Yes" is crossed out and "No" written instead, paper counts as a "Yes" vote. Two to four coopted members, if possible officials of the Fatherland Front, on returning officers' panel. In cities, no admittance for anyone not in possession of an identity card unless known personally to the returning officer. All those born in 1914 or earlier entitled to vote. Leaflets to be distributed by air. Propaganda material to be delivered to all provinces by 7.0 a.m. on Thursday under *Schutzkorps* protection. All decisions to be kept secret until 2.0 p.m. on Wednesday to forestall the Nazis.'

Both the form and style indicate that these were notes written from memory rather than a shorthand record, which in any case would have been either in shorthand or typewritten.[20] The actual regulations, as finally laid down, were in fact quite different.

Moreover as a result of another indiscretion on the part of someone present at a meeting arranged under my instructions of 4 March General Muff, the German Military Attaché in Vienna, soon came to know of a decision 'to hold elections in Austria as soon as possible'; in a secret memorandum he stated that he had been informed by a representative of Rheinmetall-Borsig that Richard Schmitz, the Burgomaster of Vienna, had been 'charged with preparing a memorandum by Tuesday March 8 regarding the necessary preliminaries'.[21] Mussolini had also advised against the project, so from the outset the omens were poor.

On 9 and 10 March intensive efforts were made through Seyss-Inquart, in so far as he still had any influence over the Austrian Nazis, to persuade them to cooperate. To this end certain provisions were agreed for the voting procedure which, on his own admission, enabled Seyss-Inquart to agree.[22] The original proposal for public employees to vote as a body in their offices was dropped; representatives of the Racio-political [*Volkspolitische*] Offices were coopted on to the electoral commissions and the secrecy of the poll was guaranteed; blank papers or those carrying any additions were declared invalid; the official security forces were made solely responsible for protection at the stations.

On 10 March Seyss-Inquart wrote to me and on the same day I replied as follows:

'Dear Minister,

In reply to your esteemed letter of 10th inst. I have the honour to inform you that my position is as follows:

1. The Berchtesgaden agreements were subject to certain well-defined limitations and there can be no doubt, particularly after our personal discussions, that authorisation for the re-establishment of political parties did not enter into the question.

2. The agreements specifically provided for the equality of all groups based on the Fatherland Front and subject to recognition of the constitution. This statement was also agreed by the German party to the agreement. The whole basis of the agreement was non-interference together with recognition of Austrian independence and sovereignty against an Austrian pledge to pursue a German policy.

3. The constitution rests upon the concept of authoritarian leadership and under Article 93 gives the Federal Chancellor the right to lay down the broad lines of policy.

4. Under the constitution, therefore, the Federal Chancellor is fully empowered to assure himself that his policy is approved by means of a plebiscite. Any opposition on constitutional grounds I regard as juridically indefensible; politically I consider it to be contrary both to the spirit and letter of the agreements. I refuse to form a coalition government; I can not recognise parties; there can therefore be no question of the formation of a second front alongside the Fatherland Front as suggested by the *Volkspolitische* Office in Styria which I hereby indict of avowed high treason; it is expressly contrary to the principles of the Berchtesgaden Agreement.

5. I have repeatedly been pressed to arrange a plebiscite; the last occasion was on 12 February by the Reich Chancellor himself in Berchtesgaden when he added that he and I should together stand as candidates in Austria. I can hardly be expected to arrange a plebiscite only on occasions when its result would in all probability be dis-

advantageous to Austria. I reserve the right to publicise this view, should circumstances force me to do so.

6. The formula chosen and the reasoning behind it show clearly that I am merely seeking approval for the path upon which we have just embarked in Austria and that my intention is to usher in the new period, which I would like to call the period of peace, with a solemn demonstration visible to all the world. Only thus can a suitable break with the past be made.

7. From the German viewpoint in particular there can be nothing objectionable in the formula since, as I have explicitly stated and wish to state yet again, it submits to popular judgement both the policy of 11 July and the Berchtesgaden Agreement. Anyone who votes against or refuses to vote shows thereby that he is not in agreement with the Berchtesgaden policy.

8. I am neither able nor prepared to play the role of puppet. I carry the political responsibility and the behaviour of the *Volkspolitische* Office in Styria is sheer mutiny.

The serious situation in the country is caused by the fact that the National-Socialists have not observed the agreements. If we had been willing to submit, nothing of what I have said would have been necessary. I hereby affirm that, as before, attempts are being made to subject both factories and the streets to terror. An end must under all circumstances be put to this once and for all – see my remarks above. Please do not forget that equality was the watchword. I have myself kept all the agreements and must insist on their observation by the other side. I cannot be expected to look on with folded hands while the country is ruined economically and politically. I am in the fortunate position of being able to call upon the world to bear witness who is right and who wants peace. I am completely determined to do this, if need be.

In any case we now know what Austrian National-Socialists mean by the "German peace". When a section of the population does not want peace I cannot unfortunately compel the remainder to conform. I am only too ready to take note of your wish to cooperate, but I must ask you most urgently, as Minister responsible for Security, to take measures to bring terrorism to an end; otherwise I shall not be able to hold the opposing forces in check.

I am at your disposal at all times and with every expression of my esteem, I remain . . .

[signed] Schuschnigg.'[23]

Seyss-Inquart's letter, to which this was a reply, had been written under the influence of his extremist advisers, including Dr Hugo Jury who had recently been appointed to the Council of State; similarly my letter was addressed more to the circle around Seyss-Inquart than to the man himself. However this may be, both are illustrative of the strained situation of the time.

On this same day, 10 March, Hitler ordered mobilisation of Eighth Army which was designated for the invasion of Austria; Globocnik flew from Vienna to Berlin and Keppler in the reverse direction. On the same evening (Thursday) I had a long talk with Seyss-Inquart as a result of which he declared his readiness to try to persuade National-Socialists to vote 'Yes' on the coming Sunday and to broadcast to this effect the next day. As regards this final discussion Seyss-Inquart stated in the witness box: 'We reached a large measure of agreement [over the plebiscite] and I hoped to overcome the remaining difficulties. But the Party was no longer interested.'[24]

On the morning of this Thursday Hitler informed General Keitel, the Chief of OKW, of his intention to intervene in Austria with military force. The officer appointed to command Eighth Army for the invasion of Austria was General von Bock, commanding Group Headquarters III in Dresden. About 4.30 p.m. on 10 March he was told of the Führer's decision 'to move into Austria, probably about midday on 12 March, to re-establish orderly conditions'.[25] Mobilisation of Eighth Army was ordered about 6.55 p.m. Major-General Ruoff was Chief of Staff of the Army which consisted of XIII Corps (Nuremberg) under General von Weichs, VII Corps (Munich) under General von Schober and a Panzer Corps under General Guderian with Colonel Paulus as Chief of Staff. Total strength of the army was over 105,000 men.[26]

At 8 a.m. on 12 March the main body of Eighth Army crossed into Austria along the whole line between Schärding and Bregenz. German units reached Bregenz and Salzburg early in the morning and Innsbruck by midday. At 9.15 a.m. *Luftwaffe* units landed in Vienna. Detachments of the army occupied Vienna on 13 March and on 14 March, on Hitler's instructions, the Austrian army was incorporated into the German *Wehrmacht* and took the oath to Hitler. The swearing-in was completed by late afternoon of the 14th; in his report General von Bock says that of about 50,000 members of the Austrian army '126 soldiers, of whom 123 were Jewish conscripts' refused to take the oath.[27] On 2 April the Austrian Legion moved into Vienna by special order of the Führer.[28]

On 20 May 1937, some ten months earlier in other words, General Ludwig Beck, the Chief of the German General Staff, had written as follows to Colonel-General Fritsch, the Commander-in-Chief of the Army: 'The occupation of Austria by force would be attended by so many warlike measures that, even should it succeed, it is to be feared that the hallmark of future Austro-German relations would not be Anschluss but highway robbery.'[29] Beck was thinking of the probable international complications which everybody thought would ensue from the Austrian Anschluss. They did not occur.

Erich Kordt, writing in retrospect after 1945, reached a somewhat similar conclusion: 'The incredible folly of the military invasion alerted the entire world to the fact that this was no voluntary association.' He describes the Anschluss, in the form in which it happened, as the result of blackmail and force.[30]

On the instructions of OKW an exchange of military courtesies took place on the ex-Austrian frontiers with Italy, Jugoslavia and Hungary; the same instructions laid down strict respect for the Czechoslovak frontier but no contact. Czechoslovakia was the only one of our neighbour states which might possibly have intervened on the invasion of Austria, though we had assumed that she would remain neutral.

In none of the speeches was Austria mentioned; in the case of the Italians and Jugoslavs this was understandable for a number of reasons, but the Hungarian Colonel too did no more than refer to battles fought twenty years ago shoulder to shoulder with German forces despite the close relations existing between the Ödenburg Hussars and their Austrian counterparts up to the last weeks and months before the Anschluss. This is perhaps to be explained by the fact that on 4 March Lieutenant-General Sztojay, the Hungarian Minister in Berlin, had told General Keitel that the Anschluss was the most sensible solution of the Austrian question; Horthy, the Hungarian Regent, basically thought the same.[31]

Austria had never been able to convince Hungary, either before or after the First World War, that in fact the destinies of the two countries were linked; this would have required complete rethinking of Hungarian national policy. It was to prove true in the long run, however. . . . On one of my trips during my twenty years in America I came across one of the last commanding officers of the Ödenburg Hussars acting as 'janitor' of a university building in Austin, Texas.

In his Order of the Day of 14 March before the Austrian army took its oath to Hitler General von Bock, the German Army Commander, had paid homage to the Austrian tradition:

> 'The Führer and Supreme Commander has entrusted me with command of all German forces within the boundaries of the province of Austria. The comradeship in arms of the hard years of war has therefore at last found its fulfilment; union of the Austrian Federal Army with the German Army is now complete.
>
> I regard it as an honour and a distinction to assume command of a force built upon the glorious traditions of the old Austrian Army. With a glad heart we will carry this proud heritage of the past into a new German future, with iron discipline, in loyal fulfilment of our soldierly duty and in selfless devotion to our Führer for the sake of the German Fatherland as a whole.'[32]

On the previous day a peremptory order from Hitler had brought Austria's existence as an independent state temporarily to an end. About 4.0 p.m. on 13 March a short cabinet meeting was held under the chairmanship of Seyss-Inquart, now Federal Chancellor; he opened it with two statements:

1. The President had invested him with full plenary powers, including those of Head of State.
2. He [Seyss-Inquart] had yesterday [12 March] been summoned to the Führer and had been instructed to pass, not later than 13 March, the law which he would now read; any resistance would be dealt with by the German *Wehrmacht*.

After reading the law the Chairman declared, without taking a vote, that it had been passed. The Ministers' meeting had lasted about five minutes.[33] The Federal Constitutional Law, which the members of the cabinet then signed, read as follows:

Article 1. Austria is a province of the German Reich.

Article 2. On Sunday April 10 1938 a free and secret plebiscite of the German men and women of Austria over twenty years of age shall be held on reunion with the German Reich.

Article 3. In the said plebiscite the decision shall be by majority vote.

Article 4. The regulations necessary for executing and supplementing this Constitutional Law shall be provided by decree.

Article 5. This Constitutional Law shall enter into force on the day of its proclamation. The Federal government is entrusted with the execution of this Constitutional Law.

This law, together with a corresponding German law, had been drafted by the German State Secretary Stuckart in Linz on 12 March. The German law ran as follows:

Article 1. The Constitutional Law of March 13, 1938, enacted by the Austrian government concerning reunion of Austria with the German Reich, hereby becomes a German law . . . (here the Austrian Law was repeated).

Article 2. The laws at present in force in Austria shall remain in force until further notice. The introduction of German law into Austria will be effected by the Führer and Chancellor or by the Minister to whom he may delegate this power.

Article 3. The Reich Minister of the Interior, in consultation with the other Reich Ministers concerned, is empowered to issue the legal and administrative regulations necessary for executing and supplementing this law.

Article 4. This law shall enter into force on the day of its proclamation.

Linz, 13 March 1938.

Thus Hitler became Austria's Head of State.

It is true that the original plan did not visualise the complete incorporation of Austria into Germany, in other words Austria's extinction. As late as 11 March the intention was to leave Austria a measure of autonomy, the two countries being united only through the person of Hitler. This presupposed, however, an internal *Gleichschaltung* in Austria as a result of seizure of power by the National-Socialists and in practice, therefore, there would have been little difference between the original plan and the full-scale Anschluss; dissolution of the previous Austrian State would merely have taken place in two successive stages. On Göring's advice and of his own volition Hitler took a snap decision to incorporate Austria completely; the reason may have been the enthusiasm of his reception in Linz, unexpected even for him, which may perhaps have given him the impression that the Austrians wanted full incorporation. In this, however, he was mistaken, for eye-witness accounts confirm that even the Nazi members of the new government in Vienna had not visualised this solution. One must, however, agree with Seyss-Inquart's statement in the witness box that the outcome of a halfway solution would have been no different. As we know, his request that the administration of Austria be left in Austrian hands was only partially met. Hitler appointed *Gauleiter* Bürckel, previously Reich Commissar in the Saar, to be Leader of the Austrian Nazi Party; Seyss-Inquart was nominated Head of the Administration with the title of *Reichsstatthalter* [Reich Regent]. The Austrian army formed part of Army Group 5 under the German General von List. The inevitable conflicts between German Party and administrative agencies and their Austrian counterparts were not long in coming and were as bitter as the previous quarrels inside the Austrian Nazi Party and its leadership; the exchange of letters between Seyss-Inquart and Bürckel in August 1939 is eloquent proof.[34]

The referendum of 10 April confirmed the already existing

situation; France and Great Britain had already voted 'Yes' by requesting the German government for an exequatur for their consulates to be installed in what had been Austria; according to international usage this implied *de facto* recognition of the Anschluss. The result was as expected – 4,273,884 'Yesses' from an electorate of 4,300,177, in other words over 99 per cent, better than earlier results in the Third Reich where Hitler had scored 95 per cent on 12 November 1933 (Germany's departure from the League of Nations), 90 per cent on 19 August 1934 (Hitler's assumption of the functions of Head of State on the death of Hindenburg) and 98·8 per cent on 29 March 1936 (occupation of the Rhineland and renunciation of the Locarno Treaty).

Hitler's electoral speech on 9 April 1938, the eve of the plebiscite, was really hardly necessary:

'Within a space of five years a world power has grown from a downcast and enslaved people; and this present-day Germany is my own personal creation. . . . After the collapse of 1918, German-Austria wanted to return to the Reich at once. . . . I am standing here because I think I can do more than Herr Schuschnigg, indeed I can prove that I am more capable than all the muddleheads who have tried to ruin this country. Who will even remember their names in a hundred years' time? . . . But my name will go down to history as one of the great sons of this land. . . . When Herr Schuschnigg broke his word on 9 March, at that moment I felt the call of Providence come to me. . . . It was my good fortune to be able to incorporate my homeland into the Reich on the day of its betrayal.'[35]

There is no reason to doubt that the result of the referendum was comparatively genuine, although no referendum can be entirely so unless some alternative choice is offered. Neither the Austrian nor the German Nazis had really doubted that the anticipated government majority in our own plebiscite planned for 13 March would be genuine; there could have been no better opportunity for the Austrian Nazis to demonstrate their alleged majority to the world. In fact we had never reckoned on 90 per cent; we had thought that there might be a safe government majority of 65–70 per cent. Dr Skubl, the State Secretary for Security and Police

President, calculated at the time that the Nazi activists in Austria numbered only 80,000.[36]

As a curiosity it should be mentioned that in the Tyrolese mountain village of Tarrenz voting took place on 13 March, since the events of the previous two days were not yet known there. One hundred per cent cast their votes for the government formula; yet on 10 April 100 per cent equally cast their votes for the Anschluss.[37]

Might the ultimate outcome have been different, had there been armed or unarmed resistance?

Unarmed resistance – passive resistance or at least a deliberately unforthcoming attitude in the early days of the occupation – would probably have had some publicity effect. But it would have changed nothing. For psychological reasons it was hardly to be expected. In any case, to the great disillusionment of the 'old fighters' among the Austrian National-Socialists and despite all the jubilation, *Gleichschaltung* was enforced at once, particularly at the centre. In the fields of civil and military administration Austrians were forthwith excluded from any participation in the real exercise of power.[38] German supervisory authorities had the last word in all matters of Party, State and economics – in everything, in other words. It could not have been otherwise. As was to be expected the Anschluss, which had come about (illegally) through occupation, after a two-day transitional period turned into annexation (equally illegal). Initially the world turned a blind eye and there was no violent resistance, but this did not alter the fact that the annexation had no cover under international law; it could be vindicated only by 'prolonged undisturbed possession', in other words over a lengthy period. Theoretically it might be possible to legalise it by 'squatter's right'.[39]

But time did not permit the Third Reich to do this. The change of mood in Austria was not long in coming. Internal resistance grew; many documents and facts exist to prove it – protests and situation reports from German government agencies in Vienna and the mounting wave of political arrests, sentences and executions. Between March 1938 and the end of the war some 6,000 political executions took place in Vienna alone, not including those who were condemned to death by the *Wehrmacht* or died in concentration camps. This figure is immeasurably greater than that for political or other executions during the whole sixty-eight years of the reign of Franz Josef and the whole First Republic up to the Anschluss. Between 1938 and 1945 some 36,000 Austrians were held in political arrest and more than 80,000 years of imprisonment were imposed on Austrians by the German Peoples' Courts.[40]

The outbreak of war and its rapid extension brought about in practice a withdrawal of *de facto* recognition of the Austrian 'Anschluss'; in the Moscow Declaration of 30 October 1943 Eden, Hull and Molotov agreed that 'the occupation of Austria by Germany on 13 March 1938 was held to be null and void'. Despite the fact that there had been no armed resistance to the military invasion of 12 March 1938, the three governments declared Austria to be 'the first free country to fall victim to the aggressive policy typical of Hitler' and therefore 'to be liberated from German tyranny' – unequivocal testimony to the illegality of Austria's incorporation into Germany. In face of a fate which at the time was inexorable, an unarguable statement such as this was the sole and ultimate object of Austrian policy in March 1938. As things were, any other course could only have ended in useless sacrifices; neither in March 1938 nor in 1945 nor later could it have changed anything. The examples of Czechoslovakia and Poland were proof enough of that.

Though it had long been planned, the German army leaders had had serious qualms about the Austrian adventure for some time. This we knew in Vienna and our knowledge was based on personal information and impressions from Hans Hammerstein-Equord, one of the most loyal and devoted Austrians, Minister of Justice for a time and later President of the Cultural League [*Kulturbund*]; his source was his cousin, General Kurt von Hammerstein-Equord, former Commander-in-Chief of the German army. After the fall of von Fritsch in February 1938, however, all scruples were clearly suppressed, as is shown by the report on 'The Situation in Austria before reunification' by General von Bock, commanding Eighth Army; though without the usual exaggerations it simply repeats the political arguments of the Third Reich's leaders; without demur it accepts the Nazi propaganda on the subject of the proposed plebiscite, showing that, even allowing for the pressure of events and the absence of any reliable independent information, news put out by the Party agencies was accepted unthinkingly. Moreover in General Muff, the German Military Attaché in Vienna, the political leaders of the Reich and the Nazi-inspired news agencies had a willing helper. Had circumstances been normal and had we followed international usage we should long since have demanded his recall as *persona non grata*.[41]

The Austrian army faced the military might of the Third Reich. Its maximum strength permitted under the peace treaty was 1,500 officers and 30,000 men but this had never been reached; up to 1933 it was about 20,000 strong. Our financial situation had necessitated the strictest economy and in addition both the Treaty limitations and the internal political situation had produced a climate unfavourable to the build-up of the armed forces. In the budget debate of 1932 Dr Deutsch, one of the deputies in the Diet, had demanded that the military vote be reduced by one third.[42]

During the twelve years ending September 1932 a Christian Social Minister, Carl Vaugoin, had been in charge of the Army Department; he had successfully built up and expanded the army and even at the time any objective critic had been forced to admit that an astonishing amount had been achieved with very modest resources; no one could have done better. During the early turbulent years the army had become tainted with politics and it was said that he had not succeeded in creating from it a non-political army; this overlooks the fact, however, that the provisions of the 1920 Defence Law, which had been passed under political pressure, remained in force throughout the parliamentary regime and could hardly have been altered without the agreement of the opposition.

In September 1933 Colonel-General Prince Alois Schönberg-Hartenstein, a highly respected First World War Army Commander, became head of the Defence Ministry. From 10 July 1934 the Federal Chancellor acted as Minister of Defence with a tried military expert, General Wilhelm Zehner, as State Secretary.

In view of Nazi Germany's mounting threat to Austria the necessity of expanding the army once more became a pressing problem. On 16 March 1935 Germany had introduced universal military service, unilaterally repudiating the provisions of the Peace Treaties. In Austria universal military service was preceded by the formation of the so-called Military Auxiliary Corps, consisting of short-service volunteers; universal military service was introduced by law in April 1936. The term of service was initially one year, extended to eighteen months on 10 February 1938. The Little Entente governments were the only ones to raise objections based on the Peace Treaties. The increase in strength was matched by various improvements in arms and equipment. Nevertheless a little country like Austria which, to keep its economy and international credit sound, had to ensure that its currency remained stable, could not afford to follow the German example and spend large sums on armaments.

Moreover the whole purpose of Austrian rearmament was totally different from that of Germany; the Third Reich's political leaders had taken a deliberate and premeditated decision to construct an instrument of offence in order to solve the German *lebensraum* problem by force, at latest by 1943–5, through expansion eastwards.[43]

The task of the Austrian army was to defend the frontiers and maintain the country's independence within the framework of the existing European order which was based on the principle of collective security as opposed to violent frontier revisions. The defence plan drafted by the Chief of the General Staff, Lieutenant-General Alfred Jansa, visualised a fighting withdrawal to the line of the Traun and Enns; unsupported, the Austrian army was not expected to resist for more than two full days of fighting on the assumption that during these forty-eight hours some relief would be provided from international sources.[44]

When the budget was stabilised through the currency reform of 1923, the army's share of total state expenditure was 5·9 per cent; in 1930 and subsequent years it fell to 4·8 per cent, but rose again to 15 per cent in 1937. In view of requirements this was a

modest sum, particularly compared to the average expenditure on
defence of nearly 25 per cent in many other European countries.

At the end of 1937 the army was still in the throes of expansion
but it had already reached a strength of seven divisions of six to
eight battalions (planning target nine), one light artillery regiment
of six batteries (planning target nine), one mobile division of four
motorised battalions, one cavalry brigade, one motorised artillery
regiment and one armoured car battalion. In addition there were
the specialist troops and a numerically small air force. The arms
and equipment which our relatively meagre resources allowed us
to obtain were of high quality as were the troops and their training. The total value of the arms and equipment taken over by the
German *Wehrmacht* on the occupation of Austria was more than
500 million schillings at the March 1938 rate of exchange.

In addition to the army the Front Militia was available; this
consisted of members of the former volunteer defence formations
and its strength was some 20,000 men. Though its discipline and
training were good, it could not be used for other than auxiliary
tasks owing to its inadequate and heterogeneous armament and
equipment.[45]

For reasons of external policy, already mentioned elsewhere,
the alert period for the Austrian army was in this case cut very
short; according to a report from the Upper Austrian Division
the first security precautions were not taken until 9 March; on 10
March the 1915 class was called up and the general alert was issued
on the 11th. From the outset, therefore, Lieutenant-General
Jansa's defence plan was inoperative, since it postulated eight days
for full mobilisation and the move of the army to the Traun line.[46]
Had we tried to organise our defence, therefore, it could only
have been improvised. As we now know, however, the Germans
were facing an exactly similar problem; the German Eighth Army
found itself suddenly confronted by a task for which it was not
fully prepared and which, as its operational report shows, it could
fulfil only with difficulty. Of course the Germans had far greater
numbers and were far better equipped, particularly in the air and
anti-aircraft defence. Supply and communications problems were
also easier to solve on the German side owing to the fact that a

fifth column existed in Austria; this would have organised risings in the cities and sabotage in the country which would have tied down our fighting troops. Nevertheless, had we resisted, the Germans would probably have been unable to keep to their time-table. According to General von Bock's report, 'Had there been a planned defence of the frontier, the army could not have moved before the morning of the 13th'. Even as it was, the Panzer Corps encountered considerable difficulties and delays in its advance due to inadequate fuel supply and, still more, traffic chaos. The German army command clearly had serious problems for its re-port says: 'There is no doubt that, had there been enemy ground or, even worse, air opposition, the incidents on the Passau–Linz–Vienna road could have led to a catastrophe.' In addition there was friction between the army and SS formations – 'The reports of some of these formations show that their commanders' ideas on many strategic problems are inadequate. . . . If it is intended to employ SS troops in war against an external enemy, it will be essential that they should be trained for it in peacetime. The prin-ciples of army training, and none other, must be followed.'[47]

The difficulties encountered by the Germans might have en-abled Austrian resistance to be longer but the ultimate outcome would have been the same; from our point of view we should have suffered heavy casualties and the country would have been devastated to no good purpose. The *Luftwaffe* would not have remained idle; Hitler's order that 'any resistance will be ruthlessly suppressed by armed force' was undoubtedly to be taken at its face value; so was the army's Order of the Day of 11 March 1938: 'Should sections of the population participate in the fighting, the laws of war are to be applied with the utmost severity. The same applies to hostile acts of any sort, including any form of passive resistance to the measures and instructions of the German army.'[48] During the Schmidt Trial someone said that it would have been better to have had a thousand casualties in March 1938 than a hundred thousand later; this assumes, however, that the thousand in 1938 would have saved the later casualties of World War II. There is nothing to support such an assumption.

Understandably, in post-1945 Austria a violent difference of opinion arose over this question of the absence of military resistance. Most people were agreed that it would not have affected the outcome, though a few thought that attempted resistance would have moved the Powers to intervene; in fact of course the intervention would have had to be rapid – within the first forty-eight hours – and on a large scale if it was to save the situation. The main argument still runs that even symbolic resistance on 11 March 1938 would have stood Austria in good stead after the liberation of 1945. If a mere hundred Austrians had fallen fighting against the German army, people say, Austria could have claimed belligerent status and these hundred casualties might perhaps have saved Austria ten years of Four-Power occupation.[49] Symbolic resistance would hardly have prevented Hitler proclaiming in Vienna that he could 'report fulfilment of the greatest aim in German history' nor would it have prevented the incorporation of Austria into the Reich; it would not have changed the initial enthusiastic reaction of the population nor the result of the referendum on 'reunion with the Reich'. Austrians would still have had to fight in the German army during the war and Austria's treatment after the war would have taken as little account of the interests and desires of the Austrians as did that of Poland or the Baltic States. The fate of General Anders' Army of Poles is proof enough of that.

These retrospective ifs and buts, interesting though they may be, in fact belong to the realm of idle speculation. It must not be forgotten, however, that in face of the stern reality of March 1938 the responsible leaders were confronted by three questions:

1. Was military resistance technically possible?
2. Was it morally and politically defensible?
3. Could its purpose have been achieved in any other way which would equally well have served the vital interests of the country and its people both in the present and future?

The answer to the first question is a guarded 'Yes'. A fighting withdrawal, spread over two days, would have been possible even on 11 March 1938. The army and gendarmerie were reliable instruments in the hands of the government. The schedule of appointments for 1938 showed that there was a total of 2,555 officers, of whom, according to lists discovered, some 5 per cent belonged to illegal organisations. It is therefore quite untrue to say that the army was riddled with Nazism.[50] Owing, however, to the absence of the necessary favourable conditions, in other words intervention by the Powers, resistance would have collapsed, particularly in rear of the front, with all the resultant consequences. Resistance begun immediately following Berchtesgaden or even instead of going to Berchtesgaden would have had the same result, primarily owing to the fact that international attitudes were governed by the desire to avoid a clash with Germany. Certain non-military circles later maintained that the army could have withdrawn to an alpine redoubt somewhere in the Dachstein area and there continued to resist, but this overlooks the ammunition and supply problems. For reasons of political psychology the situation was obviously not comparable with that of Switzerland and her defence strategy during World War II.

This brings us to the second question – the moral and political defensibility of military resistance. Politically this was linked to the continuance of that European order foreshadowed in the League of Nations Statute and the Peace Treaties. At that time, as indeed it still is, maintenance of her independence within that order was laid upon Austria as a duty and the Western Powers had insisted on strict observance of the obligation. The catastrophic chain of events which led to World War II did not spring solely from the short-sightedness of the Peace Treaties or the inadequacy of the Geneva Statute; its real cause was the failure to revise the treaties in good time or to insist on their observance when violated by a major Power, while all the time publicly proclaiming their inviolability and a policy of *status quo*. We never succeeded in obtaining an explicit guarantee of our territorial integrity, in other words a written pledge of assistance in the event of external aggression. The argument used in Berlin, that Austria depended for her existence on foreign bayonets, is not valid; she depended rather on the success or failure of the existing European order and therefore of the principle of collective security.

On 10 March 1938 the Chautemps cabinet resigned, so on the

11th France was without a government. On the afternoon of the 11th Alois Vollgruber, the Austrian Minister, spoke to the retiring Foreign Minister, Delbos, who telephoned London; after a full half hour Delbos told the Austrian Minister that he was extremely sorry to have to inform him that London refused to react in any major way to the events in Vienna and he must understand that, in these circumstances, Paris could not do anything of consequence either; in addition, as he knew, the French government had resigned. On the evening of the 11th Charles Rochat, *chef de cabinet* in the Foreign Ministry, called Vollgruber to say that London and Paris had decided to protest in Berlin, although they were convinced that this would in no way change the course of events.[51]

On the 11th Michael Palairet, the British Minister in Vienna, telephoned Lord Halifax giving him detailed information and reading him the German ultimatum. About 3.0 p.m. he telegraphed London:

> 'Situation is critical. If the Chancellor gives way it will be the end of him and of Austrian independence; if he holds firm he is faced by threat of armed action by Germany when disturbances take place (or rather are engineered) during the plebiscite. You will have learnt from Munich of semi-mobilisation taking place in Bavaria, of which Austrian government have complete information. . . . The Italian Minister was informed that Austrian government is urgently awaiting an answer from Rome.'[52]

Shortly thereafter the Minister telephoned London:

> 'Under threat of civil war and absolutely certain menace of military invasion Chancellor gave way rather than risk bloodshed in Austria and perhaps in Europe. He agreed to cancel Sunday's plebiscite on condition that tranquillity of country was not disturbed by Nazis. This was referred to Hitler by Minister of Interior (Seyss-Inquart) who was told that it was not enough and that Dr Schuschnigg must resign and be replaced by Minister of Interior. Dr Schuschnigg asks for *immediate* advice of His Majesty's Government as to what he should do. He has been given only an hour to decide.'[53]

At 4.0 p.m. on 11 March Nevile Henderson, the British Ambassador in Berlin, reported on a conversation with Tauschitz, the Austrian Minister; he (Henderson) had said that he would do his utmost to warn the German government through von Neurath against any precipitate action. On the same day he reported that a British correspondent had received the following private information from the German press bureau:

'Rumour current in Fatherland Front circles in Vienna according to which the Reich Government has demanded from the Austrian Government under an ultimatum the postponement of the so-called plebiscite is explained in political circles here as a sign of the extraordinary nervousness of the former circles. Nothing is known here of such an alleged ultimatum. The other rumour current in Vienna according to which it has been announced on the German wireless that the Reich would draw extreme conclusions if the Austrian Chancellor did not renounce his so-called plebiscite is equally pure invention and is probably to be ascribed to the fact that some foreign agitator station had put out some such news. With reference to the messages from different foreign sources that concentrations of troops and SA are taking place in Germany it is declared here in informed quarters that there can be no question of any abnormal troop movement in Germany. Individual frontier guards on the Austrian frontier have received small reinforcements, a measure which is easily comprehensible in view of the indignation of the Austrian people and the passionate sympathy of the Reich Germany [*sic*] and racially identical frontier population.'[54]

About 4.30 p.m. the British Minister in Vienna received a telegram from Lord Halifax. It ran as follows:

'Viscount Halifax to Mr Palairet (Vienna) (Received 11 March 4.30 p.m.). We have spoken strongly to von Ribbentrop on effect that would be produced in this country by such direct interference in Austrian affairs as demand for resignation of Chancellor enforced by ultimatum, especially after offer to cancel plebiscite. Ribbentrop's attitude was not encouraging but he has gone off to telephone to Berlin.

His Majesty's Government cannot take responsibility of advising the Chancellor to take any course of action which might expose his country to dangers against which His Majesty's Government are unable to guarantee protection.

Repeated by telephone to Berlin, Paris, Prague, Rome and Budapest.'[55]

Early in the afternoon contact was established with Rome but the answer was that 'under the circumstances the Italian government is not in a position to give advice'.

All Austria's defence preparations were based on the assumption that she could count on international assistance within the framework of the Powers' *status quo* policy. The only conceivable aggressor was the Third Reich. Resistance by Austrian forces alone had not the smallest prospect of success. There can therefore be little doubt about the answer to the question whether resistance in these circumstances, even symbolic resistance, made any sense and whether its inevitable consequences were morally defensible. Considering the entirely different circumstances of thirty years ago, who could say that later potential advantages bore any relation to the immediate disadvantages, sacrifices and risks and that these should therefore have been accepted?

Moreover this was no 'one-man' decision; everybody involved was of one mind – General Schilhawsky, the Inspector-General of the army, State Secretary Skubl the Inspector-General of Security Forces, Lieutenant-General Hülgerth, Commandant of the Militia, the President and myself. What we did decide was to enter a solemn legal protest before the world and before history, declaring that Austria was yielding to force. Even though no shot was fired (and I am still thankful today that none was), this did at least achieve its purpose of removing from the Third Reich's action that legal façade which Hitler wanted; it was proof positive that, however events might unfold (and at the time this was unpredictable), Austria had kept the door open for re-establishment of her independence – and developments proved that she was right.

Service to peace was the basis of Austria's existence and of her new political ideology behind the constitution. This was the answer to the ugly phrase about a 'League of Nations colony'. Even if the League had become a mere façade, it was nevertheless the first step taken in modern times to create an international organisation to prevent a repetition of catastrophes like that of 1914–18. The Third Reich thought otherwise, although many Germans suspected and the majority of professional soldiers knew that, even twenty years after 1918, an isolated Central Europe could not win another world war. We who carried the political responsibility in Austria and had not yet forgotten the last war were convinced of it too.

The European arena was, and still is, divided by geography, economics and culture into three main regions – Eastern, Western and Central; the United States is primarily interested in the West. Germany, Austria and Switzerland belong to the Centre; France, England, Belgium – and Italy too – belong to the West. Ever since the redrawing of the map in that fateful year 1918 there had been a safety curtain between East and Centre in the form of the Successor States and the Baltic States, sometimes known collectively as 'East-Central' Europe. Apart from Hungary their interest lay in maintaining the existing order and therefore, notwithstanding temporary tactical vagaries in their foreign policy, they were basically adherents of the West's political line. In view of the ratio of power potential the Centre had a vital interest in the continuance of the peace settlement and pacific neighbourly relations – quite irrespective of whether Austria introduced a new constitution or National-Socialism dominated Germany.

Dismemberment of the Centre (Austria-Hungary) had not produced the results which either its originators or its heirs had expected. No realistic observer could blink the fact, however, that the unilateral displacement of frontiers in Central Europe, disguised as re-establishment of a political order which had never existed in history, was a psychological error and a German disaster.

Ever since 1933 Berlin and Vienna had held opposite views on what the remedy was; they had differing pictures of Europe and different ideologies. Vienna thought the future lay in the Western line, Berlin in 'expansion of *lebensraum*' eastwards. From our point of view hard fact dictated that, in the interests of self-preservation, a serious clash be postponed as long as possible or averted altogether.

When, therefore, it became clear that the primary object of German policy was frontier revision, if necessary by force, the agreement given to conduct Austrian foreign policy 'in the light of the peaceful aims of the German government's foreign policy' (Point VIII of the 'Gentlemen's Agreement' of 11 July 1936) inevitably became untenable. In all our arguments with the Nazis and as counter to their totalitarian pretensions we had always emphasised that Austria was German; this we had done, not solely to refute the ridiculous, though domestically damaging, accusation of hostility to Germany, but to correct the distorted picture of German culture and the German-speaking people so prejudicial to any idea of international understanding. Basic to the Austrian ideology was the conviction that an independent Austria was in Germany's interest too, that acknowledgement of our common cultural heritage did not postulate a unified state, nor do common experiences in history and common interests in the past necessarily provide the foundations for an eventual fusion. Events have proved us right.

With the passage of time the perspective has changed. The equation 'Austrian=German' is as wide of the mark as the other extreme view whose adherents think exactly the opposite and act as though the two notions had never had anything to do with each other. Any distorted picture is the result of unconscious or deliberate forgetfulness and therefore of falsification either by negligence or design.

In March 1938 the descendants of the combatants of Sadowa faced each other once more. Although Bismarck recognised the importance of Austria and was opposed to her destruction, Sadowa marked the beginning of Austria's decline. A second Sadowa, in which Austria had no prospect of success, would have had repercussions stretching far beyond the Nazi interlude; it would have poisoned future relationships between the two nation-states and broken many human ties for years to come. Moreover in 1866 the actions of Bismarck, the Prussian, were calculated; in 1938 those of Hitler, the unwilling Austrian, were based on hatred. One has only to read his 'Second Book', published in 1928, for proof.[56]

In fact Hitler could give Austria nothing but – though he did not know it and would have been horrified – Austria took her revenge for Sadowa by making Germany a present of Hitler. The editor of Hitler's 'Second Book', Gerhard L. Weinberg of the University of Michigan, a pupil of Hans Rothfels, justifies its publication in the concluding sentence of his Foreword as follows: 'This is therefore one more proof of the fact . . . that Hitler's thinking led inexorably to the catastrophe of World War II.'

Between 12 and 15 March 1938 German army orders and the utterances of German generals laid much stress on the comradeship between the two armies during the First World War. On 12 March the Eighth Army Commander sent the following letter to General Schilhawsky, Inspector-General of the Austrian Army and the highest-ranking Austrian officer:

'To the Commander-in-Chief of the Austrian Federal Army.
Dear General,
    As I enter Austrian territory I have the honour to greet you in memory of our ancient comradeship in arms and to express to you my gratification and my thanks for the friendly attitude adopted by your troops towards their German comrades on this day.
    I hope very soon to have the opportunity of paying my respects to you in person. Until then I will forward to you my desires and my requests through the German Military Attaché in Vienna, General Muff.

In comradely association
Heil Hitler!
[signed] von Bock
General.'[57]

At the great military parade in Vienna ordered by Hitler for 15 March Austrian generals followed General von Bock on horseback. Then, after swearing its oath, the Austrian army was absorbed into the *Wehrmacht*. Considerable numbers of Austrian officers soon fell victims to the New Order. Under the chairmanship of General Muff, eagerly assisted by hurriedly reinstated Nazi officers, a Commission was assembled to deal with the expulsion or disciplinary punishment of 'politically unsuitable or undesirable' officers. No more was heard about World War comradeship or 'comradely association'. The bases of the Commission's deliberations were lists prepared by General Muff long before. The scenario, now so well known on the civil side, was re-enacted in the military field.

The first dismissals took place as early as 15 March; among them were General Zehner the former State Secretary,[58] General Schilhawsky the Inspector-General of the Army, four divisional commanders, the Commandant of the Maria Theresa Military Academy in Wiener-Neustadt, the Inspector of Infantry and numerous senior officers on the General Staff and with formations. Further waves of retirements followed. In all 55 per cent of the generals, 40 per cent of the colonels and 17 per cent of all officers serving with units or on the staff were dismissed during the early months; in addition individual retirements took place all the time. During 1938 a further 18 per cent of the officers, including 14 colonels, 137 other staff officers, 65 captains and subalterns and 80 officers of the specialist services were demoted to lower-grade posts (in replacement units for instance) and removed from active duty. All the long-service NCOs (900 of them) were dismissed or retired.

Of the officers subjected to disciplinary action more than thirty were consigned to concentration camps or sentenced to imprisonment in spite of efforts by the German *Wehrmacht* to stop this in individual cases; eighteen were punished by drastic reduction of pension – simply because they had obeyed the law and been loyal to their country. Six officers died in concentration camps or prison.

The lot of officers dismissed under the new regime, most of whom were declared 'unworthy to serve', was particularly distressing. In the early days retired generals with the First War Gold Medal for Valour were to be seen street-sweeping in Vienna. Archduke Josef Ferdinand, an elderly Colonel-General and ex-Army Group Commander of 1915, was sent to Dachau, whence he was rescued only by German military intervention.

Austrian officers remaining in service were distributed to German regiments and transferred to the Reich; the troops joined the general stream of German replacements. A considerable percentage of officers accepted into the German *Wehrmacht* were subjected to every form of slight, their reliability being said to be doubtful.

It should not be forgotten that these extremes should be laid at the door of the Party and its leaders – Hitler was, after all, Supreme Commander; moreover, as we know, the more senior German professional officers, both in formations and on the staffs, became increasingly estranged from the Party and its leaders as time went on.[59]

The twelfth of March 1938 closed a chapter of Austrian history, the tragic outcome of which the Austrian army could do nothing to alter. The sequel, written seven years later and declaring the act of force null and void, showed that of the two opponents of Sadowa, Prussia and Austria, the vanquished was the one to survive.

THE VISION AND THE REALITY

Who could blame the German, even if he were no hardened Nazi, when he saw in the Austrian Anschluss the fulfilment of a long-cherished dream? He had, after all, been taught that historically it was a foregone conclusion and in modern times an essential, something both advantageous to Germany and desired by Austria. Barely twenty years had passed since 1918 and fifteen of these had reinforced his belief that the majority of Austrians clearly wanted nothing else but the Anschluss. In addition many, though not of course all, Germans of all walks of life thought themselves superior to the 'indolent Austrians' and looked down on them. This was true despite the paradox that the German Führer was an *émigré* Austrian and in recent times, including the troubled years preceding the Anschluss, many of the most ardent Austrian patriots were German born.

I can myself remember an incident early in 1933;[1] though among friends ideologically akin to us, we encountered passionate opposition when we attempted to correct the current historical viewpoint by putting the Austrian case and arguing against the idea of the Anschluss in the interests of Germany, Austria and Europe as a whole. Conversely German visitors were astounded when the political slogans of 1922 failed to evoke the anticipated response some ten years later – before Hitler's seizure of power, be it noted. At the Christian Social Party Rally in Klagenfurt in 1931, for instance, Franz von Papen, then a representative of the Centre Party, was taken aback by the silence with which the delegates received his speech of greeting; Friedrich Funder, one of the leading Austrian writers, says that it was 'the respectful silence of the host who cannot quarrel with his guest of honour'; when the injured Papen asked him, he explained that 'we Austrians genuinely wish to pay tribute to and cultivate friendship with Germany; it would be a mistake, however, to draw from this the conclusion that we are prepared to renounce our identity and the freedom of our country'.[2] This was an apt description of the basic attitude to which we steadfastly adhered until 11 March 1938, in so far as we were allowed to do so.

People in the Reich had become accustomed to believe that Germany had some prescriptive right to Austria based on history, economic common sense, nature's law of nationalism and political expediency. When, therefore, National-Socialism began to thump its propaganda drum and finally came to power with an ominous din, many people found the easiest excuse for conformism to be agreement with the new nationalist dynamic. Here, after all, was an extremist political mass movement whose leaders for the first time thumbed their noses at Versailles and the League and reached out boldly across the frontiers, making no secret of the fact that they intended to follow their own rules. They cannot be accused of having left the world in doubt about their aims, their methods or their concept of right and wrong. Everyone should have known without the 'extrication of Germany from international entanglements', her exit from the League of Nations, for instance, or her refusal to attend the disarmament conference of October 1933,[3] without the St Bartholomew's Night of 30 June 1934 'to preserve the unity of the Reich'. All had been set out with brutal clarity ever since 1923 in Hitler's *Mein Kampf* – and it had been translated into all major languages.

Even before the 'seizure of power' in January 1933, therefore, German public opinion believed in the Anschluss and was strengthened in that belief by a number of voices from Austria; in the years which followed, this belief became even more intense but in addition changed in character.

If the Anschluss could come about on Austrian initiative, so much the better; if not, then it would be annexation. Germany's alleged right to Austria was now the cry and to assert this, even the use of force was justified, if that proved necessary.

According to the report of the 'Reichsführer-SS Historical Commission' submitted by Heydrich to Himmler on 9 December 1938 the necessary instructions and announcements for the 25 July 1934 *putsch* were drafted by Weydenhammer and Wächter in the apartment of Günther Altenburg on the evening of 24 July in Vienna – one German, one Austrian and the Counsellor of the German Embassy.[4]

The object of the 'evolutionists' was to avoid the use of force if possible, particularly after the attempt to use it on 25 July 1934 had proved ineffective; instead they hoped to make Austria ripe for take-over from within. This is the tenor of reports from Vienna by declared Nazis such as Keppler, Stein and Veesenmayer and non-Nazis such as von Papen. On 27 July 1935, for instance, a year after the death of Dollfuss, von Papen reported to Hitler:

'In order to form a clear judgement it is essential too to obtain a picture of the repercussions on internal affairs caused by the German-Austrian policy of recent years. Persons in Austria who genuinely take a Greater-German attitude have never been particularly numerous. . . . Particular importance attaches to cultural problems. . . . Over and beyond these questions, a matter of decisive importance will be the manner in which the policy of the Third Reich gives intellectual momentum to the German-Austrian question from the constitutional angle. The "new Austria" has got stuck in the mental atmosphere of particularism and has sacrificed the primacy of the nation to it. . . . *National-Socialism must and will overcome the neo-Austrian ideology.* Should some Austrians now object that the NSDAP is only a centralised Reich German Party and therefore unfit to transmit the ideology of National-Socialism to peoples of differently constituted states, then we may with justice reply that the national revolution in Germany could only be brought about in this way and no other. . . . A Nuremberg Party Rally, described as it used to be as the "German Day", and the proclamation of a "National-Socialist Peoples Front" would be a revolutionary event for all beyond the frontiers of the Reich. By such an approach we would also win over particularist Austrian circles. . . .'[5]

In the German view the Austrian question was an entirely internal German affair; any attempt by Austria to obtain international support or indeed pursue any Austrian foreign policy was labelled as treason to the nation, particularism and separatism – yet this policy had never been directed against Germany except in so far as Austria's continued existence as an entity was concerned. Non-interference in internal matters had been guaranteed by treaty, but the Embassy's and other reports prove that interference continued after the July 1934 *putsch*, different in form but not in substance.

Even German Party circles found the large-scale interference as practised prior to July 1934 to be too glaring. In November 1933 Röhm, then Chief of Staff of the SA, and Putzi Hanfstaengl, the Party Foreign Press Officer, attempted to remove Theo Habicht, a member of the German Reichstag who had been appointed leader of the Austrian Nazis; they were supported by certain Austrian Nazis including Dr Franz Riegele, Göring's brother-in-law. Hitler, however, said that if Habicht could not bring about a settlement with Austria, nobody could.[6] Habicht was in fact relieved of his appointment on 26 July 1934, but even after the July 1936 agreement Austrian *gauleiters* were still appointed, confirmed and recalled by German Party authorities.

In June 1937 Wilhelm Keppler was appointed Commissioner for the Austrian NSDAP.[7] Dr Friedrich Rainer and Odilo Globocnik, two Austrian Nazi functionaries, were continually receiving directives from the Obersalzberg for the political penetration of Austria.[8] On 3 June 1937, following a quarrel with Captain Josef Leopold, the Austrian Nazi leader, von Papen issued the following confidential instruction:

'If the Austrian NSDAP were a purely Austrian affair, any criticism of my person would leave me unaffected. But since its leaders to a large extent shape their policy in accordance with instructions from the Reich, it is completely impossible to characterise the political course pursued here by the special envoy of the Führer and Chancellor as being out of harmony with theirs and to publish this in the official organ of the Party throughout the country. My opinion of this kind of political leadership does not enter into question here. But it is absolutely essential for the advancement of the Austrian policy ordered by the Führer that we avoid giving the Austrian

Government even the slightest impression that two different official policies are being pursued by the Reich.'

In the same instruction von Papen points out that the May issue of the *Österreichische Beobachter*, the official organ of the Austrian Nazi Party, had stated that in the opinion of the Austrian NSDAP the Ambassador's mission had ended on 11 July 1936.[9]

Immediately after the Berchtesgaden meeting Hitler appointed as leader of the Austrian Nazis Major Hubert Klausner who had been cashiered from the Austrian army for political reasons; this he did in spite of the fact that he had just signed an agreement providing that:

1. Austrian National-Socialists should have opportunity for political activity on an equal footing with all other groups in accordance with the constitution (Art. II.3 of the Protocol). The constitution did not permit the formation of political parties.
2. The future Minister of the Interior (Seyss-Inquart) was the only person authorised to carry out Article II.3.
3. The Reich Government would take measures to prevent interference in the internal affairs of Austria on the part of Reich-German Party organs.[10]

All international conflicts start with an alleged or actual violation of some treaty obligation. From the German side, therefore, increasingly strident accusations were made against Austria for alleged non-fulfilment of her obligations under the agreement of 11 July 1936; the process was clearly linked to the Italian swing over to the German side which developed gradually as a result of her African involvement. The German complaints were summarised in a memorandum drafted on 11 February 1938, the eve of the Berchtesgaden meeting therefore, by Günther Altenburg, Austrian desk officer in the German Foreign Ministry, and signed by Hans Georg von Mackensen, the State Secretary, and Ernst von Weizsäcker, Director in the Ministry. It was submitted to the Foreign Minister and read as follows:

'The Agreement of July 11 1936 constitutes the basis of the present relations between Germany and Austria. The Austrian Government has thus far delayed the execution of this Agreement in spite of all efforts on the part of the German Government to hold it to the observance of the treaty obligations assumed. In the main these are: Complete amnesty for all persons who took part in the July *putsch* of 1934, extension of this amnesty to the refugees in the Reich, removal of economic and other forms of discrimination against the members of the movement in Austria (including reinstatement of their pensions) and participation of persons of the National Opposition in the shaping of the political will of the State.

The resistance to the cooperation so often promised stems mainly from the person of the Federal Chancellor himself, who said recently in the well-known interview that a wide gulf separates him from National-Socialism. He considers it his objective to gain time again and again through definite promises and half-promises. . . .'[11]

In fact there had never been agreement on a complete amnesty for persons involved in the July *putsch* or refugees in the Reich. Point IX of the Gentlemen's Agreement, it will be remembered, read:

> 'The Federal Chancellor declares that he is prepared: (a) To grant a far-reaching political amnesty, from which persons who have committed serious public crimes shall be excluded. Also covered by this amnesty shall be persons who have not yet been sentenced by judicial decree or penalised by administrative process. These provisions shall also be duly applied to *émigrés*.'[12]

In so far as persons specified in the agreement were concerned, the amnesty had been carried out in full.[13] At the end of November 1935, before the Christmas amnesty, the number of Nazis under detention (in internment camps) was 1,528; of these the majority (955) were given a conditional release before 1 January 1936; of the total of 911 persons arrested in connection with the July *putsch*, only 471 were still in prison at Christmastime 1935.[14] In any case, under the Berchtesgaden agreement the *émigrés* were excluded.[15] On 21 December 1937 von Papen reported that 'the July *putsch* was now almost liquidated by Austria, as only 45 persons were still in gaol and the only existing internment camp at Wöllersdorf had 105 inmates'.[16]

It should also be remembered that Nazi activities subsequent to 11 July 1936 had inevitably led to further judicial and political proceedings; at the end of 1937, therefore, people under detention included some to whom the July 1936 agreement did not apply at all. Moreover that agreement had made no mention of 'reinstatement of pension' for officials dismissed. As far as 'participation of persons of the National Opposition in the shaping of the political will' was concerned, when Altenburg wrote his report (11 February 1938), Glaise-Horstenau was still in the cabinet, Seyss-Inquart and Jury were members of the Council of State and leading 'Nationals' had been appointed to the *Volkspolitische* Offices of the Fatherland Front.

From the German point of view there were three reasons for the Anschluss:

1. Austria was accused of treaty violation; this ostensibly gave some legal basis for interference in internal Austrian affairs and this interference could be escalated until an acknowledged or camouflaged Anschluss was achieved.

2. For years German propaganda had emphasised that the aim was to unite the German people in accordance with history, the law of nature and the genuine desires of the Austrians; these desires had hitherto been denied expression by brutal oppression and the inadmissible interference of anti-German Powers.

3. The real, and ultimately decisive, motive behind the pressure for the Anschluss was strategic and economic in nature and of this neither in Germany nor Austria was public opinion aware. From the point of view of German officialdom the Austrian Anschluss 'by hook or by crook' was an essential prerequisite to further development of their plans for territorial expansion, strategic security and economic strength. Economically in particular Austria was by no means a negligible asset; Professor Wilhelm Taucher, the former Austrian Minister of Commerce, has pointed out that Germany's primary object in her trade treaties was to obtain raw materials but that she had no foreign currency with which to

pay. In 1938, however, Austria's gold and currency reserves stood at 2·7 milliard gold schillings (more than 2 milliard marks at the 1969 rate of exchange).[17]

In its concept of the interpretation of and obligations imposed by international treaties the Third Reich was no different from the earlier absolute and later totalitarian systems so far as the conduct of power policy was concerned. Any bilateral treaty with a small state was therefore of problematical value – everyone realised that. Helmut Krausnick says:

'In foreign policy Hitler's thinking was governed by a "realism" not really worthy of the name. Particularly as a principle of foreign policy, Hitler believed in the theory that Might can temporarily triumph over Right. In his view the object of treaties was to pin down the other side; as far as he was concerned they could be broken at any time and as the interests of the moment dictated. Political credit, the good name of the State, which Frederick the Great had described as more important than power, clearly meant nothing to Hitler. In foreign policy he played by no rules; a despairing British diplomat once said that it was impossible to play chess with a man who used his knights like castles.'[18]

In spite of all this the world at large grasped the nature of Nazi foreign policy and its treaty technique only when, after his bloodless conquest of the Sudetenland, Hitler broke his word and marched into Prague.

As already pointed out, for Germany the Austrian question was an internal matter and it was dealt with as such not only so far as internal policy was concerned; in its language the German Foreign Ministry followed the rule implicitly. In the first half of 1935 Germany was still afraid that the Western Powers might conclude a Pact to guarantee Austrian independence. The developments leading up to the Three-Power Conference in Stresa in April 1935 and the efforts to draw Russia into the European concert through the Franco-Russian Consultation and Assistance Pact of May 1935 were followed by the Wilhelmstrasse with anxiety, all the more acute since they seemed to be a retort to Germany's introduction of universal military service in March 1935 and her consequent renunciation of important provisions in the Peace Treaty.[19]

In June 1935, however, the Anglo-German Naval Agreement represented a break-through for Germany *vis-à-vis* the 'Stresa front'; Great Britain had thereby given unilateral recognition to the abrogation of the naval clauses in the Peace Treaty and re-establishment of a German submarine fleet hitherto forbidden.

Further relief for German foreign policy was provided by the Italian attack on Abyssinia on 2 October 1935. In the August Italy had ostentatiously held major manœuvres in South Tyrol to show the world that Italian interest in maintenance of the *status quo* on the Brenner was unchanged. Renunciation of the Locarno Treaties on the pretext that they had already been violated by France and the risky unilateral occupation of the Rhineland demilitarised zone also contributed to dissipation of the anxieties of the Third Reich's diplomats. In German eyes, therefore, the July 1936 treaty with Austria was analogous to a stand-still agreement, primarily intended to facilitate the formation of the future Rome-Berlin Axis.

Subsequent developments were governed primarily by internal politics in the West; they included the aggravation of the Spanish conflict and the massive, openly-admitted, German rearmament. By about mid-1937 they had produced a situation in which Hitler was justified in assuming that he could deal with the Austrian question as he wished. He still did not want to intervene by force but, if this proved unavoidable, it did not appear to imply any immediate danger. Berlin simply assumed that it would be possible, without incurring the risk of another *putsch* and simply by providing large-scale support for Austrian National-Socialism, to enable it to seize power based on the existing Austrian constitution, in other words semi-legally. This would result in *Gleichschaltung* and so, as in the case of Danzig and quite irrespective of the external façade, Austria could be exploited, not initially as an integral part of Germany, but at least as a sphere of interest and influence exclusive to the Third Reich. Nothing was therefore lost by assurances of respect for the Austrian constitution and declarations of recognition of her independence.

The fact that a section of the Austrian Nazis did not believe in this internal development without the use of force produced a split in the Austrian Party. The paradoxical result was that the revolutionaries had to be repeatedly called to order by German Party and government authorities in order to avoid being compromised in the eyes of the outside world. Finally, however, it was the supporters of revolution who called the tune and, despite their numerical weakness, forced the decision of March 1938 just at the moment when Hitler and Göring had reached the same conclusion. The end result was quite different from that visualised by the revolutionaries and they were bitterly disappointed to find themselves pushed on one side – but that is another story.

In Austrian eyes, on the other hand, the Anschluss, or rather what ultimately emerged from it, was both an indication and a consequence of a diplomatic revolution in the chancelleries of the major powers. The starting point was the change in Italian policy which ruptured the Great Power alliance based on the League of Nations; with it went the principle of collective security in defence of the European *status quo* against any attempt at unilateral change by violent means. Rome's new aims, which contrary to Italian expectations led to a break with London, had nothing to do with Central Europe. Like London, though for different reasons, Rome would in principle have preferred to maintain Austrian independence. The same was undoubtedly true of Paris and Moscow, the former for politico-military reasons and the latter primarily on ideological and pragmatic grounds.[20]

As things were, both London and Rome, with whom the decision primarily lay, were prepared, if needs must, to sacrifice the Central European *status quo* and with it the existing peaceful order for the sake of what they considered to be the overriding interests of their countries. Italy did so in order to obtain German backing for her Mediterranean plans, Britain because she thought that it offered the best chance of keeping the peace or at worst would give her the necessary time to catch up in the arms race and so enable her to carry more weight diplomatically. In view of this situation, whatever Austria might do or whatever risks she was prepared to take could do nothing to alter the position.

To understand what the Anschluss looked like to Austria through the spectacles of 1938 one must not forget that for us the enemy was not Germany but the NSDAP-Hitler Movement. Even though in retrospect it may not appear to be so, this was in fact the truth. In retrospect one is apt to forget that, although in Germany the Movement and the State had become identical, for historical, humanitarian and politico-psychological reasons we could not accept this in Austria, even at the risk of temporary submersion. In the light of geography, the ratio of forces and the close economic and cultural connections between the two countries no one could seriously pretend that Austria's existence threatened Germany's interests.[21]

Torquato Tasso the sixteenth-century Italian poet said: 'If sheltering in a small state, be content calmly to look on, as if from the shore, on the turbulent course of the world.' In the Ballhausplatz this was all we could wish for in the circumstances, but neither friend nor foe was prepared to allow us to do it. The idea of an international guarantee of Austrian neutrality would have aroused enthusiasm nowhere at the time. So we were forced to conclude treaties with our great neighbours, with Italy in the Rome Protocols of March 1934 and March 1936 and with Germany on 11 July 1936.

We were entirely genuine in our assurance that Austria was ready 'to conduct its foreign policy in the light of the peaceful aims of the German government's foreign policy' (Point VIII of the Gentlemen's Agreement). Austria had never adopted a position opposed to Germany on any question of revision of the Versailles Treaty or removal of discrimination against Germany; she had never participated in any anti-German alliance. The limit of our cooperation with Germany lay in our basic aversion to any acts of force designed to change the map of Europe, since in our view these must sooner or later lead to a breach of the peace. Naturally too we were prepared to defend ourselves against any direct or indirect assault on our existence as a state and to protest against flagrant violations of international law; among many examples of such violations two will suffice: the arrest on 14 June 1933 of Dr Erwin Wasserbäck, the Austrian Press Attaché in

Berlin, and the formation and arming of the so-called Austrian Legion on the territory of the Reich.

The Third Reich, however, was dissatisfied with the conduct of Austrian foreign policy. On 21 December 1937, for instance, von Papen commented:

> 'By exerting the best and strongest energies of the Reich and by utilising the present international situation, the Führer was trying to restore the world position of the Reich. In this process *Germany had to demand more than mere passive assistance from Austria*; she had to demand that Austria, with heart and soul, wherever possible under existing circumstances, support this struggle of the German world for its existence. Though the Federal Chancellor had told me repeatedly that his foreign policy nowhere interfered with the policy of the Reich, I had to tell him that this was not enough. *This passive attitude was in itself* [!] *a negation*. Particularly so when every act of foreign policy ended with a new appeal to the world for the maintenance of Austria's independence. . . .'[22]

The Anschluss descended on Austria like a storm, yearned for by many but a thunderclap for all; it was yearned for as a relief from the overheated atmosphere of tension which had mounted to an intolerable level; the Anschluss seemed to put an end to this – and without the catastrophe which had been thought inevitable. It looked as though peace were assured. But it came like a thunderclap because, both for Austrians and Germans, events tumbled over each other with such surprising rapidity. Everyone was longing for the fog to lift; everyone wanted to believe that the blue sky was coming, though in some cases against their better judgement.

So at first there was jubilation, partly genuine, partly as a sort of premium on a freedom- and life-insurance policy, frequently in an effort to protect friends and dependants and safeguard one's own livelihood. People hoped that everything would be all right once the initial turmoil was over; one would be able to 'put things to rights . . .'.

Many outside the country knew better; on 15 March 1938 Harold Nicolson, the well-known British diplomat, wrote in his diary: 'A sense of danger hangs over us like a pall; Hitler has completely collared Austria; no question of an Anschluss, just complete absorption.'[23]

However this may be, enthusiasm was soon to be followed by disillusionment – and very quickly too, for the Third Reich's propaganda machine made one or two serious gaffes only explicable by total ignorance of Austrian conditions and mentality. Louis Weinberger, later Vice-Burgomaster of Vienna and a respected leader of the Christian Workers' Movement, was an eye-witness of what happened and he says:

'German propaganda ought not to have allowed the affair of the "Bavarian Aid Train" to slip through. Of course there were indigent folk in Austria before 1938. Where are there not and where will there not be? At the time, however, there was hardly anybody who was really hungry and certainly no one longing for the bread and sausages distributed by the "Bavarian Aid Train".... This does not alter the fact that even here there were people prepared to be photographed and filmed eating from this soup kitchen and carrying its loaves of bread about. In contrast to the "Third Reich" Austria was a land of plenty at this time; she possessed everything which had long since become only a memory "over there" or at best was obtainable only by privileged people.

In the first few days many idealists were sadly disillusioned and many eyes opened by the tragi-comic contrast between the "Bavarian Aid Train" and the brazen looting of the "poor hungry" Ostmark. It was too ludicrous. On one side were sentimental pictures and reports about the poor Austrians, on the other a descent on the shops and warehouses of every kind. For every wagon in the "Bavarian Aid Train" one hundred others laden with loot of all sorts rolled into the "Old Reich" from the very first moment of "liberation". "Home to the Reich" in the literal sense! . . .'[24]

There were plenty of similar stories; some of them I even learnt from the gossip of my guards while I was in prison. One of these anecdotes appeared in the *Eugen-Roth-Buch*, for instance, under the heading 'An SOS':

'The Viennese were by no means all pro-Anschluss after 1938. They took their revenge by pinpricking the "Prussians" who streamed into their city – by misdirecting strangers for instance.

One German whom we knew gave a weary cry of desperation: "Please! I am a Catholic and a Bavarian. For God's sake tell me where the Herrengasse is." '25

The first organised resistance groups were formed immediately after 13 March; their members were of every political colour from monarchists to extreme left-wingers. Their heroism has received no publicity. And yet they were the ultimate victors, even though they did not all live to see their victory. Ninety of their leaders were executed or shot or died in prison; in Vienna alone 631 persons were executed on political grounds between 6 December 1938 and 4 April 1945, and 156 in Graz; in addition both inside and outside the country many thousands were condemned to death by court martial.26

Even some German National-Socialists realised the difficulties; this is shown by a report from Dr C. Koenig of Berlin, an agent of the SS Security Service, commenting on his impressions of the work of the Gestapo in Austria. It says:

'During the revolutionary events in Austria the Gestapo far exceeded its true role. As a result the impression has been given in many quarters both at home and abroad that the basic concepts of law, sanctity of property and of freedom are no longer assured in certain important fields of economic life. The more law and order are re-established in Austria, the more distasteful and untenable must the position of the Gestapo, in its present form, become. It must expect many suits for restitution of property from aggrieved persons. It is absolutely essential, therefore, that the Gestapo should draw in its horns and as quickly as possible; it should confine itself to its political role as in Germany. The problem today is to find an adequate face-saver for this retreat. Detailed examination of the mountains of files seems impossible and, if we stick to the rules, would only produce further injustice by keeping the aggrieved persons in prison. I regard it as urgently necessary for the Security Police Inspector in Austria to be instructed by *Gruppenführer* Heydrich to get in touch at once with *Gauleiter* Bürckel, who carries the overall responsibility, or with Vice-President Barth and discuss the possibilities of a solution to existing difficulties. In my view there must be a generous amnesty and it should be possible quickly to reach agreement on its scope. It should be based on the Führer's

promise that we have come, not to exact vengeance, but to be
generous. A check of the files to see whether a case was serious or not
would only take a few days, if we really intend to be generous. This
would only leave the serious cases and they will give the Gestapo
quite enough to do. This would quickly put an end to the state of
fear in which Vienna in particular is living.

Confiscations of property are a more difficult case. My advice
here is that the Gestapo should hand over all files on confiscations to
a new agency to be set up outside the Hotel Metropol and free from
any Gestapo influence, perhaps under the supervision of Welsch, the
State Attorney; goods would then be returned to their owners
without prejudice to the claims of the State.'[27]

A letter written on 30 December 1938 by P. Bruno Spitzl, the
pastor of Dornbach, to Seyss-Inquart, now the *Reichsstatthalter*,
who had been one of his parishioners, shows the crisis of conscience through which many were passing:

'Any unprejudiced observer will agree with me when I say that
the misery caused to many families by disciplinary regulations,
judgements of the courts or measures decreed by authorities of
greater or lesser importance is immeasurably greater than anything
for which the previous regime was responsible. I do not know how
the men who are responsible for all this misery, for all these tears
from innocent women and children and for the real penury of so
many families will answer for their deeds before posterity or, even
more, before the judgement of God. I cannot imagine that you,
Herr *Reichsstatthalter*, know about all this. If you knew it as I and
others know it, then you would not be able to hold your tongue
and would do your utmost to make good the Führer's promise
given before the revolution and bring true domestic peace to our
people. That would be a patriotic and a christian act worth the
sweat of all men of goodwill, the only act which could lay the
foundation for what has always been your aim, Herr *Reichsstatthalter*,
the community of the German people.

The second point about which I am most anxious is our people's
faith in Christianity and the Catholic Church. I have no fears for
the Church itself. She is bound to no one people; she can lose a
whole people, even the German people, but they will be the losers,
not the Church. Despite all her temporal trappings she is still the
work of God and, as such, indestructible until the end of our earthly

days. In this case too, therefore, my anxiety is for my country and has no egoistic background. . . .

The Party is said to stand for "positive Christianity". I cannot believe that you, Herr *Reichsstatthalter*, can find what has happened and is happening daily to be compatible with this Party principle. Equally I cannot believe that you, with your spiritual and moral principles which, as you told me on the Sunday before the revolution, you have explained clearly and unequivocally to the Führer, will fail to find some equitable solution to the claims of Catholicism and of the Church. . . .'[28]

Even the new Nazi leaders in Austria were among those for whom the Anschluss had its unpleasant side. This is shown by the violent quarrel which developed between *Gauleiter* Josef Bürckel, the 'Reich Commissar for Reunification', and Seyss-Inquart who was a Minister of the Reich; it reached its peak in August 1939.[29]

On 23 June 1939 Seyss-Inquart wrote to Bürckel voicing certain criticisms of the situation in Vienna and Austria in general and referrring to a crisis of confidence; as he later told Himmler the letter was couched in 'comradely and confidential terms'. On 8 August Bürckel replied with a series of violent accusations including personal insinuations; his letter, sixteen pages long, culminated as follows: 'So what's it all about? Simply the question of preservation or liquidation. You, Doctor, are for preservation. I have been commissioned by the Führer to liquidate. . . . Our ways have parted.' Seyss-Inquart replied no less sharply: '*Gauleiter*, I acknowledge with thanks receipt of your letter of 8th inst. At least I now know what I am and have been up against. . . .' Seyss-Inquart thereupon sent a 24-page report on this correspondence to Himmler, summarising his reply to Bürckel with the words: 'A knave can only think like one.'

Seyss-Inquart had accused Bürckel of causing a crisis of confidence, saying that it was unreasonable to behave in the 'Ostmark' like a Governor in a sort of Alsace-Lorraine and install 'Reich Germans, or rather Saarlanders, in all important Party, State and local government offices'. In his reply Bürckel accused Seyss-Inquart, who was then Reich Minister without Portfolio located in Vienna, of disloyalty to the Party and the Reich; in pleading for the maintenance of an Austrian provincial government he was doing Catholic Action's dirty work; he was thereby seeking to postpone the liquidation of Austria as long as possible, whereas he, Bürckel, regarded this as the most urgent task of the Reich Commissar. For similar reasons, he continued, once plans for an Austrian provincial government had come to naught, Seyss-Inquart had supported the formation of a Ministry for Austria as 'a sort of Ministry of Culture for the Ostmark'. Bürckel then accused Seyss-Inquart of having corresponded in the spring of 1939 with 'a vile *émigré*' in Prague and continued: 'These are all things which should perhaps merit clemency on grounds of high policy'.

Finally Bürckel's reply dealt in detail with Seyss-Inquart's political past – after the first abortive attack on Dollfuss (3 October 1933) he had sent the Chancellor a congratulatory telegram and expressed his abhorrence of the would-be assassins; he had believed that National-Socialism could be 'purified' from inside Austria and had been favourable to the attempted establishment of a Union of National-Socialist Catholics; in the critical days of March 1938 he had kept himself in the background and had hardly been seen (Bürckel here referred to a memorandum from Globocnik with whom Seyss-Inquart had quarrelled meanwhile). Bürckel then drew a sharp distinction between 'Seyss and his circles' on the one hand and the 'Old Fighters' on the other, saying: 'The confidence of my men is ennobled by the sacrifices which they have had to make because *émigré* traitors have been trying to prevent them remaining loyal to the Reich. You, Doctor, take a more lenient view than I. That is why I say to you today: Our ways have parted.'

In his defence to Himmler Seyss-Inquart attacked Bürckel no less sharply – during 1939 the Reich Commissar had spent barely two-fifths of his time in Vienna; if Bürckel denied filling all posts with Saarlanders, this was mere subterfuge; any child knew that the problem arose not in connection with the official administration but in the Reich Commissar's own agencies, particularly in Vienna, which were 'run by generally mediocre people who had not integrated here' – hence 'the malicious joke about a new

Wehrmacht regiment called the "Saarland Job-hunting Rifles"'. He, Seyss, had never demanded the preservation of an Austrian identity but rather its elimination. 'If political catholicism in the Ostmark has today been liquidated to a far greater extent than in the Old Reich, this is in no way due to the efforts of the Reich Commissar but to the energetic action of my own expert Plattner. On my instructions, with my knowledge and over my signature he has initiated all those measures which are today regarded as a pattern for the future in the Old Reich.'

Seyss-Inquart then emphasised that he had never been a member of Catholic Action; to connect him with the *émigrés* was an 'impudence' and he had already demanded from Bürckel an explanation on this point; he had never sent a congratulatory telegram to Dollfuss; he knew that in 1934 a Workers Association of Catholic National-Socialists had been formed but he did not know what Bürckel was referring to. 'If he is perhaps thinking of Professor Eibl's[30] vagaries, it is really an insult to ascribe to me so little political acumen in such matters.' Early in 1932, Seyss-Inquart continued, he had become a member of the Styrian *Heimwehr*; he had been largely instrumental in bringing this organisation into the Party and Habicht had declared that members of the Styrian *Heimwehr* were to be regarded as members; he had paid his membership contributions ever since December 1931 and from this time on had felt himself in every respect a member of the Party owing allegiance to it.

Contrary to Bürckel's statement, he went on, he had been at his post during the critical hours of 11 March 1938. Only after handing the ultimatum to Miklas had he gone out for a short while, about 4.0 p.m. or 4.45, to get a breath of fresh air. He 'realised that he would not be required before 5.30 since he knew that the people of the former system would not make up their minds one second before they had to'. He had the impression that Bürckel's extraordinary energy and initiative in personnel matters 'had already overstepped the bounds of what would medically be called a complex'. Bürckel should one day confess how many of his office staff he had dismissed either permanently or temporarily and how many members of the Party he had had arrested or locked up, even if only for a time. Seyss-Inquart's letter to Himmler ends:

'My initial reaction was to submit Bürckel's letter to the Führer and I still think that the Führer must have the last word in this matter. The Führer is so preoccupied with foreign policy questions these days, however, that I hesitate to approach him at the moment, although for me this affair has an importance greater than anything else which affects me personally. I therefore turn to you and ask you to investigate these matters most thoroughly and to decide who is responsible. Heil to the Führer.'[31]

In retrospect this correspondence is still of interest since it illustrates the inefficiency, indeed the absurdity, of all the strivings of the Anschluss supporters, whether on the German or the Austrian side. The cases both for the prosecution and the defence prove that Seyss-Inquart's Nazi team of March 1938 had split once more. Of the main participants in the events of 11 March Globocnik, Rainer, Klausner and Dr Hammerschmied were on Bürckel's side, whereas Mühlmann, Plattner, Wimmer, Fischböck and, interestingly, Dr Wächter too backed up Seyss-Inquart.

Undoubtedly the outcome of the Anschluss was a severe disappointment for Seyss-Inquart and for Leopold and the 'Old Fighters' too. They had placed all their hopes on Hitler; Seyss-Inquart, after all, had said: 'Our whole existence is directly inspired by the Führer'.

The executor of the Führer's will, however, was Bürckel and so, after a bare fourteen months, there could no longer be an Austria, even under another name. Austria could only be a district [*Gau*] of the Reich; there could be no Reich Regent [*Reichsstatthalter*], still less a provincial government; there could only be a *Gauleiter*.

Long afterwards (in 1946) von Papen said: 'How easy it would have been then (1937) to create a relationship with the German Reich similar to that of Bavaria between 1871 and 1918 – full governmental and administrative autonomy and an independent parliament. Only foreign policy and military command in wartime need have been matters of common concern.'[32]

Any such idea was, of course, quite unacceptable and for supporters of Austrian independence not even a subject of discussion; in any case how could anyone seriously consider such a 'solution' in view of Bavaria's fate since 1933 and in the light of the methods employed by Hitler and his satraps? There were now no more Embassy reports from Austria to write, so Papen goes on:

'In Austria there was no trace of autonomy. The Party machine was in charge and its rule was governed by hatred and the desire to persecute those who had said "No". Hitler appointed as High Commissioner the most unsuitable man he could find, *Gauleiter* Bürckel from the Saar and Pfalz. I knew the man personally. In 1934 I had handed over to him my office as "Reich Commissar for the Saar Territory". He was an arrogant school-teacher without knowledge of administration and politically incompetent; in addition he had some murky periods in his past.'

Von Papen had a high opinion of Seyss-Inquart which he rightly says that I had once shared. Unfortunately he has to admit that Seyss-Inquart was the greatest disappointment of his life. Here perhaps Papen is too harsh in his judgement.[33] All available evidence goes to show that, had Seyss-Inquart managed to assert himself in Austria, the barbarism associated with the Anschluss would probably never have occurred. But precisely because it did so, the end result was the death of the Anschluss idea.

Internationally the Anschluss was a highly undesirable development and the way in which it had been done questionable in the extreme; in the light of the relative power positions, however, there was nothing anybody could do to change it. In practically every country press comment was critical, though it was basically concerned less with the fate of Austria than with possible menacing future developments, especially as regards Czechoslovakia. Particularly in Paris anxiety was unconcealed. German propaganda did its best to calm down the 'storm in a teacup' raging in the world press.

On 15 March Fumimaro Konoye, the Japanese Prime Minister, congratulated the Führer and Reich Chancellor on 'the reunification of Austria with the German Reich for which he had striven for years'.[34] A telegram from the German Ambassador to China reported that Chiang Kai-shek had welcomed the union of Austria with Germany in accordance with the motto 'One People, One Reich', though he had added a critical reference to the fact that with regard to Manchukuo Germany's attitude had not accorded with this motto.[35]

In Berne Giuseppe Motta, head of the Political Department in the Swiss Foreign Ministry, told the German Minister that 'he had long regarded the Anschluss as inevitable', and that it had 'removed the elements of international conflict'. On 22 March the Swiss President issued a statement on the Anschluss, saying prosaically:

'On 13 March the Federal State of Austria, with which Switzerland has maintained warm neighbourly relations, ceased to exist as an independent state. . . . This change in the political map of Europe cannot result in any deterioration of the political position of Switzerland.'

The President then referred to the indispensability of the independence and neutrality of the Confederation and said that solemn assurances on this point had been received from all sides. 'Any attack on the inviolability of its territory would be a shameful crime against international law.'[36]

On 16 March Paul-Henri Spaak, the Belgian Foreign Minister, spoke in the Chamber:

'The union of Austria with Germany seems to be established fact. For various reasons neither Italy, France nor England have been able or willing to oppose it. I am a determined supporter of the independence of peoples and their right of self-determination. . . . I have long thought that the Anschluss was in accordance with the logic of facts and, if it had been carried out in a normal manner, then I should not have been surprised about it.'[37]

Döme von Sztojay, the Hungarian Minister in Berlin, transmitted to the Berlin Foreign Ministry on behalf of his government 'heartiest congratulations to the Führer and Reich Chancellor on the reunion [!] of Austria with the German Reich'.[38] The Hungarian reaction and the absence of any protest from Budapest – despite repeated assurances about adherence to the Rome Protocols

– was not surprising. Although in influential Hungarian legitimist circles the 'German line' was anything but popular, the Hungarian government and Koloman Kanya, its unyielding Foreign Minister, had left Vienna in no doubt that for reasons of national interest Hungary could not risk a conflict with Germany. Just as Italy finally opted for Germany because of her East African and Mediterranean policy, so Hungary did likewise primarily because of her irreconcilable differences with Czechoslovakia.

In Prague public opinion had markedly swung over to the Austrian side since the end of February. This was especially noticeable in the tone of the press, which in the last days before the German invasion made no secret of its support for the Austrian position. The attitude of Hodza, the Prime Minister, was ostentatiously friendly to Austria in contrast to that of Krofta, his Foreign Minister, who was much more reserved; it must be remembered, however, that in the country's extremely delicate situation Czechoslovak diplomacy was at pains to avoid anything which might irritate its German neighbour. Czech public opinion was only too well aware of the increased danger which the disappearance of Austria portended for the nation.

Prague's official attitude is clearly shown by the reports from Eisenlohr, the German Minister there. On 11 March he reported Krofta as saying that he did not anticipate any final solution from the Austrian plebiscite and he agreed to take steps to discourage the pro-Austrian attitude of the Czechoslovak press. In a further telegram to Mackensen next day Eisenlohr reported that Krofta had assured him that Czechoslovakia had no thought of taking military steps and wanted a *détente* with Germany. About 1.0 a.m. on 12 March Eisenlohr telegraphed again to say that the Czech cabinet had met and shortly before midnight Krofta had told him that 'no one here is contemplating intervening in Austrian affairs'.[39] Finally at 10.35 a.m. on 12 March Woermann, the German Chargé d'Affaires in London, reported that the Czechoslovak Minister there had officially informed the British government that all the rumours about Czech mobilisation were untrue and that Czechoslovakia had no intention of intervening on account of events in Austria.[40]

Mussolini's reaction on 13 and 14 March is well known: 'My attitude is determined by the friendship between our two countries, which is consecrated in the Axis.'[41] This was preceded on 11 March by a letter from Hitler to Mussolini handed over in Rome by Prince Philipp of Hesse; the text given below is that published in Rome (the sentences concerning Czechoslovakia were omitted in that version).[42]

'In a fateful hour I am turning to Your Excellency to inform you of a decision which appears necessary under the circumstances and has already become irrevocable.

In recent months I have seen with increasing preoccupation how a relationship was gradually developing between Austria and Czechoslovakia which, while difficult for us to endure in peacetime, was bound, in case of a war imposed upon Germany, to become a most serious threat to the security of the Reich.

In the course of these understandings the Austrian State began gradually to arm all its frontiers with barriers and fortifications. Its purpose could be none other than:

1. to effect the restoration at a specified time;
2. to throw the weight of a mass of at least twenty million men against Germany if necessary.

It is precisely the close bonds between Germany and Italy which, as was to be expected, have exposed our Reich to inevitable attacks. Incumbent on me is the responsibility not to permit the rise of a situation in Central Europe which perhaps might lead to serious complications precisely because of our friendship with Italy. This new orientation of the policy of the Austrian State does not, however, reflect in any way the real desire and will of the Austrian people. . . .'

There then followed the standard accusations about oppression and mistreatment of the 'Germans in Austria' by a regime which 'lacked any legal basis'. 'The sufferings of innumerable tormented people know no bounds.' He (Hitler) had therefore decided to make a last attempt to reach an agreement in order finally to establish full equality for all under the law. At the Berchtesgaden meeting he had drawn Herr Schuschnigg's attention most seriously to the facts that Germany was not prepared to permit a hostile power to establish itself on her borders and could no longer tolerate mistreatment of the nationally-minded majority in Austria by a negligible minority. He himself was a son of this soil; Austria was his homeland and from his own relatives he knew what oppression and sufferings the overwhelming majority of the people had to endure. He had told Herr Schuschnigg that, if the equality of all Germans in Austria were not restored, he would one day be forced to assume the protection of these abandoned kinsmen.

The letter continues:

'My demands were more than moderate. In fact according to all principles of reason, right, and justice, and even according to the precepts of a formalistic democracy, Herr Schuschnigg and his Cabinet should have resigned to make room for a government enjoying the confidence of the people. I did not demand this. I was satisfied with a number of assurances that henceforth, within the framework of the Austrian laws – which, although they had been enacted unjustly, were in force at the present time – all inhabitants of the country were to be treated in the same way, receive the same privileges or be subject to the same restrictions and, lastly, some security was to be established in the military sphere in order that the Austrian State might not one day become a dependency of Czechoslovakia.

Herr Schuschnigg made me a solemn promise and concluded an agreement to this effect.

From the very beginning he failed to keep this agreement.

But now he has gone so far as to deal a new blow against the spirit of this agreement by scheduling a so-called plebiscite which actually is a mockery.

The results of this newly planned oppression of the majority of the people are such as were feared.

The Austrian people *are now finally rising against the constant oppression*, and this will inevitably result in new oppressive measures. *Therefore the representatives of this oppressed people in the Austrian Government as well as in the other bodies have withdrawn. Since the day before yesterday the country has been approaching closer and closer to a state of anarchy.*

In my responsibility as Führer and Chancellor of the German

Reich and likewise as a son of this soil, I can no longer remain passive in the face of these developments.

I am now determined to restore law and order in my homeland and enable the people to decide their own fate according to their judgement in an unmistakable, clear and open manner.

May the Austrian people itself, therefore, forge its own destiny. Whatever the manner may be in which this plebiscite is to be carried out, I now wish solemnly to assure Your Excellency, as the Duce of Fascist Italy:

1. Consider this step only as one of national self-defence and there-fore as an act that any man of character would do in the same way, were he in my position. You too, Excellency, could not act differently if the fate of Italians were at stake and I as Führer and National-Socialist cannot act differently.
2. In a critical hour for Italy I proved to you the steadfastness of my sympathy. Do not doubt that in the future there will be no change in this respect.
3. Whatever the consequences of the coming events may be, I have drawn a definite boundary between Germany and France *and now draw one just as definite between Italy and us. It is the Brenner.* This decision will never be questioned or changed. *I did not make this decision in 1938*, but immediately after the end of the World War and I never made a secret of it.

I hope that Your Excellency will pardon especially the haste of this letter and the form of this communication. These events occurred unexpectedly for all of us. Nobody had any inkling of the latest step of Herr Schuschnigg, not even his colleagues in the Government, and until now I had always hoped that perhaps at the last moment a different solution might be possible.

I deeply regret not being able to talk to you personally at this time to tell you everything I feel.

Always in friendship,   [signed] Adolf Hitler.'

The letter made no mention of military occupation or indeed of the Anschluss. The explanation for the association of the Austrian question with that of Czechoslovakia is to be found in the Hoss-bach Minutes and Hitler's later statements on political and military strategy. Few other documents show more clearly than this letter the sort of opponent Austria, and later the world, was up against.

Prince Philipp of Hesse's telephone conversation with Hitler on the night of 11 March after receipt of this letter has often been recorded.[43]

Nevertheless all this did not reflect the true feeling, certainly not that of Italy; this was primarily one of uncertainty. The satisfaction officially expressed in the regimented Italian press about strengthening of the Rome-Berlin Axis and the Duce's public statement did not accord with the real facts. General Emil Liebitzky, the former Austrian Military Attaché in Rome, testified that the German invasion of Austria made an immense impression on the Italians. Even Mussolini was 'thunderstruck', he said. Particularly in army circles there was consternation. Finally people concluded that: 'If something had to happen, better that it should do so with Italy rather than against her.'[44]

Ciano, the Italian Foreign Minister, said that the Anschluss was no 'joy' to Italy but realism demanded that she retain the friendship of eighty million Germans, onerous though that might perhaps be.[45] In 1940 he said to Sumner Welles, the American Under-Secretary of State:

'No country would want to have Germany as a neighbour. Italy now has her as a neighbour and we must do the best we can to get on with her. . . . An independent Austria can be successful only if the Austrian people are given a real chance to live and a new opportunity to develop a stable and prosperous country. If any country could logically desire the reconstitution of an independent Austria, it would be Italy.'[46]

A report dated 25 March 1938 from von Plessen, the German Chargé d'Affaires in Rome also gives a very realistic appreciation of the Italian attitude.[47]

In Paris and London things were little different, though at first the tone of the press was outspoken. On 12 March, for instance, the *Echo de Paris* headline read: 'The Murder of Austria – a pure Scandal.' *Homme Libre* said: 'To estimate the dramatic events of 11 March we must be further away from them. All that one can say now is that a new order has been introduced into Europe.' *Ère Nouvelle* lamented that the international 'drama' had overtaken France in the midst of an internal political crisis. It was serious, indeed, tragic, that in the circumstances France was in danger of having to look on from the sidelines without being able to say a word either in Berlin or in London. *Le Jour* simply said: 'Austria is reaping what France has sown.' *Journal* wrote: 'In the course of twenty years a criminal game has brought France from the glorious sunrise of the armistice to a menacing dusk.'

On 12 March the London *Times* said that the previous day had brought complete triumph for the National-Socialists. Their superiority was such that Austria could offer no further resistance. The *Daily Mail* reported that on the Friday, via Franckenstein, the Austrian Minister in London, Schuschnigg had asked what support he could count upon if necessary. Franckenstein had been told that of course England was interested in events in Austria but that there could be no question of military support for Schuschnigg's policy. It was understood that Schuschnigg had asked the same question in Paris. The *Daily Telegraph* printed a five-column report on events in Austria. The *Daily Herald* also sounded the alarm both in its headlines and columns.[48]

On 11 March the Austrian Consul-General in New York received from the 'Non-Sectarian Anti-Nazi League' a telegram for transmission to the Federal Chancellor in Vienna:

'The undersigned citizens of the United States join with the defenders of democracy the world over and welcome your brave efforts to preserve the autonomy and independence of Austria. We assure you that you have all our moral support in your courageous stand against German Nazi aggression, in hope and confidence that under your leadership the Austrian people will stand firm behind you.'

The telegram was signed by fifty well-known people including Upton Sinclair, Harry Elmer, Ernest Barnes, Franz Boas, Oswald Garrison Villard and Johannes Steel. They were primarily well-known left-wing writers and journalists.[49] Because of the six-hour time-lag, however, when this telegram was drafted Austria's fate was already sealed.

On 12 March the *St Louis Globe Democrat* wrote:

'Austria has capitulated to Hitler this night; under the pressure of the German war machine the Austrian Government has given up its five-year struggle against Hitler's tyranny. German troops, concentrated on the frontiers, marched into Austria at three points. On a German ultimatum demanding the reconstitution of the government the previous Chancellor resigned.'

A cable of 11 March from the Washington correspondent of the *New York Times* ran:

'Government offices are very exercised over the Austrian crisis. Secretary of State Hull stated, however, that the United States had no intention of doing anything in the matter. . . . Hull added that nothing had happened directly affecting the United States. . . . The United States Government had exerted no restraining influence on the German Government. . . . People here are of the opinion that the majority of Austrians are opposed to German policy and this would presumably have been voiced if the Austrian plebiscite had been held. Now, however, a majority of Austrians have clearly accommodated themselves to the new situation.'[50]

Up to 14 March the American press in general had been somewhat pro-German. From this date, however, a change appeared. Dieckhoff, the German Ambassador in Washington, reported a noticeable shift of public opinion.[51] German militarism, the rape of small states and the glaring breach of agreements now became the object of violent criticism and the State Department was cold and reserved towards German diplomats. The Ambassador thought that the change could be ascribed to some initiative on the part of President Roosevelt, who was worried about future repercussions in Europe (Czechoslovakia); in addition, the Ambassador said, the political climate was very much influenced by London; there was much talk about Gestapo methods and the wave of arrests of Catholics, Jews and socialists was very adversely commented on.[52] Weeks passed before the public mood calmed down and the Anschluss was accepted as an accomplished fact; the declarations of loyalty from Cardinal Innitzer and the Evangelical Church in Austria were also a contributory factor.[53]

The only formal protests against the occupation of Austria

came from Chile, China (Chiang Kai-shek), Mexico, Republican Spain and the Soviet Union.

On 14 March in the House of Commons Neville Chamberlain, the Prime Minister, set out the views and policy of the British government:

'On Wednesday of last week Herr von Schuschnigg decided that the best way to put an end to the uncertainties of the internal situation in his country was to hold a plebiscite under which the people could decide the future of their country. Provision for that plebiscite is made in the Austrian Constitution of 1934. . . . His Majesty's Government have throughout been in the closest touch with the situation. The Foreign Secretary contacted the German Foreign Minister on the 10th March, and addressed to him a grave warning on the Austrian situation and on what appeared to be the policy of the German Government in regard to it. In particular Lord Halifax told him that His Majesty's Government attached the greatest importance to all measures being taken to ensure that the plebiscite was carried out without interference or intimidation. Late on the 11th March our Ambassador in Berlin registered a protest in strong terms with the German Government against such use of coercion, backed by force, against an independent state in order to create a situation incompatible with its national independence. Such action, Sir Nevile Henderson pointed out, was bound to produce the gravest reactions, of which it would be impossible to foretell the issue. Earlier that day I made earnest representations in the same sense to the German Minister for Foreign Affairs. . . . To these protests the German Government replied in a letter addressed to His Majesty's Ambassador in Berlin by Baron von Neurath.'

Von Neurath's letter says that in the name of the German government he must state that 'the British government is not within its rights in claiming the role of a protector of the independence of Austria'. In the course of diplomatic conversations regarding the Austrian question the German government had never left the British government in any doubt that the form of the relations between the Reich and Austria could only be regarded as an internal affair of the German people and no concern of third Powers. It was superfluous to recapitulate the historical and political bases of this standpoint. For this reason the German government must from the outset reject as inadmissible the protest lodged by the British government.

Von Neurath then reverted to the events leading up to 11 March and observed that the object of the proposed plebiscite could only have been the political repression of the overwhelming majority of the population of Austria and that it was in flagrant contradiction to the Berchtesgaden agreement. As a result those members of the Austrian government who had taken no part in the decision to hold a plebiscite, raised the strongest protest. There therefore ensued a cabinet crisis in Vienna which, during 11 March, led to the resignation of the former Federal Chancellor and the formation of a new government. It was not true that forcible pressure had been exercised by the Reich in this situation. In particular the statement subsequently spread by the former Federal Chancellor to the effect that the German government had delivered an ultimatum with a time-limit to the Federal President, failing which German troops would march into Austria, was 'pure imagination'. In fact the troop movements were the result of an urgent telephone request from the newly-formed Austrian government for assistance in the re-establishment of peace and order and the prevention of bloodshed. The telegram had meanwhile been published. Faced with the imminent danger of a bloody civil war in Austria, the government of the Reich decided to meet the appeal addressed to it. . . . Under these circumstances dangerous consequences might ensue if an attempt should be made by any third party, in contradiction to the peaceful intentions and legitimate aims of the Reich, to exercise on the development of the situation in Austria an influence inconsistent with the right of the German people to self-determination. . . .

So much for the letter from Konstantin Freiherr von Neurath, former German Foreign Minister and at the time President of the Secret Cabinet Council. Chamberlain's comment was that he did not wish to deal with the historical narrative of events as described by von Neurath and he continued:

'But I am bound at once to refute his statement that His Majesty's Government were not within their rights in interesting themselves in the independence of Austria and that, as in the opinion of the German Government relations between Austria and Germany are a purely internal affair, His Majesty's Government, as a third party, has no concern in them. . . .

In the first place Great Britain and Austria are both members of the League and both were signatories, as was also the German Government, of treaties which provided that the independence of Austria was inalienable except with the consent of the Council of the League of Nations. Quite apart from this His Majesty's Government are, and always must be, interested in developments in Central Europe . . . if only for the reason, as I stated in the House only a fortnight ago, that the object of all their policy has been to assist in the establishment of a sense of greater security and confidence in Europe. . . . Throughout these events His Majesty's Government have remained in the closest touch with the French Government who, I understand, also entered a strong protest in Berlin. . . . It seems to us that the methods adopted throughout these events call for the severest condemnation and have administered a profound shock to all who are interested in the preservation of European peace. . . .

It might seem unnecessary to refute rumours that His Majesty's Government had given consent if not encouragement to the idea of the absorption of Austria by Germany. . . . There is of course no foundation whatever for any of these rumours. . . .

We were under no commitment to take action *vis-à-vis* Austria, but we were pledged to consultation with the French and Italian Governments in the event of action being taken which affected Austrian independence and integrity, for which provision was made by the relevant articles of the peace treaties. This pledge arises from agreements reached between the French, Italian and United Kingdom Governments first in February 1934, then in September of the same year and finally at the Stresa Conference in April 1935. . . . We have fully discharged the pledge of consultation. . . . The hard fact is . . . that nothing could have arrested this action by Germany unless we and others with us had been prepared to use force to prevent it. I imagine that according to the temperament of the individual the events which are in our minds today will be the cause of regret, of sorrow, perhaps of indignation. They cannot be regarded by His Majesty's Government with indifference or equanimity. They are bound to have effects which cannot yet be measured. The immediate result must be to intensify the sense of uncertainty and insecurity in Europe. Unfortunately, while the policy of appeasement would lead to a relaxation of the economic pressure under which many countries are suffering today, what has just occurred must inevitably retard economic recovery. . . .

As regards our defence programmes, we have always made it clear that they were flexible and that they would have to be reviewed from time to time in the light of any developments in the international situation. It would be idle to pretend that recent events do not constitute a change of the kind that we had in mind. Accordingly we have decided to make a fresh review, and in due course we shall announce what further steps we may think it necessary to take.'[54]

If Chamberlain's speech to parliament was an accurate analysis of the Austrian affair, von Neurath's reply was a travesty of the facts in almost every word. Between the lines of Chamberlain's statement, however, could be read the admission that the then international organisation had not come up to expectations and, given similar circumstances, no more can the present one. It is idle to speculate whether the British protest would have had any more lasting effect if, in these critical days, the British government had been able to speak through an Ambassador willing to represent its views more faithfully.[55]

In the Commons on 14 March Winston Churchill made a speech which attracted much attention. Extracts are repeated here because in large measure they are still applicable today:

'The gravity of the event of 12 March cannot be exaggerated. Europe is confronted with a programme of aggression, nicely calculated and timed, unfolding stage by stage, and there is only one choice open, not only to us but to other countries, either to submit like Austria or else take effective measures to ward off the danger and, if it cannot be warded off, to cope with it. . . . If we go on waiting upon events, how much shall we throw away of resources now available for our security and the maintenance of peace? How many friends will be alienated, how many potential allies shall we see go down one by one into the grisly gulf? How many times will bluff succeed until behind bluff ever-gathering forces have accumulated reality? Where are we going to be two years hence, for instance, when the German army will certainly be much larger than the French army and when all the small nations will have fled from

Geneva to pay homage to the ever-waxing power of the Nazi system and to make the best terms that they can for themselves? . . .

Vienna is the centre of the communications of all the countries which formed the old Austro-Hungarian Empire and of the countries lying to the south-east of Europe. . . . The mastery of Vienna gives to Nazi Germany control of the whole of the communications of south-east Europe. . . . What is the effect of this on . . . the balance of power – upon what is called the Little Entente? . . . Taken singly, the three countries of the Little Entente may be called powers of the second rank but . . . united they are a Great Power. . . . Together they make the complement . . . of the military machinery of a great Power. Rumania has the oil, Jugoslavia has the minerals and raw materials. Both have large armies, both are mainly supplied with munitions from Czechoslovakia. To English ears the name of Czechoslovakia sounds outlandish. No doubt they are only a small democratic state, no doubt they have an army only two or three times as large as ours, no doubt they have a munitions supply only three times as great as that of Italy. But still they are a virile people. . . . They have their treaty rights, they have a line of fortresses and they have a strongly manifested will to live, a will to live freely.

Czechoslovakia is at this moment isolated, both in the economic and military sense.'[56]

In the House of Lords on 15 March Lord Halifax stated that on the Austrian question the attitude of the different British governments had always been the same; they had never assumed that the *status quo* in Austria could be maintained for all time and they had been perfectly prepared to concede the special interests of the German government in Austro-German relations; hence their readiness to consider a revision of the Peace Treaties. Lord Halifax denied rumours to the effect that he had encouraged Germany to use force against Austria; on the contrary he stressed that he had pointed out that changes in Europe should not be brought about by force or something akin to force. Germany's behaviour had struck a most severe and serious blow to Europe's confidence. He emphasised that it was no good bringing the Austrian question before the League. This was an accomplished fact and only war could change it – and the members of the League were not prepared to go to war.[57]

The views of British governments in the preceding years, however, did not tally with Lord Halifax's speech. Neither in Geneva, Vienna, Paris, nor Rome had there been any indication of any reversal of British policy as regards Central Europe. There were no signs of it during the crisis over the Austro-German Customs Union in 1931 nor at the time of the Stresa Conference in 1935 nor later. Even Berlin could not have had any such impression, at least until Sir Eric Phipps had been relieved as British Ambassador in the spring of 1937.[58] Sir Eric had been British Minister in Vienna and was known as a firm supporter of Austrian independence, as were his successors in Austria, Sir Walford Selby and Michael Palairet.

The Soviet Union's line differed from that of the other Powers. On 18 March 1938 they proposed an international conference to consider the new situation and, by reinforcing the Franco-Soviet Treaty of 1935, to meet any possibly more serious threat to peace from the Third Reich within the framework of the League. The plan evoked little response.

Chamberlain found Churchill's idea of a 'grand alliance' theoretically attractive but not feasible in practice. Geography alone made it impossible for France and England to protect Czechoslovakia against a German attack. Chamberlain therefore dropped the idea of a renewed guarantee for Czechoslovakia as also for France in connection with her alliance obligations *vis-à-vis* Czechoslovakia.[59]

In its issue of 19 March the German News Bureau (DNB) referred to a historical paradox, with the Soviet Union of all people calling for 'collective action to save the peace'. In fact, each in their own way, both Soviet diplomacy and that of the Third Reich were working for similar aims using similar methods; so far as the West was concerned in each case there was what later came to be called a considerable 'credibility gap'. Neither Washington, Paris nor London took any further notice of the Soviet suggestion. In September 1938 the League did in fact meet and, the Soviet Union alone dissenting, merely took note that with the promulgation of the reunification law Austrian membership of the League had lapsed. But by that time Austria was past history and hardly referred to. The Sudeten crisis had taken over.

Some time earlier than this, however, both Poland and Italy had had second thoughts about possible future developments in the Danube basin – but too late. This is shown by a report from the United States Ambassador in Warsaw dated 29 March 1938, which reads as follows:

'Warsaw, No 38, March 29, 4 p.m.

One. I learn following in strictest confidence from Beck [Polish Foreign Minister] and his associates:

(a) Beck gained distinct impression in conversations with Mussolini and Ciano during Beck's recent Rome visit that they both shared Beck's view in respect to Danubian Valley: Whereas Italy focussed its attention on the Mediterranean and Poland on the Baltic, neither would like to see the hegemony of any country develop further in the Danubian Valley.

(b) Of pertinent interest, moreover, during the adjournment of Anglo-Italian conversations Mussolini had recently pointed out Italy was fundamentally interested in ascertaining the extent to which Britain would be interested in doing something to bring about economic and other appeasements in that area which had been disturbed by recent events (such as Austria). My informants added that in other words Mussolini's soundings on this score indicated Mussolini's interest in embarking on a potential counter policy *vis-à-vis* Germany's suspected aspirations in Danubian Valley, the counter policy envisaging economic assistance to rescue the Danubian and Balkan States from being swept into the German camp.

Two. My informants added their opinion that Britain would probably be inclined to leave treatment of this problem in abeyance until current obstacles still retarding an Anglo-Italian solution of the problem in Spain will have been eliminated.

Ambassador Anthony J. Drexel Biddle, Jr'[60]

Both before and after 1938 Soviet diplomacy was in fact far more occupied with Central European questions, and therefore with that of Austria, than was generally believed. As early as 1935 the Soviets had seen the approach of that great turning point in European policy which in 1936 led to unconcealed crisis and in 1937 to that major revision which opened up the political prospects set out in the Hossbach Minutes of 10 November that year.[61]

The result was a major diplomatic revolution involving among other things the rejection of Geneva and the Geneva principles of collective security. During the critical years 1936 and 1937, however, Soviet international influence was small, largely because of the impression made by the internal power struggles which culminated in the forcible suppression of the anti-Stalin opposition (execution of Marshal Tukachevsky). The first results were to be seen in 1938, the final consequence in 1939.

A bare four years before, on 14 May 1935, the Franco-Russian Mutual Assistance Pact had been signed in Moscow. It had been followed on 16 May by signature of a similar Franco-Czecho-slovak Pact in Prague. The signatories had been the Soviet Foreign Minister, Maxim Litvinov, the French Foreign Minister, Pierre Laval and the Czech Minister, Eduard Benes. The background, without which both the pact system and subsequent developments are barely comprehensible, reveals a chain of events both grim and grotesque:

In February 1935 the Western Powers proposed to the Third Reich conclusion of an Eastern and a Danube Pact on the lines of the Locarno Treaties of 1925; in parallel with this was to be an armaments convention and a revision of the military clauses of the Treaty of Versailles; further conditions were recognition of the principle of collective security and Germany's return to the League of Nations. On 14 February 1935 Germany replied with a non-committal note. On 4 March 1935 there appeared in London a White Paper, approved by Ramsay MacDonald, the Prime Minister, dealing with national defence questions; it proposed an increase of ten million pounds in the British defence estimates, to be used for modernisation of the army and the fleet and accelerated air rearmament. The reason given was the new situation created by German rearmament; if, the Paper stated, this continued at its previous level, this must inevitably increase anxiety among Germany's neighbours and 'as a result a situation might arise which would endanger peace'. A large section of British public opinion and the Opposition in parliament with Clement Attlee as its spokesman strongly opposed any rearmament since it was 'completely at variance with the spirit in which the League of Nations was created to establish a collective world peace'.[62] The German press took issue with the reasons given in the British White Paper and labelled the suspicions cast upon the Third Reich as an insult.

Meanwhile for similar reasons France increased the term of military service to two years on 15 March 1935, stressing the necessity for further measures of defence. On 16 March Hitler replied with the reintroduction of universal military service, his first unilateral defiance of the military clauses of the Peace Treaty.[63]

When Sir John Simon and Anthony Eden visited Hitler at the end of this month (25 March) they asked how strong the German *Luftwaffe* was; after some hesitation Hitler admitted that it had already reached parity with the RAF – at a time when Germany officially possessed no air force at all. When the two Britons asked what peace strength he wanted for his army Hitler replied: 36 divisions (500,000 men); he laid special stress on the threat from Russia, describing Czechoslovakia as a projection of the Soviet Union; in addition he stated that Germany needed an army of this strength for her defence since she had undertaken at Locarno to keep the Rhineland zone demilitarised.[64] One year later the conclusion of the Franco-Russian and Franco-Czechoslovak Pacts served as a pretext for renunciation of the Locarno Treaties.

All this was an obvious foretaste of the diplomatic methods used to implement measures long prepared and planned. March 1938 in Austria and the events leading up to it are but a further example.

Moscow followed these developments with anxious attention and supported the efforts to conclude an Eastern and Danube Pact; but Hitler would have none of it precisely because it would have served to maintain the *status quo* and thereby Austria. In 1935 Hitler's reason for rejection of this pact, as given with much emphasis to Sir John Simon and Anthony Eden, seemed entirely credible: 'There can be no question of any association between National-Socialism and Bolshevism.'[65]

As it so happens a series of illuminating documents concerning the Soviet view on Central European policy including Austria are available from the year 1935. A Soviet intelligence agency had been set up in Vienna under the direction of a lawyer who later emigrated to Paris; somehow the German Embassy came to know of it and so von Papen was able to transmit to Berlin a whole series of confidential directives issued by the *Politburo* in Moscow;[66] they are dated 2, 4, 8, 14, 19, 22, and 27 August and 8 October 1935. Extracts are as follows:

1. *Politburo* instructions, 2 August 1935:

'The *Politburo* is convinced that the Italo-Abyssinian conflict, the localisation of which has proved impracticable, will spill over into Europe and will inevitably lead, in one form or another, to war between the Franco-Soviet coalition and Germany. The formation of a Franco-British front and the undoubted rapprochement between Great Britain and the United States make it probable that . . . Italian policy will swing in the direction of an understanding with Germany' (pp. 128–30).

2. *Politburo* instructions 4 August 1935:

'The *Politburo* subscribes totally to the declaration of Comrade Stalin which says:

"Three imperialist powers – Germany, Japan and Italy – are deliberately guiding developments towards a new world war, calculating that in any fresh distribution they would be able to seize those territories which would inevitably be lost to them in the event of agreement on a system of international guarantees for peace and of mutual support."

It is in the interest of the Soviet Union that *Italian expansionist tendencies should once more be centred around the Danube basin* and that, as a result, the conflict between Rome and Berlin over the Austrian question should again become acute. Soviet diplomacy must direct all its efforts towards ensuring that the focus of the inevitable European conflict be transferred back from Eastern to Central Europe; this is all the more necessary in that a considerable change in German-Polish relations has taken place in connection with the Danzig question and those in charge of Soviet foreign policy must utilise this to reinforce the barriers against German pressure in the East . . . the Soviet Union must adhere firmly and unswervingly to the political line already adopted of rapprochement and cooperation with Great Britain; even the contact already established with France is subject to this condition. The *Politburo* reminds the People's

Commissariat for Foreign Affairs and Comrade Litvinov personally that a settlement with Italy, desirable though it may be, must in no case be allowed to affect relations between the Soviet Union and Great Britain which are at last entering upon a phase of rapprochement.'

3. The directive forwarded by von Papen on 8 August 1935 set out the standard Soviet policy line: that the military collapse of Nazi Germany was one of the most important conditions for proletarian revolution in Central Europe and that the Soviet object was to utilise any war to promote world revolution.

4. *Politburo* instructions 14 August 1935:
Germany was firmly determined to refuse any participation in the system of security and mutual support pacts and would have no part nor lot in an East of Danube Pact. It was absolutely necessary, therefore, that the Comrades responsible for Soviet foreign policy should initiate widespread diplomatic activity designed to bring about the Eastern and Danube pacts; at the moment efforts should be directed primarily towards the Danube pact, since on this point there were no important differences of opinion between Italy, France and Great Britain. Tactically it was expedient that Soviet diplomacy should show itself active in the negotiations for the conclusion of the Danube pact and in particular should assume responsibility for bringing the views of Italy and the Little Entente states into consonance. The directive then continues:

'The *Politburo* comes to the unanimous conclusion that in his negotiations with Dr Benes in Marienbad Comrade Litvinov should bear particularly in mind methods of eliminating the Habsburg restoration question, since this constitutes the main obstacle to realisation of the Danube pact. The *Politburo* does not wish to tie Comrade Litvinov's hands by issuing precise directives on this point but it considers two points of importance as possible solutions for the removal of the above difficulties:

1. To induce Italy, France and Great Britain to make a simultaneous and adequately decisive stand against restoration of the Habsburg monarchy in any form in Austria or in Hungary.

2. To induce the Little Entente states to declare themselves in favour of a Habsburg restoration under certain conditions and with definite guarantees, thus facing German National-Socialism with the threat of a South German Catholic Empire.

The *Politburo* has no wish to conceal the fact that, in its opinion, the second solution represents a more serious danger to German National-Socialism since it would also provide the Vatican with a firm base from which to pursue its struggle against the Third Reich'. (pp. 148–50)

5. *Politburo* instructions of 19 August 1935:
The collapse – not wholly unexpected – of the Three-Power Conference in Paris (France–Great Britain–Italy) on the Abyssinian question had revealed a far greater Anglo-Italian difference of opinion than expected. Comrade Litvinov's view that the three Powers were playing a pre-arranged game, was wrong. The British government had simply discovered what Italian plans for East and North-East Africa and the Mediterranean were. This would explain British obduracy in defence of Abyssinian independence. It (the British government) knew that the conflict could not remain localised.

6. *Politburo* instructions 22 August 1935:

'*The* Politburo *especially welcomes the readiness of the Prague government to persuade the Little Entente to agree to any form of regime in Austria apart from a National-Socialist one, on condition that effective international guarantees are given for the territorial status quo in the Danube area.*

The *Politburo* fully and completely approves the assumption of mutual obligations between the Soviet Union and the Czechoslovak Republic visualising support for the most rapid possible realisation of the Eastern and Danube pacts; it welcomes the readiness of the Prague government to find a compromise between the Little Entente and Italy over the Austrian question provided the Italian government is prepared to adhere unreservedly to the policy and principles of the League of Nations.' (pp. 148–50)

7. *Politburo* instructions of 27 August 1935:
Under no circumstances must the Soviet Union appear, even temporarily, in opposition to Great Britain and the USA; efforts

should be made to ensure that France and the Little Entente also remained in line.

8. Finally a statement by the *Politburo* forwarded by von Papen on 8 October 1935:

'The *Politburo* considers it necessary to draw attention to the fact that as a result of existing circumstances:

1. A rapprochement between Italy and Germany does not figure in the plans of German foreign policy.
2. Improbable though it may be, the formation of a bloc Germany–Poland–Italy–Hungary–Austria would be preferable than an Anglo-German agreement giving Germany a free hand in Central and Eastern Europe.
3. A bloc Great Britain–France–Soviet Union–Little Entente–Balkan States would be stronger than any other European power grouping.' (p. 167)

These instructions show what the views of the Soviet leadership on the power politics game were at the time; they also illustrate the rapidity with which the various combinations developed and changed.

After the Anschluss, presumably late in 1938 or early 1939, an attempt was made to reactivate the Soviet intelligence agency in Vienna. The task was entrusted to a manufacturer from Horni Počernice near Prague, but he applied to Keppler and offered his services to him. He presented himself as an Aryan, a Sudeten German, an ex-Lieutenant in the *Deutschmeister* Regiment, a Czech reserve officer, a member of the 'Rising Sun' Lodge in Dresden since 1927 and a convinced pacifist. Leading Freemasons and communists had been in touch with him, he said, about transmission of information for the benefit of an independent American organisation. After 10 November 1938 (*Kristallnacht*)[67] he had moved to Vienna; while there he had been disillusioned by the treatment of the Jews and had kept his master in Prague informed of his unfavourable impressions. His employer in Prague had proposed that he should take over the Prague agency. He was prepared, however, to work for Germany, for which he required no personal reward. He had meanwhile learnt that he was really expected to carry on espionage for Moscow and had been told at the same time that there had previously been a Soviet intelligence agency in Vienna. His master in Prague was a communist idealist and had the entrée to the highest Czech government circles. A new organisation was now to be built up in Vienna, money being no object. A sum of 30,000 dollars had been allocated to Prague alone. His job was to bribe small craftsmen, railway workers, etc. and persuade them to transmit coded messages across the frontier.

The general directive given to him was as follows, he said: There was great discontent in Vienna, particularly in officer circles; it was comparatively easy to obtain information; it would be given either on the grounds of monarchist or other political views or to gain some personal advantage. The objectives were:

1. To discover the general strategic principles governing German foreign policy (the Ukraine, colonial problems).
2. What was the food situation; what was the mood among the population and in leading circles; could much be achieved with money?
3. At all costs Moscow wished to buy a Volkswagen, having heard that they were already being manufactured.
4. Moscow was interested in the reason for the reported arrests of officers.[68]
5. Extent of change in the Austrian armed forces, quality of the rations, morale among the men, organisation of the air force. Primary interest lay in plans for movement eastwards, mobilisation plans and all other preparations for a move. His special task had been to recruit suitable agents in Vienna, Moscow reserving the right to judge and decide on his proposals. Very significant sums in dollars would be paid for valuable information.

His Prague master had told him that very senior Party functionaries in Berlin were among the providers of information: 'You would be astounded if you knew who was in it. You would simply not think it possible.' This had annoyed him very much and he hoped that, if he took over the Prague office, he would get to know the names. He would then report them at once.

So ends the report.[69] It includes the names of the organiser in Prague, of his representative in Vienna and finally that of the alleged organiser of the Soviet intelligence agency in Vienna before 1938, all with addresses. They are unimportant, however, and so are not given here. Available sources do not reveal what became of the proposal. In any case the affair shows that, both from the Austrian and international angles, the Anschluss had its peculiar sides.

On 2 April 1938 Great Britain received the exequatur for her newly-appointed Consul-General; the United States followed suit on 6 April – before Hitler's plebiscite, in other words. So official recognition was given to the new situation; official documents confirmed it, referring to the union of Austria with the German Reich. Occupation turned into incorporation, annexation in fact. Only as a result of the Second World War was it officially registered as a breach of international law and the recognition accorded in April 1938 finally revoked.

EPILOGUE

A word remains to be said on all this from the point of view of the individual Austrian. In retrospect how did it all look to him and what did he go through?

It is not easy to know where to begin. Reactions were very varied, ranging from an emotional elation born of a sense of release, through a hard-headed acceptance of the inevitable to bitter opposition based both on sentiment and reason. To some extent everyone was elated and everyone accepted, even those who were by no means of the Party, simply because no one could avoid hearing the noises off and feeling their effects. But there was something else people soon came to realise – the frequency with which others started enthusiastically but after years of eye-opening and wavering ended in opposition – and for a long time this was tantamount to despair.

The intervening period was one of struggle, hatred and bedevilment. How could it be otherwise? And then began the endless argument about blame and responsibility, which was both understandable and indeed useful provided people were both able and willing to remember and also could bring themselves to listen. Inevitably opinions clashed and everyone tried to prove himself right because everyone is a prisoner of his past – it is only human.

When it was all over, however, and for good or ill we were together again, we were all fifty years richer in experience, whether we liked to admit it or not. Despite all the differences of interpretation, however passionately argued, and despite all the heated debates, what happened in the twenty years before and the thirty years after the Anschluss was established and proved. Of course there will always be 'ifs and buts'; one is as good as another and none can be proved.

What people discuss, however, is not how better service could have been rendered to the 'historical evolutionary development' of which there was so much talk in the Vienna Embassy reports from 1934 to 1938 and in the plans and programmes of Austrian National-Socialism;[1] their subject is: what more could anyone have done to prevent the Anschluss?

Until about 1943, the year of Stalingrad and the Moscow Declaration, there may have been many, both at home and abroad, though not including those in concentration camps and prisons, who still believed that some other form of Anschluss might be possible in future. But on one thing practically everybody was agreed – in its existing form, 'no'. Since then, for the vast majority of Austrians, wherever they may be, the Anschluss idea has become merely a reminder of a temporary aberration.[2] They are united in the conviction that 'the Anschluss has been surmounted'.[3]

Since all this, the world has taken on yet another aspect – very different from the dreams of those who balkanised the Danube basin fifty-two years ago; allegedly they did so with their eyes open but their calculations went awry; in their inability to agree on any overall concept, they liquidated Austria as a Power. But the world of today bears even less relation to the crazy picture of the men who, thirty-two years ago, their vision distorted by lust for power, proceeded to balkanise even what remained and attempted, by means of the Anschluss, to destroy the concept of Austria. Today we know that both fifty-two and thirty-two years ago the methods adopted to re-draw the map of Europe were wrong and so Europe missed a great historical opportunity.

Anyone writing the history of the Second World War is bound to deal with the Anschluss in his opening chapter; it was a fore-taste of everything to come – including even the Soviet tanks in Prague and Hungary, the Berlin Wall, divided Germany and, notwithstanding much factitious optimism, a future not of un-relieved gloom.

Prophecies must be made with caution. Fifty-two years ago,

however, when few people gave Austria much chance of survival, no one would have dared to prophesy that a generation later Austria would be the most successful of all the Central European successor states, at least as seen through Western spectacles.

This is a fact, even though the present-day Western argument runs that a calm peaceful atmosphere is equivalent to intellectual stagnation, that resistance to the rush of events is to be decried as bigotry and fascist restriction of liberty, that pleasure in an ancient culture is a waste of time and enjoyment of the famous higher standard of living is a factor of social disintegration and mere empty official verbiage.

This is not to say that there should not be freedom of speech, still less that we should not strive for something better; that has always been the guiding principle of social development. But it is to say that, for the sake of this 'something better', we should not cast overboard the good things we already have.

People sometimes think too little about this in Austria, although we have seen and suffered the result of adopting a negative attitude to everything in our own country and welcoming unquestioningly everything originating from across the frontier. Now, peaceably and without becoming suspect, we can once more refer to the true history of Austria, and we can do so with pride and respect, as we can of our past. We now know, and must recognise that geographically, politically, socially and in human terms, we are a country of the Centre and that, despite all our vicissitudes, we do belong and shall belong culturally to the Centre.

It may well be that Austrian history is not too easy to understand.

'It is apparently more difficult to make the concept of Austria comprehensible. If you ask a good average series of Austrians what Austria is, you will get some more or less intelligent answers, the majority facetious, and a large number of "don't knows"; hardly one will be comprehensive or satisfactory and none, I fear, will show any genuine belief in the idea. But if you take Austria away from the Austrians, then everyone will realise at once what he has lost. The number of those who grasp the significance of Old Austria is increasing all the time, although the generation which lived with it and grumbled about it is dying out. Austria is something indefinable, a way of life, something elementary or spiritual, like blue sky, spring or the sun, depending on the sensitivity of the person concerned. In the old days the North Germans were better able to express what Austria was than the Austrians themselves. They came here, shed their inhibitions, felt savagely well and were not afraid to say so and act accordingly. To them Austria was liberation. The Austrians looked on, shook their heads – and understood only when they had been up there and come back again. Then they were more inclined to believe in Austria. During the fifteen years since the destruction of the old Empire, when the sense of being Austrian has sometimes sunk to zero or below, the Austrian has had to receive a shock from outside to awaken the Austrian in him; a savage struggle for existence has been necessary for his sense of nationality to develop from a vague feeling into an idea and a belief. But, unfortunately, it is still difficult to make the idea of Austria comprehensible, for it is a cultural idea. Understanding of it presupposes education and a desire for culture. It is no popular slogan, no empty vote-catcher which sweeps the board at mass meetings; it has substance, depth and weight – almost too much for a period of superficiality. The tragedy of the concept of Austria lies perhaps in its brilliance. . . . I can only indicate what I understand by the concept of Austria, and I do so by a quotation from Faust which, knowing the scene from which it comes, you will understand – not superficially but spiritually and intellectually. Austria means this: "Here I am, and here is where I can really be a German." ' – Hans von Hammerstein (1935).[4]

Austria is now a small country, in area, in population and in political importance. But what do the words 'small' or 'great' signify in the era of space research and man's first real encounter with the wonders of extra-terrestrial creation?

It is certainly no accident that the first men to step on to the moon – and to do so from beginning to end before the eyes of the entire world – were non-Europeans.

This is no disparagement of Europe, without whose political and intellectual history the USA would not exist today.

But it is a disparagement of nationalism and its scale of values, for if nationalism persists, it is bound to spell the doom of the Old World, as it recently spelt the doom of one of that world's most ancient centres, Austria. Austria's example has shown that the conquest of nationalism can be followed by regeneration.

NOTES

Chapter 1. Three Flashbacks

1. Guido Zernatto was a member of the Federal Government from 1936, dealing primarily with cultural and organisational matters.
2. Dr Arthur Seyss-Inquart (1892–1946) was a Vienna lawyer. In 1937 he was appointed Counsellor of State [*Staatsrat*] and in February 1938 Minister of the Interior. From 12 to 14 March 1938 he was Federal Chancellor and then *Reichsstatthalter* [Reich Regent] in Austria. From 1939 to 1940 he was Deputy Governor-General in Poland and then, until 1945, Reich Commissar in the Netherlands. For his activities there he was condemned to death by the International Military Tribunal, Nuremberg, on 1 October 1946.
   Dr (h.c.) Edmund Glaise-Horstenau (1882–1946) was a General Staff officer who became Head of the State Archives and Director of the Institute for Military History. From July 1936 he was Minister in the Federal Chancellery and then Vice-Chancellor in Seyss-Inquart's cabinet. He committed suicide at Nuremberg in 1946 when threatened with extradition to Jugoslavia.
   On 6 March 1938 Glaise-Horstenau told me personally that he had been invited by Professor Haushofer, of the Institute of Geopolitics in Munich, to give an academic lecture, as far as I remember, in Stuttgart; he could not therefore be present at the next cabinet meeting. In view of the political situation I asked him to postpone the appointment and remain in the country, but he replied that he could not call off the lecture and, if necessary, would be compelled to resign.
   Among many accounts of events in the Ballhausplatz (the Austrian Chancellor's office) on 11 March 1938 are:

J. Benoist-Méchin: *Histoire de l'Armée allemande*, Vol. IV, 'L'expansion', Chap. XXIX.

Gordon Brook-Shepherd: *Anschluss, The Rape of Austria*.

Ulrich Eichstädt: *Von Dollfuss zu Hitler*.

Walter Goldinger: *Geschichte der Republik Österreich*.

Gabriel Puaux: *Mort et Transfiguration de l'Autriche*.

D. Wagner and G. Tomkowitz: *Ein Volk, Ein Reich, Ein Führer*.

Kurt Schuschnigg: *Austrian Requiem*; 'Als die Schatten fielen' in *Linzer Volksblatt*, 9 March 1963.

Guido Zernatto: *Die Wahrheit über Österreich*.

Legal Protocols and Records of the trial for high treason of Dr Guido Schmidt, published in Vienna in 1947. Hereafter referred to as 'Schmidt Trial'.

3. Text given in Benoist-Méchin *op. cit.* p. 542 and Zernatto *op. cit.* p. 317; also in *Weltgeschichte in Dokumente*, Vol. 5, pp. 446 *et seq.* and Schuschnigg: *Farewell Austria*, Appendix III, p. 328.

4. Telephone conversation between Göring and Keppler 8.48 p.m. 11 March:

Göring: 'Seyss-Inquart is to send us the following telegram: "Following the resignation of the Schuschnigg government the acting Austrian government regards as its task the re-establishment of calm and order in Austria. It issues an urgent request to the German government to support it in this duty and to assist it to stop bloodshed. To this end it requests the German government to despatch German troops as soon as possible. . . ." He should send this telegram as soon as he can.'

(See International Military Tribunal – hereafter referred to as IMT – Vol. XXXI, Document 2949–PS/11).

Telephone conversation between Keppler, Nazi plenipotentiary in Vienna, and Dr Dietrich, head of the Reich Press Office, Berlin, 9.54 p.m., 11 March:

Dietrich: 'I need the telegram urgently. . . .'

Keppler: 'Tell the Field Marshal [Göring] that Seyss-Inquart agreed.'

Dietrich: 'So Seyss-Inquart agrees?'

Keppler: 'Yes.'

(IMT Vol. XXXI, Document 2924–PS/12.)

In the witness box Seyss-Inquart stated, apparently truthfully, that he had never given this agreement and regarded the telegram as unnecessary (IMT, Vol. XXXII, Document 2345–PS).

5. Text of the order:
   Berlin, 11 March 1938, 20.45 hrs.
   Secret.
   High Command of the *Wehrmacht*.
   Subject: Operation Otto.
   1. The demands made on the Austrian government in the German ultimatum have not been met.
   2. The Austrian armed forces have been ordered to withdraw before the advance of German troops and to avoid fighting. The Austrian government has ceased to operate.
   3. To avoid further bloodshed in Austrian cities the German *Wehrmacht* will commence movement into Austria at first light on 12 March in accordance with Directive No. 1. I expect every effort to be made to reach the assigned objectives as quickly as possible. Signed: Adolf Hitler.
   (IMT Vol. XXXIV, Document 182–C.)

6. Full record given in Schuschnigg: *Austrian Requiem*, pp. 259–62.
7. Schmidt Trial, p. 338.
8. *Ibid.*, p. 229.
9. Zernatto *op. cit.*, p. 275; Schuschnigg *op. cit.*, p. 39.
10. Erich Kordt: *Nicht aus den Akten*, Union Verlag, Stuttgart 1950, pp. 192 *et seq.*
11. Puaux, *op. cit.*, p. 114.
12. As a result of the Berchtesgaden discussions the former illegal *Gauleiter*, Captain Leopold, and his closest associates had been summoned to the Reich at Austrian request.
13. I am particularly grateful to Dr Habsburg-Lothringen for releasing copies of these letters to me from his papers.
14. See Schuschnigg *op. cit.*, p. 50. Hans von Hammerstein was a cousin of the German Colonel-General Kurt von Hammerstein who was Chief of the German Army Staff from 1930 to 1934. The family comes from the old Hanoverian aristocracy.
15. SD stands for *Sicherheitsdienst*, the SS Security Service, first under Heydrich and then Kaltenbrunner, under overall command of the *Reichsführer-SS*, Himmler.
16. Report by ex-Captain Wichard von Alvensleben to Bishop Neuhäusler, Munich, dated 23 March 1968; see also Dulles and Gaevernitz: *The Secret Surrender*, pp. 242–4.
17. Best: *The Venlo Incident*, pp. 226, 228 *et seq.*
18. Written report dated 20 October 1968 by Wichard von Alvens-

leben 'on the liberation of prominent concentration camp prisoners on 29 April 1945 at Niederdorf, South Tyrol, submitted in support of a plea for mercy for Karl Wolff filed with the Bavarian Ministry of Justice'.

19. Schuschnigg, *op. cit.*, pp. 227 *et seq.*
20. Best *op. cit.*, pp. 235, 243 *et seq.* In November 1939 Best had been lured over the German–Dutch frontier by the SD and taken prisoner, see Schellenberg: Memoirs, pp. 85 *et seq.*
21. See *Südtiroler Nachrichten*, 3rd year, No. 7 of 15 April and No. 8 of 30 April 1965; *Der Spiegel*, 21st year, No. 9 of 20 February 1967, pp. 54 *et seq.*; *Neue Illustrierte*, Cologne, 16th year, No. 8 of 19 February 1961, pp. 33 *et seq.*; *Befreiung in den Südtiroler Dolomiten*, edited by Dr Reut-Nicolussi, Landesstelle für Südtirol, Innsbruck 1946.
22. Maria Dolores born in Munich on 23 March 1941 while I was in the Gestapo prison in Munich.
23. On 11 July 1952 Dr Ignaz Tschurtschenthaler of Klagenfurt sent me a letter transmitting greetings from Julius Raab, the ex-Chancellor, then leader of the Austrian Peoples Party; it included this: 'Raab informs me that Schärf, the Vice-Chancellor, said to him: "If Schuschnigg enters Austria I will file a case against him at once." ' (Tschurtschenthaler was Deputy Governor of Carinthia from 1945 to 1949, then deputy in the National Assembly; prior to 1938 he had been Federal Economic Counsellor; he died on 16 December 1954.)
24. Professor Wilhelm Bauer; born in Prague; until 1938 professor of dentistry at the University of Innsbruck, died in St Louis in 1956.

Chapter 2. A People in Affliction

1. In Budapest people would talk of the Hungarian nation, meaning thereby not the ethnic (Magyar) community, but the nation-state, in other words the inhabitants of all countries under St Stephen's Crown.
2. For the significance and growth of the *Ethnie française* see Theodor Veiter: *Das Recht der Volksgruppen und Sprachminderheiten in Österreich*, Part I, pp. 41 *et seq.*
3. Georg v. Schönerer – Pan-German member of the Austrian parliament.

4. See Erik Kuehnelt-Leddhin: *Freiheit oder Gleichheit*, p. 381; Alan Bullock: *Hitler, A Study in Tyranny*, pp. 39–40.
5. *Staatslexikon*, Herder, Vol. I, 1926 edition.
6. Benoist-Méchin, *op. cit.*, p. 394, note 2.
7. Stefan Varosta: *Geschichte der Republik Österreich*, edited by Heinrich Benedikt, p. 585.
8. Otto Bauer was Austro-Marxism's leading ideologist.
9. Shorthand record of third session of the Provisional National Assembly for German-Austria, 12 November 1918.
10. 72 Social Democrats, 69 Christian Socials, 26 German Nationals and 3 independents.
11. Friedrich Funder: *Vom Gestern bis heute*, pp. 607 *et seq.*; Julius Deutsch: *Ein weiter Weg*, p. 129.
12. Shorthand record of 33rd session of the National Diet, 15 April 1921.
13. Benoist-Méchin, *op. cit.*, p. 396.
14. On 1 July 1919 the rate of exchange for 100 Swiss francs was 567 Austrian kronen; on 1 July 1921 the figure was 12,200 and on 1 July 1922 300,000.
15. Shorthand record of 138th session of the National Diet, 12 October 1922.
16. Julius Braunthal: *Auf der Suche nach dem Millenium*, Vol. II, p. 455; Otto Bauer: *Die österreichische Revolution*, p. 102.
17. For the opposite view see Friedrich Hertz: *Zahlungsbilanz und Lebensfähigkeit Österreichs*.
18. See Friedrich Thalmann: *Die Wirtschaft in Österreich*; Heinrich Benedikt: *Geschichte der Republik Österreich*, Part III, pp. 493, 506.
19. The Grossglockner Pass road, for instance, was started in 1930 and opened to traffic in 1935.
20. For the *Creditanstalt* rescue operation see Alexander Spitzmüller: *. . . und hat auch Ursach' es zu lieben*, pp. 356 *et seq.*; on the German bank and currency reforms see Schacht: *My first seventy-six Years*, pp. 177 *et seq.*, 300 *et seq.*
21. As in other states a time limit was set for unemployment pay.
22. Eichstädt, *op. cit.*, pp. 13, 22.
23. When I met him in New York in 1947 Brüning, who was Chancellor when the Customs Union plan came up, told me that he had not been informed about the proposed Customs Union Treaty before it was signed. On 3 September 1931 Schober, the Austrian Foreign Minister, stated in Geneva that the Austrian Government

was withdrawing the Customs Union plan. On British initiative the plan was referred to the League of Nations which passed the case on to the International Court of Justice. This declared, by 8 votes to 7, that the Customs Union plan was incompatible with the obligations undertaken by Austria under the Geneva Protocol of 1922. Only six of the judges, however, considered that it was incompatible with the relevant provisions of the Peace Treaty.

24. Copy of the memorandum in the possession of the author.
25. Friedrich Adler was the son of the founder and leader of the Social Democrat Party who died in November 1918. On 21 October 1916 he murdered Count Stürgkh, the Austrian Minister-President, as a protest against the war and a demonstration of the necessity of social revolution. He was condemned to death but the sentence was commuted to one of 17 years imprisonment; he was amnestied before the proclamation of the Republic. See Goldinger, *op. cit.*, p. 22 and Braunthal, *op. cit.*, Vol. II, pp. 381 *et seq.*, 442 *et seq.*
26. Bauer, *op. cit.*; Bourdet, *op. cit.*, pp. 87 *et seq.*
27. Otto Bauer: *Zwischen zwei Weltkriegen*; Bourdet, *op. cit.*, Part III, pp. 179, 276 *et. seq.*
28. Bauer: *Der Weg zum Sozialismus*; Bourdet *op. cit.*, Part II, p. 91.
29. Bourdet, *op. cit.*, pp. 93–126.
30. Otto Bauer: *Zwischen zwei Weltkriegen*, quoted in Bourdet, *op. cit.*, Part III, p. 242.
31. In the US, for instance, Roosevelt was attacked in Miami on 15 February 1933, the Mayor of Chicago being killed in the process. In May 1932 Inukai, the Japanese Prime Minister, was murdered in Tokyo.
32. In August 1932 five National-Socialists were sentenced to death in Beuthen for killing a communist worker in Potempa. The violence of the Nazi reaction caused von Papen, the Chancellor, to commute the sentence to one of life imprisonment. [Translator]
33. Vienna State Archives, Political section, K 467.
34. Braunthal, *op. cit.*, Part II, pp. 453 *et seq.*
35. When Dollfuss banned the Austrian Nazi Party Hitler's retort was an attempt to ruin the Austrian tourist trade by requiring all Germans travelling to Austria to deposit a bond for 1,000 marks. [Translator]

36. Deutsch, *op. cit.*, pp. 151 *et seq.*
37. The arms came partly from indigenous stocks and partly from foreign deliveries.
38. In Bavaria, for instance, *Einwohnerwehren* [Inhabitants Defence Forces] were formed to deal with the bolshevists; they were followed by Escherich's organisation and the *Oberland* League ex Silesia, etc.; in Hungary was the Arrow Cross, in Lithuania the Iron Wolf, in Latvia the *Perkonkrust*, in Estonia the *Vaps* (League of the Freedom Fighters), in Finland the *Lapua* movement. All were anti-parliamentary and aimed at constitutional reform.
39. Otto Bauer: *Kampf um die Macht*; see also Bourdet, *op. cit.*, p. 158; also the Social Democrat Party's programme announced in Linz on 3 November 1926, Chap. 2, paras. 1 and 2.
40. Lois Weinberger: *Tatsachen, Begegnungen und Gespräche*, p. 49.
41. I was parliamentary rapporteur at the time. The Social Democrat spokesman during the compromise negotiations was Dr Otto Danneberg.
42. Korneuburg is a township near Vienna where a *Heimwehr* rally took place at which a fascist-type programme was decided upon.
43. Othmar Spann was professor at Vienna University and a well-known sociologist; his doctrine was welcomed with enthusiasm by the students; he died in Neuburg, Burgenland, in 1950.
44. Vienna State Archives, GZ Germany I/1, Zl. 21.635; the article was probably written by Virginio Gayda.
45. Vienna State Archives, Folio 467, Austria II/10, Secret 1, 31.785/467.
46. Vienna State Archives, Folio 467.
47. Documents on German Foreign Policy (henceforth referred to as DGFP). Series D, Vol. 1, No. 251.
48. *Allianz Hitler-Horthy-Mussolini*, edited by Lajos Kerekes, p. 143; see also Ludwig Jedlicka: 'Der 13 März 1938' in *Der Donauraum*, No. 3 of 1968, p. 147.
49. See Josef Buttinger: *In the Twilight of Socialism*, pp. 422 *et seq.*
50. *Ibid.*, pp. 495 *et seq.*
51. Information from war records and files of the Federal Defence Ministry quoted by Ursula Freise in her dissertation for the Faculty of Philosophy, University of Vienna.
52. Hugo Gold: *Geschichte der Juden in Wien*, pp. 62, 98.

53. Karl Renner: *Österreich von der ersten zur zweiten Republik*, pp. 93 *et seq.*, and Note 22.

54. Richard Charmatz: *Deutsch-Österreichische Politik* (Leipzig, 1907), p. 181, quoted by Dr Oskar Karbach 'Die politischen Grundlagen des Österreichischen Anti-semitismus' in *Zeitschrift für die Geschichte der Juden*, 1964, p. 4.

55. Born in Vienna in 1907, now working in the Institute for Jewish Affairs. In the inter-war period was involved in the formation of a Jewish League of Nations Association in Austria.

56. Karbach, *op. cit.*, pp. 5, 107.

57. Buttinger, *op. cit.*, p. 80.

58. Dr Emmerich Czermak: 'Verständigung mit dem Judentum?' in *Ordnung der Judenfrage*, No. 4. *Sonderschrift der Berichte zur Kultur- und Zeitgeschichte*, edited by Nikolaus Hovorka, Vienna 1934, pp. 45 *et seq.*

59. See pp. 101–105 below.

60. Vienna State Archives – Report by Ambassador Franckenstein dated 15 February 1934 and draft of Foreign Ministry's reply in Austria 2/3 Secret, G.Z. 51194–13 pol.

61. *The Call* – weekly newspaper of the US Socialist Party published in New York, Vol. XIV, No. 7 of 17 February 1947, p. 1.

62. Charles Gulick: *Österreich von Habsburg bis Hitler*, Vol. IV, p. 197, Vol. V., p. 149 and Note 38; see also 'Proofs of official and semi-official Austro-fascist anti-semitism' in *The Facts*, published in New York, March 1947 issue edited by the 'Antidefamation League B'nai B'rith', also Vol. V, pp. 234 *et seq.*

63. Transcript of Göring's speech in the author's possession.

64. Karbach, *op. cit.*, p. 178.

65. Buttinger, *op. cit.*, pp. 179, 276 *et seq.*, 289, 294, 423 *et seq.*

66. Johannes Messner: 'Staat und berufständische Ordnung' and 'Zur Österreichischen Staatsideologie' in *Monatschrift für Kultur und Politik*, 1936, Vol. I, No. 7, p. 869; also *Das Naturrecht*, Innsbruck 1949, pp. 322 *et seq.*; see also August M. Knoll: 'Antwort auf Josef Dobretsberger' in *Civitas* (Swiss Students Union periodical) Nos. 8–10 of 1949 – 'Woran scheiterte der österreichische Ständestaat 1934–1938?'.

67. Alexander Novotny: 'Der berufständische Gedanke in der Bundesverfassung des Jahres 1934' in *Österreich in Geschichte und Literatur*, No. 5 of 1961.

68. Karbach, *op. cit.*, p. 174.

NOTES

Chapter 3. Civil War – Actual and Potential

1. Renner, *op. cit.*, p. 42.
2. Julius Deutsch: *Alexander Eifler – Ein Soldat der Freiheit*, p. 22.
3. Bourdet, *op. cit.*, Chap. 2, p. 156.
4. *Ibid.*, p. 157.
5. *Ibid.*, pp. 148, 159
6. Linz (Upper Austria) was where the German Nationalist movement's programme was drafted in 1882 by Georg Schönerer, Viktor Adler and Karl Lueger. Here again in 1926 the Social Democrat Party programme was decided under the influence of Dr Otto Bauer, the doctrinaire leader of 'Austro-Marxism'.
7. Karl Karwinsky: *Aufzeichnungen*, pp. 5 *et seq.*; Gulick, *op. cit.*, Vol. V, pp. 43 *et seq.*; Adam Wandruska in Benedikt, *op. cit.*, pp. 447 *et seq.*
8. See pp. 55–6 above.
9. Vienna State Archives, Folio 467, Austria II/10 secret, dated 23 March 1933.
10. Franz Winkler: *Die Diktatur in Österreich*, p. 13; Alfred Kasamas: *Österreichische Chronik*, p. 505. The *Landbund* was a Pan-German liberal group. [Translator]
11. Richard Schmitz: *Das christlichsoziale Programm*, quoted in Wandruska, *op. cit.*, p. 331.
12. *Volkszeitung*, Sunday 6 March 1927, p. 1. Author's italics.
13. Renner, *op. cit.*, p. 78.
14. See Julius Deutsch: *Lebenserinnerungen*, p. 190 – 'Without beating about the bush Starhemberg, who was then Vice-Chancellor of Austria, demanded two million schillings from the Italian Government.' Starhemberg became Vice-Chancellor on 1 May 1934.
15. Julius Deutsch: *Alexander Eifler*, p. 26.
16. Buttinger, *op. cit.*, p. 2.
17. Report by Police Headquarters Vienna dated 28 February 1934, S.B. 931/34, p. 15, 093/34.
18. During the *Creditanstalt* crisis the Bank of England granted Austria a short-term credit of 150,000,000 schillings.
19. See Note 10, also Renner, *op. cit.*, p. 108.
20. Winkler, *op. cit.*, p. 15.
21. Minutes in the German Federal Archives, Koblenz, R 43/II–1475. I have relied here on Ludwig Jedlicka's account in 'Der 13 März

1938 in der Sicht der historischen Forschung' in *Der Donauraum* No. 3 of 1968, p. 145 and 'Die aussen- und militärpolitische Vorgeschichte des 13 März 1938' in *Österreichische Militärische Zeitschrift* No. 2 of 1968 (March).

22. Buttinger, *op. cit.*, p. 3.

23. Winkler, *op. cit.*, p. 59.

24. The *Reichsbanner* was formed in 1924 as a defensive organisation of the Weimar coalition parties. It was under primarily Social Democrat leadership.

25. For a differing view see Renner *op. cit.*, p. 128. He maintains that the Social Democrat leadership arranged that he should resign so that his vote might be available when the House divided; the government party 'replied to the opposition's manœuvre promptly and adroitly' by causing their President, Dr Ramek, equally to resign; the failure therefore lay with Straffner, the No. 3. To judge from the record of the sitting, this account is inaccurate at least so far as Dr Ramek is concerned.

26. Federal Archives, Koblenz, NS 10/50; see also memorandum by Counsellor Altenburg, Berlin 22 September 1936, DGFP, Series D, Vol. 1, No. 165.

27. Cf. speech over Munich Radio on 18 March 1933 by Hans Frank, Head of the Legal Department of the Nazi Party headquarters and a Minister: 'If the Austrian government continues to restrict the rights of Austrian National-Socialists, the German NSDAP will undertake to protect the freedom of our German compatriots in Austria'; see also Eichstädt *op. cit.*, p. 28.

28. The occasion was the discovery of considerable stocks of *Schutzbund* weapons in Styria and a bloody clash in Bruck an der Mur on 17 March 1933; see Karwinsky *op. cit.*, p. 70.

29. See Kurt Schuschnigg: *Farewell Austria*, pp. 198–200.

30. Vienna State Archives, Folio 466.

31. In November 1933 Hitler said: 'Habicht will produce a settlement with Austria or no one can', Vienna State Archives, Folio 466 DI/12.

32. Report on the National-Socialist rising of 25 July 1934 in Vienna by Rudolf Weydenhammer – known as the Weydenhammer Report. Vienna Institute of Contemporary History.

33. Kerekes *op. cit.*, p. 156.

34. Adolf Schärf: *Geheimer Briefwechsel Mussolini-Dollfuss*, p. 32.

35. *Ibid.*, p. 35.

36. Brook-Shepherd: *Dollfuss*, p. 204.

37. Personal information from Suvich to the author, November 1968; Italy never regarded Fey as a possible successor to Dollfuss; she did think, however, that the Republican *Schutzbund* was preparing to revolt and that a government commissar should therefore be installed in Vienna for security reasons.

38. See Goldinger in Benedikt *op. cit.*, pp. 215 *et seq.*; Wilhelm Böhm; *Februar 1934, ein Akt der österreichischen Tragödie*; Friedrich Funder: *Als Österreich den Sturm bestand*, pp. 138–60; Emil Ratzenhofer: 'Die Niederwerfen der Februarrevolte' in *Militärwissenschaftliche Mitteilungen*, Vienna 1934; Brook-Shepherd: *Dollfuss*, pp. 132–47; Julius Deutsch: *Bürgerkrieg in Österreich, Lebenserinnerungen*, pp. 203–24; *Alexander Eifler*; Buttinger *op. cit.*, pp. 1–20; Karl Karwinsky, unpublished notes 'Ein Beitrag zur Geschichte des 12 Februar 1934'.

39. Report by Police Headquarters Vienna, 28 February 1934.

40. Gulick, *op. cit.*, Vol. IV, pp. 316 *et seq.*; Karwinsky: *Aufzeichnungen*, p. 24.

41. Winkler, *op. cit.*, p. 99.

42. Brook-Shepherd, *op. cit.*, p. 132.

43. Buttinger, *op. cit.*, pp. 152 *et seq.*

44. Kerekes, *op. cit.*, pp. 181 *et seq.*

Chapter 4. Between Hammer and Anvil

1. He said this to me himself when I met him officially in Venice in April 1934. Dr Anton Rintelen (1876–1946) was professor of Roman Law at the University of Graz, Governor of Styria and Christian Social deputy in the National Diet from 1919 to 1926 and 1928 to 1932, Minister of Education 1932–3 and Minister in Rome from summer 1933 to July 1934.

2. DGFP, Series C, Vol. 2, Nos. 308, 328, 389.

3. See also Brook-Shepherd *op. cit.*, p. 150 and Helmut Andics: *Der Staat den keiner wollte*, pp. 449 *et seq.*

4. See Brook-Shepherd *op. cit.*, pp. 204–5 where he refers to personal information from Ambassador Hornbostel who was diplomatic adviser and interpreter at the Dollfuss-Mussolini negotiations.

5. 'Germany has neither the intention nor the desire to interfere in internal Austrian affairs, to annex or incorporate Austria' –

extract from Hitler's speech to the Reichstag on 21 May 1935.

6. Schärf *op. cit.*, pp. 55 *et seq.*: Brook-Shepherd *op. cit.*, pp. 224–5; DGFP, Series C, Vol. 2, No. 255.

7. Kerekes *op. cit.*, pp. 151 *et seq.*; Schärf *op. cit.*, p. 28.

8. Kerekes *op. cit.*, pp. 160 *et seq.* quoting from secret political files of the Hungarian Foreign Ministry 1934–20–49. During the Second World War Colonel Rendulic became Colonel-General commanding a German Army Group on the north-eastern front.

9. Austrian Yearbook 1933–4, Series 15, Vienna 1735, p. 19.

10. Kerekes *op. cit.*, pp. 187 *et seq.*, quoting political files of Hungarian Foreign Ministry 1934–23–81. For Hungarian anxieties over the Habsburg question see DGFP, Series C, Vol. 2, Nos. 444, 455.

11. Brook-Shepherd *op. cit.*, pp. 221–3; DGFP, Series C, Vol. 2, Nos. 299, 332.

12. On 30 June 1934 an alleged revolt prepared by the SA was suppressed by Hitler with much bloodshed – the 'Röhm putsch'.

13. Austrian Government's 'Brown Book', pp. 72 *et seq.*

14. *Ibid.*, p. 77.

15. Report of the Historical Commission of the *Reichsführer-SS*: *Die Erhebung der österreichischen Nationalsozialisten im Juli 1934*, introduction by Ludwig Jedlicka, published in Vienna in 1965.

16. *Weltgeschichte der Gegenwart in Dokumenten*, Part I – International Politics, 3rd edition, p. 265.

17. DGFP, Series C, Vol. 3, No. 125.

18. Hungarian document from Austrian resistance records; all the above documents appear in an annex to the SS report written by Ludwig Jedlicka and entitled *Die Lage in Österreich 1934*.

19. Dollfuss' speech on the Trabrennplatz, Vienna, on 11 September 1933.

20. Dr Wächter in *Österreichischer Beobachter*, No. 2 of July 1938, reproduced in Ludwig Jedlicka: *Die Lage in Österreich*, p. 287.

21. Brook-Shepherd *op. cit.*, pp. 270–1; see also Goldinger in Benedikt *op. cit.*, p. 230.

22. Zernatto *op. cit.*, pp. 83, 85 *et seq.*

23. Dr Irmgard Bärnthaler: *Geschichte und Organisation der Vaterländischen Front* – Dissertation (unpublished), University of Vienna, 1964, pp. 105–17.

24. Buttinger *op. cit.*, pp. 152–3.
25. *Ibid.*, p. 152.
26. *Ibid.*, p. 291.
27. Austrian Year Book 1933–4, pp. 400 *et seq.*
28. Buttinger *op. cit.*, pp. 424 *et seq.*
29. Von Papen's report on the 'May Rally of the Freedom League' dated 12 May 1936 – document D. 703 in the Schmidt trial, pp. 404 *et seq.*
30. Buttinger *op. cit.*, p. 451.
31. *Ibid.*, pp. 152 *et seq.*
32. Telegram of 1 August 1934 from Sir John Simon to Drummond, the British Ambassador in Rome – copy in the notes of an Italian ex-diplomat.
33. See Chapter 5.
34. German Federal Archives, Koblenz, Folio 0218.
35. Arnold J. Toynbee: *Survey of International Affairs*, 1938, Vol. 1, Royal Institute of International Affairs, 1941.
36. Report by von Papen, 14 January 1937, DGFP, Series D, Vol. 1, No. 198.
37. Report by von Papen, 21 December 1937, *ibid.* No. 273.
38. Buttinger *op. cit.*, pp. 457–8.
39. *Ibid.*, p. 471.
40. *Ibid.*, pp. 341, 438 *et seq.*
41. See Hans Huebmer: *Dr Otto Ender*, p. 193.
42. At a personal interview in November 1968 Fulvio Suvich, who was Italian Under-Secretary for External Affairs at the time, assured me that he could remember Mussolini giving this advice.
43. Text in *Neue Freie Presse* of 13 May 1936 (morning edition) – quoted in Gulick *op. cit.*, Vol. 5, pp. 442 *et seq.*
44. Written information to the Chancellor on 27 May 1936 from Edmund Weber, director of the official news agency – in Federal Archives, Koblenz, Seyss-Inquart section, No. 15.
45. Signed Appunto, Rome 15 May 1936 – in Federal Archives, Koblenz, Seyss-Inquart section, 15.
46. Federal Archives, Koblenz, Seyss-Inquart section, 15.
47. Gulick *op. cit.*, Vol. 5, p. 471; on Fey's press conference see radio script issued by the German news agency in Federal Archives, section Seyss-Inquart, 16.
48. Gendarmerie report of 7 October in Federal Archives as above.

49. Information from Dr Fulvio Suvich to the author, November 1968.
50. *Ibid.*
51. Elizabeth Wiskemann: *The Rome-Berlin Axis*, p. 57.
52. From my own memory of my visit to Florence, August 1934.
53. DGFP, Series D, Vol. 1, No. 1.
54. Information from Dr. Fulvio Suvich to the author, November 1968.
55. Sir Samuel Hoare was British Foreign Secretary and Pierre Laval French Foreign Minister. The Hoare-Laval plan proposed a compromise satisfactory to Italy but it was indignantly rejected by British public opinion, leading to Hoare's resignation and his replacement by Anthony Eden.
56. Report by von Papen, 4 October 1934, Federal Archives NS 10/50, Appendix 4.
57. Kerekes *op. cit.*, p. 4.
58. *Ibid.*, report on the negotiations in Rome on 21 March 1936, document 10, pp. 124 *et seq.*
59. DGFP, Series D, Vol. 1, Nos. 254, 259.
60. *Ibid.*, Series C, Vol. 2, No. 389. Benes' comment was made in a speech to the Prague parliament on 21 March 1934.
61. *Ibid.*, No. 393.
62. My own testimony at the Schmidt trial (p. 432) and that of Theodor Hornbostel (p. 168).
63. Hornbostel's testimony at the Schmidt trial, p. 168.
64. *Ibid.*, pp. 174, 177.
65. See letter from Andor Wodianer, Hungarian Chargé d'Affaires in Madrid, to Gabor Apor, acting Foreign Minister, dated 28 July 1936. Kerekes *op. cit.*, Document 12, p. 128.
66. From Federal Chancellor's Office – subject: Foreign policy matters concerning Austro-German discussions on 8 July 1936; see Schmidt trial, pp. 482 *et seq.*
67. Guido Schmidt was born in Vorarlberg in 1901. He studied at university and then joined the foreign service. Both his friends and his enemies agree that he was of above-average ability. As a result, and thanks also to his tireless energy and his ambition, his promotion was rapid. Schmidt was a civil servant, not a politician. He owed his appointment in July 1936 as State Secretary for Foreign Affairs to three facts: first, following the July agreement it seemed advantageous to put forward a new diplomatic personality unknown in Germany and not hitherto

conspicuous in the political struggle; secondly, as Deputy Director of the Presidential Chancellery he was fully *au fait* with government business and personalities; thirdly, both the President and I had particular confidence in him, having known him personally for years.

In spite of rumours to the contrary, he fully justified this confidence up to 11 March 1938. He was thoroughly opposed to National-Socialism, a firm supporter of Austrian independence and never joined the Nazi Party even after 1938. Although, unlike some of his colleagues and many of his subordinates, he did not suffer political persecution, he had no official position under the Nazi regime.

On the debit side he has been rightly reproached for succumbing to the temptation to join the board of the Hermann Göring Works in the spring of 1939. This position he owed to the goodwill of Göring who knew him personally and, as Schmidt admitted at his trial, wished to protect him from arrest by Himmler. Schmidt was held in prison from 1 July 1945 until his acquittal on 12 June 1947 by the Vienna People's Court after a four-month trial. He later became Managing Director of the Semperit Company in Vienna, where he died in 1958.

68. Vienna State Archives, Folio 466, NPA, K 466.
69. *Ibid.*, GZ 2269 *et seq.*
70. DGFP, Series D, Vol. 1, No. 152.
71. Note by Altenburg of the Berlin Foreign Ministry dated 22 September 1936 – DGFP, Series D, Vol. 1, No. 165.
72 Report by Papen 5 June 1937, DGFP, Series D, Vol. 1, No. 229.
73. *Ibid.*, No. 160.
74. Vienna State Archives, Folio 466, 2158 *et seq.*
75. Report from Papen to Hitler, 1 July 1937, DGFP, Series D, Vol. 1, No. 233.
76. See *inter alia* von Stein's report of 7 October 1937 in DGFP, Series D, Vol. 1, No. 259, and Papen: *Memoirs*, pp. 381 *et seq.*
77. Hoffinger's evidence, Schmidt trial, p. 137.
78. Statement by Ambassador Hornbostel, Schmidt trial, pp. 176, 184.
79. Evidence by Professor Wilhelm Taucher, Schmidt trial, pp. 214 *et seq.*
80. Official Trade Ministry figures published in the *Wiener Zeitung* of 25 February 1938 – 'Bundestagsrede vom 24 Februar 1938'.

81. DGFP, Series D, Vol. 1, No. 155.
82. Federal Archives, Koblenz, NS 10/50–422082, p. 250.
83. DGFP, Series D, Vol. 1, No. 162.
84. *Ibid.*, No. 165.
85. *Ibid.*, No. 166.
86. *Ibid.*, No. 167.
87. Signed by Karl Ritter, Ministerial Director and head of the Trade Department in the Foreign Ministry, *Ibid.*, No. 172.
88. *Ibid.*, No. 193.
89. Report by von Stein dated 7 October 1937, *Ibid.*, No. 259.
90. *Ibid.*, No. 251.
91. Note by von Neurath on a talk with Guido Schmidt in Brand, Vorarlberg, *Ibid.*, No. 247.
92. Kerekes, Lajos: *Akten des ungarischen Ministeriums des Äusseren*, pp. 378 *et seq.*, quoted by Ludwig Jedlicka 'Der 13 März in der Sicht der historischen Forschung' in *Der Donauraum*, No. 3 of 1968, pp. 141–55.
93. Papen, *op. cit.*, pp. 370–1.
94. See Zernatto *op. cit.*, pp. 173 *et seq.*
95. *Weiner Zeitung*, 27 November 1936, p. 327; see also Papen *op. cit.*, p. 380.
96. DGFP, Series D, Vol. 1, Nos. 186, 187.
97. Vienna State Archives, Folio 466, NPA, K 466.
98. Federal Archives, Koblenz – Section Seyss-Inquart 1.
99. Vienna Archives, Z.22, General folio 305/766; see also Ludwig Jedlicka, 'Der 13 März 1938' in *Der Donauraum* No. 3 of 1968, p. 150, where reference is made to Household, Court and State Archives NPA, K 309/1968.
100. Vienna Archives, Z.22, Gen. 1/452/46.

Chapter 5. Parting of the Ways

1. Both when I met Göring in 1936 and when Schmidt visited him in 1937 the general tenor of the conversation was: We can easily agree on Austrian requirements for air force equipment – 'you don't need the Italians for that'.
2. Letter from Göring to Guido Schmidt of 11 November 1937 and reply dated 23 November – Schmidt trial pp. 311 *et seq.*
3. See Chapter 3, p. 95.

NOTES

4. The Stresa conference in April 1935 between Italy, Britain and France had adopted resolutions against further unilateral German violations of the Treaty of Versailles, had declared Austrian independence to be in the common interest and had emphasised the importance of the Locarno policy. The so-called Stresa front, however, was soon relegated to impotence by Italian policy in Abyssinia.

5. Report by Papen 4 November 1936, DGFP, Series D, Vol. 1, No. 171.

6. Official *aide memoire* dated 8 January and office minute dated 26 January 1938 – Schmidt trial, pp. 556–7; Papen *op. cit.*, pp. 406 *et seq.*; Eichstädt *op. cit.*, pp. 267 *et seq.*

7. Report by Wimmer, the Austrian Minister in Belgrade, dated 29 January 1938 (Z.7/Pol) – Schmidt trial, pp. 549 *et seq.*

8. Report by Wimmer dated 12 June 1937, *ibid.*, p. 548.

9. Reports by Wimmer dated 12 February, 26 February and 2 March 1938. (Z.10, 16, 18/Pol), *ibid.*, pp. 551 *et seq.*

10. Telegram from von Papen in Papen Report file, Federal Archives, Koblenz.

11. Schuschnigg: *Farewell Austria*, p. 228; *Austrian Requiem*, p. 118.

12. Papen *op. cit.*, p. 408.

13. The Hossbach Minutes of 10 November 1937, quoted in Schmidt Trial, p. 575.

14. *Ibid.*, pp. 574 *et seq.* At the conclusion of the Berchtesgaden meeting Hitler said that, if the agreement was observed, there would be peace for five years, in other words until 1943 – 'By then the world will look very different in any case'.

15. Secret reports from Ambassador von Papen in the Federal Archives, Koblenz, Folio NS 10/50, partially reproduced in the Schmidt Trial and published in DGFP Series D, Vol. 1.

16. Report from Baar, the Austrian Minister in Budapest, dated 25 February 1938 (Z1.23/Pol), Schmidt Trial, p. 569.

17. See Chapter 4.

18. Papen *op. cit.*, p. 396.

19. *Ibid.*, p. 412.

20. Schmidt Trial, p. 338.

21. Office Minute, G.Z.50943-13, Subject: Interview with Ambassador von Papen, 26 January 1938 – Schmidt Trial, p. 557.

22. See p. 144 above.

23. Eichstädt *op. cit.*, p. 274 and Note 12.

24. Guido Zernatto: *Die Wahrheit über Österreich*, p. 200.
25. Paul Schmidt: *Hitler's Interpreter*, p. 59.
26. The Earl of Avon: *The Eden Memoirs – Facing the Dictators*, p. 435 (US edition), p. 387 (British edition). [Future references will be to the US edition with reference to the British edition in brackets – Translator]
27. Schmidt *op. cit.*, pp. 76 *et seq.*; see also Schuschnigg: *Austrian Requiem*, p. 24.
28. Eden *op. cit.*, pp. 576 (509) *et seq.*
29. Schuschnigg: *Austrian Requiem*, pp. 20 *et seq.*
30. *Ibid.*, p. 26.
31. P. Friedrich Muckermann was born in Bückeburg, Lower Saxony in 1883 and died in Montreux in 1946. He was a member of the Order of Jesuits, a well-known literary historian and preacher and editor of the periodical *Gral*. At this time he was living in Rome and Luxemburg; he had spend a few days in Vienna in 1937. So far as I remember, the last time I had seen him was in 1933. A report from von Papen dated 12 February 1938 (DGFP, Series D, Vol. 1, No. 292) says:

'As the Legation is informed from a reliable source Count Coudenhove-Kalergi, the head of the pan-Europe movement, recently gave a tea at his home in honour of the exiled Father Muckermann. A relative of the host's, Countess Marietta Coudenhove, who is known for her National sympathies, was present at this reception. Since her political attitude is evidently not known to Count Coudenhove, however, they spoke quite freely in her presence.

Muckermann himself said that he was in Vienna by order of the Vatican in order to organise the defence against National-Socialism and to exterminate the Austrian National-Socialists. As matters now stood, there could be no doubt at all of the success of his mission.

The wife of the host, the Jewess Ida Roland, later brought the conversation around to the subject of the Führer's trip to Italy. On this Muckermann expressed himself somewhat as follows: "That is all prepared. While he is inspecting the Capitol, they can get close to him. I am convinced that the great Austrian plan will succeed entirely." Thereupon Ida Roland said: "Then we shall have reached our goal."

I am passing on this information with reservations despite the reliability of the source. As a result of a conference I had with a member of the clergy who is very close to Cardinal Innitzer, I can state as follows: Cardinal Innitzer has considered taking steps toward imposing silence on Father Muckermann and has to this end contacted the Superiors of his

Order. There could be no question of an order from the Vatican to Father Muckermann. This lie was due to Father Muckermann's need to make himself important. I expect that my efforts in this direction will be successful, since the Cardinal too views the political activity of Muckermann with obvious displeasure.

I can take no definite stand on the statements indicating an attempt at assassination. That the Freemason Coudenhove and his set are among the bitterest foes of National-Socialism, there is no doubt.'

32. Dr Kajetan Mühlmann's evidence at the Schmidt Trial, p. 250.

33. For the opposite view see Eichstädt *op. cit.*, p. 303.

34. The Keppler Protocol is to be found in DGFP, Series D, Vol. 1, No. 294, and the final protocol as signed in No. 295. The mention of General Böhme in the latter is an error; he was Chief Signal Officer at this time.

35. *Ibid.*, No. 295.

36. *Ibid.*, No. 298.

37. *Ibid.* (Editor's note).

38. See Schuschnigg: *Austrian Requiem*, p. 24; Churchill: *The Second World War – The Gathering Storm*, pp. 191 *et seq.*

39. DGFP, Series D, Vol. 1, No. 273.

40. *Völkischer Beobachter*, South German edition, 31 January 1939.

41. Statement by Dr Rainer before the International Military Tribunal, Nuremberg, record of session 11–13 June 1946.

42. Evidence by Dr Rainer at the Schmidt Trial, p. 340.

43. Mühlmann's evidence at the Schmidt Trial, p. 249.

44. Churchill's Mansion House speech, 10 November 1942, referring to British victories in Egypt.

45. Papen *op. cit.*, pp. 409 *et seq.*

46. *Ibid.*, p. 422. The agreement, it will be remembered, explicitly referred to non-interference.

47. DGFP, Series D, Vol. 1, No. 293.

48. Reports by Dr Ludwig Jordan, Austrian Consul-General, Munich, dated 16 October 1937, 21 January, 8 and 24 February 1938 – Schmidt Trial, pp. 489, 507 *et seq.*

49. Amnesty 1938, Federal Archives Koblenz, Folio 0218.

Chapter 6. To the Brink

1. Sumner Welles: *The Time for Decision*, p. 32.

2. Nuremberg document 3300/PS. – Schmidt Trial, pp. 345–86.
3. DGFP, Series D, Vol. 1, No. 327.
4. See the Hossbach Minutes, Nuremberg document 386, p. 573 in the Schmidt trial.
5. Apart from the numerically insignificant group led by Dr Walter Riehl, the Vienna advocate, who was a leading member of the War Veterans [*Frontkëmpfer*].
6. Papen Memorandum of 3 May 1945 – see Note 2 above.
7. State Archives Vienna, L 466 – Germany 1/12E; reproduced in Schmidt Trial, p. 507.
8. Vienna Archives, 22 Gen. 2 Pol. 38 – Schmidt Trial, p. 507.
9. Schmidt Trial, pp. 508 *et seq.*
10. DGFP, Series D, Vol. 1, No. 255.
11. *Ibid.*, No. 138 (author's italics).
12. *Ibid.*, No. 139.
13. Eden *op. cit.*, p. 570 (504).
14. Testimony on the economic situation in 1937 given by Professor Wilhelm Taucher, Schmidt Trial, p. 217.
15. The relevant parts of the speech are quoted in Papen *op. cit.*, pp. 421–2.
16. DGFP Series D, Vol. 1, No. 328.
17. Churchill *op. cit.*, p. 206.
18. Schmidt Trial, pp. 561 *et seq.*
19. *Ibid.*, p. 180 – statement by Theodor Hornbostel, Head of the Political Division of the Austrian Foreign Office.
20. *New York Times*, Sunday 12 December 1938, p. 66.
21. Keesing's Contemporary Archives, 18th year, 16 December 1948, p. 1739A (German edition).
22. *New York Times*, 16 December 1948 (see Note 20).
23. For another view see Brook-Shepherd: *Anschluss*, pp. 65 *et seq.*
24. Puaux *op. cit.*, pp. 103 *et seq.*
25. DGFP, Series D, Vol. 1, No. 313. At this time Veesenmayer was staff officer to Keppler, the plenipotentiary for Austria and representative of the SD; he later had a special part to play as German Minister in Budapest.
26. DGFP, Series D, Vol. 1, No. 309.
27. The German version, however, was that Hitler and Mussolini had agreed at their meeting that Germany would not obstruct Italian policy in the Mediterranean whereas Italy would not oppose the special German interests in Austria – DGFP, Series

D, Vol. 1, No. 1; see also Ludwig Jedlicka: *Ein Heer im Schatten der Parteien*, p. 162.

28. Evidence by Dr Emil Liebitzky at the Schmidt Trial, p. 223.
29. DGFP, Series D, Vol. 1, No. 34.
30. Eden *op. cit.*, p. 653 (575).
31. *Ibid.*, p. 657 (579).
32. *Ibid.*, p. 658 (579).
33. DGFP, Series D, Vol. 1, No. 122.
34. Eden *op. cit.*, pp. 701 *et seq.* (616).
35. See Churchill *op. cit.*, Chaps. 5–8.
36. See Keith Feiling: *Life of Neville Chamberlain* and the Hossbach Minutes.
37. Ciano's *Diary*, 1937–8 – entries for February 1938.
38. DGFP, Series D, Vol. 1, No. 129.
39. For another view see A. J. P. Taylor: *Origins of the Second World War* where he supports Hitler's claim to national integration.
40. Nuremberg document NG 3578 in the archives of the *Institut für Zeitgeschichte*, Munich.
41. After the July 1934 *putsch* Reinthaller, an engineer, was Director of the pacification campaign which bears his name; he was leader of the Nazi peasants. Dr Langoth had been a Pan-German deputy in Upper Austria and Director of the *Hilfswerk* [Voluntary Aid] which was approved by the Austrian government. Dr Rainer was an aspirant notary public and later *Gauleiter* in Carinthia and Salzburg. Odilo Globocnik was illegal Nazi *Gauleiter* for Austria.
42. See Note 40.
43. Nuremberg document NG 3282, Archives of *Institut für Zeitgeschichte*.
44. Papen *op. cit.*, p. 403.
45. DGFP, Series D, Vol. 1, No. 289. In my opinion Leopold must have been told about the preparations for Berchtesgaden by his informant in the German Embassy, the Counsellor von Stein.
46. *Ibid.*, No. 313.
47. Minutes in the *Institut für Zeitgeschichte*, Munich.
48. DGFP, Series D, Vol. 1, No. 313 (see Note 25 above) – author's italics.
49. Seyss-Inquart's evidence in Nuremberg, IMT, Vol. XV, p. 621; see also Benoist-Mechin *op. cit.*, p. 498.
50. DGFP, Series D, Vol. 1, No. 328.
51. Zernatto *op. cit.*, pp. 239 *et seq.*

52. Cabinet minutes in Vienna archives.
53. DGFP, Series D, Vol. 1, No. 289.
54. Papen *op. cit.*, pp. 423–4.
55. DGFP, Series D, Vol. 1, No. 329.
56. *Ibid.*, No. 124.
57. *Ibid.*, No. 132.
58. Reports from Alois Vollgruber, Austrian Minister in Paris, dated 22 and 26 February 1938 – Schmidt Trial, pp. 542, 570; see also Eichstädt *op. cit.*, pp. 341 *et seq.*
59. Notes by Vollgruber – Schmidt Trial, p. 572; Eichstädt *op. cit.*, pp. 344 *et seq.*
60. DGFP, Series D, Vol. 1, No. 305.
61. Telegraphic report from Franckenstein 17 February – Schmidt Trial, p. 565.
62. Hansard.
63. Hansard; see also DGFP, Series D, Vol. 1, No. 331.
64. Brook-Shepherd: *Anschluss*, p. 86.
65. See report by von Papen on 17 April 1937 forwarding two secret instructions from the Austrian Foreign Ministry to the Legations in London and Rome – DGFP, Series D, Vol. 1, No. 220; also a report of Stein, the German Counsellor, reporting a journey to Steenockerzeel by Karwinsky, the former State Secretary, to see Archduke Otto – DGFP, Series D, Vol. 1, No. 337.
66. See Holldack *op. cit.*, p. 26; *Ambassador Dodd's Diary*, pp. 238 *et seq.* (not in English edition); François-Poncet: *The Fateful Years*, p. 224.
67. Papen *op. cit.*, pp. 227–8.
68. *Ibid.*, pp. 381–2.
69. In *History of the Austrian Republic*, Part III, published in 1954; Friedrich Thalmann: *Die Wirtschaft in Österreich*, pp. 498 *et seq.*
70. DGFP, Series D, Vol. 1, No. 333.
71. *Ibid.*, No. 334.
72. Schuschnigg: *Austrian Requiem*, p. 54.
73. DGFP, Series D, Vol. 1, No. 335 – author's italics.

Chapter 7. Across the Rubicon

1. See memorandum by Colonel-General Ludwig Beck dated 5 May 1938 quoted by W. Foerster in *Ein General kämpft gegen den Krieg*, pp. 82 *et seq.*

2. Walter Goldinger in *Geschichte der Republik Österreich*, edited b Heinrich Benedikt, p. 264.

3. *Ibid.*, pp. 265 *et seq.*; see also A. J. P. Taylor: *Origins of the Secon World War*, and David Hoggan: *The War forced on us*.

4. DGFP, Series D, Vol. 1, No. 328.

5. *Ibid.*, No. 313.

6. See von Stein's reports in DGFP, Series D, Vol. 1, Nos. 259 (Oct. 1937), 264 (22 Oct. 1937), 290 (10 Feb. 1938), 306 (17 Fe 1938), and 341 (10 Mar. 1938).

7. Situation report in *Der Einsatz der 8 Armee 1938 zur Wiedervereinigun Österreichs mit dem Deutschen Reich* in archives of *Institut f Zeitgeschichte*, Vienna – henceforth referred to as *Einsatzbericht*.

8. DGFP, Series D, Vol. 1, No. 295.

9. Evidence by Wilhelm Miklas at the Schmidt Trial, p. 260.

10. DGFP, Series D, Vol. 1, No. 264.

11. *Ibid.*, footnote.

12. *Ibid.*, No. 138.

13. Telegram from Halifax to Henderson, 10 March 1938 – *Documen on British Foreign Policy*, Series III, Vol. 1, No. 9 (hereaft referred to as DBFP).

14. Puaux, *op. cit.*, p. 110, Note 1.

15. DGFP, Series D, Vol. 1, No. 295.

16. Zernatto, *op. cit.*, p. 272.

17. Eichstädt *op. cit.*, p. 357, Note 34.

18. Papers in the archives of the *Institut für Zeitgeschichte*, Vienna.

19. For authentic version of proclamation and speech see *Tirol Gewerbe*, Innsbruck – special edition of 9 March 1938.

20. Papers in archives of *Institut für Zeitgeschichte*, Vienna.

21. DGFP, Series D, Vol. 1, No. 338.

22. Letter from Seyss-Inquart to Zernatto of 9 March 1938, quoted i Zernatto *op. cit.*, pp. 290 *et seq.*

23. Reproduced in Zernatto *op. cit.*, pp. 290 *et seq.*

24. Evidence by Seyss-Inquart at the Schmidt Trial, p. 338.

25. *Einsatzbericht* (see Note 7 above), dated 18 July 1938, p. 2.

26. *Ibid.*, p. 21 and Annex 3, 'Order of Battle of Eighth Army for th invasion of Austria'; see also Friedrich Fritz: 'Der deutsch Einmarsch in Österreich 1938' in *Militär-historische Schriftenreih* edited by the Army History Museum (*Militärwissenschaftlich Institut*), Vienna 1968, pp. 3 *et seq.*

27. *Einsatzbericht*, p. 14.

28. *Ibid*, p. 20.
29. Fritz *op. cit.*, p. 3.
30. Erich Kordt: *Nicht aus den Akten*, p. 194.
31. Ludwig Jedlicka: '11 März – Der "Fall Österreich" ' in *Die Furche*, No. 11 of 14 March 1953, p. 3.
32. *Einsatzbericht*, p. 15.
33. This account is taken from a letter to me dated 2 February 1951 from Dr Rudolf Neumayer, ex-Minister of Finance.
34. See Chapter 8, pp. 302–305.
35. Hitler's speech of 9 April 1938 quoted in Benoist-Mechin *op. cit.*, pp. 585/6.
36. Evidence by Max Hoffinger at the Schmidt Trial, p. 144; evidence at the same trial (p. 164) by Dr Hans Becker, the Fatherland Front recruiting officer, who calculated on an average majority of 80 to 85 per cent; evidence by Dr Michael Skubl, IMT Vol. XVI, p. 178.
37. Information to the author from Kuprian, the ex-Burgomaster, 8 May 1968.
38. See Chapter 8 below.
39. Verdross: *Völkerrecht* (4th edition), p. 225.
40. Figures from a memorandum dated 8 February 1947 on Austrian resistance during the Hitler period written by Dr Gruber, the Austrian Foreign Minister and quoted in Kasamas *op. cit.*, p. 695.
41. *Einsatzbericht*, p. 1.
42. A minority motion introduced in the Army Committee of the National Diet by Dr Julius Deutsch demanded the reduction of the effective strength of the armed forces and the number of military appointments from 18,300 to 15,000. In the preliminary discussions of the army budget for 1932 he had already demanded reduction of the sum proposed to the 1928 figure. Speaking for the opposition in the National Diet on 16 December 1931 Dr Deutsch had said: 'With our 18,000 men how are we to defend frontiers over 600 miles long if we are attacked by a major power? . . . This army budget before us now is still far too high for our modest state with its modest size.' Budget debate, 64th sitting of the National Diet, 4th Session, Army proposals 1932 – record of National Diet of 20 February 1931, p. 644 and 16 December 1931, pp. 1767 *et seq.* and 1802.
43. The Hossbach Minutes; Helmut Krausnick: 'Vorgeschichte und

Beginn des militärischen Widerstandes gegen Hitler' in *Die Vollmacht des Gewissens,* p. 261.

44. Evidence by Lieutenant-General Jansa at the Schmidt Trial, pp. 217 *et seq.*; Ludwig Jedlicka: *Ein Heer im Schatten der Parteien,* pp. 130, 164.

45. Data on the Austrian army comes from two unpublished memoranda, copies of which were sent me on 26 March 1952 by the author, General Emil Liebitzky.

46. Jedlicka *op. cit.,* p. 180; Jansa's evidence, Schmidt Trial, p. 217.

47. *Einsatzbericht,* pp. 24 *et seq.*

48. Document C 102 in the Schmidt Trial, p. 576; *Einsatzbericht,* p. 6.

49. Gordon Brook-Shepherd in a letter to the author, 1 February 1962; see also his book *Anschluss,* p. 169.

50. Evidence by General Liebitzky and Lieutenant-General Jansa at the Schmidt Trial, pp. 221, 223; data on the Austrian army from General Liebitzky's memorandum (see Note 45 above).

51. Information from ex-Ambassador Vollgruber in a letter to the author, 6 November 1967.

52. DBFP, Series III, Vol. 1, No. 20.

53. *Ibid.,* No. 19.

54. *Ibid.,* No. 24.

55. *Ibid.,* No. 25.

56. *Hitler's Secret Book,* Grove Press, New York 1962.

57. *Einsatzbericht,* p. 9.

58. General Zehner was murdered in his house by the Gestapo on 10 April 1938, the day of the referendum. An attempt was made to simulate suicide.

59. From a memorandum drafted by General Liebitzky in 1952 entitled *Daten über das österreichische Bundesheer 1920–1938.*

Chapter 8. The Vision and the Reality

1. Address at the Görres-Ring, Köln, 16 January 1933 on Austro-German relations; see *Österreichisches Adenblatt,* Serial 63, p. 7, 21 June 1933.

2. Friedrich Funder: *Als Österreich den Sturm bestand,* pp. 16 *et seq.*

3. See Hitler's exposé to the Commanders-in-Chief Conference on 23 November 1943 – Nuremberg document 789/PS in the Federal Archives, Koblenz, and reproduced as Document XLIX in Holldack *op. cit.,* p. 458.

4. Report of the 'Reichsführer-SS Historical Commission': *Die Erhebung der österreichischen Nationalsozialisten im Juli 1934*, p. 80.
5. DGFP, Series C, Vol. IV, No. 232 – author's italics.
6. Evidence in Austrian State Archives, Vienna, Folio 466.
7. See Chapter 5, p. 181.
8. Evidence by Rainer at the Nuremberg Trial, session of 11–13 June 1946; evidence by Rainer at the Schmidt Trial, p. 340.
9. DGFP, Series D, Vol. 1, No. 229.
10. DGFP, Series D, Vol. 1, No. 295. The mention in this document (and also in Eichstädt *op. cit.*, p. 303) of the replacement of Lieutenant-General Jansa by General Böhme is in error. The new Chief of Staff, appointed in January 1938 before the Berchtesgaden meeting, was Lieutenant-General Eugen Beyer, ex-commander of the Salzburg-North Tyrol-Vorarlberg Division. See also Field Marshal Jansa's evidence at the Schmidt Trial, p. 220.
11. DGFP, Series D, Vol. 1, No. 290. The interview referred to was given on 5 January 1938 to Kees von Hoek, the *Daily Telegraph* correspondent. Subject was the problems of Austrian policy with particular reference to Austria's relationship to National-Socialism. Text in German Press Agency issue No. 4 Anglo of 5 January in Federal Archives, Koblenz, R 43 II/1474a.
12. DGFP, Series C, Vol. 5, No. 446.
13. According to the figures of the Ministry of Justice, in July 1936 15,457 persons had been amnestied – 958 cases of suspension of sentence, 1,881 of quashing of proceedings and 12,618 of discontinuance of enquiries against minor participants in the July *putsch*. On 9 July 1937 109 National-Socialists were still in detention for crimes committed before 11 July 1936 involving bloodshed or the use of explosives.
14. *Reichspost*, 24 December 1935, No. 355.
15. Berchtesgaden Protocol Article II, 4 – DGFP, Series D, Vol. 1, No. 295.
16. *Ibid.*, No. 273.
17. Professor Taucher's evidence at the Schmidt Trial, p. 316.
18. Helmut Krausnick in 'Unser Weg in die Katastrophe von 1945' in the supplement 'Aus Politik und Zeitgeschichte' to the periodical *Das Parlament*, No. 19 of 9 May 1962.
19. Report by von Papen, 27 July 1935, Nuremberg document 2248/PS, reproduced in Holldack *op. cit.*, p. 299.
20. See report by Johann Graf Welczek, the German Ambassador in

Paris, 11 February 1938 – DGFP, Series D, Vol. 1, No. 291.

21. In his Second Book (or 'Secret Book'), however, Hitler thought otherwise—'In the very fact of her [Austria's] existence there already lies an easing of the military strategic position of Czechoslovakia' (p. 198).

22. DGFP, Series D, Vol. 1, No. 273 – author's italics.

23. Harold Nicolson: *Diaries and Letters 1930–1939* (Collins, London 1966), p. 331.

24. Louis Weinberger: *Tatsachen, Begegnungen und Gespräche*, pp. 72 *et seq.*

25. Das Eugen-Roth-Buch (Munich 1966), p. 255.

26. These and other detailed data come from Otto Molden: *Der Ruf des Gewissens* (Vienna 1958), pp. 330, 345. For further details on Austrian resistance see Friedrich Engel-Janosi: 'Remarks on the Austrian Resistance 1938–1945' in *Journal of Central European Affairs*, Vol. XIII, No. II, July 1953.

27. Letter from Dr Koenig to Vice-President Barth 6 August 1938 – Federal Archives, Koblenz, EAP 106/1, p. 2347 *et seq.*

28. Original in Federal Archives, Koblenz, Folio Seyss-Inquart 13.

29. Josef Bürckel was originally a school-teacher in the Saar. In January 1935 he managed the Saar plebiscite and then continued as Nazi *Gauleiter* in the Saar territory. On recall from Vienna in August 1940 he became Head of Civil Administration in Lorraine until he joined the *Wehrmacht*; he committed suicide in 1944.

30. Hans Eibl, Professor of Philosophy at the University of Vienna.

31. Copies of letters, Bürckel to Seyss-Inquart, 8 August 1939, and Seyss-Inquart to Himmler, 19 August 1939, in Federal Archives, Koblenz, Folio Seyss-Inquart 13.

32. See Chapter 6, Note 2; Schmidt Trial, p. 377.

33. *Ibid.*, p. 379.

34. German News Bureau, No, 407, 15 March 1938; see also DGFP, Series D, Vol. 1, No. 387.

35. DGFP, Series D, Vol. 1, No. 379.

36. Report by German Minister in Berne, 14 March 1938 – DGFP, Series D, Vol. 1, No. 382; German News Bureau, No. 449 of 23 March.

37. German News Bureau, No. 418, 17 March 1938.

38. *Ibid.*, No. 409, 16 March.

39. DGFP, Series D, Vol. 2, Nos. 67, 69, 70.

40. *Ibid.*, No. 71.
41. Text in *Weltgeschichte der Gegenwart in Dokumenten* (Essener Verlagsanstalt, Berlin, Essen & Leipzig 1936–1938), Vol. V, p. 468.
42. DGFP, Series D, Vol. 1, No. 352 – author's italics.
43. Schuschnigg: *Austrian Requiem*, pp. 258–9; IMT Document 2949.
44. Evidence by General Liebitzky at the Schmidt Trial, p. 223.
45. Ciano Diary, entries for 13 and 15 March 1938; Eichstädt *op. cit.*, p. 443.
46. Sumner Welles: *Time for Decision*, pp. 81–2.
47. DGFP, Series D, Vol. 1, No. 399.
48. German News Bureau summary, 12 March 1938 – *Das Ausland zu Österreich*.
49. Federal Archives, Koblenz, Folio R 43, II/1360.
50. *St Louis Globe Democrat*, No, 297, 12 March 1938.
51. DGFP, Series D, Vol. 1, Nos. 391, 401; Eichstädt *op. cit.*, p. 440.
52. *Ibid.*
53. Solemn declaration by the Austrian bishops, 18 March 1938 – German News Bureau (DNB) No. 486, 28 March; letter from Cardinal Innitzer to *Gauleiter* Bürckel clearing up and correcting Havas reports on the Bishops' declaration – DNB No. 536, 1 April; statement by the Evangelical Church of Austria on 'Our attitude to the Führer's act of rescue', signed on behalf of the Church Council by Dr Kauer – DNB No. 536, 1 April.
54. Documents of British Foreign Policy, Series III, Vol. 1, Nos 79, 56; Eichstädt *op. cit.*, p. 437; Brook-Shepherd: *Anschluss*, p. 207.
55. See Chapter 6, pp. 214–5.
56. Churchill: *The Second World War – The Gathering Storm*, pp. 244–5.
57. See report by Woermann, the German Chargé d'Affaires, 17 March 1938 – DGFP, Series D, Vol. 2, No. 88.
58. Eden *op. cit.*, p. 570 (502).
59. Churchill *op. cit.*, p. 246.
60. See Chapter 6, Note 20.
61. See Chapter 5, pp. 176–7; also Karl Scheidl: 'Vor 25 Jahren' in *Österreich in Geschichte und Literatur*, No. 3 of 1963, p. 113.
62. Eden *op. cit.*, p. 139 (127).
63. Schmidt *op. cit.*, p. 24.
64. Eden *op. cit.*, pp. 156–7 (140–1); Schmidt *op. cit.*, p. 24.
65. Schmidt *op. cit.*, p. 20.
66. Photostat copies of the German translation of these *Politburo*

directives found their way from Vienna into the Federal Archives Koblenz – Folio Papen Reports, NS 10/50, pp. 128–71. Author's italics. See also report in the Keppler folio in the Federal Archives (10379–10384) on an offer to spy for Germany against Russia after 1938.

67. An officially inspired anti-Jewish pogrom in Germany. [Translator]

68. This presumably refers to the large-scale disciplinary measures taken against officers during 1938 – see Chapter 8, pp. 284–5.

69. In Keppler folio in the Federal Archives, Koblenz, file No. 10378A, ZZ 10379–10384.

Chapter 9. Epilogue

1. See Papen *op. cit.*, p. 426: 'Where we differed was in our conceptions of Austria's role within the framework of the future of the German peoples; a conception with which Schuschnigg's international policies seemed to me irreconcilable'; see also p. 438; also DGFP, Series D, Vol. 1, No. 328 (Chapter. 7, Note 4).

2. A public opinion poll conducted by the Vienna socialist periodical for politics, economics and culture, *Die Zukunft*, in November 1967 showed 73 per cent against the Anschluss, 9 per cent for, and 18 per cent don't know – see Keesing's Archives, 26 November 1967, p. 13.554.

3. See Stephan Verosta: 'Die geschichtliche Kontinuität des österreichischen Staates' in Benedikt *op. cit.*, p. 610; Weinberger *op. cit.*, pp. 148 *et seq.*; Julius Deutsch: *Ein weiter Weg*, p. 372; Renner *op. cit.*, p. 233 (he says that in 1945 he proposed a plebiscite on non-acceptance of the Anschluss and was 'completely convinced that, apart from a tiny minority, the entire people, including all who were not fanaticised Hitler disciples, would have voted for Austrian independence by an overwhelming majority'); Adolf Schärf: *Österreichs Erneuerung*, pp. 20 *et seq.* ('The Anschluss is dead. All love for Germany has been banished from Austrians') – from the discussion between Schärf and Wilhelm Leuschner in spring 1943; Molden *op. cit.*, pp. 148 *et seq.*

4. Hans von Hammerstein, address to the Vienna *Kulturbund*, 21 October 1935 – 'Österreichs kulturelles Antlitz', pp. 14 *et seq.*

SELECT BIBLIOGRAPHY

1 *Books*

Andics, Helmut: *Fünfzig Jahre unseres Lebens*, Vienna, 1968

Ball, Mary: *Post-war German-Austrian relations*, London, 1937

Bauer, Otto: *Der Weg zum Sozialismus*, Vienna, 1919; *Die Revolution in Österreich*, Vienna, 1923; *Der Kampf um die Macht*, Vienna, 1924; *Zwischen zwei Weltkriegen?*, Bratislava, 1936

Benedikt, Heinrich: *Geschichte der Republik Österreich* (Beiträge von Walter Goldinger, Friedrich Thalmann, Stephan Verosta, Adam Wandruszka), Vienna, 1954

Benoist-Mechin, J.: *Histoire De l'Armée allemande, Vol 4 – L'expansion*, Paris, 1964

Best, S. Payne: *The Venlo Incident*, London, 1950

Böhm, Johann: *Erinnerungen aus meinem Leben*, Vienna, 1953

Bourdet, Yvon: *Otto Bauer et la Revolution*, Paris, 1968

Braunthal, Julius: *The Tragedy of Austria*, London, 1948; *In Search of the Millenium*, London, 1945

Buttinger, Josef: *In the Twilight of Socialism*, New York, 1953

Ciano, Galeazzo: *Diary 1937/38*, London, 1952

Churchill Winston: *The Second World War: The Gathering Storm*, London, 1948

Deutsch, Julius: *Ein weiter Weg. Lebenserinnerungen*, Vienna, 1960

Diamant, Alfred: *Austrian Catholics and the first Republic*, Princeton, 1960

Dodd, William E.: *Ambassador Dodd's Diary 1933–1938*, New York, 1941

Dulles, Allen and Gaevernitz, Gero v. S.: *The Secret Surrender*, London, 1946

Eden, Anthony: *The Memoirs: Facing the Dictators 1923–1938*, Boston and London, 1962

Eichstädt, Ulrich: *Von Dollfuss zu Hitler*, Wiesbaden, 1955

Franckenstein, George: *Facts and features of my life*, London, 1939

Fritz, Friedrich: *Der deutsche Einmarsch in Österreich 1938*, Vienna, 1968

Funder, Friedrich: *Von Gestern ins Heute*, Vienna, 1952; *Als Österreich den Sturm bestand*, Vienna, 1957

Gedye, G. E. R.: *Fallen Bastions*, London, 1940

Görlich, Josef Ernst: *Die österreichische Nation und der Widerstand*, Vienna, 1967

Gold, Hugo: *Geschichte der Juden in Wien*, Tel-Aviv, 1966

Gulick, Charles: *Österreich von Habsburg bis Hitler*, Vienna, 1949

Hantsch, Hugo: *Geschichte Österreichs, Band II*, Graz, 1950

Hitler's Secret Book, New York, 1962

Hoor, Ernst: *Österreich 1918–1938: Staat ohne Nation, Republik ohne Republikaner*, Vienna, 1966

Jedlicka, Ludwig: *Ein Heer im Schatten der Parteien: Die militärpolitische Lage Österreichs 1918–1938*, Böhlau, 1955

Kerekes, Lajos: *Abenddämmerung einer Demokratie*, Vienna, 1966; *Allianz Hitler–Horthy–Mussolini: Dokumente zur ungarischen Aussenpolitik 1933–1944*, Budapest, 1966

Kordt, Erich: *Nicht aus den Akten*, Stuttgart, 1950

Kun, Béla: *Die Februar-Kämpfe in Österreich und ihre Lehren*, Moscow–Leningrad, 1934

Leichter, Dr Otto: *Zwischen zwei Diktaturen*, Vienna, 1968

Mikoletzky, Hanns Leo: *Österreichische Zeitgeschichte*, Vienna, 1962

Molden, Otto: *Der Ruf des Gewissens; der österreichische Freiheitskampf 1938–1945*, Vienna, 1958

Papen, Franz v.: *Memoirs*, New York & London, 1953

Puaux, Gabriel: *Mort et Transfiguration de l'Autriche*, Paris, 1966

Renner, Karl: *Österreich von der Ersten zur Zweiten Republik*, Vienna, 1953

Romanix, Felix: *Der Leidensweg der österreichischen Wirtschaft 1933–1945*, Vienna, 1957

Schärf, Adolf: *Geheimer Briefwechsel Mussolini–Dollfuss*, Vienna, 1949

Schuschnigg, Kurt: *My Austria*, New York, 1938; (*Farewell Austria*, London, 1938); *Austrian Requiem*, London & New York 1947

Seipel, Ignaz: *Der Kampf um die österreichische Verfassung*, Vienna, 1930

Selby, Walford: *Diplomatic Twilight 1930–1940*, London, 1953

Shell, Kurt L.: *The Transformation of Austrian Socialism*, New York, 1962

Shepherd, Gordon Brook: *Austrian Odyssey*, London, 1958; *Engelbert Dollfuss*, London, 1961; *The Rape of Austria*, London, 1963

Stadler, Karl: *Österreich 1938–1945 im Spiegel der NS-Akten*, Vienna, 1966

Taylor, A. J. P.: *The Origins of the Second World War*, London, 1962

Wagner, D., Tomkowitz, G.: *Ein Volk, Ein Reich, Ein Führer*, Munich, 1968

Weinberger, Lois: *Tatsachen, Begegnungen, Gespräche*, Vienna, 1948

Winkler, Franz: *Die Diktatur in Österreich*, Zürich–Leipzig, 1935

Wolf in der Maur: *Guido Zernatto: Vom Wesen der Nation*, Vienna, 1966

Zernatto, Guido: *Die Wahrheit über Österreich*, New York, 1938

2 *Periodical and Document-Collections*

Donauraum, 13 Jg., 3 Heft, 1968: Ludwig Jedlicka: 'Der 13 März 1938 in der Sicht der historischen Forschung'

Österreich in Geschichte und Literatur, 10 Jg., 1966: Johann Auer: 'Antisemitische Strömungen in Wien, 1921–1923'

Zeitschrift für die Geschichte der Juden, Tel-Aviv, 1964: Dr Oskar Karbach: 'Die politischen Grundlagen des österreichischen Antisemitismus'

Akten des Ungarischen Ministeriums des Äusseren zur Vorgeschichte der Annexion Österreichs, edited by Lajos Kerekes, Budapest, 1960

Documents on German Foreign Policy 1918–1945, Ser. C, D

Documents on British Foreign Policy, III Series, Vol. 1, 1938

Institut für Zeitgeschichte Vienna: *Einsatzbericht der 8 Deutschen Armee im März 1938*

International Military Tribunal, Nuremberg (IMT), 1947–9

Protokolle im Hochverratsprozess gegen Dr Guido Schmidt, Vienna, 1947

Weltgeschichte der Gegenwart in Dokumenten 1934–35, Essen, 1936–8

INDEX

Abyssinia (Ethiopia), Italian campaign in, 125, 128–9, 130, 141, 148, 164, 168, 171, 190, 216, 226, 227, 228, 229, 295, 324, 326
Action française, 69
Adam, Colonel Walter, 112, 196, 198
Adamovich, Professor Ludwig, 206
Addis Ababa, 125–6
Adler, Friedrich, 45, 46, 70, 339 n
Adler, Max, 46, 72
Adler, Dr Viktor, 28, 342 n
Alexander, King (of Jugoslavia), 111, 112, 129–30
Allied and Associated Powers, 31, 32
Allied HQ, Caserta, 23
Allizé, Henri, 31
Altenberg, Günther, 149–50, 289, 291–2, 293
Alvensleben, Captain Gebhard von, 20
Alvensleben, Captain Wichard von, 17–18, 20, 21, 22, 336 n
Anders, General, 277
Anfuso, Philippo, 164
Anglo-German Naval Agreement (1935), 246, 295
Arbeiterwehren (Workers' defence forces), 51, 52, 61; *see also Schutzbund*
Arbeiterzeitung (Social-Democrat newspaper), 64
Army Department (Austrian), 273
Army of Poles, General Anders', 277
'Arsenal affair', 77–8, 83
Attlee, Clement, 132, 322
Atwell, Captain John, 20
Austria, American diplomatic reports on, 220–3; Anschluss movement after World War I in, 27–36; anti-semitism in, 61–6; Army officers

dismissed and imprisoned in, 284–6; 'Arsenal affair' in, 77–8; Berchtesgaden Agreement with, 5, 6, 123, 145, 172, 173–4, 176, 178, 180, 186–205, 207–8; Britain and, 57, 108, 163–5, 174, 190–1, 211–15, 279–81; burning of Palace of Justice in, 179–81; coalition collapses in (1931), 184–5; conflicting ideologies of Germany and, 217, 281–3, 287–98; conflict within Nazi Party of, 202–3, 208, 233–7; currency crisis in, 37–8, 84, 225; deteriorating relations between Germany and, 150–6; diplomatic documents on crisis in, 57–60; disillusionment after Anschluss in, 299–306; Dollfuss government of, 87–112; economic viability of, 36–8; European involvement in, 82–5, 242–7; evolutionary v. revolutionary socialism in, 121–2, 123–4; Four-Power occupation of, 277; France and, 30–1, 32, 108, 132–3, 222, 278–9, 296; Germany increases military pressure on, 210–11; German political demands rejected by, 247–51; government cooperation with workers in, 118–21; *Heimwehr* movement in, 54–6, 126–8; Hitler changes tactics (after Berchtesgaden) towards, 238–9; Hitler's views on, 90, 176–7, 211–16; Hungary and, 53–4, 60, 72, 104, 108, 131–2, 136–7, 266–7; identification of 'German' with National Socialism in, 232; instructions to foreign representatives after

367